INSIGHT GUIDES

CHANNEL ISLANDS

Discovery
CHANNEL

APA PUBLICATIONS

Part of the Langenscheidt Publishing Group

INSIGHT GUIDE
Channel Islands

Editorial

Editor
Brian Bell
Principal Photography
Alain Le Garsmeur, Glyn Genin

Distribution

UK & Ireland
GeoCenter International Ltd
The Viables Centre, Harrow Way
Basingstoke, Hants RG22 4BJ
Fax: (44) 1256 817988

United States
Langenscheidt Publishers, Inc.
36–36 33rd Street 4th Floor
Long Island City, NY 11106
Fax: 1 (718) 784 0640

Australia
Universal Publishers
1 Waterloo Road
Macquarie Park, NSW 2113
Fax: (61) 2 9888 9074

New Zealand
Hema Maps New Zealand Ltd (HNZ)
Unit D, 24 Ra ORA Drive
East Tamaki, Auckland
Fax: (64) 9 273 6479

Worldwide
**Apa Publications GmbH & Co.
Verlag KG (Singapore branch)**
38 Joo Koon Road, Singapore 628990
Tel: (65) 6865 1600. Fax: (65) 6861 6438

Printing

Insight Print Services (Pte) Ltd
38 Joo Koon Road, Singapore 628990
Tel: (65) 6865 1600. Fax: (65) 6861 6438

©2006 Apa Publications GmbH & Co.
Verlag KG (Singapore branch)
All Rights Reserved
First Edition 1988
Third Edition 2000
Updated 2006

CONTACTING THE EDITORS

We would appreciate it if readers
would alert us to errors or out-
dated information by writing to:
**Insight Guides, P.O. Box 7910,
London SE1 1WE, England.
Fax: (44) 20 7403 0290.**
insight@apaguide.co.uk

www.insightguides.com
In North America:
www.insighttravelguides.com

ABOUT THIS BOOK

The first Insight Guide pioneered the use of creative full-colour photography in travel guides in 1970. Since then, we have expanded our range to cater for our readers' need not only for reliable information about their chosen destination but also for a real understanding of the culture and workings of that destination. Now, when the internet can supply inexhaustible (but not always reliable) facts, our books marry text and pictures to provide those much more elusive qualities: knowledge and discernment. To achieve this, they rely heavily on the authority of locally based writers and photographers.

The book is carefully structured to convey an understanding of the islands and their distinctive culture as well as to guide readers through their sights and activities:

◆ The **Features** section, indicated by a yellow bar at the top of each page, covers the islands' history and culture in a series of informative essays.

◆ The main **Places** section, indicated by a blue bar, is a complete guide to all the sights and areas worth visiting. Places of special interest are coordinated by number with the maps.

◆ The **Travel Tips** listings section, with an orange bar, provides a point of reference for information on travel, hotels, shops and restaurants.

Fresh flowers on sale in St Helier's central market.

The contributors

This edition of *Insight Guide: Channel Islands* has been comprehensively revised by **Susie Boulton**, author of *Insight Compact Guide: Jersey*, **Christopher Catling**, author of *Insight Compact Guide: Guernsey*, and **Peter Body**, a Jersey-based editor. Boulton also revised the Travel Tips listings section for the entire book – no small task, given the ever-changing hotels and restaurants scene.

This edition builds on the strong foundations created by the writers of previous editions.The turbulent history of the islands was recounted by **Brian Bell**, Insight Guides' editorial director. An insight into how the islands are run was provided by **Edward Owen**, the Guernsey-based former correspondent of London's *Financial Times*, who wrote the chapters on Government, Tax Exiles and Financiers. His wife, **Willa Murray**, a fellow journalist, wrote on archaeology and described the Little Islands such as Jethou and Lihou.

Two Jersey writers provided many of the remaining features. **Chris Lake** wrote on Food and Drink, Policing and Folk Legends, plus the Places chapter on Herm. **Rob Shipley** wrote the chapters on Fishing and Sailing.

Tim Earl, a Guernsey journalist who has travelled the world leading birdwatching trips, provided the chapter on Birds and also profiled Alderney, which he rates highly among ornithological wonders.

Stuart Ridsdale, an intrepid traveller and former Insight Guides editor, wrote the chapters on Jersey and Guernsey. **Colin Smith**, who began his journalistic career on Guernsey before becoming a foreign reporter for Britain's national newspapers, profiled the feudally-run island of Sark.

Stuart Abraham, a Jersey writer and photographer, wrote on the islands' renowned cows, and **Diane Fisher** described the remarkable zoo created on Jersey by Gerald Durrell.

Most of the photographs for the original edition were provided by Jersey-born **Alain Le Garsmeur**, one of Britain's most respected photojournalists. For this edition, much additional photography came from **Glyn Genin**, formerly picture editor of the *Financial Times*.

Susie Boulton and **Peter Pannett** were the contributors for the 2006 update, which was edited by **Alexia Georgiou**. The indexer was **Elizabeth Cook**.

Map Legend

▬ ▬ ▪	International Boundary
▬ ▪	National Park/Reserve
▬ ▬	Ferry Route
✈ ✈	Airport: International/Regional
🚌	Bus Station
P	Parking
ℹ	Tourist Information
✉	Post Office
† ⸸	Church/Ruins
†	Monastery
☾	Mosque
✡	Synagogue
▦ ▦	Castle/Ruins
∴	Archaeological Site
∩	Cave
𝟏	Statue/Monument
★	Place of Interest

The main places of interest in the Places section are coordinated by number with a full-colour map (e.g. ❶), and a symbol at the top of every right-hand page tells you where to find the map.

INSIGHT GUIDE
Channel Islands

Maps

CONTENTS

Introduction

History

Features

Beauport
Bay, Jersey

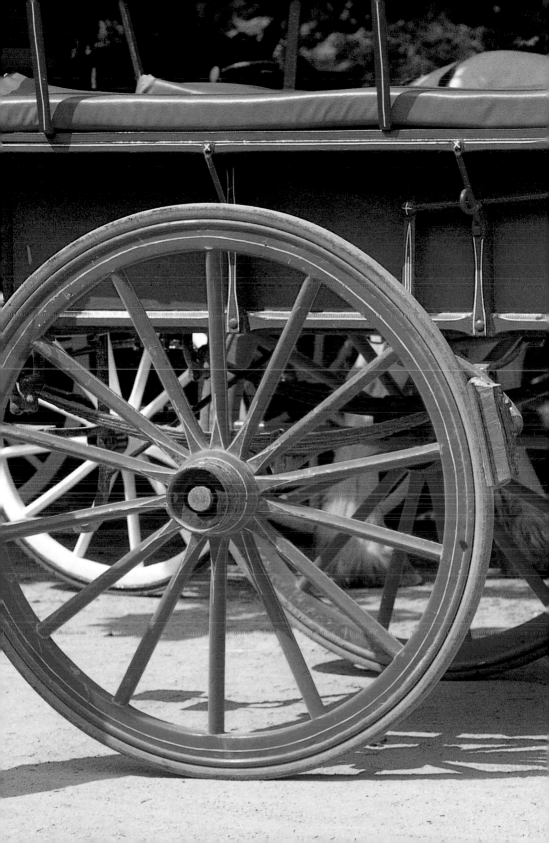

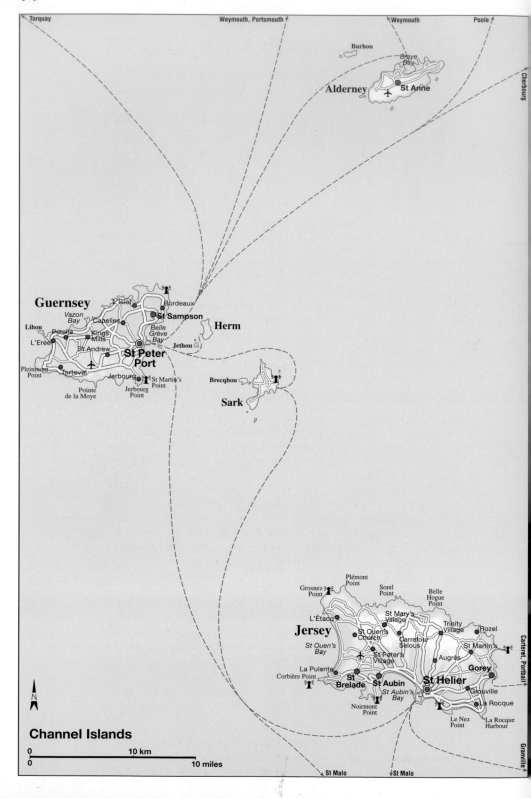

Torquay   Weymouth, Portsmouth   Weymouth   Poole

Cherbourg

Burhou

Braye
Bay

Alderney   St Anne

Guernsey

L'Islet   Bordeaux
Vazon
Bay   Capelles   St Sampson   Herm
Lihou   Perelle   Kings   Belle
Mills   Grève
Bay
L'Erée   St Andrew   Jethou
Pleinmont   St Peter   St Martin's
Point   Torteval   Port   Point   Brecqhou
Jerbourg
Pointe   Jerbourg
de la Moye   Point   Sark

Cherbourg

Carteret, Portbail

Plémont
Point
Grosnez   Sorel
Point   Point   Belle
Hogue
Point
L'Étacq   St Mary's
Village
Jersey   St Ouen's   Trinity   Rozel
Church   Village
St Ouen's   Carrefour
Bay   Selous   St Martin's
St Peter's   Augrès
Village
La Pulente   Gorey
Corbière Point   St Aubin   Grouville
St   St Helier
Brelade   St Aubin's   La Rocque
Bay
Noirmont   La Rocque
Point   Le Nez   Harbour
Point

Channel Islands

0   10 km
0   10 miles

Granville

St Malo   St Malo

THE TUG-OF-WAR ISLANDS

It's a winning recipe: take traditional English ingredients,
add a few French spices and lots of international finance

The Channel Islands are not really in the English Channel at all, but lie scattered along the Gulf of St Malo, their closest point to France being just 8 miles (13 km) from the Cherbourg peninsula. They are not sovereign states, nor are they colonies. They are British, but do not belong to the United Kingdom. They are partly in the European Union, partly outside it. They do not bow the knee to Her Majesty's government in Great Britain, but loyally (if anachronistically) toast the Queen of England as "Our Duke of Normandy".

Such contradictions multiply to give Jersey, Guernsey, Sark, Herm, Alderney and their smaller brethren a distinctive appeal. They have their own language, but everyone speaks English. They have their own banknotes, but deal in familiar pounds and pence sterling. They hold elections, but as yet there are no party politics. They flourish in a democratic age while preserving the western world's last bastion of feudalism. They formed the setting for *Bergerac*, a popular British television detective series of the 1980s, yet they have one of the lowest crime rates in Europe. They attract international financiers and rich tax exiles who drive Porsches and Jaguars, yet nowhere does the speed limit exceed 40 miles an hour (64 kmph).

Victor Hugo, who wrote *Les Misérables* during his 16-year exile in Guernsey, called the Channel Islands "pieces of France which fell into the sea and were gathered up by England". Geographically, he was right: the islands belong naturally to France rather than to England. Yet they were ruled by France for only 200 out of the 900 years during which they were at the centre of a tug-of-war between the two countries. No matter; they have absorbed a distinct Gallic flavour from their immediate neighbour.

Renoir, for example, who appraised Guernsey's light with a painter's eye, also noticed how "the Anglo-Saxon miss sheds her prudery when she arrives in Guernsey". Hugo, for his part, was prepared to broaden her mind still further: ignoring Anglo-Saxon decencies altogether, he lived on the island with both wife and mistress, introducing them respectively as *"Madame, la mère de mes enfants"* and *"Madame, mon amie"*.

Aside from these cultural contradictions, the Channel Islands have a more direct appeal to holidaymakers, offering towering cliffs, Atlantic surf, solitary beaches, country walks, majestic castles, quaint cottages, fascinating wildlife, and an equable climate. Jersey, Guernsey, Sark, Herm and Alderney tempt visitors with a menu that's nothing if not varied. ❏

TITLE PAGE: *Enfants au Bord de la Mer*, by Renoir, who praised Guernsey's light.
PRECEDING PAGES: coping with the boom in boating; a carriage on Sark, where cars are banned; the horse provides reliable island transport; car-free lanes in Sark.

TOADS AND DONKEYS

Jersey and Guernsey may look similar to visitors, but try convincing the natives that they have much in common. Old rivalries run deep

It's the Gallic flavour that is most attractive to the taste of English visitors, who still dominate the tourism statistics. Street names like Colomberie (Dovecot) and Rouge Bouillon (Red Spring) give them the feel of an English-speaking province of France. So do the croissants and long French loaves in the bakeries.

The Channel Islands have a combined population of just 160,000, yet rivalries – as ferocious as the tides that pound their shores – exist between them. When natives of the two largest islands, Jersey and Guernsey, refer to each other as *ânes* (donkeys) and *crapauds* (toads), the humour in their remarks is laced with a touch of contempt. To an outsider, these attitudes can be baffling. After all, the two islands have more similarities than differences – so why does each behave as though the other does not exist?

History is partly to blame, but today's insecurities can probably be traced to the realisation that good times can always turn bad, that there may not always be enough tourists to go round, that offshore financiers may find a more appealing home for their money.

Feudal chic

The past has a strong appeal for many tourists and in no other part of Britain is the tradition of preserving tradition so stoutly established. The telephone directories of the islands are littered with names like de Carteret and de Veulle, descendants of the Norman knights rewarded with land by William the Conqueror 10 centuries ago. Michael Beaumont, the Seigneur who rules Sark today, is successor to the feudal lords of the manor who held sway in Norman times – though, before succeeding his formidable aunt, Sybil Hathaway, who was Dame of Sark from 1927 until her death in 1974, he had led a thoroughly 20th-century existence as a guided weapons engineer with the British Aircraft Corporation.

A Norman-French patois is still spoken in

LEFT: maintaining a French flavour on Jersey.
RIGHT: sunbathing on Jersey at La Maison de Garde, built in 1765 and now run by the National Trust.

both islands, but its use is in decline. The most recent census revealed that of Jersey's population only three percent speak it and about 15 percent has "some understanding".

The result is that they are "tight little islands" – unsurprisingly insular in outlook, more than a little complacent, sometimes a bit illiberal.

When "Swinging London" was at its height in 1969, Jersey made the headlines by expelling a 21-year-old Portuguese girl who had come to work, quite legally, in a knitwear factory. The reason for her unacceptability: she was about to become an unmarried mother. Sark lagged even further behind the times. Only in 1974 were married women given the right to have their own bank accounts and to own property.

To many visitors such differences stir feelings of nostalgia. In the dusty lanes of Sark, where cars are banned, it is refreshing to encounter horse dung rather than petrol fumes. In the age of the jumbo jet, you fly to Alderney in a tiny 18-seater Trislander of Aurigny

Air Services, whose in-flight magazine includes a diagram of the cockpit layout – on the assumption, perhaps, that you might wish to reach forward and take over the controls.

As a holiday destination, the islands can exploit two valuable resources: sea and sunshine. There are unspoiled bays and coves, with shellfish in rock pools. Hugo mused poetically about the "Aegean of the Channel" and Queen Victoria, visiting Jersey in 1846, found that St Aubin's Bay reminded her of Naples.

Then there is the contrast between the superb shoreline and the lush rural interior. The farmland has been subdivided between heirs for so

euphemism would be "offshore finance centres" or "special tax regimes".

In the narrow lanes of St Helier and St Peter Port, brass plaques list the international bankers, insurance agents, trust administrators and multi-currency fiduciary deposit managers who thrive in the bracing financial atmosphere of these offshore city states. St Helier has over 50 international banks and as someone said, has become like a scaled-down financial centre – little Zurich.

Nor have the smaller islands failed to benefit from the financial boom. The so-called "Sark Lark", abolished for Channel Islands companies but still available for companies registered in tax

many generations that there is a patchwork profusion of small fields and scattered dwellings. Pretty cottages have a bygone charm and the towns are undisfigured by skyscrapers. The restaurants offer lobster and fresh vegetables.

Money talks

But the islands aren't just playgrounds. Traditionally they have been a market garden, providing England with early fruit, new potatoes and fresh cream. They are a breeding ground for Jersey and Guernsey cows, among the world's leading milkers. And, in recent decades, they have become tax havens; not that any resident would dream of describing them as such – the preferred

A CHOICE OF LANGUAGES

The English language, first introduced to Jersey in the 18th century, is now spoken by all the islanders. Street names in St Helier still carry French names, often very different from their later English names, e.g. La Rue de Derrière (King Street), La Rue des Trois Pigeons (Hill Street) and La Rue Trousse Cotillon (Church Street, but in French "Pick up your Petticoat Street"). Most districts retain their French names, and pronounciation still confuses English visitors. Ouaisné, for example, is pronounced *Waynay*, and St Ouen, *Saint Wan*. Language groups are anxious to keep the historic Jersey-Norman patois alive and the signs at the airport and harbour now wish visitors *"beinv'nue a Jèrri"*.

havens such as Liberia, allowed companies to minimise tax liability if they were prepared to hold annual directors' meetings on the island, so that the well-dressed passengers you would see on a horse-drawn carriage might very well have popped over from London for the day to attend a statutory board meeting in somebody's house. Alderney, meanwhile, has done its best to mimic its larger neighbours by welcoming a range of offshore businesses and has become a centre for e-commerce, in particular for Internet betting shops.

A HIGH ENTRANCE FEE

Immigration in Guernsey is controlled by dual house prices. A house costing £235,000 on the local market would cost an outsider around £900,000.

like their counterparts in Hollywood who identify film stars' mansions, will point out the homes of TV personality Alan Whicker, thriller writer Jack Higgins, golfer Ian Woosnam and former racing driver Nigel Mansell. For a while, Guernsey could even lay claim to a fully-fledged film star, the late Oliver Reed, whose memory lives vividly on in many island pubs.

Whatever the virtues of tradition, the islanders are ever adapting to change. Having been farmers, fishermen and innkeepers, they

But the easy-going image of a tax haven could not be more misleading. The islands are crawling with customs and immigration officials, determined to deny smugglers and illegal immigrants a back door into Britain and the entire European Union. Foreigners entering the Channel Islands are entering Britain, and their image of tax haven life is quickly shattered.

Seeing stars

There is a glamorous side to being special tax regimes. Tour guides in Jersey and Guernsey,

became expert in the 1960s and 1970s in fitting brass nameplates to bankers' doors. They have passed through those doors to become accountants, advocates and computer programmers. Now they are having to adjust to new government structures, fiscal reforms and imminent tax rises. With pressure to bring them into line with the rest of Europe, the islands are struggling to maintain their identity. The traditional way of life is gradually disappearing and controversial new measures – in Jersey at least – are emerging. But while the islands' alluring image as anomalies is threatened, their distinct Gallic flavour, beautiful scenery and fascinating heritage persists.   ❑

LEFT: the traditional Jersey bonnet.
ABOVE: a Sark fisherman.

Decisive Dates

8,000 BC Stone-age nomadic hunter-gatherers migrate to the islands, which were cut off from the mainland of France by rising sea levels at the end of the Ice Age.

4,850–2,850 BC The Neolithic Period. Settlers plant crops, raise animals, create flint tools, stone axes, pottery and querns (hand-mills for grinding cereals). Megalithic tombs or dolmens are erected.

2,250–600 BC The Bronze Age. Bronze is used

for weapons, jewellery and other luxury items.

600 BC – AD 350 Iron Age. Larger settlements develop. Hoards of 1st century BC. coins may have been buried as news came of Romans sweeping northwestwards through France.

56 BC Channel Islands become part of Gaul, but there is little evidence of the Roman Occupation.

6th and 7th centuries AD Britons, fleeing from the Saxons, arrive via Brittany, bringing with them Christianity.

9th century Vikings ravage the islands.

933 William Longsword, the 2nd Duke of Normandy, annexes the Channel Islands, which become part of the Duchy of Normandy.

1066 William the Conqueror, the 10th Duke of Normandy, conquers England and establishes the first constitutional links between Britain and the Channel Islands.

1204 King John loses Normandy to King Philip of France. Channel Islands remain loyal to the English sovereign.

1215 In return for their allegiance, King John grants the Channel Islands customs and privileges, tantamount to self-government, which have since been confirmed by every English monarch. France is now the enemy.

1338 The French capture Jersey and hold on to it for seven years in just one of the many skirmishes between France and England that disrupt life and trade on Guernsey.

1484 An Act of Neutrality is granted by the Pope to the Channel Islanders, so that their ships are free, in theory, to sail unmolested, even during times when England is at war.

1564 With Queen Elizabeth I's approval, Sark is colonised by Helier de Carteret.

1500–1600 Construction of Elizabeth Castle on the islet of St Helier. Sir Walter Raleigh, Governor of Jersey from 1600 to 1604, names it after Queen Elizabeth I.

1560s Trade in wool between Southampton and the Channel Islands leads to the rapid growth of the knitwear industry, with the islands exporting high-quality sweaters, stockings and gloves to England and France. So profitable is the trade that local laws are passed to ensure that essential agricultural work is not neglected.

1642–47 In the English Civil War, Jersey and Guernsey support the Royalists

1649 Charles I is beheaded. Charles II, then Prince of Wales, who takes refuge in Jersey, is proclaimed king by Sir George Carteret, Governor of the island. As a reward, he gives Smith's Island and some neighbouring islets off Virginia to Sir George Carteret with permission to settle. These are renamed New Jersey.

Mid-1700s The era of privateering, whereby Channel Islands ships are licensed to capture enemy shipping and confiscate their cargoes. This becomes a major source of revenue.

1770s Methodism gains a strong foothold in the Channel Islands following the visit of John Wesley to Alderney and Guernsey, replacing the older Huguenot-influenced Calvinism.

1779 Construction of coastal towers begins on Jersey and Guernsey as the islands try to defend themselves from the French.

1781 The French, under the command of Baron de Rullecourt, attempt to take over Jersey. The heroic Major Francis Peirson leads the local militia to victory in the Battle of Jersey, which takes place in St Helier's Royal Square. Both Peirson and De Rullecourt are killed in action.

1815 After the French defeat at Waterloo, attacks from the French cease. Influx of British army officers, retired on half-pension.

1836 Silver is discovered on Sark, but the mines are worked out by 1847 and abandoned.

1840s Granite begins to be quarried on Alderney, Sark and Herm in great quantities, and shipped to England for use in construction.

1847 Construction work begins on the breakwater on Alderney, designed to create a secret base for the English navy, close to France.

1870 The Jersey railway is opened. St Helier is linked to Grouville in 1873 and to St Aubin in 1884, extending to Corbière in 1899.

1900 Guernsey's parliament adopts English as its official language.

1920 The novelist Compton Mackenzie leases Herm and Jethou and writes *Fairy Gold* while living on Herm.

1936 The Jersey Railway is forced to close because of competition from buses and a fire which destroys most of the rolling stock.

1937 Airport opens at St Peter in Jersey.

1939 Guernsey Airport opens, a few months before the outbreak of World War II.

1940–45 Channel Islands demilitarised and thousands evacuated. The Germans occupy the islands, building substantial fortifications, most of which survive, as part of the Atlantic Wall devised by Hitler to fend off attack by Britain and the United States.

1944 The neutral Swedish vessel, the SS *Vega*, brings Red Cross food parcels and other essential provisions.

1945 The islands are liberated by British forces on 9 May. King George VI and Queen Elizabeth visit in June.

1948 French ceases to be the official language of Jersey's parliament.

1949 Peter Wood, the first Tenant of Herm, takes on a 100-year lease of the island, and begins to transform it from a bramble-choked wilderness into today's island paradise.

PRECEDING PAGES: the Battle of Jersey, portrayed in John Copley's *Death of Major Peirson*. **LEFT:** Henry VIII's ships of war. **RIGHT:** the Germans arrive in 1940.

1950s Tourism booms in the Channel Islands, partly because UK visitors are curious to see the only British island to have been occupied during the war.

1970s The era of cheap air travel ushers in even more of a tourist boom.

1973 Britain joins the European Community. Special terms agreed for the Channel Islands.

1980s Offshore finance becomes the dominant source of revenue.

1996 Construction starts on a major new project in St Helier, west of Albert Pier on land reclaimed from the sea. The development com-

prises a marina, gardens, a leisure centre, five-star hotel, new housing, shops and restaurants.

1997 Jersey's £23 million airport terminal building is completed.

2004 Channel Islands celebrate 800 years of allegiance to the Crown. Guernsey changes from a committee system of government to a Council of Ministers, headed by a Chief Minister; and work ends on the new airport terminal building.

2005 Jersey's Democratic Alliance Party is launched and the island receives a visit from the Queen to mark the 60th anniversary of the liberation of the Channel Islands.

2006 Jersey changes to a ministerial system of government. ❑

BEGINNINGS

*Given their vulnerable location, it was inevitable that the early history
of the Channel Islands would be a catalogue of invasions*

The Channel Islands today are regarded as romantic places, ideal destinations for holidaymakers looking for relaxation. The image isn't always utterly accurate, but it is at least an improvement on their traditional role. Because of their location, the islands, throughout history, have served as stepping stones for plundering armies on their way to new conquests. Like many similar places around the world, the Channel Islands were, for centuries, prey to scourges of nature, easy pickings for passing pirates, and reluctant pawns passed between warring rulers. If today's inhabitants seem occasionally to overemphasise their proud independence, it is because they are well-informed about their turbulent past.

As elsewhere, earliest recorded history celebrates the survival of the fittest. More than 100,000 years ago, Stone Age men in Jersey banded together to hunt for game. Their prey included the elephant and the woolly rhinoceros. Various excavations at La Cotte de St Brelade, a cave on Jersey's southwest coast, have provided tantalising traces of palaeolithic activity on the island, which was then still connected to the French mainland.

It wasn't until around 6,500 BC, when the great Ice Cap melted, that the Channel Islands were separated from the rest of Europe. Today, at very low tide, evidence can still be seen in Jersey's St Ouen's Bay of a "submerged forest" that dates back to early neolithic times.

Detective work

Farmers supplanted hunters in about 5,000 BC. Villages began to take shape. The remains of pottery and flint tools resemble those found in northern France. Burial mounds, containing passage graves, survive. One Jersey burial mound, at La Hougue Bie *(see panel, right)*, is an impressive 177 ft (54 metres) in diameter.

Excavations at the Les Fouaillages mound on Guernsey have unearthed the work of

builders spread over 1,500 years. Fragments of tools and weapons and a large gold neck-ring (on display in the Jersey Museum) provide clues to the trading links and relative prosperity of the Bronze Age, which came shortly before 2,000 BC.

As with much of Western Europe, the Channel

SECRETS OF LA HOUGUE BIE

Labour was cheap 5,000 years ago, but the building skills needed to construct La Hougue Bie's massive burial mound are still impressive. The 40-ft-high (12-metre) mound covers a chamber 65 ft (20 meters) long. The heavy slabs of the roof are supported by granite uprights, strengthened by dry-stone walls and the larger stones may have been hauled from 4 miles (6 km) away, perhaps on sledges or on rollers.

These megalithic mounds served not only as family vaults but also as temples – a communal focal point for the peasant farmers who had come on foot from Normandy before rising sea levels turned Jersey into an island.

LEFT: L'Étacq in Jersey, where seaweed has long been harvested. **RIGHT:** the west coast of Sark.

Islands' early history is a catalogue of invasions. Defensive earthworks on the coasts of Jersey and Guernsey date back more than 5,000 years and were augmented in the Iron Age by the Celts, who arrived in 800 BC from France and Germany. Their success in developing iron weapons turned the Celts into fearsome opponents, and subjugating the horse had made them mobile. Hoards of buried valuables, including more than 15,000 coins, suggest that the Celts felt threatened. Certainly, they were no match for the might of the Romans.

When Rome's conquering legions marched across Europe in 56 BC, they swept the islands, along with what is now France, into their province of Gaul. Jersey, it is thought, became "Caesarea", Guernsey "Sarnia" and Alderney "Riduna". They were ruled from what is now Lyons, but the evidence is that rulers such as Mark Antony and Justinian left "the islands in the sea between Gaul and Britain" largely to their own devices, much as the British parliament does today.

The Romans left surprisingly few traces; only a few coins and trinkets which were unearthed centuries later, and the excavated remains of a Gallo-Roman settlement which was found in Alderney show that they visited

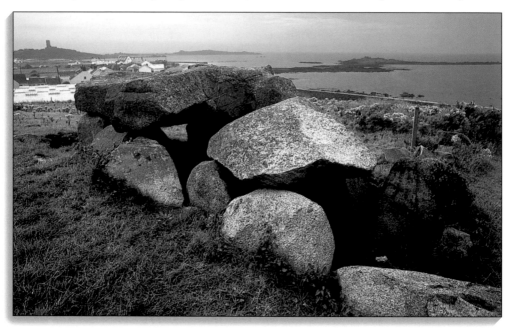

THE NORMANS' LASTING LEGACY

The ruthless efficiency of the Norman conquests, which extended from the Channel Islands in the 10th century to England in the 11th, can be traced to their origins as the Viking pirates from Denmark, Norway and Iceland who plundered their way down the western coasts of Europe.

Having converted to Christianity and adopted the French language, the Normans (or "Northmen") rapidly picked up the French skills of cavalry warfare, which they used to extend their influence as far as southern Italy and Sicily. Just as their reckless courage and brutal violence served them well as conquerors, their ability to adapt and improve the institutions they conquered gave them a lasting significance. They made feudalism efficient and added a ruthless professionalism to the cult of knighthood. They took Christianity seriously, embarking on pilgrimages, promoting religious orthodoxy and developing Norman monasteries as important centres of Benedictine life and learning.

In a classic case of the poacher turning gamekeeper, the former pirates had an acute sense of the value of money and set great store by fiscal competence, introducing the notion of an exchequer to the previous feudal system. In the case of Jersey and Guernsey, the Normans' respect for financial institutions was a harbinger of the islands' eventual success in today's offshore finance industry.

the islands at all. Occasionally Roman coins are still found, usually dating from the third century and identifiable as originating in Alexandrian mints.

Christians and Vikings

The early Christian era was a period of comparative peace. Parishes grew up around stone churches and missionaries gave their names to areas such as St Sampson in Guernsey and St Brelade in Jersey. St Helier founded a hermitage on a rock near the present town. St Magloire established a monastery on Sark, which had been inhabited from early times.

In AD 911, Charles the Simple of France, tiring of the endless devastation, tried to buy off Rollo, chief of the most feared band of raiders, by giving him land that was later to become the Duchy of Normandy. It was not enough: in AD 933 Rollo's son, William Longsword, wrested more territory from the Breton lords, probably including the Channel Islands. The end result was that the feudal system was firmly in place.

Rollo lives on today in the curious *Clameur de Haro*. An islander who feels that someone is damaging his property can summon two witnesses, kneel before the offender and call out: *"Haro, Haro, à l'aide mon Prince, on me fait*

tort"* (Rollo, Rollo, my Prince, come to my aid, I am being wronged), followed by the Lord's Prayer, also in French. The offender must then stop whatever he is doing until the case is heard in a court of law.

The peace was shattered in the 9th century as the Vikings arrived in their Scandinavian long ships in search of booty. Again and again, houses were burnt, people murdered, crops and cattle carried off and prehistoric tombs rifled. Norse words began to enter the language, not least the word *ey*, meaning "island", which provided the last syllable for Jersey, Guernsey and Alderney. The Norsemen were also expert sailors and farmers – skills which they left the islanders as a permanent legacy.

The medieval cry, originally used to prevent murder or robbery, is far from defunct and can still be effective. It has been uttered in recent times to stop people felling trees and, in a more contemporary context, to force a building contractor to remove a crane that was violating the air space of a newsagent's shop in St Peter Port.

William Longsword's successor, William the Conqueror, captured the English crown in 1066 when he won the Battle of Hastings, thus

LEFT: Le Trépied Neolithic dolmen in Guernsey, reputed to be the meeting place of witches.
ABOVE: a cavalry charge by the indomitable Normans.

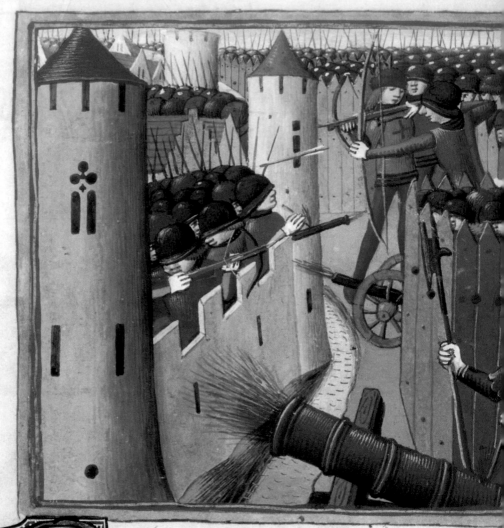

Puis assiegerent ozlean
Les contes de salesbzy suff
Talbot et aultres leurs gen
Qui y trauaillerent moult
la firent de grans ba
Du coste de beausse et soule

bringing England within the same jurisdiction as the Channel Islands. The sequence of events has not been forgotten: because England was added relatively late to the Duke of Normandy's offshore properties, islanders today jokingly refer to their dominant neighbour as "a possession" of Les Isles Anglo-Normandes – a reverse of what most people would think.

After 1066, the centre of power shifted to London. But the islanders went on paying their taxes to Rouen, William's Normandy capital, and the islands changed hands frequently within the families of the dukes of Normandy. Sark, for example, was handed over to the monks of St Michel.

A stark choice

The enlarged kingdom, however, lacked stability. When Richard the Lionheart died in 1199, his brother, John, succeeded him; but Brittany preferred the claim of his cousin, Arthur. Fighting broke out and Arthur disappeared, presumed murdered on the orders of John.

In 1204, Normandy broke away to become part of the kingdom of France and John fled to England. The islanders were torn: should they swear allegiance to England or would they be better off throwing in their lot with France? It was a particularly difficult decision for families who had possessions in both countries.

The better offer came from King John, who promised the islanders "the continuance of their ancient laws and privileges", thus laying the foundation for the self-government they still enjoy. There were other considerations, too. First, the islanders had to consider that England, with its superior naval power, might defend them more effectively against raiders; and second, that the King of England, being farther away than the King of France, might interfere less in the islands' affairs.

The theory was sound. But in fact the tug of-war between England and France was just beginning and Mont Orgueil Castle, built early in the 13th century on a Jersey promontory overlooking the French coast, became a lasting symbol of the islands' beleaguered state. Geography, too, dictated their plight: they were strategically placed to shelter the opposing fleets from each other and from the elements. They were, therefore, fated to remain at the centre of a struggle that would continue for centuries. ❑

LEFT: the Normans created a powerful war machine.

CAUGHT IN THE MIDDLE

For more than five centuries, the islands were a pawn in the political and military strategies played out by England and France

Like the Third Reich's invaders in 1940, England's 13th-century rulers found that the islanders had infuriatingly independent minds. They insisted, for instance, on being governed according to their ancient customs; but English administrators, who were by now used to laws being formally codified, could never quite be certain what those customs meant in practice.

What became known as the Hundred Years' War between Britain and France subjected the islands to frequent hit-and-run raids between 1337 and 1453. At the outset, the French dangled a tempting carrot in front of the islanders: join France in return for a firm confirmation of self-government. England's Edward III was forced to match the offer. In a charter which was profoundly to affect the islanders' future, he allowed them to "hold and retain all privileges, liberties, immunities and customs granted by our forbears or of other legal competency, and that they enjoy them freely without molestation by ourselves, our heirs or officers".

Even so, the raids continued. France invaded twice in 1338, capturing Guernsey, Alderney and Sark. In 1373 the Constable of France, Bertrand du Guesclin, overran all of Jersey except for Gorey Castle, which withstood a siege from July until September, when it was relieved by the English fleet. In 1380 the French captured Jersey again and held it for two years.

Reversals of fortune

Within four years of Henry V's triumph over the French at Agincourt in 1415, virtually all of Normandy except for Mont-St-Michel was an English province. His dream was to unite the two kingdoms, which would have oriented the Channel Islands permanently towards the closer of the two cultures, the French.

But after Henry's death the tide was turned by a 17-year-old peasant, Joan of Arc, who inspired the French forces to rout the English. By the end

of the Hundred Years' War in 1453, the tables of history had been turned again and Calais was the only part of France held by England.

Peace was short-lived. In 1455 the islands were caught up in an internecine English feud, later dubbed the Wars of the Roses after the emblems of the two combatants, the House of

York (white rose) and the House of Lancaster (red rose). The conflict dragged on for 31 years, with the loyalties of entire families bitterly split between the two Houses. The French, taking advantage of the diversion, mounted a successful attack on Mont Orgueil (Mount Pride) in 1461 and held the islands as part of Normandy for the next seven years.

In 1483 Edward IV of England and Louis XI of France agreed that the Channel Islands should be neutral territory in any ensuing conflict between their countries. Pope Sixtus IV reinforced the treaty by issuing a Papal Bull pronouncing "sentence of anathema and eternal damnation with confiscation of goods" on anyone who

LEFT: Du Guesclin attacks Mont Orgueil Castle.
RIGHT: Grosnez Castle on Jersey.

infringed this neutrality. Soon, the islands were divided for administrative purposes into two bailiwicks: today's Jersey and Guernsey.

The Papal Bull of Neutrality didn't rule out preemptive strikes. Even Sark couldn't escape the feuding and in 1549 was seized by the French. The island, which had prospered in the 13th century, had been abandoned by the monks in 1412 when they could no longer withstand the countless pirate raids, and belonged more to the birds than to either Britain or France.

For the next nine years the French proceeded to fortify it. Their presence there was a thorn in the side for the larger islands. Finally Sark was

liberated by Flemish adventurers who returned it to the English crown. Elizabeth I later granted it to Helier de Carteret, a member of one of Jersey's leading families, under a typical condition of feudal tenure: that he kept at least 40 loyal subjects there. He found willing colonists and provided them with housing, the titles to which still give the owners the right to a seat in the island's parliament, the Chief Pleas.

De Carteret found Sark "so full of rabbit-holes and heather, briars, brambles, bracken and undergrowth that it looked impossible to cultivate. There were no tracks down which a cart could safely pass, nor harbour where a boat could unload safely." Nevertheless, farming was developed and a safe harbour (the tiny Creux Harbour) was cut from the rocks.

Alderney, meanwhile, had been a pirate stronghold throughout the Middle Ages. The buccaneers were finally driven out during Elizabeth I's reign, a period of consolidation for the islands. As trade flourished, Sir Walter Raleigh, while governor of Jersey for a brief period, oversaw the building of another addition to the island's skyline: Elizabeth Castle in St Aubin's Bay. Every monarch added to the fortifications. In Henry VIII's time a stolid fortress, Les Murs de Haut, came to dominate the approaches to Alderney's Longey harbour; rebuilt, it was to become Fort Essex in the 19th century.

God's law

By now the islands had evolved legislative assemblies, known as the States, which helped stabilise internal affairs when anarchy reigned in neighbouring nations and were to be the foundation of eventual self-government. Their religious orientation had changed, too. During the Reformation from 1547 until 1558 "the venom of Martin Luther's heresy", as the Roman Catholic church called it, swept through Normandy and across to the Channel Islands. Roadside crosses were smashed and Latin services swept away. Few of the islanders spoke English and the new English prayerbook had to be translated into French for Edward VI's subjects in the Channel Islands and Calais.

Responding to the influence of the Huguenots, the islanders adopted the Calvinist model of the new Protestant faith. Dancing or gossiping on Sundays, which were reserved for church-going, meant a jail sentence. Absentees from the quarterly communion were thrown in the stocks. If anyone at a party sang lascivious songs or told licentious stories, everyone present was fined. The unrepentent were excommunicated, "cut off as septic limbs from the body of Christ, as Adam was expelled from Paradise by a flaming sword".

The Presbyterian ethic didn't drive out the ancient beliefs in witchcraft, which lingered through the 17th century and into the 18th. At best, someone might whisper of a neighbour: "She has the hidden knowledge." At worst, someone might be flogged or executed.

KNITWEAR AS FASHION

The Tudors made knitted stockings fashionable and it is recorded that Mary Queen of Scots went to her execution wearing a pair of white weatherproof Jersey stockings.

both men and women. Jean Poingdestre, a lieutenant bailiff of Jersey, wrote: "The greatest part of the inhabitants are knitters. There be many houses where man, wife and children, beginning at the age of five or six, have no other employment, and may be said to make everyone a pair of stockings every week; which must, according to my account, come to more than 10,000 pairs weekly." Rectors forbade knitting in churches because the noise of the needles drowned out the sermon. And the authorities began to get

The knitwear boom

On the economic front, though, things were improving. The islands' fishing fleets had discovered the rich waters off Newfoundland and at home the knitting of stockings and fishermen's sweaters – still known as "jerseys" and "guernseys" – became the most important industry. Strict quality control was enforced, with inspectors being appointed to ensure that three-ply rather than two-ply wool was used in their manufacture.

Knitting became so profitable that it employed

LEFT: a woman is burnt at the stake in the witch hunts of the early 17th century. **ABOVE:** Essex Castle on Alderney, begun in 1546 by Henry VIII.

worried: so irresistible were the profits that men were beginning to neglect the harvesting crops and collecting seaweed (*vraic*) used for cooking and heating. In 1608 a new law was framed: "During harvest and *vraicing* seasons all persons shall stop making stockings and work on the land on pain of imprisonment on bread and water and the confiscation of their work."

There was comparative peace until England was torn apart by its Civil Wars, the bitter conflict between Parliament and Charles I over freedom in politics and religion. Jersey's sympathies were with the King; Guernsey's with Parliament. On two occasions Jersey's Elizabeth Castle gave sanctuary to the King's children, Charles, Prince of Wales, and James, Duke of York. When the King was beheaded in 1649, Jersey proclaimed the Prince Charles II and he spent much of his time on the island with a generously large group of courtiers, including a jester. As a reward to their supporters, Charles and James granted them land on the eastern seaboard of America; it was to become known as New Jersey.

Jersey's loyalty to the monarchy incurred the wrath of Parliament. In 1651, after the Royalists were defeated by Cromwell's Roundheads, Charles became a true vagabond prince. A fleet of 80 vessels under Admiral Blake was despatched to crush the Royalist resistance. The

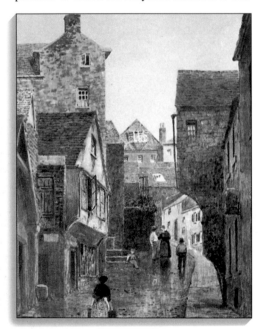

Roundhead troops landed at St Ouen's Bay and quickly took St Aubin's Fort and Gorey Castle. Elizabeth Castle capitulated after a 50-day siege, but Castle Cornet held out for nearly nine years.

It was not an easy occupation: the troops billeted themselves in churches and ignored ancient charters by press-ganging able-bodied men into the forces. Jersey remained under Parliament's rule until the monarchy was restored in 1660.

Methodism and martello towers

Towards the end of the 17th century, the islands steadily grew more prosperous and, in an uncanny echo of today's concerns, the States complained that too many houses were being built. With the French fleet less of a threat, fishing business with Newfoundland flourished.

In Jersey, new ploughing methods improved the yield of parsnips. St Peter Port, now a free port, profited by acting as middleman to smugglers, who were tolerantly regarded by most islanders. Tobacco was a favourite commodity, shipped secretly by night to the Devon coast; customs men realised what was going on when they noticed that the islands were importing far more tobacco than their inhabitants could possibly hope to smoke on their own.

Sark's fortunes began to fluctuate. The de Carteret family remained rulers until 1720, strengthening their holding by giving support to Charles II. But the sixth Seigneur, Sir Charles de Carteret, got into debt and, with Queen Anne's permission, sold the island. It then changed hands regularly.

Methodism became popular in the 1770s and the church's founder, John Wesley, visited Guernsey and Jersey. But a more telling indicator of the times were the dozens of round towers (later called martello towers) springing up around the coasts.

The Battle of Jersey

As various wars erupted between England, France and Spain, enterprising sea captains grew rich as armed privateers, licensed to plunder merchant vessels of the current enemy. Scores of brigantines and cutters prowled the seas around the islands, most often preying on French traders. Jersey's fine martello towers were built as beach defences in anticipation of more trouble from France.

It was a wise precaution: in January 1781, Jersey was invaded during the night by French troops led by a soldier of fortune, Baron de Rullecourt, who lost his life in the hard-fought contest that came to be called the Battle of Jersey. The island's lieutenant-governor, Moses Corbet, was taken prisoner in bed and capitulated. Major Francis Peirson, 24, disregarding the surrender, led the local militia successfully against the French but died at the moment of victory.

As a protection against further attacks, the imposing Fort Regent was built on a granite hill overlooking St Helier, but proved to be redundant: the French never invaded again. ❑

LEFT: Guernsey's capital, St Peter Port, as it once was.
RIGHT: Major Peirson, hero of the Battle of Jersey.

HIGH SPIRITS AND LOW TAXES

The 19th century was a time of prosperity and well into the 20th century the old traditions kept modern life at bay. All that changed in 1940

When the French returned in 1789, they came as refugees, fleeing from the French Revolution. Thousands of aristocrats sought refuge from the guillotine and were joined by an estimated 3,000 priests who refused to swear loyalty to France's new constitution. It was a lucrative time for the islands' boatmen who ferried them across. Builders benefitted, too, as the aristocrats invested whatever wealth they had salvaged in erecting manor houses.

When France declared war on England in 1793, Jersey became a counter-espionage centre and an operation based at Mont Orgueil was set up to smuggle fake banknotes into France to undermine confidence in the Republic's currency.

The brigands were having a heyday. By now piracy was promising such guaranteed profits that old ladies were known to invest their savings by buying shares in the privateers. As a business, it required little capital since some of the ships themselves were vessels taken in combat: the *Union*, for instance, had started life as the *Los Dos Amigos*. So much French brandy was plundered that Guernsey was dubbed the bonded warehouse of British merchants.

Eventually, Napoleon Bonaparte's patience ran out. "France can tolerate no longer this nest of brigands and assassins," he fumed. "Europe must be purged of this vermin. Jersey is England's shame." Taking him at his word, the English built Fort Regent as a defence. But the threat never materialised and the privateers survived, finding new opportunities during Britain's war with the United States in 1812.

Peace breaks out

The French threat finally ended with the English victories at Trafalgar in 1805 and at Waterloo in 1815, and a period of prosperity began. Retired army and navy officers began to settle on the islands, attracted by the low cost of living, and a few French arrived to open hotels.

One helpful consequence of the islands' strategic importance was that the roads had to be improved to allow soldiers to be moved more easily from place to place. Usually it was far faster for Jerseymen to get from St Helier to St Aubin by boat round the coast than to travel through the narrow, meandering country lanes. "Two carts meeting each other could not pass;

one or the other must back until it reached the nearest field or gateway or some other recess to which it might retreat during the passage of the other," said a report to Britain's Board of Agriculture. "To this little circumstance in their internal economy, and the disputes which it engenders, may perhaps in part be attributed to the remarkable proficiency of the Jersey populace in swearing." Such a situation would not be unfamiliar to drivers in today's car-clogged lanes.

The military's attempts to upgrade the roads were not appreciated by the farmers. One resisted with a gun, and another raised the ancient *Clameur de Haro*, forcing the issue to be taken to court. (He lost.)

LEFT: portrait of a traditional Guernsey flower seller.
RIGHT: a 19th-century water trough in Jersey.

Another cause for frequent dispute in Jersey was the bitter rivalry between the politically radical party, whose symbol was a rose, and the conservatives, who wore a laurel leaf. A guidebook of the time reported that Laurel and Rose supporters hated each other "more bitterly than do rival actors or singers. They seldom intermarry, seldom salute each other in the public ways; and they, for the most part, carry their mutual animosities into every transaction of their lives, legislative, judicial, municipal and private."

Yesterday's bitter rivalries could not be more removed from today's scene, when politicians are elected as individuals and confront-

William the Conqueror to the Augustinian Order of Cherbourg, who farmed it; but the religious community had all but died out by the 16th century and Guernsey's gentry began using Herm as a game preserve. But in 1815, granite quarrying became big business, bringing in its wake shops, a school, a hotel and a lilliputian beehive-shaped jail.

Thereafter, Herm passed through the hands of wealthy men who liked the idea of owning an island. One famous tenant in the 1920s was the novelist Sir Compton Mackenzie; another tenant raised wallabies there. Finally, in 1946, the island was bought by the States of

ational political parties as such do not exist.

Economically, great changes were taking place. Stocking-making didn't survive Britain's Industrial Revolution and was largely replaced by a large entrepot trade which exploited the islands' ability to sail under the UK's tariff barriers. Thus, leather might be imported tax-free from France and exported as shoes to England. Tomatoes, introduced in 1865, flourished, eventually accounting for 75 percent of Guernsey's income and employment of the local people.

Shooting parties

The 19th century brought important changes to Herm. The tiny island had been given by

Guernsey, and it has since been let to tenants, but only on the condition that the public has access to the foreshore and many other parts of the tiny domain.

The smuggling business, known colloquially as *La Fraude*, was changing too in the 19th century as customs men tightened their grip. As in Devon and Cornwall, violence often erupted on moonless nights as the authorities pounced on contraband cargoes of spirits and tobacco.

An advertisement placed by the British customs in a Jersey newspaper in 1823 gives a graphic account of one such encounter. The advert offered a £50 reward for information about an incident in which "Humphrey Oxenham, being out on duty about one o'clock of the morning of Thursday, 19 June, saw a smuggling vessel in the offing and some carts on the beach, which were accompanied by upwards of 40 smugglers, armed with bludgeons, who surrounded him, struck him a violent blow above his eyes, which knocked him down, and, whilst on the ground, beat him severely, until James Hudie, an extra boatman, came to the assistance of Humphrey Oxenham, on which the smugglers dispersed."

A RED REVOLUTION

Guernsey's first glasshouses, built in 1792, were used for growing dessert grapes but became a source of huge wealth as tomatoes, introduced in 1865, took over.

putting an end to the venture. The 16th Seigneur, the company's principal shareholder, was forced to mortgage the island to pay off his mounting debts.

Tourists of the time, denied the inducement of a silvermine, looked to Alderney where they marvelled at the massive fortifications. Napoleon Bonaparte called the island "England's shield". The English began building an ambitious 3,300-ft (1,000-metre) breakwater in 1847 to counter a French naval build-up at Cherbourg. Alderney, they said,

The silver rush

Nor were the smaller islands exempt from the pressures of the age. Sark's idyll was disrupted when traces of silver and copper were discovered and the Sark's Hope Mining Company began trading in 1834. But early dreams turned to tragedy when a cutter carrying the first silver to England diverted to Guernsey when the captain returned to visit his sick wife. The vessel ran on to the rocks, sinking with the loss of both crew and cargo. On the same day, seawater flooded the mine's profitable lower galleries,

SAILING THE SEVEN SEAS

Shipowning in Jersey and Guernsey expanded rapidly in the first half of the 19th century, ranking the islands 10th among British ports in 1865, ahead even of Hull and Bristol. The growth was powered intially by oyster fishing and the cod trade, but gradually international shipping became more important, with Channel Islands vessels, many of them built locally, travelling as far as Australia.

When iron steamships began to dominate the seas in the 1870s, the islands were badly hit: local shipbuilders couldn't afford to build them and local shipowners couldn't afford to buy them. The great seafaring days were over and the islanders turned to agriculture and tourism.

LEFT: smugglers at work in a deserted Jersey cove.
ABOVE: history captured in a Guernsey art gallery.

would become the Gibraltar of the Channel. It was a project so worthy of the mighty British Empire that Queen Victoria herself paid two visits to see its construction.

But the architects hadn't bargained for the pounding of the seas and the ferocity of the westerly gales. By 1864, the project was abandoned as being hopelessly expensive and England agreed "temporarily" to bear the cost of maintaining the incomplete breakwater. The arrangement turned out to be more than temporary: by the 1980s, maintaining the Victorian white elephant was costing the British government more than £500,000 (US$800,000) a year,

though responsibility for repairs has since been assumed by the Bailiwick of Guernsey as a contribution to the defence of the realm.

Waiting for war

Fort building was, all in all, a safer business to be in. Military architects specified the finest quality of stone, selected shades of granite to set off their design and, to keep that traditional touch, included arrow slits and moats that had very little to do with 19th-century warfare. In Alderney an impressive half-circle of coastal forts was created, from Fort Clonque to Essex Castle.

The islands' reputation as a place of refuge

JERSEY'S FOOD RIOTS

A high birthrate in the mid-19th century meant that there was not enough work for the island's population, and even those in work were paid barely enough to feed their growing families. In 1847 the States of Jersey opened a bakery to supply bread to the poor more cheaply than existing shops. But they closed it after a few months and, after unsuccessfully demanding a pay rise, workers staged a protest march, which swelled to 1,000 people by the time it reached St Helier's Royal Square. The military was called out to stop protesters breaking into the Town Mills. The price of bread was reduced, but many islanders decided to emigrate to North America and Australia.

brought in exiles from many countries – Poles, Hungarians, Italians, French – during 1848, when revolutions erupted all over Europe. The most celebrated refugee, Victor Hugo, a politician as well as a novelist, poet and playwright, arrived with a price on his head in 1852 from Paris, where he had violently opposed the rule of Louis Napoleon.

Typifying the traditional rivalry between Jersey and Guernsey, both claim to have pioneered Britain's distinctive posting box. Jersey says its octagonal model was adopted by the English novelist Anthony Trollope, at the time a Post Office surveyor; Guernsey claims its first pillarbox appeared in St Peter Port in 1853.

New, fast steamships were making the islands more accessible to both tourists and wealthy new residents. The first railway lines were built in the 1870s. Telegraphic communication with England followed. Hotels sprang up, schools and libraries were opened, and cattle farming flourished. However, industries such as knitting, oyster fishing and cider-making were dying out.

Peace reigns

The 20th century was ushered in on an exuberant note. A Battle of Flowers, held to commemorate Edward VII's coronation in 1902, became a regular festival, symbolising the islands'

houses with spacious grounds and ran smart cars about the islands.

Modern life was kept at a distance. Electricity didn't come to Alderney until the 1930s and, apart from the telegraph service, instant communication with the outside world depended on one radio-telephone. Sark's Court of Chief Pleas outlawed cars and motorcycles, on the grounds that they would ruin the island's charm. When one persistent doctor shipped in a car, he was forbidden to use it unless it was pulled by a horse.

The Channel Islands might not have been Britain's South Sea Islands, as one guidebook claimed, but they were a delightful and hospitable

fecundity. Even World War I failed to spoil the tranquillity: although many natives joined the forces and Guernsey-based French seaplanes kept watch for U-boats. The war passed the islands by and they were even considered safe enough to house German prisoners-of-war. Only sugar and petrol were rationed.

In the 1920s, buses put the railways out of business and many retired English people, attracted by the genial climate, easygoing lifestyle and low taxes bought comfortable

LEFT: French workers provided the islands with much needed immigrant labour.

ABOVE: making lobster pots in Jersey in the 1930s.

little world. By 1939 Guernsey's modern and efficient tomato industry was producing 35,000 tons a year and Jersey's potato yield was 10,000 tons. Both islands did well from cattle exports. As Europe talked of war, the Channel Islands regarded themselves as the safest place on earth.

World War II

When war was declared the States of Jersey and Guernsey pledged to King George VI the services of "Your Majesty's Norman subjects" and many islanders, although exempt from UK military service, joined the British armed forces. His Majesty's government, however, had given so little thought to the position of the

Channel Islands that it was unsure whether to communicate through the lieutenant-governors of the bailiwicks, both militarymen, through the War Office or the Home Office.

When, in September 1939, Jersey asked London for anti-aircraft and coastal defence guns, the War Office, unable to supply even a Bren gun for at least a year, said the chances of an attack on Jersey were "somewhat remote". Certainly, the conflict seemed far away as 1939 gave way to 1940. Ration books were prepared, and a few elderly gentlemen with ancient firearms stood guard over power stations and reservoirs.

However, life went on as usual; cargo boats

still called, the mail still arrived. And Jersey felt so unaffected that it advertised the island in newspapers as "the ideal resort for wartime holidays this summer".

The question of evacuation

By the middle of 1940, things looked less rosy. All British troops had been driven out of France. The Channel Islanders, realising that German forces were now just 8 miles (14 km) to the east of Alderney, felt utterly vulnerable. What support could Britain offer given their defeats? Perhaps total evacuation ought to be considered?

Since the 1920s, Army chiefs had argued that the islands had no strategic value for Britain –

and, anyway, they would be impossibly expensive to defend. On 19 June 1940, the long-awaited decision was taken: they would be demilitarised. All army personnel were evacuated. So were the lieutenant-governors. Civilians were ordered to hand in all weapons to their local parish constable. But in London the military experts were reassuring: "There need be no fear of the Germans taking any advantage from the British decision to demilitarise the islands."

There was a great deal of dithering about whether to evacuate the islanders to the UK. Finally voluntary evacuation was offered, but without any guidance as to the wisdom of accepting it. Initially shipping offices were besieged and there was a run on the banks. Defiant posters appeared: "Why run away?" In the end, 90,000 people chose to leave the islands and 80,000 stayed. Many found themselves packed like cattle on boats normally used to haul coal or potatoes.

On Jersey valuables were buried; savings withdrawn from banks; houses, farms and cars abandoned; several thousand pets destroyed. In Guernsey a publican abandoned his bar, inviting his neighbours to help themselves to the liquor.

The stark options

In Alderney, communications were particularly bad: the telegraph cable to England was out of order and radio silence was obligatory. A meeting of the States was convened and the town crier invited the island's 1,400 people to assemble. A notice from the island's *de facto* leader, the autocratic Judge F. G. French, set out the stark options: "I have appealed to Admiralty for a ship to evacuate us. If the ship does not come, it means we are considered safe. If the ship comes, time will be limited. You are advised to pack one suitcase for each person, so as to be ready. If you have invalids in your house, make arrangements in consultation with your doctor. All possible notice will be given."

Enough fishing boats arrived at Alderney on 23 June to take off the entire population; so people, expecting the worst, took to the boats. During the voyage to England, three children were born on one ship. Only 19 islanders stayed behind – and 12 of those were soon persuaded to flee to Guernsey. On Sark, reassured by the example set by the Dame, Mrs Sybil Hathaway, a forceful lady who had ruled over the feudal island since 1926, hardly anyone left.

In London, the authorities were divided on one question: should the Germans be told the islands were undefended? If they knew, they might invade. If they didn't know, they might attack. Either way, the islands were sitting ducks.

The first shots

On 28 June, a gloriously warm summer day, the Luftwaffe put an end to the dithering: it first bombed and machine-gunned Guernsey, then Jersey, killing 33 people. The government asked the US ambassador in London, Joseph P. Kennedy, to inform Germany through the American Embassy in Berlin that the Channel staged the cautious German naval command by touching down on Guernsey. There was no resistance. Satisfied that the island was defenceless, the Germans flew in a platoon of soldiers. The next day a detachment of naval assault troops and a company of Infantry Regiment 396 flew into Jersey. Troops on motorbikes and officers in cars drove into St Helier and St Peter Port. Alderney was occupied on 2 July and Sark on 4 July.

For the first time, a part of the British empire – one just 90 miles (140 km) from the English coast and the monarchy's oldest possession – had been abandoned to an enemy, without a shot having been fired in its defence. ❏

Islands had been demilitarised and were no longer a legitimate target for bombardment.

The invasion seemed to the Islanders a long time in coming. Every day German planes flew overhead on reconnaisance missions, but none landed. The Germans expected to find the islands defended because aerial photographs revealed columns of lorries, assumed to be troop carriers, approaching the harbours of both main islands. The lorries were, in fact, transporting Jersey potatoes and Guernsey tomatoes, not British troops.

Then, on 30 June, a lone Luftwaffe pilot up-

LEFT: a German gunner gets the islands in his sights.
ABOVE: armed Nazi guard meets unarmed British bobby.

FIRST ENCOUNTER WITH THE ENEMY

Ralph Mollet, Secretary to the Bailiff of Jersey, kept a diary throughout the war, and published it in 1945 as *Jersey Under the Swastika*. In it, he recorded his first encounter with a German officer, Captain Gussek: "The Captain saluted and shook hands. I said that the Bailiff expected him at 10 o'clock. He replied that it was already 10am, Central European Time… He asked me how long the British had occupied the Island. I replied that we conquered England in 1066. He smiled. He produced to me an ordnance map of Jersey, and asked where he could obtain similar maps. I sent the porter out to purchase some; he said he would pay for them."

THE GERMAN OCCUPATION

It lasted for four years, ten months and seven days, and was by far the most traumatic event in the islands' often turbulent history

Life under the Wehrmacht, Germany's armed forces, began in a cordial enough way. True, a curfew was imposed, the sale of spirits was banned, listening to any radio station not German-controlled was forbidden, carrier pigeons were outlawed, and clocks were put forward one hour to conform to Central European time. But church services were still allowed, prayers for the Royal Family and the British Empire could be said, and civilians could travel between Jersey and Guernsey.

Such "correct" behaviour, it was reasoned, would counter propaganda about German barbarity and reassure the English that they had little to fear when England fell, as it inevitably would, under Hitler's rule. Anticipating that day on celluloid, the Germans filmed their army invading the virtually deserted island of Herm and claimed, for propaganda purposes, that it was the Isle of Wight.

Soon there were more Germans per square mile on the islands than in Germany, and there was no question about their purpose. Major-General Count Rudolph von Schmettow, Commander of the Channel Islands, a Silesian nobleman, was generally regarded as being courteous and civilised – but he was under direct orders from the Führer to turn the islands into "strong naval fortresses as quickly as possible, employing all forces and means available". After the war, Hitler had decided, Alderney would become part of France, while Jersey and Guernsey would remain German outposts.

Chalk and cheese

The Germans began to administer the islands as part of France, believing the islanders would be glad to be liberated from the British colonial yoke. They found it hard to understand the people's loyalty to Britain, and soon found much to disapprove of in their easy-going ways: the high illegitimate birth rate, the heavy consumption of alcohol, the presence of retired

plutocrats who devoted their time to golf and bridge. The Germans deplored the wide gap between rich and poor and regarded social provisions as being much behind the times. Reform, they vowed, must be a priority, and by 1943 they were able to report: "The face of the islands has been changed completely; it has

become more serious and more European."

But they found it almost impossible to come to grips with the islands' feudal system of government. What sense did it make to judge a 20th-century traffic offence by reference to 11th-century practices? Reluctantly, they decided to leave untouched this "constitutional nature reserve". For one thing, they were too thin on the ground to change everything overnight; for another, it soon became clear that it was in their interests to let the locals go on running their everyday affairs while the troops concentrated on making the islands impregnable.

Even so, the inexperienced German chiefs issued many unworkable orders. All photo-

LEFT: the redoubtable Dame of Sark confronts German officers. **RIGHT:** the swastika is unfurled.

graphic apparatus had to be handed in, they decreed; they were deluged not only with cameras but also with lenses, tripods and developing tanks. All weapons must be surrendered, they ordered; a strange selection of hunting weapons such as spears, tomahawks and blunderbusses descended on them – the legacy of the colonial careers of former administrators who had retired to the islands.

Many such people, who had devoted their life to the British Empire, now felt abandoned by Britain. Why, they asked bitterly, were the Channel Islands mentioned so seldom in BBC broadcasts? Had they been totally forgotten? In fact, the Home Office had advised the BBC not to make direct broadcasts to the islands for fear of reprisals by the Germans, who might, it was argued, confiscate all radio sets and so leave the islanders in complete ignorance of what was happening in the outside world. The argument was probably correct: when the war started going badly for the Germans, they did confiscate all radios. At first there was more than enough food on the islands for those remaining; too much, London thought, since the surplus would help sustain the invaders. Financially, things looked less rosy: many taxpayers had left, taking their bank accounts with them.

Curiosity about the Third Reich's new acquisition ran high in Germany. The Military Commander bought all the local literature he could find and imported a student of history, Dr Hans Auerbach, to write an account of the islands. This book, *Die Kanalinseln, Jersey, Guernsey, Sark*, was printed in Paris at the end of 1941 and sold well in St Helier to soldiers wishing to send copies to their families in Germany. In 1943, a book of photographs of the islands was published, *Ein Bilderbogen von den Kanalinseln*.

To inform troops of local affairs and keep them posted on the progress of the war, a daily newspaper, *Deutsche Inselzeitung*, began appearing in July 1940.

When the troops first arrived, they rapidly bought up everything they could find in shops – clothes, jewellery, clocks, gas fires – to send to their families in Germany. Since they paid in *Reichskredit* currency, issued only in occupied territory, this was in effect a form of respectable looting. Cars were requisitioned in return for eventual and inadequate compensation in *Reichsmarks*.

Prices soar

As the shops emptied, some were converted to other uses, such as soldiers' canteens. Others began selling secondhand goods, such as old kettles and worn clothes, at fancy prices. Soon flour, sugar and butter had to be imported from France. So did two-thirds of the meat ration.

The Germans took a particular interest in food production, bombarding experienced farmers with unwanted advice and demanding regular supplies of statistics. Glasshouses in Guernsey had to start producing green vegetables instead of flowers and tomatoes. Wheat, oats and barley largely replaced potatoes in Jersey's fields. "Agricultural commandos" were appointed to ensure that farmers were not supplying a black market.

Fishermen were closely supervised. Permits were issued only to those "who for family rea-

concocting such delicacies as carrot jam.

Smokers turned to substitutes such as watercress leaves and dried rose petals. They also tried cultivating tobacco plants and found, to their joy, that they flourished in the Channel Islands' soil. The States tried unsuccessfully to license the growers, some of whom were raising thousands of plants, and then turned their attention to how best to tax the tobacco grown. As a result the black market price of tobacco soared to 10 times its controlled price.

As fuel supplies diminished, vehicles were restricted to transporting troops or to essential services such as distributing milk. Bicycles

sons are unlikely to flee" and, unless escorted, they had to stay close to shore. As a result, catches were inadequate. The regulations governing fishing boats became so restrictive that, even when the seas were teeming with mackerel and mullet, the fishmongers had little to sell. In June 1942 fish was rationed.

Tea ran out within a year of Occupation. By 1943 black market supplies were costing £25 a lb (less than a half-kg). Soap ran out early in 1941. Soon sugar was short. With each deprivation, the islanders became more inventive,

were requisitioned, and soon rusty old crocks that might once have fetched a few shillings were changing hands for £10. Collisions involving German troops became frequent after driving on the left was abandoned in favour of the continental system of driving on the right. Gradually road-signs were translated into German, turning Castle Cornet into *Hafenschloss* and Petit Bot Bay into *Grüne Bucht*.

Close screening

Schools had to add German lessons to their curriculum, but not enough teachers could be spared from Germany to ensure it was effectively taught. When the few English language films

LEFT: the occupiers march into St Helier.
ABOVE: a German band concert.

trapped on the islands – such as *The Barretts of Wimpole Street* – at last lost their appeal through repetition, German films were imported. A galvanised pipe ran down the centre of cinemas; Germans sat to the right of it, locals to the left. Cinema-goers were instructed that it was in order to applaud comedians and heroes. Many locals turned, instead, to amateur theatricals, although the choice of plays had to be approved.

For lovers of military bands, there was no shortage of entertainment. For frustrated lovers among the military, official brothels were opened in St Helier and St Peter Port; the girls, imported from France, were permitted the more generous

rations usually reserved for heavy workers.

Respecting the Hague Convention, the Germans did not insist that Channel Islanders undertake any war-related jobs which might indirectly harm their fellow countrymen. But they did tempt some workers, particularly from the local Irish community, with high wages and better food rations. In reality, of course, anyone who grew potatoes or produced milk on the island was indirectly working for the enemy.

The grip of rationing tightened. An adult was allowed half a pint of milk a day and 7 lbs (3 kg) of potatoes. Gradually the amounts decreased: by the end of the war the bread allowance had fallen from 4 lbs (2 kg) a week

to 1 lb (0.5kg); the meat allowance from 12 ozs (330 gm) a head to 1 oz (28 gm) a week, and a 1-lb (half-kg) packet of tea cost up to £30 on the black market. Thievery became commonplace. Crops were stolen and some took advantage of the curfew to sneak into farms and milk the cows. Ingenuity (and necessity) produced parsnip coffee, blackberry leaf tea, carrot pudding and seaweed jelly. Curtains were made into clothes. Shoes were soled with wood.

The black market in food smuggled in from France began flourishing early in the Occupation. "It was interesting," remembered one doctor, "to watch people who lost weight at the early part of the Occupation gradually put it on again as they overcame their scruples."

Friend or foe?

The moral question faced by everyone was: to what extent should they cooperate with the enemy? Clearly the islands were too small for an effective resistance movement to develop, as it did in France. But at what point did passive cooperation shade into cordial collaboration? It was a delicate balancing act.

One resident remembered many years later: "There was no organised resistance as there was in France, because in a small country like this there would have been nowhere for them to hide. In France you could blow up a train and be hundreds of miles away by nightfall. There was not much sabotage, but plenty of passive resistance. Our motto was: if you couldn't hinder you didn't help. There was a great deal of hiding of food, of falsifying returns of potato crops, that sort of thing."

As so often in such situations, however, some girls cooperated closely enough to become pregnant. They were derided as "Jerry bags". Some personal grudges were settled as people informed on neighbours who had kept a radio set hidden or hoarded too much food. There were small acts of defiance, too. When supplies of Jersey's postage stamps ran out, the artist Edmund Blampied designed a new set with King George VI's cipher "GR" hidden in the scrollwork.

Soon the islanders became pawns in the battle of wills between Winston Churchill and Adolf Hitler. When Britain detained German citizens working in Iran, Hitler threatened to deport all British-born inhabitants of the Channel Islands. Unknown to the islanders, lists were drawn up.

The *Wehrmacht* were unenthusiastic about the idea: they had more than enough women and children on their hands in refugee camps and, with 36,000 much needed troops pinned down in the Channel, were already referring to Hitler's "island madness". But the Führer's personal orders could not be ignored for ever and in September 1942 the threat was finally carried out. More shiploads followed; eventually 2,000 British-born islanders were interned in Germany.

Even more ruthless retaliation was feared.

A RETURN TO HORSES

As fuel became scarce, horse-drawn traffic increased, with animals being imported from France at more than £200 each – a large sum, Bicycles cost £30.

---

and child could have been gassed and incinerated in a single day in one of the larger and more efficient German concentration camps".

Such a grim prospect didn't stop Churchill from planning nuisance raids on the islands. Bad weather put an end to most of these operations before they even began, but one Royal Navy action ended in disaster when E-boats sank *HMS Charybdis* in October 1943 with the loss of 462 lives. At the burial of the 21 bodies washed up on Guernsey, virtually the entire

The Germans reserved the right "to nominate certain members of any parish who will be liable to the death penalty in the event of any attacks against communications, as for instance harbours, cranes, bridges, cables and wires, if these are made with the assistance or the knowledge of the inhabitants of the parish concerned". The threat was not taken lightly. As Charles Cruickshank points out in his official history, *The German Occupation of the Channel Islands*, it was realised that "every man, woman

---

LEFT: before the food shortages began to bite, some old favourites were still on sale.

ABOVE: Jersey displays a defiant Victory sign.

---

population of around 5,000 people turned out to mourn. The Germans were surprised by such uncompromising loyalty to Britain.

Gradually the face of the islands changed as up to 15,000 imported slave workers, including Russians, Poles, Spanish Republicans and European Jews, poured in 17½ million cubic feet (half a million cubic metres) of reinforced concrete. Anti-tank walls 6 ft (2 metres) thick appeared on beaches. Gun emplacements ringed the coast: Jersey had 16 coastal artillery batteries, Guernsey 15, Alderney five and Sark one. Old granite towers and mills were turned into observation posts. Concrete strongpoints were surrounded by fixed flame-throwers and barbed-wire entanglements. Narrow-gauge railways were built to transport the concrete. More than 150,000 mines were laid.

Hard labour

The human cost was appalling. On Alderney, where an SS concentration camp (Sylt) was set up, as well as three labour camps (Norderney, Borkum and Helgoland), there were no civilians to witness the ruthless regime. It was "work, hard physical work for 12 to 14 hours a day, building the fortifications," one French survivor said later. "Every day there were beatings and people's bones were broken, their arms or their legs. People died from overwork." A Russian recalled that the German guards "tried to get out of us every ounce of labour and energy they could on as little food as possible. Our term of usefulness was generally accepted by the Germans to be six months. After that we were expended." Soon Jakob, Gustav and Adolf – as Jersey, Guernsey and Alderney were coded in the construction plan – were far better fortified than the coast of France. At one point there were 42,800 enemy personnel on the islands – two to every three remaining native islanders. Yet the islands, which were eating up one-twelfth of the

WHEN STARVATION STALKED THE ISLANDS

As autumn turned to winter in 1944, the situation looked bleak for the beleagurered islands and their captors. There was no coal and no gas and not enough wood for fuel. Supplies of electricity looked certain to cease at the end of the year. Communal kitchens were set up. The bailiff of Jersey summarised the stark facts to the German commander:
Butter: 2 oz. weekly ration. Sufficient to last until 31 Dec.
Sugar: 3 oz. weekly ration. Sufficient to last until 18 Nov.
Salt: for bakers only. Sufficient to last until 30 Nov.
Macaroni: Sufficient to last until 15 Nov.
Dried beans: three rations of 7 oz. remaining.
Cheese: 4 oz. ration. Sufficient to last until 15 Oct.

Tinned vegetables: one ration remaining in stock.
Tinned fish: one ration remaining in stock.
Tinned milk: one ration remaining in stock.
Matches: one ration of four boxes per household remaining in stock.
Dripping: not enough for one ration.
Oil (cooking): enough for one ration of under half-pint remaining.
Saccharine: enough for two rations of 100 tabloids remaining.
Soap: None.

Soon, one milkless day a week was announced. This was extended in January 1945 to three days.

Wehrmacht's resources, had little military significance, even as a jumping-off point for Operation Sealion, the invasion of England. The Occupation was about prestige. Commonsense was a low priority.

As supplies of soap ran out and medicines became scarce, it wasn't just the morale of the islanders which deteriorated. The Germans, at first delighted by their posting to such a pleasant location, soon became bored. Apart from occasionally turning the anti-aircraft guns on overflying RAF planes, there wasn't much to do. Also, as postal deliveries became less frequent towards the end of the

The action on D-Day, 6 June, was concentrated elsewhere: on the beaches of Normandy. With rations down to three months' supply, the islanders were left to wait out the rest of the war and found themselves in a frustrating situation: besieged by the British navy. Because fuel was scarce for the supply vessels that hadn't already been destroyed, the Germans began using Rhine barges to supply their "beleaguered Atlantic fortresses". These boats were low enough to creep under British radar screens but they couldn't be used in rough seas, so supplies became more uncertain than ever.

In the autumn of 1944 there were more than

war, the German troops, hearing of British bombing raids on Germany, worried increasingly about the fate of their families.

The tide turns

By the beginning of 1944, the tide of war had turned decisively against Hitler. But, worried that the Channel Islands might still be used as stepping-stones for an Allied assault on Europe, he repeated the order: the islands must be held to the last man and the last bullet.

LEFT: the Occupation Tapestry in the St Helier's Maritime Museum building recalls wartime conditions. **ABOVE:** relics in Guernsey's German Occupation Museum.

90,000 mouths to feed. Jersey contained 39,000 civilians and 12,000 troops, Guernsey 23,000 civilians and 13,000 troops, and Alderney had 3,500 Germans plus the slave workers. The poor diet encouraged ill health: tuberculosis, arthritis, jaundice and diptheria became common. Some troops were on the verge of revolt. Islanders listening into BBC broadcasts on illegal home-made crystal sets heard of food being sent by the Allies to Russia, Greece and Italy. What about the Channel Islands, they wondered. Had they really been abandoned?

At this point, Hitler had a dilemma. On the one hand, he couldn't let civilians starve; nor did he have the resources to move them to

Europe. So, he reasoned, it would be best to hand them over to Britain. On the other hand, three-quarters of the people were working for the troops, directly or indirectly, growing food and running utilities such as electricity and water – so how could they be spared?

In the end, Hitler asked Britain to evacuate all islanders except those fit to bear arms. This created a dilemma for Churchill. Naturally, he wanted to liberate as many Channel Islanders as possible; on the other hand, leaving the Germans with most of

NO TIMES FOR TIDES

As 1945 began, almanacs were impossible to obtain, so islanders had no information about the tides or the times of sunrise and sunset.

were raided to ensure that this order was obeyed.

In January, telephones were finally cut off. Electricity supplies, which had been limited to one kilowatt per house per week, ended completely. It was forbidden to cut wood for fuel. Down to their last few matches, people tried to keep alight a paraffin-soaked piece of string. To conserve food, no household was permitted to keep more than one dog; all others were killed. There seemed to be fewer pets, anyway, and people began to notice the increasing number of advertisements for

the food would prolong the Occupation longer than necessary. An alternative was to send food parcels and medical supplies to the islands. However, the same dilemma had to be faced: the Germans might take more than their share and again the Occupation would be prolonged.

But the risk had to be run, and food parcels were duly delivered at the end of 1944 by the International Red Cross. The German response was to hand over the parcels but seize locally grown potatoes and cereals. They also told the islanders that, if they were accepting free gifts of food, they could not justify hoarding secret stocks of tinned soup or fruit or bottles of wine and that all such stocks must be handed over. Houses

missing animals in the "lost and found" columns of local newspapers. The horrifying answer to the mystery soon emerged: hungry troops were catching and cooking cats and dogs.

Ironically, if the Germans had shipped in fertiliser as well as cement and grown more of their own food to start with, the islands might have become self-supporting. One plan, early in the Occupation, had been to turn Herm over to cattle fattening, but the idea came to nothing. As the end of the war neared, they turned desperately to planting potatoes and fishing. But it was too late.

When Hitler's death was announced on 1 May 1945, a German Army newspaper printed in Guernsey ran the headline: "Führer dies a hero's death". The islanders reached for their Union Jacks, but they weren't able to wave them in public for another week, until surrender documents were signed. Churchill had ruled that Operation Nestegg, as the liberation of the Channel Islands was called, should not involve an assault that might cost civilian lives.

Free at last

There were scenes of jubilation but also of violence as *HMS Beagle* and *HMS Bulldog* liberated the islands after four years, 10 months and seven days of Occupation. In Jersey, some girls who had consorted with the Germans were

Home Secretary, Herbert Morrison, praised Mrs Hathaway for having been "almost wholly mistress of the situation" throughout the Occupation.

Alderney, the ultimate fortress which, according to one estimate, would have cost a quarter of a million lives to capture by force, was liberated peacefully on 16 May. Four days later, 2,332 Germans were taken as prisoners-of-war to Britain, leaving 500 behind to begin the massive clean-up. A *Guernsey Press* editorial caught the mixture of jubilation and apprehension: "As the gates of Liberation and Freedom swing upon their hinges, the durance of captivity passes like a dreadful dream, and there

rough-handled and a few black marketeers were beaten up. But, mostly, ecstasy was in the air as British soldiers handed out lemonade, chocolate, cakes and soap. A child given an orange started bouncing it: never having seen one before, she thought it was a ball.

On Sark, British soldiers could not be spared to guard the German prisoners and the task was left to the redoubtable Dame of Sark. From 10 May until 17 May, she took charge of 275 Germans, ordering them to return confiscated radio sets and to remove mines from the harbour. The British

LEFT: a gun emplacement camouflaged as a house.
ABOVE: Red Cross supplies helped stave off starvation.

opens before us a prospect impossible, as yet, either to realise or to visualise."

Now, more than 50 years after the end of World War II, memories of the German Occupation are fading. In recognition of this, the ceremonies arranged in 1995 to mark half a century of freedom in Jersey and Guernsey left lasting memorials to the courage and fortitude of islanders. Both islands have imposing liberation sculptures. Jersey also has a hugely detailed Occupation tapestry – rivalling in scale the more famous one in Bayeux – which charts the story of the war years from the arrival of the Germans to their surrender to the British liberators of Force 135 in 1945. ❏

BRAVE NEW WORLD

Rebuilding the islands after the war meant encouraging three new waves of invaders: tourists, tax exiles and bankers

Hitler's plan, had he won the war, was to turn Jersey into one giant holiday centre as part of the Third Reich's "Strength through Joy" programme. What happened, some would say, was not all that different.

The economic need to win back holidaymakers was evident from the first day of peace – even though the islands were in no state to receive them. The economies of Jersey and Guernsey had to be rebuilt and Alderney needed a complete overhaul. Many houses were damaged, some beyond repair. House rents, living costs and taxation had all gone up and domestic servants, the more affluent discovered, were practically unobtainable. Some shrewd UK businessmen, seeking to escape from the grim economic prospects on the mainland, snapped up houses at inflated prices, leaving returning ex-servicemen and the poorer evacuees unable to find affordable accommodation.

One major problem was what to do with the fortifications, air raid shelters, munitions dumps, gun emplacements and subterranean hangers. Were they an eyesore, a unique tourist attraction or both? One islander in exile in the UK had written with prescience in 1944: "What is a disfigurement of the landscape today will be a historic monument tomorrow." In many cases the problem was theoretical anyhow, since the concrete was solid enough to defeat the demolition teams. In glasshouse-covered Guernsey, the dynamiters didn't dare try.

Reclaiming Alderney

Alderney, evacuated in 1940, had suffered most. So great was the devastation that some observers thought her best left abandoned. But soon the islanders started drifting back. The first contingent arrived on a stormy December day to be greeted with "Welcome Home" placards made by German prisoners of war on the orders of the British army. Surprisingly, relations were tolerably good between the remaining Germans and

the returning islanders, and the Germans, before they were finally shipped out in June 1946, gave a farewell concert in the Lyceum Cinema.

Prompted by the UK, Guernsey assumed financial and administrative responsibility for Alderney. For the individual, though, picking up the pieces after more than five years was

heartbreaking. It certainly wasn't made any easier by the curious decision of Judge French to allocate the islanders' scattered furniture and belongings by means of a free-for-all; the people lined up and, when a whistle was blown, ran forward to grab whatever goods they could. It was a sure way to create ill-feeling, and it did.

Nor could the past be easily forgotten. There were demands that known collaborators – mistresses of Germans, profiteers and informers – should be punished. But from whom should the pound of flesh be extracted? At what point did disgraceful behaviour become treachery? It was easy enough to claw back profits made from the Occupation: a 60 percent levy on such

---

LEFT: joy as the islanders are liberated in 1945.
RIGHT: Sybil Hathaway, the Dame of Sark.

profits was imposed in Jersey; in Guernsey, 80 percent of the first £10,000 of profits were seized, then 100 percent. But, in identifying traitors, the British authorities found it difficult to separate hearsay from hard evidence, and there were no criminal prosecutions.

Calls for reform

In facing the challenges of peacetime, many of the islanders who had spent the war in the UK were determined not to return to the prewar rule of a paternal establishment; they had experienced a more robust political climate in the UK and demanded reforms in the States. More

activities formalised themselves into "The Society for the Preservation of German Occupation Relics". This became the Channel Islands Occupation Society, which runs filmshows and talks about wartime life and publishes a magazine.

One last territorial squabble between Britain and France was played out in 1953. It centred on ownership of the offshore reefs, the Minquiers and Ecréhous, and was fought out in the International Court at the Hague. England won. But, although the lawyers seemed satisfied as to who owned the reefs, some Frenchmen were unwilling to accept the decision with good grace. There have been a number of symbolic

democratic election procedures were introduced. These brought experienced businessmen into government, laying the foundation for the prosperity to come. Due concession was made to tradition, however: it was decided to keep French as the language for formal and ceremonial occasions, so that, even today, the islands' parliaments vote *pour* or *contre*.

As older people tried to forget the Occupation, a younger generation began to discover it. Two Guernsey schoolboys began collecting some of the relics still to be found in bunkers, tunnels and slit trenches: gas masks, satchels, helmets with the original owner's name inside. As their collection outgrew their attics, their

occupations of both reefs, and as recently as 1998 an attempt was made to replace the Union Flag at the Ecréhous with that of the "Republic of Patagonia". A Frenchman was arrested and a Jersey policeman hoisted the Union Flag again.

The television age

Even TV had to tailor itself to island life. The commercial station, Channel Television, became Britain's nearest equivalent to community TV, closely reflecting the needs of the people. Adding to the constitutional anomalies, the Independent Broadcasting Authority Act became the only Westminster legislation applying to the islands. It decreed that Channel Television must produce at least 3½ hours a week of local programming, buying the rest from the network. Making a virtue of its size, the station avoided trade union opposition to new technology and became the first ITV station to benefit from the flexibility of electronic newsgathering equipment.

In the early 1960s, as more and more of the British Empire's colonies were granted independence, many expatriates in those countries, fearing for the future, looked around to find a safer haven for their capital. With the abolition of a 200-year-old law limiting interest rates to a maximum 5 percent, Jersey made its bid to become a tax haven – or, as it prefers to call itself, an international finance centre.

KEEPING OUT BUTLIN'S

Keen to retain its quiet image, Jersey refused to let one of its most celebrated tax exiles, Sir Billy Butlin, build one of his holiday camps on the island.

selves with more middle-aged couples, who demanded a better class of hotel and restaurant and who were looking for alternatives to sunbathing. About half the holidaymakers were return customers – an enviable endorsement of the islands' popularity, but a worry to the tourism authorities because that meant the average visitor was getting older; even today, more than 60 percent of tourists are over 45. Would the next generation of tourists forsake the Channel Islands?

Jersey began wooing the more sophisticated

Gradually the face of tourism changed. In the old days, the Channel Islands had catered for honeymooners and the conventional family holiday: two weeks living in a guesthouse, with most days spent on the beach. It was "going abroad" made easy. In the 1960s, however, as cheap package tours lured many British families to the Mediterranean, the Channel Islands found them-

visitor. Capitalising on its abundant seafood and fresh vegetables, it started a gastronomic festival in 1965. Activity holidays – walking, windsurfing, horse riding – were designed to appeal to the health-conscious younger set. To give tourists something to visit, museums were spruced up and cottage industry attractions, such as glassblowing, were created. Both States discovered that there was money to be made in the low season from the conference trade and soon busloads of nurses, teachers, salesmen and Rotarians were being discharged into hotel lobbies. Guernsey's tourism chief echoed the words of countless other populations throughout the world: "The islanders hate tourism, but they like visitors."

LEFT: a Jersey cow joins the export drive in 1956.
ABOVE: celebrating Jersey's Black Butter night.

Jersey, meanwhile, has tried to increase its up-market appeal by focusing attention on heritage and the arts. Medieval castles, a wealth of museums and an international festival which has featured the Royal Shakespeare Company and the Royal Liverpool Philharmonic now feature prominently in the island's advertising copy.

Relations with Europe

When Britain joined its old foe, France, in the European Economic Community in 1974, the Channel Islands were uncertain which way to jump. Accepting the EEC's rules could undermine their agricultural and financial services

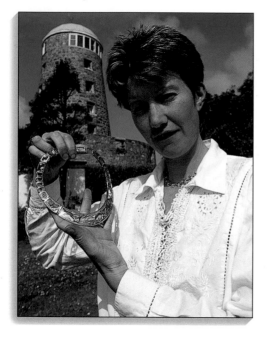

industries. In the end, a compromise was hammered out: the islands became subject to the EEC's external tariff on industrial goods and to certain parts of its byzantine Common Agricultural Policy; but they did not have to harmonise their taxes or conform to the rules governing the free movement of workers and capital, and cattle were exempted from the CAP so that the purity of the Channel Islands strain could be preserved. The States, having gained the best of both worlds, congratulated themselves on beating the bureaucrats of Brussels.

Also, aware that 80 percent of Jersey's visitors and 90 percent of Guernsey's came from Britain, the tourist chiefs saw an opportunity

to spread their net wider. The average French visitor, for instance, was younger and spent more. When other Europeans began expressing interest in the islands' history, the States, which had never been particularly conscious of their heritage, opened a maritime and wrecks museum in an old Guernsey fort and revived the noonday gun-firing ceremony at the 13th-century Castle Cornet.

In the 1970s, the oil crisis gave a new significance to the islands' sunshine statistics as solar panels began appearing on rooftops. As inflation ravaged Britain, Jersey's prices still looked cheap to Continentals. The French in particular came to buy English woollens and pop records and to eat gourmet food at affordable prices.

Crisis point

But population pressures were stretching the islands to breaking point. The water supply was inadequate. So were rubbish disposal facilities. Roads weren't good enough. The well-heeled immigrants were demanding efficient services, but Guernsey had more cars than workers. Jersey erected that familiar totem to modern living, a multi-storey carpark (it now has six). Hospital, police, fire and ambulance services all required expansion. The tourism industry had to import seasonal staff, such as waiters and chambermaids, first from Madeira, then from Poland.

Even Sark's tranquillity as an offshore Ruritania began to be eroded by day-trippers. Did such visitors, the locals asked, benefit anyone except the wagonette owners? Many brought packed lunches and were rushed around so fast by their tour guides that they didn't have time to buy a postcard.

Other aspects of the modern world impinged. In 1979, an automatic telephone exchange was installed on Sark because spare parts could no longer be found for the old manual exchange. The new technology was not welcomed. The islanders liked the old days when you didn't have to remember phone numbers; when you simply told the lady operator who you wished to speak to and she would connect you, even if the person was in the grocery shop or visiting neighbours.

Also, you could have too much of a good thing, even millionaires. Tax exiles such as golfer Tony Jacklin and boxer Billy Walker had brought the islands useful publicity, but too many rich people, the States felt, would unbalance their economies. Restrictions were imposed. Suddenly it seemed easier for a rich man to get into the kingdom of Heaven than to settle in the Channel Islands.

Immigrants to Jersey were expected to buy an expensive house and had to be able to contribute £10,000 a year in taxes to the island's coffers. Even then, the number was limited to 15 a year and all applicants had to be interviewed. Guernsey adopted a two-tier approach to housing: there was to be a fixed stock of 1,200 houses on an open market, available to newcomers; the rest, in a closed mar-

PROVING YOUR WORTH

Becoming a tax exile isn't easy. Jersey made even a former Governor of the Bank of England reveal his bank balance to prove his tax liability would be suitable.

tise their profession. One couple who had kept a house on Guernsey while they worked abroad for 20 years were denied residents' licences when, on retiring, they tried to return to the house.

Alderney, too, encountered its fair share of problems. An influx of middle-aged wealthy settlers unbalanced the population; there were too few children on the island. In addition, some natives felt that the rash of new housebuilding was making the island look suburban, detracting from its rural appeal.

ket, could be bought only by natives. What's more, the newcomer could expect to pay between three and five times as much for a house on the open market than the native would pay for a comparable house.

The rules defining residents became so complicated that native-born students who had left for long study courses (such as medicine) found it hard to get permission to return home to prac-

LEFT: Guernsey jeweller Catherine Best, one of the many talented craftspeople on the islands.
ABOVE: La Visite Royale, a twice-yearly check on behalf of the Queen ("Our Duke of Normandy") that the hedgerows are not obstructing her highways.

Who pays for defence?

Alderney was unexpectedly hit by an aftershock from the 1982 conflict between Britain and Argentina over the Falkland Islands in the South Atlantic. The States of Jersey, in a spontaneous act of charity to people who had suffered a similar occupation to that of the Channel Islands in World War II, immediately sent £5 million to the Falkland Islands Fund and Guernsey followed with a contribution of £100,000 towards sheltered accommodation for the elderly. Within weeks both islands were formally asked for a contribution towards the UK defence bill.

Similar requests had been batted off with ease in the past but this time the demand was definite:

the islands would be protected in the same way as the Falklands, an act generously acknowledged by Guernsey and Jersey, and the contribution had to be paid. Having let the cat out of the bag, there was no catching it. A number of methods of payment were considered but eventually Guernsey said that they would make no contribution. The independence and constitution of the bailiwick was clearly laid down in ancient royal charters and would not be jeopardised. Instead they would take over the expensive maintenance of Alderney's defensive breakwater (*see page 264*).

This was bad news for Alderney. With its economy booming and its accounts with Guern-

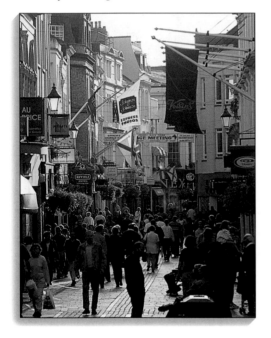

sey showing a healthy surplus, many islanders had been talking about seeking political independence. But the "Falklands factor", which added the cost of maintaining the breakwater to the annual budget, wrecked such hopes.

Alderney's prosperity stemmed from the 1980s financial bonanza and was shared by the other islands. Margaret Thatcher's new Conservative government in London relaxed exchange controls. This meant that British residents no longer needed Bank of England permission to move money to the Channel Islands and enabled them to use the islands as a base from which to trade on world money markets. Non-resident company registrations soared.

The banking and fund management industries attracted billions of pounds. As unemployment soared in most of Europe, the islands enjoyed virtually full employment, no public debt and healthy budget surpluses.

The recession of the early 1990s eventually had a significant impact, but in spite of a downturn in the fortunes of tourism and agriculture and a slight weakening of the economies in general, finance remained largely unscathed and continued to prosper.

The financial dilemma

Although the States owe allegiance to the Queen rather than to the UK government, they realised that they could be harmed by politicians at Westminster. One Labour spokesman accused the islanders of living off the proceeds of tax avoidance and encouraging "fraudsters, shysters and tricksters". It was intolerable, the party stated, that British territory should be "a bolthole for money that shuns the light". Nonsense, said the States, most investment money comes from non-UK sources and boosts the UK's balance of trade by adding to its invisible earnings. Prudently, though, they drew up plans to break the monetary union with the UK if necessary.

They also resolved to keep their image clean, expertly juggling the two sometimes contradictory qualities demanded of a tax haven, confidentiality and respectability. An investigation was quickly mounted in 1985 when the US alleged that millions of dollars of Mafia drug money was being laundered through the Channel Islands. No evidence of organised crime transactions was found.

Embarrassments occur regularly, however. Eleven bars of gold bullion from Britain's biggest robbery, a £26 million raid on a Brink's-Mat warehouse in 1983, turned up in Jersey. And, in 1987, it was discovered that Channel Island companies had handled part of the wealth of Ferdinand Marcos, the deposed president of the Philippines. One top banker neatly summed up the situation when he said: "You will notice the corollary between crime and secrecy, and therein lies our dilemma." More recently, despite constant vigilance, there have been other reports that the Channel Islands have been used as repositories for "money which shuns the light", but their reputations for probity remain relatively undamaged in comparison with some other offshore finance centres.

This was confirmed by an extensive review of the islands' finance laws carried out by a former Treasury official, Andrew Edwards, at the request of the Home Secretary, who is the UK Government minister with responsibility for the islands. The Home Secretary failed to consult the islands before ordering the review, which is against constitutional convention and, although that caused some fuss in the islands, the eventual Edwards report was very flattering to the islands and claimed that in some respects they were ahead of the UK.

ECLIPSE OF THE "TOM"

Guernsey tomato growers, unable to compete with cheap exports from Spain and Portugal, began cultivating cut flowers.

Financial institutions wishing to set up shop on the larger islands today are confronted with a "No Vacancies" sign. At best, they must wait patiently, as they might after applying to join a select gentleman's club in London. Hoping to take advantage of this situation, Alderney began trumpeting its wares in display advertisements: "Looking for a new offshore base? There are no house purchase restrictions, and the lack of red tape makes it ideal for the smaller business."

Short of space, both principal towns have

The head hunters

There are other dilemmas. The finance industry in Jersey, for instance, employs 12,000 people, and finding sufficient suitably qualified staff is a constant problem. As often happens on small islands, many of the brighter young people leave to build careers on the mainland, and immigration restrictions mean that the banks can import only specialists. As a result, local school-leavers are often offered jobs in finance before they have even taken their examinations. Poaching staff from rivals is the other common solution.

LEFT: easy shopping in St Helier's pedestrian precinct.
ABOVE: one of the high-speed ferries to England.

been clawing land back from the sea. St Helier, already using 14 acres (nearly 6 hectares) of reclaimed land east of the harbour, has added 35 acres (14 hectares) west of the harbour, created by infilling. St Peter Port has reclaimed 30 acres (12 hectares) for a marina, car park and container marshalling yard.

Now, as ever, there is a new wave of French invaders. But, as befits the islands' affluence, the newcomers are hoteliers and chefs, seeking to replace tomato soup and cod steaks with *escargots à la Bourguignonne* and *truite Grenobloise*. It's the latest of many revolutions, but at least it is being realised with the kitchen knife, not the sword. ❑

GOVERNMENT BY AMATEURS

The islands' tradition of appointing unpaid volunteers as politicians and policemen has been put under strain by the realities of modern life

The Channel Islands' system of government provokes very varied reactions from outside observers. Visiting international bankers praise it for its virtually unshakeable political stability. A former British Conservative member of parliament with a holiday home on Sark has spoken admiringly of the islands' non-party "consensus" style of poli-

tics. On the other hand, left-wing critics at Westminster tend to see the system as an unholy alliance of surviving feudalism and freebooting capitalism, lacking many of the elements of modern democracy.

Local politicians feel that some of their detractors, ignorantly or wilfully, ignore the islands' constitutional history, treating them as a corner of the United Kingdom that has obtained home rule, whereas in fact they have never been part of mainland Britain. Channel Islanders, it is pointed out, have been running their own affairs for centuries – ever since, in fact, they chose to be linked to the English Crown rather than to France.

That choice was a lucky historical chance (or perhaps shrewd 13th-century thinking) because, if the islands had remained part of Normandy, as they were at the time of the Norman Conquest of England, they would have long since been absorbed into metropolitan France. As it was, in return for staying loyal to the English Crown when King John lost his French possessions, they were granted, in 1215, rights and privileges that amounted to self-government, subject only to Royal assent through the Privy Council.

Creeping democracy

The islands' parliaments evolved gradually from the Royal Courts established by the constitutions of King John. The bailiff, who presided over a court of 12 *jurats*, began to consult other leading members of the community – Les Etats, or the States, as they came to be called – about the running of the island. It was not until the mid-18th century that the separate functions of the Royal Court and the legislative body, the States, were clearly defined, and not until the 19th century that elected representatives began to sit in the States.

Under a postwar reform that followed the German Occupation in World War II, the number of elected deputies was increased, and the *jurats* and rectors who had previously sat by right in the States were dropped.

The parishes continued to be represented, and the *jurats* (magistrates) were replaced by 12 senior statesmen, known as senators in Jersey and *conseillers* in Guernsey, whose purpose was to bring political maturity and continuity to the more democratic island parliaments.

Jersey's States Assembly currently consists of the bailiff or deputy bailiff sitting as Speaker, 12 senators, 12 parish constables, 29 deputies, the dean of Jersey, attorney-general and solicitor-general. Until recently Guernsey's States of Deliberation comprised the bailiff or deputy bailiff, 12 *conseillers*, 10 *douzaine* (parish council) representatives, 33 people's deputies, two Alderney representatives (since that island comes partly under Guernsey's administration), HM Procureur (attorney-general) and HM Comptroller (solicitor-general).

Pressure for reform

In December 2000 a government review body recommended an overhaul of Guernsey's constitution, reporting a need for clearer leadership and the implementation of a more efficient and accountable system of government. Since then the structure of the States has undergone major change: 12 new deputies replaced the *conseillers*, the role of *douzaine*

Port, though the States of Alderney, which consist of a popularly elected president and 12 people's deputies, remain as they were and their two members who sit in the Guernsey States will continue to do so.

Sark – frequently referred to as the last feudal constitution in the western world - is updating its laws following pressure from the European Court of Human Rights. Many of the existing laws have hardly changed since they were enacted under Queen Elizabeth I over 400 years ago. The ban on divorce has been repealed and the death penalty (which according to the records has never actually

was abolished and in 2004 the island adopted a ministerial system with a Chief Minister elected by the States (the Bailiff was previously appointed by the Crown). Forty-three separate committees have been replaced with a Policy Council, 10 departments and five 5 specialist committees – including a new scrutiny committee.

The changes have impacted on other islands of the Bailiwick of Guernsey. Herm and Jethou now come under the district of St Peter

PRECEDING PAGES: farmers in Jersey; tourism in Sark.
LEFT: States ceremonial in St Peter Port, Guernsey.
ABOVE: Jersey's coat of arms, in St Helier's market.

been carried out on the island) is likely to be given the heave-ho. Sark's Chief Pleas currently provides more representatives per head for its 500 inhabitants than anywhere else in the British Isles, since besides 40 tenants or landowners, it includes 121 people's deputies. However this will all change on 1st January 2006 when the Chief Pleas will consist of 16 tenants elected by their peers and 16 deputies elected by the remainder of the population.

The atmosphere of the courtroom persists in the island parliaments, and this sets the tone of political life. Visitors find the debates remarkably disciplined compared with the barracking and background chatter of the House of Commons in London.

Proceedings in the States are opened in French – and a member could still address the House in French at the risk of not being understood by many of his colleagues. As the Queen's representatives, the lieutenant-governors of Jersey and Guernsey normally attend States meetings (though with no vote), and in Guernsey, for example, an official is asked if "His Excellency" is present in the words: "*Monsieur Le Prévôt de la Reine, son excellence le Lieutenant-Gouverneur assistera-t-il à la séance d'aujourd'hui?*".

Hands-off policy softens

States meetings are like a mixture of a national parliament and a town council, as members have to deal both with weighty affairs and very parochial matters. There is no written agreement setting out the relationship between the islands and the UK Government, but by constitutional usage it is accepted that Britain is responsible for the islands' defence and international relations but does not interfere in their internal government. Whether the islands could take a major decision that conflicted with British policy is an open question. Guernsey abol-

"THE BEAST OF JERSEY"

Despite the impression given by the 1980s television cops series *Bergerac*, the Channel Islands are a relatively law-abiding place. An exception to this rule, however, was the series of sex crimes committed by the notorious "Beast of Jersey", Edward Paisnel.

Between 1960 and 1971, "the Beast" terrorised the island and, in so doing, highlighted one of the main flaws in Jersey's police system: the lack of cohesion between the island's unpaid honorary police *(see page 71)* and the paid variety. During any investigation after a crime, an honorary policeman had to be in attendance because only he had the power to enter a home without a warrant – a priv-

ilege denied the paid officials. Only an honorary policeman (usually the Centenier) could formally charge a man and so, for a decade, the paid and unpaid police got in each other's way in trying to unmask the Beast.

Even when Paisnel was caught, it was more through luck than judgement. His excuse that he was "on his way to a fancy dress party" when he was arrested (initially for a traffic offence) seemed tame when a mask, wig, gloves and large blue coat with inch-long nails protruding from the shoulders were found in his car. As the "Beast of Jersey" affair unfolded in court, the States were encouraged to rethink their policing policy.

ished the death penalty before the UK did – but opinion in British government circles was already leaning that way. The view of the 1973 Royal Commission was that the Westminster parliament "has, and should retain, the right in the last resort to legislate for the islands". By and large the relationship has worked amicably, partly because potential problems are quietly sorted out behind the scenes. Insular legislation is sent to the Home Office for comment before it goes before the States and, once passed, has to go back to the Privy Council for Royal assent.

However all this is likely to change in step

A broadening of opinion

A new political party, the Jersey Democratic Alliance was launched in April 2005 and is campaigning to reintroduce party politics. The party aims to boost local industries such as tourism and agriculture which have lost out to finance. With regard to party politics, their thinking runs counter to that of the pressure group Elect Jersey 2005, set up in May 2005, which believes Jersey is not ready to go down that route.

Lack of an official opposition has been held up by outside critics as evidence of political immaturity, but most islanders see it as just the reverse. At a Commonwealth Parliamentary Association

with constitutional reform. In 2002 the Clothier Report, akin to the review body that urged an overhaul of Guernsey's constitution, came up with similar recommendations for Jersey. The move from the existing committee system towards ministerial government is scheduled to go ahead once the autumn 2005 elections are over. This is to be a cabinet-style government headed by a Chief Minister; the number of Deputies will be reduced and a handful of Scrutiny Panels, as well as a Public Accounts Committee, will be established.

LEFT: riding to a States of Jersey ceremonial.
ABOVE: Royal Square, St Helier.

conference in 1987, the Guernsey delegation asked: "Is party politics desirable in the government of small countries today?" The majority of Channel Islanders think not; they believe that non-party parliamentary debate enables MPs to get on with their job without wasting endless time in scoring off each other. Indeed, some islanders think there would have been far less trouble in the post-imperial Commonwealth if the former colonies had adopted the Channel Islands' system instead of Westminster's. Others are hoping to see the back of the anachronistic government structures and look forward to a more streamlined system.

Non-party politics have certainly produced

stability – a feature of the Channel Islands that the offshore financiers value as much as, or even more than, their low taxation. Up to now there has been no risk of an election bringing a swing from Right to Left, let alone a drastic change of regime. The islands are virtually revolution-proof.

Paying for politics

Until recently States members were, in theory at least, unpaid (as MPs were in England at one time), although they received a substantial allowance. This payment countered the criticism that running the community was the

prerogative of the better-off. Voluntary public service is a tradition of which the islands are particularly proud, however, and it runs right through their institutions. Jersey still has honorary parish police forces operating alongside the States police, and Sark's law enforcement is carried out by unpaid feudal officers.

In practice, Jersey and Guernsey have compromised to some extent with their belief in honorary service, partly to enable the less well-off to enter parliament and partly because States work has become increasingly time-consuming. In Guernsey members could claim a taxable allowance of just over £7,000

(US$10,500) a year plus expenses of £1,400. In addition, there was a means-tested payment of £20 for every half-day spent on States business and supplementary allowances for committee presidents. In Jersey, States members could claim an allowance of £8,000 plus a means-tested income supplement of up to £10,000. A few members managed to live mainly on the allowance and were in effect full-time politicians. The majority (like many Westminster MPs) combined parliamentary duties with careers as lawyers, accountants, estate agents and farmers.

With the growing complexity of island affairs, and the increasing pressure placed on members' time, the hallowed tradition of honorary States service is changing. Up to now there had been no central policymaking cabinet; the States comprised a number of committees, each responsible for a particular sector such as agriculture or tourism, which independently brought forward propositions to the House.

The system had its advantages in the past. It strengthened political stability by ensuring that no single States committee could push an unpopular policy through the House. And, under the honorary system, it rewarded those prepared to give their time to public service with their own little political empires. However the lack of co-ordination was revealed to have severe drawbacks when it came to social and economic planning.

Settling into the new system

Even so, local politicians remained very suspicious of anything that looked like greater central control. When in 1987 the Jersey States commissioned a review of the island's government machinery from accountants Peat Marwick McLintock, the consultants were asked not to propose reforms that would undermine the committee system and introduce a cabinet. Nevertheless, they concluded that the island's "cumbersome" system of government needed restructuring.

Now that both Guernsey and Jersey have jettisoned their committee-style governments and that the days of "amateur" politicians are numbered, the old systems may finally be on their way to becoming historical curiosities. ❏

LEFT: the Bailiff of Jersey, Sir Philip Bailhache.

Policemen in Pullovers

For the first half of the 20th century (and for many centuries before) 11 of Jersey's 12 parishes policed themselves without paid assistance from men in blue uniforms. The philosophy was that each parish was an extended family and looked after its own. This meant that, if someone committed a crime, the head of the parish (the Constable, or *Connétable*) and his honorary, part-time policemen – including the *Centenier* (his right-hand man), Constable's officers and *vingteniers* (the on-the-beat kind of PCs) – would be called out. But the paid police of St Helier would not be alerted unless the crime was too large for the parish to handle.

In simpler terms, the Constable was the father; his men, elected within the parish, were big brother; the rest of the parish were family; and, as in all families, if a younger son got out of hand the older, wiser lads would quickly bring him to heel. The system dominated crime prevention and fighting. In 1950 there were 233 honorary police in Jersey and only 50 full-time, uniformed professionals. If a crime took place outside the town or if a criminal hid in another parish, the uniformed branch could not arrest that man without the permission of the other parish's Constable or Centenier.

As far back as 1919, Guernsey had abolished such a system. After all, for every Sherlock Holmes that emerges from a volunteer, unpaid police force whose members could be farmhands or quarrymen, how many ponderous Dr Watsons might there be? The States allowed a "real" police force to be established in the 1950s. By the 1960s, it was dealing effectively with most of the major crime committed on Jersey.

In the 1970s the paid police force were given more power. Nowadays they operate from the main police station on Rouge Bouillon (there are smaller sub-stations at Halkett Place and St Aubin) and nearly all serious charges are made here. Only an honorary policeman (often the Centenier) can formally charge a suspect. This means, for example, that if a St Clement man is arrested, the Centenier of St Clement will be invited to St Helier police headquarters to charge the man. The next morning

RIGHT: the British-style uniform still persists.

the Centenier will present the case at St Helier's magistrate's court. If the crime is a serious one, it will be referred to the Royal Court; if not, it will be dealt with by the presiding magistrate.

The main arbiter of justice in Jersey, the Bailiff, presides over Royal Court, aided by his deputy and a panel of Jurats. A similar panel operates in Guernsey, whose courts have the power to pass judgement on criminals arrested in Sark (which has no professional policeman), Alderney (which has two) and Herm.

Jersey's honorary police have a wide range of powers which would be the envy of many UK officers. They can order petty criminals to attend an

inquiry at the parish hall where, depending on the severity of the crime, the offender will be warned, fined, or referred to the magistrate's court for a sterner sentence. They can also set up road blocks and can flag down a car if they think the driver is breaking the law.

While Jersey's paid police are now the real threat to big-time crime in the island, visitors should never underestimate the powers of the honorary police. If you find yourself involved with the law, don't ignore the little man with the rollneck sweater, pipe and carpet slippers who shuffles his way alongside the burly, blue-uniformed police sergeant and into your cell. He's the man who's going to charge you. ❑

THE TAX EXILES

You have to be seriously rich to be accepted as a resident. Once you're in, there's no lack of charitable causes to help part you from your money

The homes of the rich and famous are among the sights of Jersey. Coach drivers taking visitors on island tours will often point out the clifftop house overlooking Bouley Bay where the television celebrity Alan Whicker has lived since 1973 – or Villa Devereux, the £1.5 million high-tech house in St Brelade built by the inventor Ron Hickman, who made his fortune from the Black & Decker Workmate bench.

Sometimes it is the price paid for a property that is the guide's talking-point. Nowadays Jersey's wealthy settlers are unlikely to buy anything under £1 million. Lord Matthews, former deputy chairman of Britain's Trafalgar House group, paid nearly £1 million for his Jersey home in 1985, but many more recent wealthy immigrants have cheerfully broken the million and even the £5 million barrier. Given that some residents are among the nation's super rich – the Barclay Brothers on Brecqhou have a fortune estimated at £1.2 billion – finding a suitable house scarcely ranks as a major problem.

Eagle's nest

No-one except the Comptroller of Income Tax knows exactly how many millionaires live in Jersey, but there are believed to be at least 250. The only statistic available is that quoted by States adviser Colin Powell, who estimates that wealthy immigrants contribute 20 percent of the island's gross domestic income. Just one of them, best-selling author Jack Higgins (real name Harry Patterson), who moved to Jersey in 1976 after hitting the jackpot with his novel *The Eagle Has Landed* and* lives in a house with an indoor pool overlooking St Aubin's Bay, paid about £500,000 in tax over one three-year period.

No-one can say, either, how rich you have to be to get accepted as a "K" resident in Jersey – a term taken from section 1(1) K of the housing law, which admits a newcomer on "social or economic grounds" (the other main category is "J", for non-islanders taking up essential jobs).

Wealth is not the sole criterion for a "K" resident; someone with a dubious past would be turned away, but anyone with a positive contribution to make to the community is in with a chance. Basically, however, the would-be settler has to satisfy the chief executive of the States that he or she has sufficient safe assets to make

a substantial tax contribution. Applicants need to demonstrate realisable assets of around £20 million and an income likely to produce £150,000–200,000 a year.

Racing driver Derek Warwick and pop singer Gilbert O'Sullivan passed the means test in the 1980s. More recently, golfer Ian Woosnam and racing driver Nigel Mansell have been welcomed into the community.

Until 1986, Jersey was allowing in 15 new wealthy immigrants a year. Although it is accepted that controls have since been tightened, there is now no quota, but it is officially acknowledged that only a "handful" of K-category applicants are considered each year.

LEFT: the marina at St Peter Port, a playground for the islands' wealthy. **RIGHT:** golf constitutes another draw.

To settle in Guernsey, you don't have to be a multi-millionaire: the so-called "open market" properties start at around £300,000 for a one bedroom flat and £500,000 for a two/three bedroom house, but go up to £5 million for larger houses and up to £10 million for the top properties. The island's system is to make available about 1,700 higher-priced properties (of which about 20-120 are for sale at any one time) for occupation without restriction by newcomers, and to reserve all the remaining houses and flats either for local people or for non-islanders granted an essential worker's licence.

Millionaires' row

Guernsey has a 50-acre (20-hectare) estate set aside for wealthy settlers – Fort George, above St Peter Port, formerly the site of a 19th-century fortress garrisoned by British redcoats. Known as "Millionaires' Row", it comprises over 100 houses, many well over £1 million.

One of Guernsey's most famous wealthy residents was the film star Oliver Reed. The hell-raising actor enjoyed Guernsey's sociable pub life, and chose a local publican as his best man when he married in the mid-1980s.

Alderney and Sark do not have the same housing restrictions as the larger islands, and the only real obstacle to settling there is the limited number of properties that come on the market. Elizabeth Beresford, creator of the Wombles of Wimbledon and author of nearly 100 books, bought a home in Alderney. So did cricketer Ian Botham, though he left in 1996. Botham, who still visits to enjoy the island's fishing as well as the privacy it offers, wasn't the first cricket enthusiast to settle in Alderney. He was preceded by commentator and wine connoisseur John Arlott, who lived just outside the island's small capital, St Anne, until his death in 1991.*

The Channel Islands can boast a mini-Debrett of titled residents on Jersey, for example Lord Brownlow bought a six-bedroom house for £225,000 in 1983 when he had to sell the ancestral home, Belton House in Lincolnshire, because of death duties and rising costs.*

Brecqhou's Brothers

Brecqhou, the tiny island just off Sark, is owned by the reclusive Barclay twins, Sir David and Sir Frederick, who bought it for a reported £2.3 million in 1993. From humble origins in London they built up a huge business empire through property and shipping, later moving into publishing. Their press acquisitions include *The Scotsman*, *Edinburgh Evening News* and *The Telegraph Group* (which assembles *The Daily Telegraph*, *The Sunday Telegraph* and *The Spectator*). They are also owners of the London Ritz hotel, the Littlewoods stores and mail order chain, and many other business interests. In 2000 the brothers were knighted for their services to charity, having donated around £40 million. In 2005 they came 33rd in *The Sunday Times* Rich List with a fortune estimated at £1.2 billion, having already divested Guernsey's David Rowland of the title of wealthiest Channel Islands resident in the previous year. The son of a scrap dealer, Rowland made his first million in 1969 at the age of 23 and is today worth £660 million, nonetheless lagging behind the Barclay brothers by over £500 million.

No sooner had they become lords and masters of the tiny island than they began building a huge, castle-like house. Isolation was clearly one of the reasons they chose this site for their £60 million home, and since their arrival they have taken pains to ensure that their privacy is not disturbed. They also caused controversy by their campaign to overturn Sark's ancient property laws, which dictated that daughters could inherit only if there were no male heirs. The Barclays, who wished to will their castle to all four of their children, three boys and a girl, won their case in 1999.

While there are settlers who treat the islands just as a port of convenience, spending much of their time away and taking little interest in local affairs, many have become strongly attached to their adopted homelands. Newcomers are quickly recruited into the enormous amount of voluntary and charitable work that goes on.

There have also been notable individual donations, such as the wealthy Jersey resident who put up the entire £750,000 needed to build a day hospital for the elderly.

his hugely popular cops and robbers show was televised. And the resident authors, of course, tend to write about the islands; Jack Higgins's novel, *The Night of the Fox*, is set in Jersey during the German Occupation, and Elizabeth Beresford has used Alderney as a background for some of her stories.

As for celebrities born and bred on the islands, these are few and far between. Apart from Lillie Langtree, Jersey's main claim to fame is the football player Graeme Le Saux, who was born on the island in 1968. He played locally for St Paul's club before moving to Chelsea FC in 1987. ❑

Whicker's world

The famous among the *rentiers* (or wealthy settlers) help the islands by lending glamour to local events and promoting them in press interviews and TV appearances when they are travelling abroad. Alan Whicker used Mont Orgueil castle in Jersey as the backdrop for the relaunch of one of his travel series, and comedian Cyril Fletcher presented gardening programmes for Channel Television. *Bergerac* actor John Nettles, meanwhile, was at one time a one-man PR machine, putting Jersey on the map wherever

LEFT: television personality Alan Whicker. **ABOVE:** Tom Scott, a major player in the Islands' retail industry.

HOW LOCALS SEE THE TAX EXILES

In the anglicised Channel Islands, the British tax exiles do not form any distinct expatriate set, and their presence provokes no noticeable resentment. Most native-born islanders see them as a positive asset, adding colour and sophistication to local life, handsomely refurbishing old farmhouses that the natives no longer want, and providing welcome business for the shops, bars and restaurants. The ill-feeling is directed more towards the other end of the social spectrum, the so-called "illegal immigrants" – the seasonal workers and imported labourers who manage to stay on in defiance of the housing regulations.

THE FINANCIERS

The islands don't like being called tax havens, but the influx of offshore finance

has brought unprecedented prosperity – and some problems too

Probably nowhere in the British Isles, outside the City of London, do financial activities loom so large in daily life as in the Channel Islands. Eavesdrop on a conversation in any upmarket bar or restaurant in St Helier or St Peter Port, and the chances are that the topic will be money dealings of some kind. Islanders are very conscious that the banks, legal firms and trust companies are now the power in the land, and anyone seeking sponsorship for a charitable cause or for a musical or sports event looks first in that direction.

The banking boom

Over the past 50 years and largely in the past two decades, the Channel Islanders' life-style has become almost unrecognisably urban and affluent. The standard of living is higher than that of Britain or any other EU country bar Luxembourg. In the simpler days of the 1950s, the only banks were branches of Britain's high street clearers, along with the Jersey and Guernsey Trustee Savings Banks. Islanders would have laughed in disbelief if they had been told that, within 30 years, their harbour capitals would be bristling with banks of every nationality and that finance business would be the mainstay of the economy.

Although Jersey's rate of income tax had been unchanged at four shillings (20p) in the £ since 1940, and Guernsey had reduced its rate from 5s. 2d. (26p) to the same level in 1960, the finance era was really ushered in by Jersey's decision in 1962 to abolish a usury law restricting interest rates to 5 percent. This was a calculated move by the island's pioneering finance minister, the late Senator Cyril Le Marquand.

Merchant bankers looking for a low-tax base from which to service clients, especially ex-colonials and expatriates, began to see the potential of islands that had low taxes, were conveniently close to the City of London but outside UK jurisdiction and had a political system that ensured long-term stability. The first to move in were Kleinwort Benson, Hill Samuel and Royal Trust of Canada, followed not long afterwards by N. M. Rothschild and Hambros.

Even in the 1970s, however, offshore finance business was seen just as a useful extra leg of the economy. No one foresaw how dominant it

would become, outstripping traditional industries like horticulture and tourism as a source of States revenues. Today, as Channel Islanders are reminded every Budget day, it has grown into the golden egg that is largely paying for education, healthcare and other social services.

Bank deposits totalling over £173 billion are held in Jersey, and Guernsey is also the custodian of mind-numbing sums of money. Many billions are invested in the hundreds of offshore funds run from the islands and yet more billions are handled by local trust companies. There are branches or subsidiaries of many of the world's top banks here.

None of them is just a nameplate, although

LEFT: polishing the nameplates of companies registered in the islands.

RIGHT: the Royal Bank of Scotland's modern atrium.

some are known as "managed" banks which means they do not have their own staff but are managed by an existing financial institution, probably another bank. Many of the building societies in Guernsey fall into this category. However there are no brass plate banks as there are in many Caribbean tax havens, and most occupy substantial, fully-staffed buildings. Virtually all of the recent developments in St Helier and St Peter Port have been for banks and finance firms.

Shady dealings

In the early days, the prestigious names of merchant banking traded alongside a number of

smaller so-called "banks", some of them shaky, one or two positively shady. There were financial scandals, such as those involving the Merchant Bank of Guernsey, linked with motor insurance fraud, and the notorious Bank of Sark, centre of a multi-million-dollar offshore swindle. Gradually, through protection of depositors' legislation and stricter vetting of would-be entrants, the islands were able to weed out the undesirables.

The Jersey and Guernsey authorities have always repudiated the description of "tax haven", arguing that their low-tax economies evolved naturally to serve the needs of small – and originally quite unsophisticated – communities, and that their tax structures have never been deliberately manipulated, as in some offshore centres, to attract financial business. They can trace their low tax status back to 1240, while some Caribbean and Pacific tax havens have grown up virtually overnight.

Such arguments have not saved the islands from repeated charges by certain Labour members of Parliament in London that they are leeches on the British economy, enjoying the advantages of British citizenship without paying their share of taxation and then requiting this privilege by draining off untold millions of pounds from the British exchequer by providing a haven for tax-avoiders. The critics however have quietened since Jersey and Guernsey were given a clean bill of health by the International Monetary Fund in 2003, and, after pressure from the EU, agreed to change their tax system.

The threat from drug money

London MPs investigating drug abuse visited Guernsey and Jersey in 1985 and went away apparently satisfied that both the local law enforcement agencies and the banking community were as vigilant as their UK counterparts in the face of the growing threat from drug trafficking. Nevertheless no one pretends that "dirty" money does not find its way into the islands – if only because, as one Westminster MP put it, "if laundering is successful, you won't know it has been laundered, like a perfect murder." Local bankers, however, argue that it is probably easier to launder money in the City of London.

This does not stop the bad publicity, though. A BBC TV documentary castigated the islands for their lax attitude towards money laundering. But a few weeks later the US Government announced that it was giving Jersey $1 million because of the good co-operation the US authorities had received from Jersey in tracking down the proceeds of crime. That rather left egg on the faces of the TV programme makers.

The islands have followed the United Kingdom in introducing legislation to empower courts to get more information from banks and to confiscate assets where the handling of drug money is suspected, and they have taken steps to try to prevent local companies being used to cloak "insider trading" operations in the City of London. Both Jersey and Guernsey have also introduced new legislation to combat the laundering of money earned from any criminal activity, including tax fraud.

A new challenge

Changes are crucial in assuring the future stability and success of the islands. While the second half of the 20th century saw an almost continual rise in economic growth, the first years of the 21st century have seen low to zero growth. Moreover, recent tax reforms will result in huge holes in the offshore centres' budgets and ultimately higher taxes for islanders.

In response to fierce competition from other offshore centres and pressure from the EU, both economic growth has led to wage freezes and job losses, particularly in the financial sector. But with agriculture and tourism both in decline, the financial industry remains the only real source for expansion.

Proposed reforms in taxation and government spending policies are being driven through at the same time as major constitutional reform and will no doubt succeed in making the systems more streamlined, accountable and efficient. For investors from the outside world, the islands are likely to lose their 'tax haven' attraction. ❏

> ### TIME TO DIVERSIFY
>
> Both Jersey and Guernsey, knowing they are so dependent on the finance industry, have been backing tourism and information technology as alternative sources of revenue.

Jersey and Guernsey have finally agreed to do away with preferential tax treatment for foreign companies and move to a standard zero rate corporation tax, as from 2008. Guernsey, which has already overspent £26 million on its new airport, St Sampson's marina, New Jetty, main fire station and prison, estimates an annual 'black hole' of £45 million in the not too distant future; in Jersey this may be as great as £120-150 million.

Economic growth and savings made by the new ministerial governments are hoped to partly meet the shortfall. At present, the levelling off of

---

LEFT: Jersey's distinctive banknotes and coins.
ABOVE: keeping up with the *Financial Times*.

> ### WHAT THE LOCALS THINK
>
> The average Jerseyman and Guernseyman seems to have something of a love-hate attitude to the industry that has made his community rich. He knows that the islands cannot do without the massive tax revenues generated by the financiers and that it would be a disaster if ever they went away. At the same time, he laments the loss of the old, more innocent way of life and dislikes the idea that everything must now be done with one eye on the bankers. And perhaps, subconsciously, the traditionally hard-working, self-reliant Channel Islander feels just a little bit guilty that something as meretricious as dealing in money is now his main economic support.

FOOD AND DRINK

There's an abundance of fresh ingredients, from potatoes to lobsters.

But it's harder to find top-class restaurants than you'd think

In total the Channel Islands cover just 100 sq. miles (259 sq. km), an area not much larger than a city and its suburbs. Yet, included in that area are more than 300 restaurants and cafés, over 400 hotels and guest houses and 60 inns.

Such odds in the diner's favour would spell death to restaurants anywhere else in the world. But in the Channel Islands, the population is more than 1 million in summer, giving the restaurateurs a chance to make their money. Many, however, have been trying to extend their restaurant's life by earning a good local reputation that will stand them in good stead for the rest of the year. This means a visitor will often enjoy a better meal out of the tourist season than in it and, what's more, stand less chance of coinciding with a party of fussy, old age pensioners on a strictly guided tour and a strictly limited menu. Autumn or spring (particularly during the food festivals) are seasons for the gourmand.

Local specialities

Guernsey and Jersey import a great deal of food from the continent. Their markets and shops (including supermarkets) offer tremendous selections of cheese, fish, shellfish and fruit. The islands' unique position of not being owned by the British and not being part of the European Union gives them access to a range of foodstuffs hard to find elsewhere, although recent initiatives by both islands have tried to emphasise the unique flavour of local foodstuffs.

In Jersey, for example, restaurateurs are coaxed by the tourism authorities to include on their menus traditional dishes prepared under the "Genuine Jersey" label. If a menu includes Black Butter and Apple Tart with a Calvados Sabayon, for example, it means that the chef has prepared a special dessert with a Jersey theme.

Alderney also takes pride in its local produce, including sea bass and crab, and because the island is as much a retirement island as it is a holiday resort, islanders who want to make the

best of their tax-free retirement want to enjoy on occasions a slap-up meal. Not surprisingly, therefore, Alderney possesses at least one superb restaurant and one or two others that wouldn't look out of place in London or Paris.

Herm *has* to offer good food to its visitors, even if choice is limited. Without tourism, the

island would die and the island manager, Adrian Heyworth, demands dedication from his staff. Even when the food is disappointing, therefore, the waiter is sure to be servility personified.

The last of the major islands, Sark, remains an enigma. Repopulated by Jersey in the 16th century, it has watched the other islands move firmly into the 20th century. Good food may be found there; the price it will cost you is another matter.

Fruit and vegetables

Of all Channel Island recipes, *des pais au fou* is most renowned, although its Jersey-French name hides a dish which is hardly glamorous. If ever a cheap meal of various beans, pig's

---

LEFT: Channel Islands potatoes are a big export.
RIGHT: visitors enjoy the local produce.

trotters and belly has been refined by count-less generations of cooks into something finer, this is it. The dish sounds better in French than in the islanders' name for it – bean crock.

So, too, do other dishes, including *d'la soupe de congre* (conger eel soup), *d'la Bouanne soupe* (Sark pottage, traditionally made with mackerel, gooseberries, shredded cabbage, milk and ham) and *d'la soupe de caboche* (cabbage soup). If the soup doesn't appeal, try the bread. Cabbage loaves (*des pains à caboche*) are superb. The bread is baked wrapped in cabbage leaves which are then pulled away to leave a sweetish, doughy bread.

Other local vegetable dishes include Guernsey baked potato pudding (*houichepoté à patate*), Jersey baked carrot pudding (*du podin d'carotte*), tomato soup (*d'la soupe des tomates*) and parsnip pottage (*panais à la Graisse*). Such dishes were extremely popular during the German Occupation, when meat was rare and vegetables scarce.

Jersey's culinary claim to fame is the royal potato, cultivated here for over 120 years. The potatoes are ready for digging as early as April – well before the earliest in the UK. Many are grown for export, but for those who happen to be in Jersey in spring there is nothing to compare with a Jersey royal straight from the soil.

WHERE TO FIND THE BEST FOOD

True to their claim of providing something for everyone, the Channel Islands have some of the best restaurants in the British Isles outside London – and some of the worst.

Traditional holidaymakers from England, while enjoying the climate and slightly foreign atmosphere, demanded their customary "meat and two veg" and "pub grub", and unimaginatively overcooked food is all too easy to find. Given the relatively short tourist season, it therefore fell to the retired tax exiles and prosperous resident financiers and lawyers to provide enough year-round business for a few first-class restaurants. To promote better standards of cuisine and boost low-season tourism, both Jersey and

Guernsey run food festivals each year, featuring cookery contests, lectures by leading cookery writers and TV chefs, and special gourmet menus at many restaurants and hotels.

Jersey's capital, St Helier, has a surprising dearth of gourmet restaurants and the best places tend to be scattered around the island, mostly on the coast. At the lower end of the scale, there's no shortage of places serving fast food and snacks. Most beaches have at least one café, some serving seafood, crab sandwiches, home-made cakes and cream teas. The latter can vary from the dreary pre-packed variety to freshly-made scones with lashings of thick Jersey cream and strawberry jam.

Sweetmeats

Another apple-based dish the islanders are known for is *bourdelots* or apples baked in shortcrust pastry. They are delicious and, like cabbage loaves, should be cooked wrapped in cabbage leaves – the island's version of modern-day tinfoil.

Jersey black butter, another delicacy, sounds best in the native tongue (*du nier beurre*), although in either language the name is confusing: black butter isn't made from milk but from apples. Before 1914, most islanders made it regularly and looked forward to autumn when a huge brass pan of new cider would be placed

November they spend 24 hours or more making enough black butter to last them and their families from one end of a year to another. It tastes sweet and syrupy and can be spread quite happily on toast or *gâche* (pronounced "gosh") one of the tastiest sweetmeats in the islands, and consisting of flour, butter, eggs, candied peel, sultanas, milk and sugar.

Guernsey *gâche* in Jersey tastes different to Guernsey *gâche* in Guernsey. This is because each island jealously protects the purity of its own distinctive breed of cattle, which means that the milk of each island tastes slightly different to that of the other.

on the outhouse stove. To this would be added peeled, cut apples, sugar and liquorice, plus a variety of spices. The pan would be stirred constantly, day and night and the spices added right at the end of the marathon. Two or three brawny young, farmers would be called to stir the stiff, tacky mixture.

The phrase "brawny, young farmers" is used deliberately because the Jersey Young Farmers Club is the mainstay of the traditional *sethe d'nière beurre* (black butter night). Every

Because of the high cream content, Channel Islands milk has a tendency to leave grease marks on top of tea or coffee. But it's no problem: just close your eyes and enjoy the taste. This high cream content also means the milk sours quickly and dissuades Jerseymen (but not Guernsey cheddarmen) from turning it into cheese.

Jersey wonders (*des mervelles*), Guernsey hearts (*des p'tits tcheurs*) and local biscuits (*des galettes*) are also worth sampling.

Meat and fish

Channel Islanders, being inventive by nature, have learnt to make the most of their seafood resources. Moules (mussels) and oysters are

LEFT: the rich soil of the islands and the mild climate provide excellent growing conditions for vegetables.
ABOVE: fresh flowers in St Helier's Central Market.

successfully farmed locally and appear on many menus. Ormers (similar to large limpets) are hard to find and even lobsters and crabs (mainly spider crabs) are not as plentiful as they used to be and are no longer cheap: locally caught lobster (*l'homard*) are more expensive than quality meat imported from the continent. Inevitably, demand has outstripped supply. As many as 4,000 lobsters a week were pulled from Guernsey pots in the 1860s and even a decade ago; they were so prized that Belgian business-men would fly to the islands, buy half-a-dozen, and fly back home that same day to sell them at extortionate rates in their restaurants.

Crab is getting scarcer, too, and Canadian crabmeat is occasionally flown in to satisfy the increasing demand. Limpets, although lilliput-ian compared to lobster, are an alternative treat when they are cooked for half an hour in a saucepan and served with vinegar. The prob-lem is, of course, that you have to cook an awful lot of limpets to satisfy a hungry man. What recommends them is that, along with whelks and shrimps, they are freely available.

Islanders have an extraordinary ability to turn anything that can be swallowed into food. An Alderney dish, for example, became popular when the locals, realising that all around them flew a rich source of food no-one had thought

to capture, created sparrow pie. You can still find recipes for it, or, a much more tempting prospect, *des pigaöns* (boiled pigeons).

Getting tipsy

When you can't turn your environment into meat, you may be able to turn it into drink instead. The Blayneys have done so success-fully at St Mary, in Jersey, where they reintro-duced vines to the island. The vineyard (under new management) now produces its own pass-able light white wines and sparkling wines, as well as cider and apple brandy. Other growers have followed in the Blayneys' footsteps and there are a variety of locally produced wines now available in Jersey or Guernsey, although Channel Island wine will never be as popular as imported beer.

In the 1990s the popularity of imported lager led to a sharp decline in the sales of local brew-eries. Several closed and the well known Ran-dalls, which had been brewing since 1868 (minus 5 years during the German occupation) stopped making beer and turned to the UK. The Jersey-based brewery now imports several brands of keg real ale and have invested heav-ily in their public houses in an attempt to make them "family-friendly".

Meanwhile, an upstart publican and brewer, Steve Skinner, had the audacity to set up the largest in-house brewery in Britain in the Tipsy Toad Town House in St Helier. His second in-house brewery (his first was the Star and Tipsy Toad, St Peter) soon produced beers which won awards in mainland brewing competitions. They deserved to win on their names alone: "Black Tadger", for example, and "Horny Toad". Tipsy Toad was taken over in 1997 by Mary Ann, a long-established Jersey brewery. Real ale production came to a halt at their main site in 1999, but keg beers are still brewed here and both plants were relocated under the name of the Jersey and Tipsy Toad Brewery.

Skinner was also one of the first publicans actively to encourage parents to bring their chil-dren with them into a family atmosphere pub. Others have followed suit. Parents have the option of enjoying their meals in peace while not 20 metres away, in a sound-proofed room, their young children are happily occupied. ❑

LEFT: The Good Wife at Jersey's Hamptonne Country Life Museum. **RIGHT:** oysters have become popular.

FIGHTING IT OUT WITH FLOWERS

It started when someone on a float threw flowers at an onlooker. Then the onlookers began to rip up the floats and pelt their friends with blooms...

Both Jersey and Guernsey celebrate the success of their horticultural industries with flower festivals in which huge wire-framed floats, mounted on trailers, are covered with blooms and drawn past great crowds of spectators. The festivals, a cornerstone of community life, are held on the second Thursday in August in Jersey and on the third Thursday in August on Guernsey. Years ago, the parades ended with the ultimate test of design and construction of the floats – people swarmed over them, ripping out the blooms as missiles to be hurled at each other, which is how the Battle of Flowers got its name. The winner was the float which best stood the test of destruction. Excitement was high, and a few serious injuries would occur in the carnage. Thanks to the size of the crowds these days, the battles have ended but the name lives on.

EVERGREEN MEMORIES

Naturally, there's a museum. The Museum of the Battle of Flowers (La Robeline, Mont des Corvées, St Ouen, Jersey, open daily 10am–5pm) was founded in 1971 by Florence Bechelet and houses more than a dozen of the floats that have starred in past parades. Miss Bechelet was one of the Battle's most prolific exhibitors and many of her handmade floats won prizes. Exhibits such as "Arctic Scene", "Dovecote" and "Monarchs of the Prairie" are accompanied by some evocative black-and-white photographs. The floats, made of dyed hare's tail and marram grass, date from 1953.

◁ **QUEEN FOR A DAY**
Local girls compete to become beauty queens, and a celebrity is chosen to do service as Mr Battle.

△ **COMMUNITY EFFORT**
Two or three nights before the big day, volunteers can be seen busily cutting fresh blooms and glueing them to the framework.

◁ **OLDER BATTLES**
Some of the most striking floats recall the Channel Islands' chequered history as the French and English struggled for dominance.

Class A
Second

△ PAPER DREAMS
Marigolds, carnations, asters and hydrangeas still form the basis of most floats, but less weather-prone paper flowers have recently started to appear.

◁ COMPETING QUEENS
The Jersey event is a much larger event than its counterpart on Guernsey.

△ PETROL POWER
Motor vehicles first joined the parade in 1906, though horse-drawn floats still took part as recently as the 1970s.

▽ YESTERDAY'S STYLE
The parades give islanders an excuse to show off traditional costumes as they recreate the role of the flower seller.

◁ A GOOD CAUSE
After the parade, the floats are parked around the islands and charity collecting boxes are left at the feet of the fantasy figures until they fade to become charnel caricatures of their former glory.

WHERE BLOOMS ARE BIG BUSINESS

The above display at the Guernsey Freesia Centre isn't just for the tourists – it is a reminder that the cut-flower trade plays an increasingly important part in the Channel Islands' economies. This is especially true for Guernsey, whose vast complexes of greenhouses used to grow tomatoes. But, unable to compete with the cheap tomatoes being produced by European Union countries such as Spain and Portugal, they turned to flowers, a trade that had begun in a small way as long ago as 1864 when a single consignment of fresh daffodils was sent to the London market. Now more than 1 million boxes of flowers are exported annually – Britain alone takes 40 million roses every year.

BIRDS AND BEASTS

The growth of tourism has spurred islanders to protect their rich heritage of animal, bird and insect life as well as some delicate plants

Birdwatching guides who take parties to Alderney have a money-making ruse which they work on their clients for the cost of a pint or two of beer. A few pence per person is collected for a sweepstake to benefit the party member who sees the first magpie. If none is seen, the kitty goes to the guide. The leaders always win, even when escorting Channel Islanders: the magpie, which is numerous throughout the archipelago, can't be found in Alderney.

Moles can be found, though. They also push their unwelcome mounds up in Jersey, but not Guernsey or Herm. And hedgehogs, occurring in all the islands, were introduced into car-free Sark by the Seigneur's wife, Diana Beaumont, a few years ago. They still get killed on Sark's roads – run over by horses and carts – possibly proving that rolling in front of a vehicle is the most popular way for a hedgehog to commit *harakiri*.

Inter-island differences

The differences in wildlife distribution between the islands are large and often cannot be explained. Jersey has 120 breeding species of bird but just 70 or so nest in Guernsey. Loose-flowered orchids are scarce in most of the islands, bar Guernsey, where thousands of the plants grow in old boggy meadows. A bare-footed walk across any public land can be done with impunity, except on Herm Common where the burnet rose covers the ground. Its delayed action thorns allow soft unsuspecting feet to get several metres over the inviting sward before pain strikes, making retreat an act of self-inflicted agony.

The gap between the UK's natural history and that of the islands is even wider; familiar creatures like deer, foxes, hares and badgers are missing. So too are rooks, jays and some members of the titmouse family. One ornithologist, studying dippers, arrived on a two-week research programme to find his work completed after just one telephone call. "We have no dippers," he was told by a local birdwatcher.

The Channel Islands are the nail on a finger of Mediterranean species which runs along the French Atlantic coast from Portugal and Spain, pointing at the southern counties of England. The delicate plants, insects and birds which

inhabit this strip of usually mild terrain struggle to maintain a toehold and their presence is sometimes threatened by slight shifts in climate.

One such shift occurred when a heat-seeking frost of great severity sucked all life from palms, eucalyptus trees and the rocket-like giant echiums which are cultivated in the islands. The frost also wiped out most of the Dartford warbler populations, leaving large gorse slopes in Alderney, Guernsey and Jersey all but devoid of the Burgundy-coloured songster's sharp rattling notes and is occasionally now spotted on Jersey and Guernsey. It has been seen by lighthouse keepers on Les Casquets, northwest of Alderney, attracted by the flashing beam on

LEFT: Alderney bursts into bloom.
RIGHT: a shag guards its young.

misty autumn nights. However there are signs that this diminutive warbler, which paid the price for not migrating south in winter, is returning to the Channel Islands.

The green lizards living around the skirts of Jersey's Mont Orgueil Castle and beneath the defensive walls of Fort George in Guernsey escaped the frost during their subterranean hibernation, as did the Glanville fritillary butterflies which danced over the cliff paths to lay their eggs on plantain leaves the following June. Mole crickets singing their summer love songs from burrows in the sandy soils also escaped the cold.

A marine biologist in Guernsey measures temperature changes in the ocean by calculating the ratio between a northern and southern species of acorn barnacle. They meet in the English Channel and, as the sea gets hotter or colder, their respective populations change. The northern species is winning, thanks to lower sea temperatures.

Conservation questions

Nature conservation in some islands equals much which is done in the UK, while in others it is nonexistent. Guernsey and Jersey have the best records but took opposing paths to get the

THE THREAT TO THE ORMER

Lower sea temperatures in recent years have hit the Channel Islands' most prized delicacy, the ormer (or sea ear). These huge Mediterranean relatives of the limpet are collected from beneath large rocks and, although they need 24 hours' cooking to be edible, the delicate flavour (which some compare to mushrooms, others to chicken) make them popular. To preserve stocks strict regulations apply. For example, in Jersey they can only be fished from September to April (ie only months with an 'R' in them) and only on the first four days of a new moon.

Octopus and dolphin used also to be common visitors but have almost vanished from local waters.

final results. Herm has a happy compromise between the demands of a modern farm manager and those of the vast visiting public who want to see the island's natural attractions. Alderney and Sark people tend to conserve by default, finding that leaving things wild is easier than war with nature – yet still attracts the tourists.

Both Alderney and Sark make the most of their natural assets. They have superb cliff paths which wander through natural flower gardens of thrift, stonecrop, gorse and prostrate broom. Banks of heather grow on the more exposed sites and in sheltered valleys small woods ring to the sound of singing blackcap, garden warblers, chiffchaff and even the rare golden oriole in spring.

Within sight of Alderney are Burhou, an island which boasts one of the largest puffin colonies in the Channel Islands and Les Etacs, where 2,000 pairs of gannets live within a beak's-length of each other, raising their chicks in a bird city which holds all the ingredients for a nervous breakdown. Overcrowding results in fights between neighbours, lack of a sewage system coats the rock in white, foul-smelling guano, and hot calm days force the birds to take flight, occasionally in the direction of Cocq Lihou where kittiwakes, Alderney's most recently established colony, call out their onomatopaeic names in friendly greeting.

banks overlooking the colony, opening in sunshine to justify the botanist's lens which must be used to see the full beauty of the tiny flowers. Little Sark, with its desolate-looking silver-mine chimneys, has a few puffins in Pot Bay while fulmars have included the island's cliffs in their worldwide expansion plans.

Warring factions

Jersey's conservation movement was spilt by dissension and argument, with the result that several organisations claimed that they looked after the wildlife. La Société Jersiaise pontificated, local members of the Royal Society for

The boat trip used to include a visit to Blue Stone Bay for a peek at naturists basking on the rocks, but the universal redundancy of bikini tops has ended the thrill of that sport.

Sark's seabird ledges are observed from cliffs above Port du Moulin where guillemots huddle together on Les Autlets rock like penguins. There they incubate pear-shaped eggs which roll in tight circles if kicked by a departing parent rather than drop into the sea below. Sand crocus stick their minute heads out of the grassy

the Protection of Birds could do nothing because the society's charter does not allow them to buy land in the Channel Islands – and the Jersey Conservation and Naturalists Society split the movement.

The National Trust of Jersey owns some of the best sites in the island, but like its Guernsey counterpart, is a body independent of the UK trust. As such, both are more responsive to local pressures than the National Trust and people's wishes are sometimes placed before the interests of wildlife. It was left to the States of Jersey to pick up the pieces, and to their credit the Island government initially appointed a conservation officer before, in 1994, appointing a States Environ-

LEFT: an ormer, threatened by temperature changes.
ABOVE: superb cliff paths lead to natural flower gardens among the sand dunes..

mental Advisor. His appointment means that before any project which might affect the look of the island can be implemented, he is given carte blanche to criticise it and recommend changes if it is likely to change the balance of nature, although after making his report his powers are limited. Conservationists in Guernsey have resisted the temptation to press for a similar post to be set up but the Island does employ an "administration property manager (environment)" who describes his job as "looking after public land in an environmentally-friendly way".

The work of Jersey's conservation officer led to the establishment of Les Mielles and Les

CONSERVATION SOCIETIES

Both the main islands have active bodies dedicated to studying their history, archaeology and natural history and to conserving the environment and preserving notable buildings and monuments. La Société Jersiaise was founded in 1873 and the Guernsey Society of Natural Science and Local Research, now La Société Guernesiaise, in 1882.

Special interest groups range from botany and entomology to numismatics and transport history. Regular study groups and talks are held throughout the winter, with field outings during the summer. Annual membership of the societies carries with it free admission to a number of sites and museums.

Quennevais conservation area with its information centre at Kempt Tower. The area is considered to be a naturalist's paradise with one of the richest sand dune habitats in Britain containing 1,000 plant species or more, including 16 listed in the Red Data Book of endangered species.

La Mare au Seigneur, known to Jersey folk as St Ouen's Pond, has a similar reputation for migrating birds. The very shy Cetti's warbler was observed through a telescope from her lounge by a keen naturalist who was able to record the first breeding record of the species in the British Isles. The nest is now in Jersey Museum. The pond is also used by vast flocks of swallows and martins, reed and sedge warblers, and many birds of prey which stop off in the island.

Two headlands in Jersey contrast the differences in climate and habitat between north and south. Les Landes in the north is the largest area of heath on the island. Due to the wind, few shrubs or trees are able to raise their heads high and dwarf scrub heath is the dominant vegetation. Glanville fritillary butterflies, a few remaining Dartford warblers and, according to local rumour, the protected agile frog occur. In contrast, Noirmont Headland on the south coast is covered with tall gorse, bramble scrub and a few evergreen Mediterranean holm oaks. Autumn squill, spotted rockrose and the declining Jersey forget-me-not are found in the area.

Orchid collections

In Guernsey nature conservation is shared between the National Trust, the States, who employ environmental contractors when and if the need arises, and La Société Guernsiaise, whose members provide the money, labour and political incentive to protect the island's natural resources. They became land owners when the Silbe Nature Reserve, a wooded west coast valley in St Peter's, was given to the society in 1975. Other sites were bought and La Société now own fields around L'Eree and Rue du Vicheries, which contain six of every 10 British loose-flowered orchids.

"They are called Jersey orchids in UK and Jersey," Guernsey botanists will tell you with horror in their voices. "But we call them *pougencoute* in Guernsey patois, meaning Pentecost or Whitsun orchid after the season in which they flower." The Eric Young Foundation in Jersey, a trust established by the founder, is acknowledged as one of Europe's leading orchid collections.

Splendid sites

The States of Guernsey became involved in conservation by handing management of several sites to La Société. Prize of these is a conservation area made up of a marsh, shingle bank and seashore at L'Eree. The shingle bank, owned by the States, forms a barrier to the sea at Rue de la Rocque, and has little robin, halberd-leaved orache, Cornish mallow and progenitor of the brassica family of cultivars, sea kale. It lies between the society's reserve at La Claire Mare – a reed bed with wader scrape and birdwatching hide – and a beach slated to be the island's first marine nature reserve.

La Société also advises the States on the management of Port Soif Headland with its locally rare bee orchids and the area around Fort Hommet which has a low-lying seacliff habitat. One of Guernsey's oldest companies, Bucktrout Ltd, gave the management of the Vale Pond to the society. The reserve has played host to a multitude of rare migrant birds and is the site of several botanical gems including the bulbous foxtail, a grass species not found in the other islands. A hide, with access from the main road running past, overlooks the area.

The threat of disease

Dutch elm disease has brought some of the most severe modern changes to the Channel Islands. Elms were a large proportion of the few trees found in Alderney and have died, along with huge stands in Sark and Jersey. But in Guernsey, where the States fear the effect of increased wind speeds on the cost of heating greenhouses, a strict felling programme and a scheme to give away trees have kept the disease in check and ensured that alternatives are planted. Many of the free trees died – through lack of care in the first two years: unprotected at ground level, they were killed by weed cutters and rabbits, or because they were the wrong species chosen for the site. Stakes and guards are now given with each tree.

Myxomatosis threatened to change the delicate habitats found on Herm when it was introduced a few years ago, killing the rabbits which ate the rank, coarse vegetation but leaving the more delicate species of plant. Here lay the quandary of Herm's management. Should they pursue modern farming techniques, which would

---

LEFT: following a nature trail on Guernsey.
RIGHT: Bonne Nuit's beach on Jersey.

see an end to the island's natural assets enjoyed by so many visitors, or watch pests, weeds and people put paid to a potentially prosperous farm? The compromise was fairly reached. Large sections of the island, including a skirt of scrub draping the farm and the common which has a wonderful sand dune habitat, were left wild.

But intensive farming supports a top herd of cows, providing an extra bonus for tourists who can take advantage of the 8.30am "milk boat" from Guernsey to get a full day on the island. Ravens and puffins nest on the south coast, Brent geese winter in the shallow bays along the western side of Herm and white campion grows

among the boulders which separate the fields.

Cliff paths, running along the highest parts of Jersey and Guernsey, mark a peculiar difference between the islands. Jersey's path is along the northern cliffs with views over the other Channel Islands; the land slopes away for 5 miles (8 km) to reach the sea along the sandy south coast. Jersey's farmland faces south and enjoys a milder climate than Guernsey which faces north and needs greenhouses to protect the crops from cooler winters. Jersey farmers specialise in early outdoor potatoes and vegetables while in Guernsey the cost of higher horticultural investment is met by bigger incomes from the production of flowers and tomatoes under glass. ❏

NEW ANGLES ON FISHING

*Wrasse, bass, grey mullet, black bream, pollack, garfish, mackerel and conger eel
are all caught offshore – and there's freshwater angling, too*

Limpet shells by the hundred unearthed at La Hougue Bie, the site in Jersey of a miraculously preserved New Stone Age burial chamber, suggest that Channel Islanders have always had an appetite for seafood.

At first, of course, the sea merely supplemented a meagre diet, but eventually regular contacts with mainland Britain led some medieval wide-boy to the realisation that fish could also supplement income. Conger eels abounded then, as they do now, and, salted or dried, they found eager buyers across the English Channel. The *saleries* and *éperqueries* (the centres of the salting and drying trades on shore) became such big business that Jersey during the Middle Ages was often referred to as the "Isle of the Congers".

Paradoxically, success with exports of Friday fare led indirectly to the decline of the islands' fisheries. In the 16th century the immense riches of the cod banks of Newfoundland were first discovered and canny Jersey and Guernseymen recognised that, if there were profits in moderate quantities of dried conger, there were fortunes in unlimited quantities of dried cod.

Opening up the shellfish market

While island ships were supplying Catholic Europe with cod from the other side of the Atlantic, the home fisheries declined. Declined, that is, until another rich source of revenue was found lurking on the muddy seabed between Jersey and the Norman coast: 1797 was the year of the oyster and soon after the shellfish were discovered, their lucrative exploitation was in full swing. Again, the catches were for the English market and again it looked like a triumph for the islanders' know-how and business acumen.

The French, the traditional enemy, saw things differently, and the dredger fleets working just off French beaches were often harrassed. In 1822, when 300 boats, 1,500 fishermen and 1,000 shore workers were supported by the Jersey fishery, separate fishing zones eased the rivalry.

LEFT AND RIGHT: the enormous tidal range makes possible a wide variety of fishing.

"The Battle of the Oyster Shells" of 1838 was, therefore, an insular rather than an international affair, being based on an early attempt at conservation. The "battle" was joined by 120 oyster smacks which set off to fish protected beds off Grouville, pursued – rather improbably – by the Constable of St Martin in a rowing boat.

Jersey's Lieutenant-Governor was also involved, calling out the garrison and the militia to march on Gorey, the oystermen's home port. Cannon were fired and 96 skippers found themselves in jail, but, ironically, the only serious casualty of the otherwise comic-opera episode was the Lieutenant-Governor. He caught a chill and died of complications a few days later.

Efforts at control gave way to a free-for-all and, by the close of the 19th century, Channel Island oysters had gone the way of the North American buffalo. You can still find a few oysters on the rocks, but those on your plate will have been nurtured carefully in recently established "farms" on the foreshore.

A liking for lobsters

Gradually, however, lobsters – those blue, heavy-clawed crustaceans which boiling transforms to red-shelled gourmets' delights – became the focus of the harvest of the sea, laying the foundation of today's Channel Islands fishery. A stroll nowadays around Jersey's St Helier Harbour, St Peter Port in Guernsey or Braye in Alderney will reveal sturdy wooden boats, often with flared bows that betray French origin, in the 10- to 20-metre category. These crabbers were acquired to cash in on the shellfish boom which began in the 1960s when local enterprise fixed its gaze on the prices fetched by lobsters and crabs in

high-class restaurants. The kelp-covered reefs of coastal waters were the first zones to be bombarded with string upon string of baited lobster pots, but the bigger boats soon ventured further afield, seeking their valuable quarry in the English Channel and even off the Scottish coast.

Typically, today's crabbers are based in Jersey or Guernsey but use Alderney as an operating port while fishing the Channel during neap (small) tides. During these restricted fishing periods, there's no time to lose and it's all systems go.

Setting and lifting 700 or more 50-pound (23-kg) pots each day, crewmen clad in the traditional blue denim fishing smocks of the islands or in vivid yellow oilskins carry on working in almost any condition short of a severe gale. The catch, which now consists primarily of the brown edible crab, with its flat, pie-crust shell, is stored on board in water-filled *viviers* before being unloaded in bulk. Some of the tangled, writhing mass of carapaces, claws and legs may eventually grace island tables, but most are exported to France, Spain and Portugal.

Sea angling

The shellfish fleets of the Channel Islands are the big money earners and other forms of commercial fishing – such as trawling – are relatively unimportant. This, of course, is excellent news for that other category of fisherman, the angler. Sea angling has become important in all the islands. Once a way of putting a little extra on the table, it is now a major leisure activity, for both islanders and visitors.

The main islands already have accomplished charter boat skippers who can put their clients' bait right on the fish's nose and Alderney has an international reputation as a shore fishing centre where record-breaking ballan wrasse and monster grey mullet are landed. The latter are now caught with the lightest of light tackle which would not be out of place in the hands of a freshwater coarse angler.

This is a far cry from the methods of old, when the mullet man would set off not only with his tin of *chervie* (ground bait) but also with a rod and line strong enough to yank the top lip off this delicate, shy fish. The technique in those days was to swing hooked mullet under your jacket as soon as they left the water. Loose scales from captured fish were thought to scare the rest of the shoal.

Alderney, with its half-mile breakwater as a superb vantage point, may have the premier rep-

---

WHEN TO THROW THEM BACK

The use of modern tackle is not the only way in which local sport fishing has leapt into the 21st century. There are many serious anglers, including some of the charter skippers and dedicated specimen hunters, who return a high proportion of captured fish to the sea. This is especially good news in the case of slow-growing species such as bass, but many hooked tope, congers and rays also live to fight another day.

Conservation, however, is taken far enough and no further: so far, there have been no reports of the big turbot (which are often tempted by live sand eel baits fished over offshore banks) being returned to the depths.

utation as a shore angling centre. However, the other islands should not be ignored by the fishermen who like to keep their feet on dry land. Jersey, for example, offers excellent pier fishing from St Catherine's Breakwater, and everywhere you will find rocky points from which pollack, mackerel, garfish and a host of other varieties can be caught from the shore.

Bear two things in mind, though: there's nothing but sea between the islands and America and the entire area has an enormous tidal range. The first factor means that huge swells sometimes sweep up exposed rocks; the second means that it is all too easy to get cut off as the tide rises. Care and, above all, local advice are the things to take.

Most parts of the world are content with two forms of fishing: commercial and sporting. As in so many other things, the Channel Islands are different. If you hear someone talking mysteriously about "going down the tide" he will be talking about low-water fishing, an activity made possible by the enormous tidal range which can pose such a threat to the unwary.

Low-water fishing is a complex business because it is no single pursuit but a whole range of different pursuits. These vary from putting baited lines (trots) on winter beaches to catching razorfish with salt – yes, salt. This is something visitors often try, setting out sceptically for the low-tide mark armed with a salt pot and the knowledge that they are looking for keyhole-shaped burrows in the sand. If they have been instructed properly they discover that adding the salt to the keyholes is as effective as it is meant to be and up pops the razorfish (a plump mollusc in an elongated shell) shooting out like a missile from a silo. He is, of course, a victim of chemical warfare, preferring to take his chances in the open instead of being pickled in his lair.

Hunting the ormer

In the same breath as mentioning "going down the tide", islanders are likely to speak of ormers, ear-shaped shells which stick themselves to rocks with their own brand of superglue. Tourists may be fascinated by the ormer because of its beautiful mother-of-pearl inte-

> **CLOSE ENCOUNTERS**
>
> If you'd like to meet some of the local professionals, try having a drink at one of the fishermen's pubs, such as La Folie Inn on the very edge of St Helier Harbour.

rior, but for Jersey and Guernseymen the little beasts are sought for their meat.

Anywhere but at the Minquiers, that massive reef 10 miles (16 km) south of Jersey, finding sufficient for a meal can be a real challenge, involving hours and hours of wading and rock turning. However, ormers are held in such esteem that several attempts have been made to breed them in captivity and an "adopt an ormer" scheme was launched in 1988. All sponsors got in return for their 10p contributions were a car

sticker and a sense of virtue, but they were assured that their money would be put to good use in a marine conservation area near Fort Saus-marez in Guernsey. What's more, ormers are protected by rigidly enforced closed seasons. In Guernsey, where the season is restricted to a few winter days, illegal ormering is regarded almost as seriously as an act of high treason.

As if the sea weren't big enough, both Jersey and Guernsey offer facilities for freshwater angling, game and coarse. The venues include reservoirs and, in the genuinely idiosyncratic style of the islands, Jersey's South Canal, which is a flooded German antitank defence in the meadowland bordering St Ouen's Bay. ❑

LEFT: lobsters fetch good prices in local restaurants.
RIGHT: St Peter Port is Guernsey's main harbour.

SAILING CLOSE TO THE WIND

*The islands' many sheltered bays are good for beginners
and the open sea offers challenges to the experienced*

Show a landsman a chart of the Channel Islands and you might persuade him that its printer had been incompetent. So many rocks, heads and treacherous wave-washed reefs are marked that they could be taken for the smudges of poor workmanship. The truth, of course, is that the reefs really are there, so it's lucky that today's yachtsmen have the benefit of modern cartography and a buoyage system to help them through the chaos of rugged granite and unpredictable water. Certainly, if a complete picture of its hazards were not available, the entire Channel Island sea area would be as lethal to strangers as an unmapped minefield.

That sounds like a daunting introduction to the delights of the islands' waters, but anyone who has cruised them will quickly say that the dangers ordinarily do no more than add spice to the routines of sailing. The interest of coping with the navigational challenges outweighs the inconvenience of extra vigilance.

Flood tide perils

Besides what may be described as fixed hazards, island waters also try to intimidate with their famous tides. These can have a range of well over 32 ft (10 metres) between low- and high-water and they move so many cubic miles of sea that tremendous forces are exerted by their flux and reflux.

The influence spreads throughout the area but nowhere is it felt more powerfully than around Alderney, particularly in the passages north and south of the island, the Swinge and the Race. On the flood tide the whole Atlantic Ocean does its best to force its way into the English Channel and in doing so it creates fearsome tidal streams which have been logged at almost 10 knots.

Such conditions occur only in restricted zones on the very biggest of big spring tides, but the Swinge or the Race on only average form can be monsters if the weather is less than

perfect. A wind howling against a contrary tidal flow can whip up the sea so that it looks more like a white-water river in full spate than a cruising ground for pleasure craft. Overfalls (a word which is sprinkled liberally over charts of the islands) make matters even worse where tidal runs scour rough ground on the seabed.

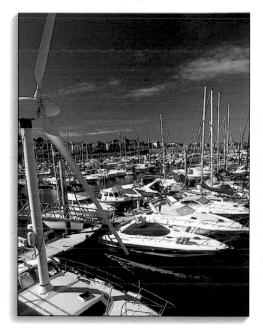

Again this sounds like bad public relations for the islands; but, in practice, conditions suitable only for Cape Horn veterans are rare. In summer the chances are that even the narrows with the most fearsome reputations will be docile. Under the influence of light airs the short, tumultuous, confused seas that make such good background for bar-room chats are transformed into glassy glides as clear as chalkland brooks.

Care is still needed if swift currents are not to push a boat off its intended heading and into trouble, yet on many days the sun will beat down, the breeze will be gentle and bikinis may even be more in order than oilskins.

LEFT: dinghy sailing off the coast of Jersey.
RIGHT: St Peter Port's yacht marina.

Serious sailing

Once the physical threats, real and imaginary, of the islands have been braved, what is left for the yachtsman visiting Jersey, Guernsey or the smaller isles? The answer rather depends on where the yachtsman is coming from, because the Channel Islands are the objective for two distinct boating invasions. One originates in France, the other in the United Kingdom.

Le yachting is a passion among many Frenchmen – including those going to sea for the first time. It's not surprising, therefore, that the passage seems to be the crucial matter for the southern visitors who pour out of St Malo and other Breton ports throughout summer.

Many take their sailing so seriously that they make it a point of honour not to use their auxilliary motors until it is absolutely necessary, so any yacht flying the *tricoleur* should be allowed plenty of searoom as she leaves or enters port. Once on dry land, of course, the Continental visitors can soak up what for them is the English atmosphere and enjoy shopping for duty-free whisky or chain-store woollens.

Merely getting afloat can also be the main concern of the British yellow wellie wearer but it is more likely to be tempered by thoughts

THE BOOM IN YACHTING

In the 19th century only the very rich could afford a yacht, and in the early 20th century, when the first yacht clubs were established on Jersey and Guernsey, the pastime was still confined to the wealthy.

It wasn't until the 1950s that yachting's popularity widened and by the early 1980s between 8,000 and 10,000 yachts a year were visiting each of the main islands. In response, Guernsey linked an old quarry on the northeast coast to the sea to form Beaucette Marina and converted several basins in St Peter Port into marinas. Jersey opened a marina in La Collette reclamation area and more recently converted parts of St Helier's harbour for yachting use.

of enjoying islands which blend with France and make an excellent staging post on the way to it. Alderney, the hospitable if slightly bleak northern isle, is the logical first landfall for the English armada, and during the summer it's not unusual for the down-to-earth pubs near Braye Harbour to be full of the patrician accents of off-duty professionals temporarily disguised as matelots.

There's nothing wrong with this, although after a particularly heavy cross-Channel influx it's easy for average holidaymakers to close their eyes and imagine that they have gate-crashed the headquarters of a more than averagely pukka yacht club.

Meeting of equals

Boating can, however, be a great leveller, and when the ketch of the retired doctor from Devon and the sloop full of students from Paris are tied up alongside each other it may be in one of the marinas in Jersey or Guernsey. The latter island has an 800-berth marina granted pride of place in a land reclamation project next to St Peter Port Harbour; this is the home of two older berthing areas, including the Victoria Marina, which is where the visitor is most likely to find himself.

In addition to these States of Guernsey facilities, there is a new 350-berth marina at St Sampson which opened in 2005. The 250-berth marina

harbour. Elizabeth Marina has around 600 berths, mainly for the use of locals or non-residents on one-, five- or 10-year leases. This has freed up space in St Helier Marina, Jersey's main visitors' marina, conveniently located in the Upper Harbour close to the Town centre. Berthing is available for 200 visiting yachts and access is three hours either side of high water. The marina has established quite a reputation for itself, having won the five gold anchors, the top award of the National Yacht Harbours Association. That might come as a surprise to those more used to five-star hotels than five-anchor marinas; the view of the crowded pontoons from the adjacent Victoria

in private ownership at Beaucette was created in the 1960s when visiting Royal Engineers were good enough to blast a channel linking a disused quarry with the open sea. The entrance they cut in the granite is less than 66 ft (20 metres) wide, so a cool head is required during the final approach to this most sheltered of havens.

Topless sunbathers

Jersey also has a new 600-berth marina, constructed on reclaimed land west of St Helier

---

FAR LEFT: sand-yachting at St Ouen's Bay, Jersey.
LEFT: riding the waves in the English Channel.
ABOVE: Guernsey has developed successful marinas.

Pier is enticing only when the decks of the yachts below are decorated with topless sunbathers. All marinas, with their craft packed together like sampans in some exotic anchorage and washing fluttering from a cat's cradle of rigging, tend to look like floating slums.

However, from the yachtsman's point of view, the sardine-can environment offers plenty of companionship of the right sort and every facility from hot showers to a café serving bacon and egg breakfasts. It's easy to see why marinas are a better bet than a drying mooring half-a-mile from the high-water mark on a featureless expanse of glutinous grey mud.

The choice of places to tie up may begin with

modern facilities but it does not end with them. Throughout what geographers (but never locals) might call the archipelago are many sheltered mooring places, a large number of which are protected by stone piers dating from the 19th century or earlier. Braye Harbour and its massive Admiralty Breakwater in Alderney is an example on the grand scale; altogether more modest, though no less interesting, are havens such as Gorey on Jersey's east coast, Creux in Sark and Herm's fittingly tiny harbour. Just what is on shore at these and other mooring places varies

SETTING FOR A NOVEL

Hammond Innes used the rocks of Les Minquiers as the setting for his novel *The Wreck of the Mary Deare*.

enormously, but the pilot books which explain in precise detail how to approach them in safety are often full of useful information.

Perhaps the best way to enjoy the sheer cliffs of Sark, Jersey's sunbaked southern coast or the low-lying, reef-strewn west of Guernsey is to find a temporary anchorage where the hook can be dropped for lunch, a swim or sunbathing. Again, pilot books explain where you can venture safely, so don't be too surprised if someone has beaten you to what the chart suggested was going to be a secluded spot. Often the first to the

THE FIRST LIGHTHOUSE

The remains of two Roman wrecks found in St Peter Port harbour were a reminder that the treacherous rocks and strong currents around the Channel Islands have always posed a deadly hazard for shipping.

A frequent problem was that, in poor weather, captains would mistake the Channel Islands for the south coast of England and steer south, intending to head into the middle of the Channel but in fact aiming straight at the reefs. The first lighthouse, using burning coals to provide the beam, began operating on the Casquets in 1724. But it didn't prevent a 100-gun warship, HMS *Victory*, being lost in a 1744 storm, drowning more than 1,000 men.

best anchorages are islanders, many of whom are just as keen on sailing as their UK and French counterparts.

Warm welcome

Happily, there's not too much "them and us" feeling, and visitors are made welcome. The welcome is extended on land as well, the islands' yacht clubs taking their tradition of reciprocal hospitality very seriously.

Perhaps this is one of the reasons why so many yachtsmen in transit decide to make the Channel Islands their cruising ground for an entire holiday instead of heading on to France or, in the case of the French, England's Channel coast. It is possible to use the islands as mere stopping-off points but much is missed in doing so. Lost, for example, would be the magical experience of slipping quietly past the rocks of Maître Ile and Marmotière at Les Ecréhous to find the peace of the offshore reef's enclosed anchorage set in the midst of a wasteland of kelp and sandbanks. Lost, too, would be the pleasure of cautiously exploring Les Minquiers, the 12-mile (19-km) long rock and shoal plateau south of Jersey. Certainly, storms in the area have claimed enough ships over the centuries to make the islands an exciting place for experienced divers.

high level of boat ownership to Guernsey's bid for publicity when it hosted international power-boat racing and the prestigious Swan European Regatta for £750,000 superyachts.

The sailboard experience

There is, though, one growth sport *par excellence* which puts sailing within almost anyone's reach. Sailboards are everywhere, both on the sheltered waters of enclosed bays and off surf beaches such as Jersey's St Ouen, where the swells roll in from mid-Atlantic. There are conditions suitable for windsurfers of all levels of competence because, in anything short of a full

Although the Channel Islands have been a classic destination for sailors from both sides of the Channel for decades, they are now the starting point for many yachting holidays. Skippered and "bareboat" charters can be arranged to begin at St Helier or St Peter Port and the charter firms are only too eager to point out that hiring an expensive hole in the water is more cost-effective than owning one and pouring money into it 12 months a year.

Evidence of how important the sea is to Channel Islanders is provided by everything from the

LEFT: learning to sail in St Peter Port's harbour.
ABOVE: surfing at St Ouen in Jersey.

gale, there always seems to be a protected shore where conditions are safe. And tuition is no problem in the main islands: there are schools where lessons are given and equipment – including buoyancy aids and wetsuits – is hired.

It's even possible to learn the rudiments of the sport without getting your feet wet. Windsurfing simulators on the beach let you get the feel of board and rig before going out on the water. And, if even that sounds like hard work, wait for the big winds and big seas and watch the funboard sailors. At home even among pounding breakers, they have adapted and extended the repertoire of ordinary surfing to suit their custom-built wave-jumping sailboards. ❑

DIGGING OUT THE PAST

The islands' strategic location meant that, even in prehistoric times, they were much visited. Archaeologists are piecing together the evidence

There is abundant archaeological evidence to suggest that prehistoric man, mysterious builder of unfathomable architecture, found the Channel Islands as attractive a base for his operations as bankers and offshore settlers do today. The geographical accident that made these little islands into stepping stones between two hazardous mainland coasts presents archaeologists with something of a bonus. The archipelago was the point where, many hundreds and even thousands of years ago, different cultures crossed and met, mainly through trading. Sometimes these influences – on pottery, for example – were given distinctive local adaptations.

Bob Burns, now retired but formerly the acting director of the Guernsey Museum, oversaw excavations establishing St Peter Port for the first time as a thriving Roman trading post. He points out that "island hopping" made good sense to our ancestors. "They were frightened of the sea, and naturally would stop off here on their way across the Channel."

The legacy of Lukis

Guernsey is particularly lucky in having sites that have been left much as their prehistoric builders conceived them. They include the impressive passage graves of Le Déhus and La Varde, 42 ft (13 metres) long and 13 ft (4 metres) wide. Preservation of the integrity of Neolithic chambered tombs, some dating to 3,000 BC, and the rescue of quantities of grave furniture found in them is due to one remarkable Guernseyman, Frederick Corbin Lukis. In the best traditions of the self-taught, Victorian "gentleman" scientist, Lukis had wide interests – conchology, natural history, geology, and archaeology above all.

When he was 23, he excavated La Varde in 1811 with his elderly relative, Joshua Gosselin, the first Guernseyman to make a study of prehistoric remains. Afterwards, Lukis dug up his native island with unflagging zeal for over half a century to unearth the secrets of a megalithic

civilization. He also made archaeological expeditions to Alderney and Jersey. In those days, when archaeology was little understood, Lukis was ahead of his time. He made detailed records of his findings, and would bribe farmers not to tamper with strange boulders found in their fields. And he astonished locals by paying cash for earthy old pots and bits of flint.

He was one of the first archaeologists to realise that megalithic remains were not "druids' altars" as was generally supposed, but the burial places of a much older people. His four sons inherited his enthusiasm and helped in the field work, and his three daughters made hundreds of drawings of stone monuments, urns, axes and other artefacts. Lukis died in 1871, leaving his entire collection and voluminous records to Guernsey.

The chances of turning up an untouched Neolithic site in a small island like Guernsey – already well worked over by the Lukis family – are pretty slim. Yet that is exactly what happened in 1978. Members of the archaeological section

LEFT: Jersey's Dolmen de Faldouet.
RIGHT: Grosnez Castle on Jersey.

of La Société Guernesiaise (the local cultural body) spotted two large stones, near the fifth green of the golf course, whose composition suggested that they had been transported there. Following an exploratory dig, Dr Ian Kinnes of the British Museum was called in. Over the next three years, he carried out a total excavation of the complex Les Fouaillages site.

The significance of the findings at Les Fouaillages – involving levels of human activity from 4,500 BC to about 2,000 BC – is still being assessed. But the strange, original level could be the first stone monument known in Western Europe – a bridge between primitive structures

of wood and the familiar dolmens. Six decorated vessels of the Bandkeramic group were discovered in association with this first stone layer. The pottery has been found so far only in conjunction with evidence of building in wood.

For lack of a Lukis, Jersey has fared less well. It was not until the opening of La Hougue Bie tomb in the 20th century that the larger island could lay claim to excavation of a significant prehistoric site that had not been pillaged, damaged or just rearranged more tastefully. In 1787, the Vingtaine de la Ville (town councillors) of St Helier actually presented a complete group of prehistoric monuments to General Henry Conway, a former Governor of Jersey, who accepted this "feeble but sincere tribute of our gratitude".

Dubbed "Little Master Stonehenge" because of its likeness to Stonehenge, the site had been discovered two years earlier during military reinforcements of what was then Town Hill, but is now the Fort Regent leisure centre. Dauntless General Conway had the capstones and 45 megaliths – each more than 23 ft (7 metres) in diameter and weighing around 140 tons – shipped across the Channel and then transported by barge up the Thames to his Park Place estate at Henley-on-Thames. The re-erected stone circle of General Conway's "Jersey Temple" stands there still – 200 miles (320 km) from the monument's homeland.

Tomb robbers

A more fitting destiny awaited the 43-ft (13-metre) man-made mound of La Hougue Bie, because it was acquired in 1919 by La Société Jersiaise, founded in 1873. The mound, crowned by a 12th-century and a 16th-century

---

THE MYSTERIES STILL TO BE SOLVED

Roman remains were unearthed at an important Iron Age site of around 100 BC at King's Road, on the outskirts of St Peter Port. Sophisticated artefacts that include a sword and sheath and a brooch point to the existence of an elite community who drank wine imported from Northern Italy before the coming of the Romans.

Guernsey archaeologists have filled in a number of blanks in the island's history from around 250 BC to AD 1250. Four seasons of excavations for the Ancient Monuments Committee at 13th-century Castle Cornet has built up a vivid profile of the stronghold's development, and supplied details of sieges and bloody battles with the French.

A pet ambition of Bob Burns, former acting director of the Guernsey Museum, is to uncover the mystery of Corbière Castle, which used to dominate the sea below the cliffs at Guernsey's west coast. Because it is below the cliffs it is vulnerable to attack from above, an obvious flaw in its situation, if not design. A sketch of the fortress, drawn in 1680 for an official survey on Channel Island defences for Charles II, is tantalising proof that it once was there. "Perhaps the Romans built it as a watch tower," says Mr Burns, "and it may well be that I will never discover its purpose. But the Channel Islands are full of archaeological goodies, and there will be plenty left for future generations to discover."

chapel, was excavated in 1924 to reveal a chambered tomb. Dr Arthur Mouran, a member of that excavation team as a 20-year-old undergraduate, later recalled that the structure of the passage grave was in such perfect condition that it was presumed to have been untouched since Neolithic times. But the contents of the tomb chambers had been scrabbled out into the middle of the floor, and the bones and pottery broken up, probably by looters.

New excavations were begun at La Hougue Bie in the early 1990s after radar studies of the mound suggested that it might hide other passages. The excavations have improved access to the tomb and have revealed the methodical way in which the mound was constructed, but as yet there have been no more major discoveries.

There are archaeological and geological displays at La Hougue Bie, but the story of Jersey's pre-history is told more fully at Jersey Museum in St Helier. An artificial rockface, complete with the figures of Palaeolithic man, helps to put into context the finds at La Cotte at St Brelade, the island's prestigious Old Stone Age site. These include the remains of woolly rhinoceros, a species which roamed Jersey 150,000 years ago (when it was joined to the Continent). The skulls alone of these animals weigh about 300 lbs (130 kgs) apiece.

The complex site encompasses a time scale of 250,000 years, and records how humans interacted with their changing environment.

Mammoth remains

The bones of mammoth and rhino found heaped at the foot of the site's 98-ft (30-metre) drop prove that primitive man used ravine systems such as La Cotte as "funnel" traps, stampeding herds of prehistoric beasts over the cliff edge to their deaths. Teeth that were discovered are believed to be the only true Neanderthal remains found so far in the British Isles, and more stone artefacts of the same period have been recovered from La Cotte than in the whole of Britain. While evidence of Roman occupation in Jersey continues to be slight, there have been dramatic discoveries on land and sea in Guernsey fixing St Peter Port firmly on the Roman map for the first time. Excavations at the town site of La Plaiderie uncovered two substantial buildings with Roman

roof tiles that were almost certainly warehouses. These, and a wealth of other items, establish St Peter Port as a waterfront trading post.

Traces of the Romans

Revelations of Roman activity on land were matched at sea by local diver Richard Keen's exciting discovery of a unique wreck in St Peter Port harbour. The Gallo-Roman merchant vessel had been preserved below the silt for 18 centuries, until propwash from a new generation of cross-Channel ferries began to expose and then to erode it.

Dr Margaret Rule, who raised the Tudor war-

ship "Mary Rose" masterminded a successful underwater excavation in 1985 so that timbers of the 23-metre long vessel could be put on public display by the Guernsey Maritime Trust. An Alderney fisherman's catch led to the discovery of yet another underwater wreck when he brought up an ancient musket entangled in his lobster pot. The 16th century *Makeshift* went down off Alderney in the 1590s and is believed to be the only wreck of an English warship from the Elizabethan era, possibly one of the ships that fought against the Spanish Armada. Over 1,000 artefacts have been raised, but substantial financial support from outside the Island is needed to do full justice to the site. ❑

LEFT: the neolithic dolmen at la Hougue Bie.
RIGHT: exploring the burial chambers at La Hougue Bie.

THE LEGENDS THAT LIVE ON

Seafarers kept the islanders entertained with tall stories, but belief in witchcraft was to cause the torture and death of innocent people

In heathen times, in Jersey, there lived a band of unscrupulous beachcombers who believed in leaving nothing to chance. If stormy weather wouldn't wreck ships and sweep their cargo to shore, then stormy weather would have to be given a hand. And so, at the height of a storm, they would build huge fires above the most treacherous rocks at Corbière and L'Etacq as a signal to worried captains that here, below, was sanctuary from the wind and waves.

As the unwary captain steered his ship closer to the shore it would be caught by the tide, thrown against the rocks and torn apart. A day or two later, and the cargo would be washed ashore by tides more kindly to the St Ouen wreckers, as they were called, than to the foreign captain and his crew. Death was inevitable: any seamen who managed to survive the raging water would be murdered by the wreckers.

This is one of Jersey's best-known legends, which has been altered dramatically over the centuries and inevitably glamorised, particularly by Victorian writers, who were determined to give their readers value for money.

Father's curse

One account, for example, tells of an old man's vain efforts to save his daughter's life as his ship, one of five on their way from America to Spain, was lured towards Corbière in 1495. The wreckers, watching from the headland, heard the old man cry out: "Save my daughter's life and all my chests of gold will be yours. Refuse my plea and I condemn you all to die within a year." They ignored his cries and calmly watched as the ships and everyone aboard them were destroyed in the howling seas below. Exactly a year later, a black, howling storm swept in from the west and tore to pieces the islanders, their homes and the forest to the north of the bay. Only sand and tree stumps remained.

Such legends were told and retold in melodramatic style. "Even as their fiendish laughter

broke out, a cresting wave swept the decks of the doomed ship and carried the young girl into the depths of the sea," was one 1856 version. But the legends contained nuggets of truth. At one time the Seigneur (lord) of St Ouen, who could claim any wreckage thrown on to the beaches bordering his property, had an arrange-

ment with his parishoners whereby they would be paid for anything brought to the manor. And contemporary records show that in 1494, or thereabouts, one Spanish ship (not five) carrying wine was wrecked off Corbière and that many hundreds of barrels were washed ashore, to be purloined by the lord.

From this story the legend grew and to it were added other elements of truth – as well as the tale of the old man's curse. For at one time there was a forest to the north of St Ouen, and old maps show a château near L'Etacq where, today, there is only sea. The forest disappeared long before the 15th century, the château in more recent times.

LEFT: old women were often suspected of sorcery.
RIGHT: stormy seas, the stuff of legends.

The legend contains a name which appears in many Channel Island stories – de Carteret, hereditary lords of St Ouen. The regularity with which their name appears should surprise no-one who knows Channel Island history: over the centuries the family has bred easily and regularly (Margaret de Carteret, for example, gave birth to 20 sons and a daughter in the 15th century) and it was Helier de Carteret who, in 1565, took 40 parishoners with him to populate Sark.

Presumably Pierre de Carteret, who (legend has it) lived in Sark in the 18th century, was some distant cousin, although the islanders hated him and branded him a witch. Known locally as

"*le vieux diable*", he was said to have employed small devils and spoken fluently to them in their own language. He built a boat in a barn one morning and the Serquiaise watched in amazement as he launched it at Creux harbour. How he managed to get it into the water they never discovered because the barn was far from the sea and the boat was too large to get through the door. They decided that he had used black magic.

However, there is no record of his having been to trial for "*l'horrible et énorme crime de sorcellerie*" although, between 1 June 1550 and the end of October 1661, over 170 Channel Island "witches" were tried. Tales about their antics abound. They danced naked at La Rocqueberg in Jersey, for example, and bewitched passing fishermen into joining in their fun. They met at Le Catioroc, in Guernsey, where they rubbed *le verjus au diable*, a hallucinatory cream, on their bodies, and would shout relentlessly across the sea to the small priory of Lihou "*Tcheit d'la haout, Marie d'Lihaou*" ("Fall from up there, Mary of Lihou").

There seems to be a shred of truth behind such tales: certain weird men and women did meet, in both Guernsey and Jersey, for devil worship. In rigidly puritanical islands, any hint of scandal was seen as a sign that the devil was in someone, and the best way of removing him, it was thought, was to burn the afflicted person and to scatter the ashes to the four winds. In Guernsey, the condemned man was burnt alive in the aptly-named "Vale of Misery". In Jersey, he was tied to a post in the market square, strangled from behind, then burnt.

The devil drops in

All such executions attracted huge crowds, not least because public execution was one of the few forms of recreation the courts allowed. In addition, there was also the remote but tantalising possibility that the devil might come down and whisk away his favourite son or daughter before the executioner had earned his pay.

A Guernsey legend, set in 1640, illustrates this belief. An old woman "of four score years and more" was sentenced to death for sorcery although she was convinced that no human hand could kill her. As she was escorted down the steps from La Tour Beauregard toward *La Vallée de Misère*, a great black raven appeared. The old woman threw a length of black cotton towards the bird which flew away, holding tightly to one end, while the woman, clinging to the other, was lifted into the air. It seemed to the waiting crowd that the witch would make good her escape until a youth, who was standing on higher ground, threw his staff at the bird which, stunned, immediately released the thread. The old woman fell back to earth where she was recaptured and burnt. The lad, lauded as a hero, enjoyed his triumph over evil but within a year he, too, had died – choked to death in his sleep.

Sadly, from a storyteller's point of view, there

KILLING OFF WITCHES

Belief in witchcraft was gradually eroded by education. The Calvinist movement, brought to the islands by French Huguenots, played a major role in setting up schools.

there was always the ultimate deterrent, death, as the *greffier* (chief clerk of the court) was well aware. While writing down the court's verdict in the ledgers, as the magistrate sentenced yet another islander to death, the *greffier* would doodle in the margin pictures of the condemned man hanging above the flames. The more people condemned (for example, three of the Massi family in 1624), the larger the picture. These sketches can be seen in the States' archives.

In Guernsey the most prominent witch-hunter

were no witch trials in 1640. But why quibble with fact when there is a good moral tale to tell?

The sting at the end of that tale served as a reminder to islanders that the devil was a vindictive loser who would exact a terrible revenge when crossed. For this reason, they heated nails in a pan over the fire on Friday evenings to deny him access to their houses, or they carried quicksilver (mercury) when they went fishing, or spat on the shadow of a passing witch in the belief that to do so protected them from evil.

If such superstitious practices didn't work,

LEFT: frogs dancing on the witches' Sabbath.
RIGHT: rituals of devil worship on Guernsey.

was Amice de Carteret, bailiff and magistrate, a member of the St Ouen de Carteret family with a tally of 35 witches burnt and 19 banished between 1601 and 1635. In Jersey, the chief scourge was George Paulet, bailiff at the end of the 16th century, who ordered the execution of 18 witches from 35 trials. Paulet's daughter, coincidentally, was married to a de Carteret.

The devil gets absolutely everywhere, of course, which is why, when making dough, Channel Island housewives traditionally make five dents in the pastry before placing it to rise, make a sign of the cross and say "*au nom de feu, soit*". Presumably, if it doesn't rise, no-one has been listening. ❑

JERSEY

A detailed guide to the island, with the main points of interest
clearly cross-referenced by number to the maps

Jersey, the self-styled "Queen of the Channel", combines a flourishing tourism industry with a traditional agricultural economy and, in St Helier, a spectacularly successful offshore finance operation. Its symbol, Mont Orgueil Castle, has been defying France for seven centuries.

For the tourist there is plenty to see and do. The island offers castles, museums, flower centres, potteries, German Occupation relics, watersports, boat trips and a celebrated zoo. But for most visitors it is the coastline which is the greatest allure. Jersey has 50 miles (80km) of shoreline, 20 miles (32km) of sandy beaches and nowhere on the island lies more than 2½ miles (4km) from the sea. Moreover, the coastal scenery is highly varied, from the towering cliffs of the north, to the Atlantic rollers of the windswept west and the spacious unspoilt sands of the south.

The most southerly of the British Isles, Jersey lies in the Gulf of St Malo, 100 miles (160km) from the south coast of Britain, but just 14 miles (22km) from France. On most days Normandy is visible from the east coast of the island. The largest of the Channel Islands, Jersey is 9 miles (14km) long, 5 miles (8km) wide and covers an area of 45 square miles (72 sq km). However, the 350 miles (560km) of roads, many of them narrow winding lanes, make the island feel much larger than it actually is.

Jersey has one of the largest tidal movements in the world and the coastal landscape undergoes dramatic changes between high and low water. During spring tides the island's surface area increases from 45 to 63 sq. miles (72 to 100 sq. km) and the vertical difference between high and low water can be as much as 40ft (12 metres). The extreme tidal movements ensure the beaches are regularly washed, but also bring strong currents around the coast.

Cheap package holidays to Spain and Eastern Europe have lured away many of Jersey's traditional summer visitors in recent years. In response, it has tried to cater for demands beyond those of the sun-and-spade brigade, focusing attention on heritage and the arts, outdoor activities, gastronomy and the environment. In 1997 the island was the first destination in the world to achieve the Green Globe destination award, as part of an environmental programme for travel and tourism developed in 1994 at the Rio Earth Summit. Jersey has some of the cleanest waters in Europe, aided by its award-winning ultra-violet sewage treatment system, installed in 1992. Green lanes, reducing the speed limit on some country lanes to 15 mph, have encouraged cyclists and pedestrians, and clearly marked cycle routes now cover 92 miles (150km) of coast and countryside. ❑

PRECEDING PAGES: Mont Orgueil Castle, Jersey; St Peter Port's harbour, Guernsey; at play in Royal Harbour, Jersey.
LEFT: golf links at Gorey, Jersey.

ST HELIER

Apart from the astonishing number of international banks, Jersey's capital has good shopping facilities, varied entertainment and rich historical associations

Map on page 122

"**A** large harbour; a maze of streets, busy and prosperous, but noted for their cleanliness; a huge fort rising perpendicularly out of the town; good shops; numerous places of worship; a miscellaneous assortment of carriages and well-appointed 'Jersey cars' plus a general air of comfort... are the prominent features of St Helier."

This description of St Helier is taken from a guide published 100 years ago. Delete "a miscellaneous assortment of carriages and well-appointed Jersey cars", substitute "a steady stream of hire-cars interrupted by the occasional tanned and carefree cyclist" and you have a fair description of St Helier today.

The original words described a relatively new community. In 1800 St Helier had far fewer streets, no large harbour and no fort. It was less prosperous, too; tourism didn't get into gear until Queen Victoria's visit in 1846.

The name St Helier has an ancient heritage; it commemorates the hermit Helerius, son of a Belgian nobleman who came to Jersey to seek an isolated spot where he could devote his life to prayer and fasting. He chose a place, today known as the Hermitage Rock, near the islet on which Elizabeth Castle stands, where he lived for 15 years in solitude and piety. In AD 555 he was murdered by axe-wielding pirates. As folklore has it, the hermit picked up his severed head and carried it for 200 yards, at which point the pirates "departed in great haste and fear". Helerius was later canonised – hence St Helier's crest, two crossed axes that recall the hermit's death.

There are other pointers to St Helier's past. Archaeologists have found evidence of habitation from the 12th century in the Old Street area of the town centre (near the Town Hall). Much of the Town Church dates from the 14th century. Elizabeth Castle provided an important focal point on Jersey's southern flank from the 16th century onwards. And there are buildings surviving from the 17th and 18th centuries. Growth was slow. In 1734, it is recorded, St Helier still contained only 534 houses.

The town expands

It was a long time before the town developed as a port. In the 17th century the main landing place was Havre des Pas. Things improved a little after 1700 with the English Harbour and the French Harbour, though there were no major facilities until 1751, when George II gave the island £200 to help with the building of a new harbour. For a long time access was restricted by the tides. Even when Victoria Pier and Albert Pier were built in the middle of the 19th century, the harbour could really only function with continual dredging. Not until 1975 was substantial work undertaken. Existing piers were strengthened and widened and the yachting marina was built.

LEFT: satyr and coat of arms at the Jersey Museum. **BELOW:** a ferry departs for France from St Helier.

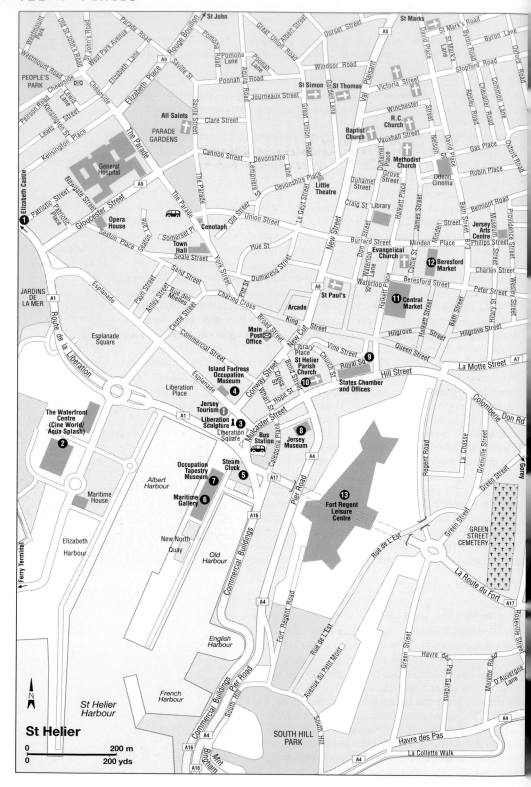

St Helier

0 ____ 200 m
0 ____ 200 yds

St Helier's real expansion began with the French and American wars in the late 18th century when privateering (legalised plundering of enemy shipping) was a major and lucrative island industry. The French Revolution brought an influx of at least 4,000 refugees to the island. And during the Napoleonic wars, the population of St Helier was swelled by the British garrison. Work on Fort Regent, begun in 1806, brought an influx of Irish workers too. Of the two Roman Catholic congregations in the town today, one is very Irish, the other very French, although the Portuguese influence grows ever stronger as more workers from Portugal and Madeira come to live on the island.

The end of the Napoleonic wars saw military men and their families settle in Jersey. The climate was good, the living was inexpensive and the introduction of steamer services to England eased communication. Yet though the Regency and Victorian houses went up and the town grew, praise for the way St Helier looked was guarded. An 1862 tourist guide stated: "The Town of St Helier is altogether wanting both in architectural and picturesque effect."

Map on facing page

Elizabeth Castle

The criticism of the town could not be made of **Elizabeth Castle ❶** (open Easter to Oct daily, 10am–6pm, last admission 5pm, admission charge). At high tide, the sight of its turrets, towers and chimneys marooned on a rock nearly a mile out at sea is nothing if not picturesque. At low tide, the visitor walking along the Esplanade can't help but notice the causeway tracing a beckoning track across the beach to the castle's outer gates.

Until the 16th century, Mont Orgueil Castle at Gorey had been Jersey's principal stronghold; but improvements in the power of cannon meant that it was no longer impregnable. The islet of St Helier was a natural choice for a new stronghold. Sir Walter Raleigh, one of Jersey's most distinguished governors, was involved in the construction, which began in 1594. It was he who diplomatically named the fortress "Fort Isabella Bellissima" (the most beautiful Elizabeth) after his Queen.

Elizabeth Castle didn't see any action until the English civil war. After Sir George Carteret, the Governor of Jersey, retreated to the castle, Charles II eventually paid his respects when Elizabeth Castle had become the last Royalist stronghold in Britain. His first visit was in April 1646, his second in November 1649. On this occasion he was proclaimed King in St Helier's marketplace by Sir George, even though the monarchy had been abolished.

A chequered history

In 1651, Parliamentary forces landed in St Ouen's Bay and the castle was bombarded by mortars set up at the foot of Mont de la Ville. One bomb broke through the roof of a chapel built inside the ruins of the old chuch and penetrated the crypt where gunpowder and two-thirds of the castle's provisions were stored. The resulting explosion was catastrophic. It demolished the Abbey and forced Sir George Carteret to surrender. The Parliamentarians held Jersey for the next nine years. A cross in the Barrack Square marks the approximate site of the Abbey church.

TIP

Elizabeth Castle can be reached either by amphibious ferry or, at low tide, on foot.

BELOW: amphibious transport to Elizabeth Castle.

*Firepower at
Elizabeth Castle.*

During the 18th century, Elizabeth Castle was always ready for an attack from France, acquiring in the process a granite barracks and various moats, gates and look-outs. When the French finally arrrived in 1781 and entered St Helier, the garrison at the castle was marooned. The French marched out to the castle with a copy of the surrender that the kidnapped Governor of Jersey, Moise Corbet, had been forced to sign. There followed a superb example of British insularity: when asked to surrender also, Captain Mulcaster, the senior officer in the castle, pocketed the documents without reading them and informed the enemy he did not understand French. It was left to troops under the command of Major Peirson to win the day in Royal Square.

Exploring the Castle

Elizabeth Castle has been dubbed "one of the finest fortified sites in Western Europe". It's actually a castle "complex" comprising three distinct sections: the Upper Ward, built between 1594 and 1601; the Lower Ward, built between 1626 and 1636; and the Outer Ward, finished in 1668. And beyond that, along the breakwater, is the small oratory known as the Hermitage, built in the 12th century to commemorate St Helier. Every year on the Sunday closest to 16 July a pilgrimage makes its way here, and a wreath is laid in the saint's memory.

You can clamber in and around four centuries worth of fortifications, though when you tire of this there's plenty to learn about the castle's past. In the Lower Ward, the Jersey Royal Militia Museum houses a display of military memorabilia stretching back several hundred years. The Jersey Militia served the island for around 600 years and in its heyday numbered over 6,000 local men, divided into four regiments. The Barracks have a permanent artillery display that includes

BELOW:
Elizabeth Castle
floodlit by night.

a short audio-visual show. To reinforce the military theme, a gun is fired daily at 12 noon and male visitors may be dragooned into marching the Parade Ground. In the Upper Ward, the Governor's House contains two elaborate tableaux depicting Sir Walter Raleigh and King Charles II. For the best views of the coast, climb up to the gunner control tower built by the Germans, who modernised the castle with guns, bunkers and battlements.

The Waterfront Centre

Back on dry land you can't fail to miss the first stages of the £150-million waterfront development. This privately-funded project, which is to become a leisure, business and residential centre, has inevitably caused a stir among islanders. Built on reclaimed land, the programme so far consists of a new marina, high-rise apartments, a multi-story international hotel, recreational facilities and American fast food joints. Recent plans for waterfront skyscrapers (of up to 20 storeys) have been reassigned to the drawing board. While some see the development as the key to Jersey's future, catapulting the town into the 21st century, the majority of islanders see it as a blot on the landscape and a threat to the essential nature of the island. So far the development is soulless and devoid of architectural merit. In addition to this, the creation of a multi-storey hotel and 750 (proposed) flats is inevitably controversial at a time when many Jersey hotels are struggling to survive and a large number of vacant apartments are on the market.

At the St Aubin's end of the waterfront development **Les Jardins de la Mer ❷** feature a water maze and central sculpture of swimmers and dolphins. To the north, Parade Garden, which attracts strollers on summer evenings, was built as a parade ground by General Don, a soldier known for the island's "Routes Militaires".

Map on page 122

TIP

There are free guided walks of St Helier twice a week during the summer months. Enquire at the Jersey Tourism office in Liberation Square.

BELOW:
Albert Harbour.

Liberation Square

The Esplanade leads eastwards to **Liberation Square** ❸, opened by Prince Charles on 9 May 1995, the 50th anniversary of the end of the Occupation. It was here that huge crowds gathered to see the British fleet sailing in to release the islanders after five long years under the Germans. The **Liberation Sculpture**, a fine bronze depicting flag-waving islanders, enlivens an otherwise unremarkable square, surrounded by a hotchpotch of architecture. Originally the focus of some controversy, the sculpture by Philip Jackson, has become a major St Helier landmark. Overlooking the square the Jersey Tourism building formerly housed the St Helier terminus of the Jersey Railway which served the south and east coasts.

Looking up from the square, you can see the walls and bastions below the modern white dome, which survive from the original Fort Regent. This was built at enormous expense between 1806 and 1814 against the threat of French invasions. Troops were stationed here for many years, but it was never actually used to defend the island. In 1958 the fort was sold back to the States for £14,500, the original price of the land, and in the 1960s the building was converted into a huge leisure centre. The mast, seen to the far left, is the last working signal station in the British Isles. Dating from 1708 it is used today to signal weather warnings, high tides, shipping movements and special anniversaries. The latest addition is the orange pennant which goes up when the plane carrying the daily national newspapers has left London and is lowered to half mast when it lands.

Occupation memorabilia

Just along the Esplanade lies the **Island Fortress Occupation Museum** ❹ (open daily 9.30am–6.30pm, 10am–4pm in winter, admission charge), one of

Philip Falle (1656–1742) described St Helier thus: "The Town is inhabited chiefly by Merchants, Shopkeepers, Artificers, and Retailers of Liquors; the Landed Gentlemen generally living upon their Estates in the Country."

BELOW:
Philip Jackson's
Liberation sculpture,
Liberation Square.

a number of permanent Occupation exhibitions in Jersey. You can inspect a large collection of German military hardware as well as field medical supplies, a field kitchen and mannequins sporting Nazi uniforms. Look closer and you'll see a host of intriguing details of life in Occupied Jersey. The most fascinating is a small bundle of blue toilet paper made from tomato tray-liners; the enterprising islander whose idea it was to provide for the convenience of others in this way is said to have made a fortune.

All the items on display are placed in a serious and proper perspective in the video room where you can sit and watch an account of the invasion, the Occupation, the resistance and the eventual liberation. Interviews with Jerseymen who survived Nazi concentration camps provide a salutary reminder of how close Hitler came to the United Kingdom.

Map
on page
122

The Steam Clock

The Maritime Museum

South of Liberation Square, don't hunt too hard for The Weighbridge, marked on some maps. It disappeared long ago and today is a bustling scene with boats in the background and cars clogging the intersection between the Esplanade and the tunnel. Overlooking the old harbour, and looking like something out of Disneyland, the world's largest **Steam Clock** ❺ is modelled on a 19th-century paddle-steamer. Wait long enough and it will start to foam, whistle and chime.

A more worthwhile development on the waterfront is the excellent **Maritime Museum** ❻ (open daily 10am–5pm, 4pm in winter, admission charge also covers Tapestry Gallery). Housed in a restored warehouse on North Quay this new museum explores every aspect of the island's links with the sea, bringing to life its former role as a seafaring state. From 1820 to 1870

BELOW: the
Jersey war Tunnels.

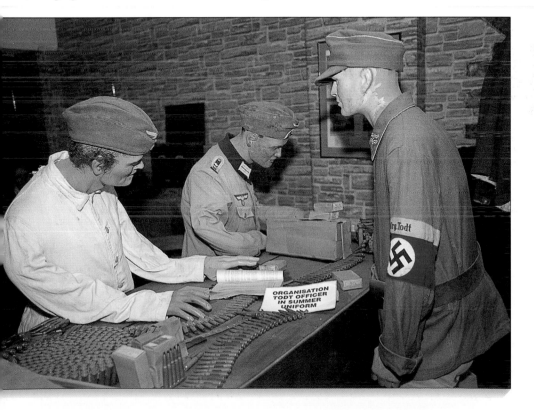

Hands-on in the Maritime Museum.

Jersey had the fourth largest shipbuilding industry in Britain and many of the island's merchants and shipowners made huge fortunes from the cod trade. The museum is split into three main sections: natural science, boat building and activities at sea. The emphasis is very much on seeing and doing. Visitors can feel the pull of the currents and the power of the sea, build a boat and sail in in the wave tank, listen to legends of the sea from a 12-ft (3.7-metre) model of a whelk and watch on a huge globe the historic sea voyages made by Jersey vessels. A speeded-up video shows tidal cycles on the island, reminiscences are related by sailors via a John Dory handset and there's a full scale construction of the prow of a historic ship, including a cabin below deck which rocks to assimilate the ship's movement.

Within the same building the **Occupation Tapestry Gallery** ❼ (Open daily 10am-5pm, 4pm in winter, included in Maritime Museum admission charge) comprises 12 separate tapestries depicting scenes from the Occupation. These historically accurate and carefully-worked scenes were created by the 12 Jersey parishes. The themes range from the Outbreak of War and Deportation to the daily life of civilians, such as the school-room scene of a boy yawning in a German lesson.

Glimpses of the past

Back at the Weighbridge, behind the bus station, lies the main entrance of the extended and greatly enhanced **Jersey Museum** ❽ (open Mon to Sat 10am– 5pm, 4pm in winter, admission charge). The core of the complex is still a magnificent four-storey merchant's house, but a café, an audio-visual theatre and a shop selling surprisingly worthwhile souvenirs also occupy the site. It is also home to La

BELOW: the Maritime Museum.

Société Jersiaise, an antiquarian and scientific organisation founded in 1873 for the study and research on all matters relating to Jersey.

Map on page 122

The museum, which has won two major national awards, tells the story of Jersey from prehistoric to present times. Exhibits cover all aspects of the island including interesting sections on traditions and trades specific to Jersey, such as oyster catching, shipbuilding and knitting. The second floor is devoted to works of Jersey artists, including John Everett Millais' portrait of Lillie Langtry and a new 3-D hologram image of the Queen. The top floor rooms comprising school room and bedroom have been carefully reconstructed to show how they would have looked in Victorian times when the house was occupied by a doctor and his family.

For many visitors, the star attraction of the museum is Emilie Charlotte Le Breton, better known as Lillie Langtry or the "Jersey Lily". Daughter of a philandering Jersey dean, she married a wealthy widower in 1874 and two years later took London society by storm with her beauty and charm. Eventually she numbered among her friends and admirers the Prince of Wales (later King Edward VII), whose intimate relationship with her provoked much gossip. One exhibit, a quote taken from a certain Lord Carrington, concerns the dubious reputation Lillie Langtry's beauty had earned her. On hearing that her parrot was missing, he punned: "I didn't know she had a parrot, though I'd heard she'd had a cockatoo."

An actress plays Lily Langtry in the Jersey Museum.

Royal Square

If the Weighbridge is a noisy focus of the town's energy, the shaded precinct of **Royal Square ❾** is one place where you can escape it. Here many strands of Jersey's history come together. Overlooked by the States Chamber (the seat of Jersey's government) and the Royal Court House, the square is also very much

BELOW:
Jersey Museum.

Royal Square

Royal Square started life as a market, though it doubled as a site for execution and incarceration. Records tell of two witches being strangled and burnt here in 1648. In the following century, prisoners being brought from Mont Orgueil Castle at Gorey were placed in an iron cage in the square to await trial. On market day, offenders were placed in the pillory (removed only in 1836) and exposed to the jeers and missiles of onlookers.

Sentencing, performed in the Court House, could entail further drama. In 1787 an unfortunate named David Brouard and his wife were both whipped by the public executioner from the Court House, along the quarter-mile route to the prison at Charing Cross. The noise and commotion of market day caused real problems: Royal Square became so crowded that it was a constant source of complaint. A particular problem was the desecration to the cemetery and the Town Church caused by wandering pigs and poultry. In response, the States pur-

chased a plot of marshy ground a short distance away – the site of today's Central Market – and by 1800 market day was no longer held in Royal Square.

The glitzy golden statue at the eastern end of the square, depicting George II in the garb of Caesar, was unveiled on July 9, 1751, and it was in honour of this regal statue that Royal Square received its name. But by the middle of the 19th century the myth was firmly established that this was a figure of a Roman emperor salvaged from a stranded ship and renamed to suit the square. (The fact that this pseudo-Caesar was wearing the Order of the Garter was overlooked).

It's worth going into the National Westminster bank, a building occupying the site of the Cornmarket. The original granite arches of this open-air meeting place have been preserved in the banking hall.

Royal Square is best known as the site of the Battle of Jersey. Both Baron de Rullecourt and Major Francis Peirson died here in the battle between an invading expedition of French soldiers and the local militia. The French were defeated within 10 minutes of arriving at the square. As Balleine's History of Jersey tells it: "Peirson sent his main force up what is now Broad Street, while he himself led another party to the Rue de Derrière, which is now the King Street precinct, to burst into the square by the opening now known as Peirson Place." The Peirson Public House is said to have borne the brunt of the shooting.

Royal Square is a reminder that Jersey's next invaders stayed much longer. From a balcony in the States offices Alexander Moncrieff Coutanche, Bailiff of Jersey, announced that the island was to be liberated after five years of German military occupation. In 1985 the Duchess of Kent unveiled a plaque in commemoration.

Unknown to the Germans, a stone-mason had already made his own discreet liberation proclamation just a few metres away. While relaying flagstones in Royal Square, he changed the position of stones to read "V" for victory and kept his efforts covered with sand. Today the sign reads "Vega 1945"; the additional letters were added to commemorate the arrival in 1944 of the Swedish ship *Vega* with urgent Red Cross supplies. ❑

LEFT: George II in the garb of Julius Caesar.

part of the present. An administration building occupied this site as far back as 1329. The first Court House was built in 1647 and rebuilt in 1764. The present buildings date from 1866.

At the western end of the States building is the old Public Library, an elegant place founded in 1736 by the Reverend Philip Falle, author of the respected *History of Jersey*, published in 1694. The contents of the old library are now to be found in a modern building in Halkett Place. This may be less imposing than its Royal Square predecessor, but it is light, cool, airy and a minor triumph of modern design.

St Helier Parish Church west of the square, is dedicated to the 6th-century hermit Helerius, commemorated by a statue above the north door. The church was formerly the hub of town life. Locals locked themselves here in times of crises, elections were held here and bells were rung when enemy ships were sited. Major Peirson, hero of the Battle of Jersey, is buried inside the church, while Baron de Rullecourt, who led the enemy, has a small stone memorial in the graveyard. The walls of the chancel are said to be the remains of an 11th-century chantry erected near what was then the seashore, but the present church dates essentially from the 14th century. Outside in Bond Street, the existing railings surrounding the church incorporate part of the chapel screen used to separate male and female prisoners attending services at Jersey's now-demolished Newgate Prison.

Continental atmosphere in Royal Square.

Central and Beresford Markets

In 1800 the town market was moved to its present site on the corner of Halkett Place and Beresford Street to relieve the congestion in Royal Square. The original building, erected in 1803, was a grand affair, closely modelled on the City of Bath market and was hailed as "one of the finest in Europe". In 1881, it was decided to build a new market to celebrate the centenary of the Battle of Jersey. The building was completed in 1882, though two of the seven entrances have elaborately adorned gates dating back to 1803. **Central Market** (Mon to Sat 7.30am–5.30pm, except Thur 7.30am–1pm) is a fine Victorian building with cast iron columns supporting a roof of slatted window panes – the sort of architectural features that went hand in hand with the coming of the railway. A favourite venue for both locals and tourists, this has 40 stalls selling fresh produce, flowers, Jersey lily bulbs, meat, cheese, bread and groceries. Its centrepiece is still the towering 15-ft (5-metre), four-tier fountain, with cherubs, foliage and live goldfish.

Beresford Market , running betwen Beresford Street and Minden Place, grew out of the Central Market. Established as a fish market in 1841, it is the best place in St Helier for fresh fish and offers lobster, squid, scallops and crab.

BELOW: the Central Market.

Pubs and plays

St Helier has more than its share of pubs, and one of them, the **Tipsy Toad Townhouse** in New Street, has its own in-house brewery, which produces a range of delicious real ales, including Jimmy's Bitter and Horny

Toad. The Townhouse, which has an out-of-town branch, the Star and Tipsy Toad in St Peter, offers food and entertainment as well as drinks. The same trend has been followed by many other pubs in town and in the countryside. Liberalisation of the licensing laws has led to the creation of facilities which are suitable for children as well as their parents.

If high culture rather than pub culture is to your liking, visit the **Jersey Arts Centre** (www.thisisjersey.com/jac) in Phillips Street. The bar there is a popular meeting place for the island's sometimes self-styled intelligentsia, but the theatre plays host to entertainment of a consistently high standard. Touring UK theatre groups perform everything from Shakespeare to Joe Orton, and the music ranges from modern jazz to Mozart. The centre is also home to two art galleries and the venue of the Jersey film society.

How today's fun-oriented Fort Regent is advertised.

BELOW: the Tipsy Toad pub sign.

Fort Regent

Although **Fort Regent** ⓭ today is dedicated to fun rather than history, it does have a fascinating past. The Battle of Jersey in 1781 concentrated the citizens' minds on the island's vulnerability. Invasion, however, wasn't a new theme. The French threat to all the Channel Islands was perceived way back when King John lost Normandy in the 13th century. In 1550, King Edward VI identified the strategic location of what was to become Fort Regent. He said: "Because on occasion of foreign invasion we be informed you have no place to retire unto, we require you to convey your Town unto the hill above the same, which we be informed may with little charge be made strong and defensible."

More than 250 years later the fear had surfaced again. In 1806, when the

Napoleonic Wars had entered their 13th year, Sir George Don, the Lieutenant-Governor, expressed his fear of imminent invasion. He said: "From the great progress of the enemy on the Continent, I must expect to be attacked in the spring". Mont Orgueil, Jersey's great castle at Gorey on the east coast, had earlier been superseded by Elizabeth Castle. Now it was the turn of Sir Walter Raleigh's fortress to fall foul of changing military capabilities. Jersey was about to embark on the third of its great trio of fortifications.

The fort falls redundant

It was John Hambly Humfrey, Commanding Royal Engineer, who drew up plans for this fort. But, when the scheme was finally agreed on, work could not start for 18 months. The delay was caused by a fierce argument over the money due in payment for the site of Mont de la Ville. The colossal sum of £11,280 was eventually settled on. The British Government then spent over £1 million on making Fort Regent (named after the Prince Regent, later George IV), well-nigh impregnable.

This fortification was the hub of a wide network of defences that General Don and Royal Engineer Humfrey had conceived. This comprised barracks, arsenals, martello towers and batteries, as well as General Don's celebrated "Routes Militaires" that were built to move soldiers around quickly. Fort Regent wasn't completed until 1814. With Waterloo just a year away, the reason for its construction, Napoleon Bonaparte was about to disappear. Nevertheless, this lofty outpost was home to the British garrison until 1927.

Map on page 122

Fort for a rainy day

Today Fort Regent (tel: 01534 500 200; www.esc.gov.je) is a bastion of sport, leisure and entertainment, a mega-facility just dying to involve you in something. With squash courts, pool and snooker tables, badminton courts, weights and fitness centre, steam rooms and the facilities for five-a-side football, basketball, bowls, and table tennis, it is an indoor sporting oasis. At the centre of the complex are a massive space under the dome of the rotunda and the chameleon-like Gloucester Hall, purpose-built to serve either as a sports arena or a 2,000-seat auditorium for occasional concerts and exhibitions.

A rather haphazard succession of bars, cafeterias and self-styled piazzas still leaves room for indoor and outdoor playgrounds. However, with the closure of the swimming pool (AquaSplash on the waterfront is now St Helier's main pool) and diminishing live entertainment and exhibitions, Fort Regent has lost something of its identity in the past few years. A number of proposals have been made for the redevelopment of the site, including a casino and hotel or a general entertainment centre. This will not affect the centre's greatest asset: its views over St Aubin's Bay, St Clement's Bay and much of St Helier.

If you leave Fort Regent and make your way via Pier Road and the Royal Square, you can easily find the heart of Jersey's shopping area. This centres on King Street and Queen Street, pedestrianised thoroughfares which are lined by shops and stores. ❑

Working out at Fort Regent.

BELOW: Saturday shoppers.
LEFT: riding high on a sculpture of Jersey cattle.

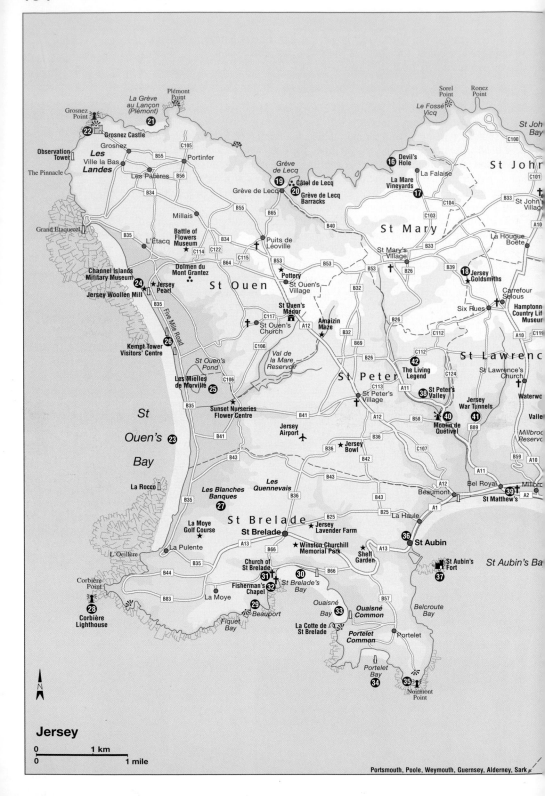

Sorel Point
Ronez Point
Le Fossé Vicq
St Joh
St John's Village
C100
C101
St John
C101
B33
St John's Village
La Hougue Boëte
C104
C103
La Falaise
Devil's Hole **16**
La Mare Vineyards
17
St Mary
St Mary's Village
B33
B26
B39
18 Jersey Goldsmiths
Carrefour Selous
Six Rues
Hampton Country Lif Museu
C112
C119
A10
St Lawrenc
C112
42 The Living Legend
C124
St Lawrence's Church
Waterwo
B89
C113
St Peter's Village
A11
38 St Peter's Valley
Jersey War Tunnels **41**
Vall
40 Moulin de Quétivel
B59
A10
Millbro Reservo
St Peter
B32
B58
B36
A12
C107
Bel Royal
Millbro
A11
A12
Beaumont
39
A2
St Matthew's
Millbro
St Aubin **36**
St Aubin's Ba
St Aubin's Fort **37**

Plémont Point
La Grève au Lançon (Plémont)
21
Grosnez Point **22**
Grosnez Castle
Observation Tower
The Pinnacle
Grosnez
Ville la Bas
Les Pâtières
Les Landes
Portinfer
C105
B55
B56
B34
Greve de Lecq
19 Câtel de Lecq
20 Grève de Lecq Barracks
Millais
B55
B65
B40
Grand Étaquerel
L'Etacq
B35
Battle of Flowers Museum
B34
C114
C122
Puits de Léoville
C115
B53
B53
B64
Dolmen du Mont Grantez
Channel Islands Military Museum
24
Jersey Pearl
Jersey Woollen Mill
B35
St Ouen
Pottery
St Ouen's Village
B32
B26
Five Mile Road
St Ouen's Manor
C117
St Ouen's Church
A12
Amaizin Maze
B32
B69
Kempt Tower Visitors' Centre
26
C106
Val de la Mare Reservoir
B26
St Ouen's Pond
C106
Les Mielles de Morville
25
St Ouen's Bay
B35
Sunset Nurseries Flower Centre
B41
Jersey Airport
B41
B43
B36
23
Jersey Bowl
B42
La Rocco
B35
Les Blanches Banques
Les Quennevais
B36
B43
B43
La Haule
B25
B25
A1
27
La Moye Golf Course
St Brelade
B25
Jersey Lavender Farm
A13
St Brelade
L'Oeillère
B35
B66
Winston Churchill Memorial Park
Shell Garden
A13
La Pulente
Church of St Brelade
B66
B44
La Moye
B83
Corbière Point
31
32 Fisherman's Chapel
30
B66
St Brelade's Bay
B57
Belcroute Bay
28
Corbière Lighthouse
29 Beauport
Fiquet Bay
Ouaisné Bay
La Cotte de St Brelade
33
Ouaisné Common
Portelet
Portelet Common
Portelet Bay
34
35
Noirmont Point
N

Jersey

0   1 km
0   1 mile

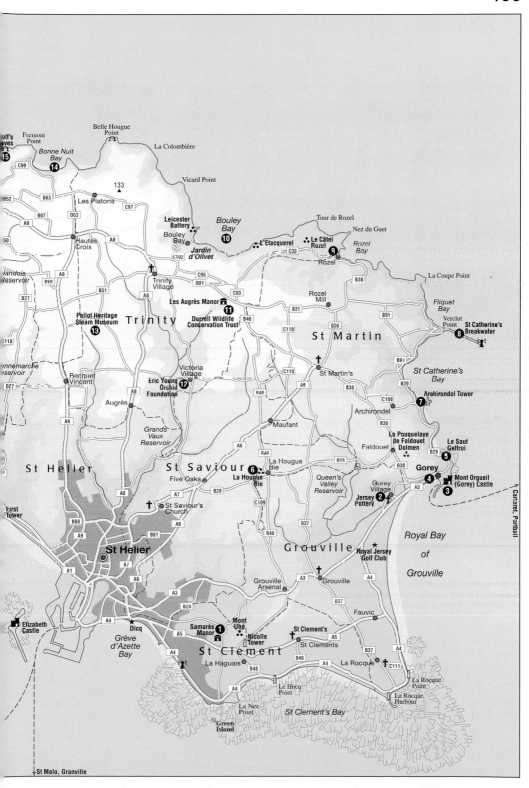

1 3 5

Golf's
Caves
15

Fremont
Point

Bonne Nuit
Bay
14

C99

Belle Hougue
Point

La Colombière

Vicard Point

133

Les Platons

B52

B63

B07

DG3

C97

A9

50

Hautes
Croix

A8

B50

B27

Jandois
Reservoir

Leicester
Battery

Bouley
Bay

Bouley Bay

Jardin
d'Ollvet

Tour de Rozel

Nez du Guet

L'Etacquerel

Le Câtel
Rozel

Rozel
Bay

Rozel

9

La Coupe Point

10

C102

C33

Trinity
Village

C95

D01

B38

Rozel
Mill

Fliquet
Bay

B51

B31

D00

Les Augrès Manor

11

Pallot Heritage
Steam Museum

13

T r i n i t y

B46

Durrell Wildlife
Conservation Trust

C110

C93

B91

B91

Verclut
Point

St Catherine's
Breakwater

8

C118

nnemarche
eservoir

D27

Becquet
Vincent

Augrès

A9

Eric Young
Orchid
Foundation

Victoria
Village

12

C110

St Martin's

S t   M a r t i n

B30

B29

C108

St Catherine's
Bay

Archirondel Tower

7

Grands
Vaux
Reservoir

A8

A6

Maufant

R66

B30

Archirondel

B30

La Pouquelaye
de Faldouet
Dolmen

B29

Le Saut
Geffroi

5

Faldouet

S t   H e l i e r

St Saviour

Five Oaks

La Hougue
Bie

6

R66

La Hougue
Bie

B28

Queen's
Valley
Reservoir

Gorey
Village

Gorey

4

Mont Orgueil
(Gorey) Castle

3

6

A3

2

Jersey
Pottery

Cartaret, Portball

A7

St Saviour's
Church

First
Tower

B60

B61

C109

B46

B37

G r o u v i l l e

Royal Bay

of

Grouville

A9

A6

Royal Jersey
Golf Club

St Helier

A1

A7

A6

Grouville
Arsenal

A3

Grouville

A4

B24

A3

Fauvic

B37

Elizabeth
Castle

Dicq

A4

A5

Samarès
Manor

1

Mont
Ubé

St Clement's

St Clements

A5

Grève
d'Azette
Bay

A4

Nicolle
Tower

B37

A4

Grève

S t   C l e m e n t

La Haguais

B48

B49

A4

La Rocque

C111

La Rocque
Point

Le Hocq
Point

La Rocque
Harbour

A4

Le Nez
Point

St Clement's Bay

Green
Island

St Malo, Granville

AROUND JERSEY

Star attractions include the imposing Gorey Castle, the neolithic passage graves at La Hougue Bie, the Durrell Wildlife Conservation Trust, and museums chronicling the German Occupation

Map on pages 134–5

The road passing through the tunnel under Fort Regent leads along the south coast into the parish of **St Clement**. St Clement's Road, just over a quarter-mile along the way, marks both the western edge of **Howard Davis Park** and the parish border. A local philanthropist, Thomas Davis, dedicated the park in 1939 to his son Howard, who was killed in World War I. Today it is one of the most appealing of Jersey's public gardens; it is also the site of a World War II cemetery.

On the coast just south of the park, a slipway called **Le Dicq** was a favourite haunt of Victor Hugo, St Clement's best-known resident *(see panel, page 139)*. A good part of St Clement lies below high-tide level, making it prone to flooding. The worst inundation, in 1811, prompted the States of Jersey to build a seawall. But the parish made good use of the low-lying land.

Samarès Manor

For several centuries, St Clement was dominated by **Samarès Manor ❶** (open Easter to mid-Oct daily 10am–5pm; admission charge), a name derived from the French for "salt marsh". The ancient way of making salt was to let the sea flood low-lying land, block the channel, and then let the sun evaporate the water. The land between Samarès Manor and the sea was certainly put to profitable use and is still known as Samarès Marsh.

Until 1763, all who held land on the Manor had to make the seigneur's hay, to fetch his wood and wine, and even to clean out his pigeon-house. Today the Manor is the best place to visit in this parish. When the garden was extensively developed in 1924, with 40 gardeners and at a cost of £100,000, it quickly earned the reputation of being one of the most beautiful of its kind in Britain. The 14 acres (5.7 hectares) of landscaped gardens incorporate a Japanese garden, ponds with swans and ducks, an ancient dovecot and a delightful walled garden full of culinary, cosmet and medicinal herbs. There are guided tours of the manor house (additional charge) and free tours of the agricultural museum as well as garden talks on weekday afternoons. Farmyard animals, horse-drawn rides, falconry demonstrations and parrot shows provide plenty of entertainment for the young; and there are various craft displays including the Jersey Woodturners who make walking sticks out of the famous Jersey Giant Cabbage.

A short distance from **Nicolle Tower** on the A5, near Samarès Manor, is a Neolithic passage-grave called **Mont Ubé**. Discovered in 1848 by quarrymen, this is the most ancient site in St Clement and is believed to be around 4,800 years old.

Directly south of Samarès Manor, **Green Island**, just a few hundred metres off the coast, is the most southerly in the British Isles – though it is only an

LEFT: the gardens at Samarès Manor.
BELOW: woodturner at Samarès Manor.

The Green Island
Restaurant facing
Green Island is one of
Jersey's best fish
restaurants.

island approaching full tide. Early in the 20th century, some rectangular prehistoric "cist" graves were discovered here but were removed for safekeeping to the Jersey Museum. The island is gradually being eroded by the sea and restorers are currently trying to prevent it from being washed away.

Inland again, along the A5, is **St Clement's Church**, from which the parish takes its name. The earliest reference to this church is from 1067. St Clement's has some of Jersey's few remaining medieval frescoes (wall paintings). These were found in 1879 by workmen employed in an extensive 19th-century restoration. Before their discovery, they had been hidden by plaster and were already damaged and defaced.

Grouville and golf

At the far east of St Clement's Bay the little harbour of **La Rocque** was the landing place of Baron de Rullecourt and his invasion force in 1781. Rounding La Rocque, you get your first view of the east coast and the Royal Bay of Grouville to Gorey and Mont Orgueil Castle beyond. Queen Victoria, so impressed by this long and spacious sandy bay, gave it the Royal prefix after her visit in 1859. Halfway round the bay is **Grouville Common**, part of which is used by the Royal Jersey Golf Club. This is regarded as *the* golf course on the island. If you've already been to the Jersey Museum you'll have heard the name of one man who played here: Harry Vardon, five times winner of the British Open Championship. And, if you and a partner get the opportunity to battle it out here, spare a thought for past losers: Gorey Common used to be a duelling ground where disputes could be settled with pistols at 20 paces.

Grouville Church was established as a parish church before 1035, though

BELOW: the Royal
Bay of Grouville.

the nave is said to be over 1,000 years old. The date of consecration, 1322, applies merely to the completion of the Chancel and the Tower. The font is a curious survivor of the Reformation. Originally part of the Town Church of St Helier, it was later recovered from a farmyard where it had been playing the undignified role of a pig trough.

The tower at La Roque Point.

Jersey Pottery

From the road to Gorey follow the brown signs and the tourist coaches to **Jersey Pottery ❷** (open Mon to Sat 9am–5.30pm, Sun 10.30am–5.30pm; tel: 01534 850 850, www.jerseypottery.com). No self-respecting tourist economy would be without its pottery and this one puts the craft very clearly and very professionally on display. It is an authentic, profit-making and highly successful enterprise. There are no guided tours, but information boards tell you about the various processes.

Modern, clean and spacious, the premises are laid out so that you can hover just a few feet away from the staff as they create the pottery. They use liquid clay, a mixture of sodium silicate, clay, soda ash and water and import the raw materials from Devon and Cornwall. In each department are large information boards describing processes such as "fettling" and "casting" and revealing the function of a machine called a "blunger". Once you tire of peering at the unselfconscious potters, you can shop in the showroom. The large range of ceramic tableware and decorative pieces include Jersey-themed items such as the bean crock, milking can and Jersey cow. Even if you aren't tempted by the wide range of pottery, you may not be able to resist the garden restaurant (lunch only, Wed to Sun) where a combination of good food, good wine and the shade of willow trees makes Jersey Pottery all the more worthwhile.

BELOW: at work in Jersey Pottery.

VICTOR HUGO IN JERSEY

Following his expulsion from France, Victor Hugo spent a year in Brussels, then foreseeing expulsion, took refuge in the Channel Islands. The romantic writer and political activist was driven from France by Louis Napoleon who had staged a coup d'état in December 1851 and dissolved the Assembly.

Hugo's exile from France lasted until the reconstitution of the republic in September 1870. He arrived in Jersey in 1852 and lived in St Clement near Le Dicq at 3 Marine Terrace, establishing his mistress, Juliette Drouais, at Le Havre des Pas. Unfortunately his house was demolished. Hugo and his compatriots used to gather in the evenings by a large rock at Le Dicq, known as Le Rocher des Proscrits, to make plans against Napoleon III, "the Sawdust Corporal". A commemorative tablet can be seen in the rock. In 1855 the writer was expelled from Jersey for his support of newspaper articles discrediting Queen Victoria for making a state visit to Paris.

The next 15 years of his life were spent on Guernsey. Much as he is said (by natives of Guernsey, at least) to have maligned Jersey, his tributes to the island were lyrical. To Hugo, Jersey was "un bouquet grand comme la ville de Londres". There were, of course, features of Jersey life he didn't care for: having to keep his shutters closed when he held Sunday billiards parties, for instance.

Mont Orgueil

When King John lost Normandy to France in 1204, work started on the castle at Gorey as a bastion against possible French invasion. Just how far-sighted this plan was may be judged from the fact that, between 1204 and 1600, the French made no fewer than 15 attacks on Jersey.

Mont Orgueil, meaning "Mount Pride", was named by Henry V's brother, the Duke of Clarence. In the middle ward, the uncovering of a huge rampart indicates that an Iron Age "hill fort" existed on this site long before this first part of the castle was built. Mont Orgueil is built on the concentric principle, with a series of defences each independent of the other. Wherever possible, the walls grow straight out of the rock so that together they are a formidable obstacle to would-be attackers.

The castle's defenders in the 14th century had every reason to strengthen it. In 1338, Sir Nicholas Behuchet, a French admiral, had successfully invaded Jersey, though he was forced

to retire when his siege of Mont Orgueil failed. In 1339, a seaborne force of 52 vessels was unable to take the castle. Another French attempt in 1374 also failed. Mont Orgueil did fall victim to a betrayal brought about by the Wars of the Roses. In 1461, Margaret of Anjou (the wife of Henry VI) sought the help of her cousin Pierre de Breze in the failing Lancastrian cause. De Breze obliged in the form of an invasion that resulted in a seven-year French occupation. In 1468, Sir Richard Harliston regained the castle after a siege.

Without treachery Mont Orgueil was invincible – as long as armies consisted of archers and armour-suited knights. Its defences were laid bare with the advent of the cannon. The round towers which had ringed the castle were too lightly constructed to withstand being shot at, and even displayed an unfortunate tendency to collapse when big guns were installed.

The last effort to strengthen the castle was the massive Somerset Tower. This, however, couldn't defeat Mont Orgueil's proximity to Mont St Nicholas: this neighbouring hillside provided an ideal position for enemy cannon.

In the 17th century, the castle served as a prison. You can still see the chamber in which William Prynne, whose writings incurred the censure of Charles I, began his sentence. Not only incarcerated, Prynne was also fined £10,000, had his ears cut off and his face branded with the initials S.L. ("seditious libeller"). In 1660, when the English monarchy had been restored, two leading parliamentarians of Jersey, Dean Bandinel and his son, were imprisoned. Their celebrated attempt to escape by tying bedclothes together and climbing out of a castle window is recalled in one of four tableaux.

By the 18th century Mont Orgueil was no longer a prison. In 1789, it regained briefly some of its former splendour as a refuge for aristocratic families fleeing the Reign of Terror and the guillotine in France.

Afterwards it faded into virtual obscurity until the early part of the 20th century when the stronghold was formally handed over by the Crown to the States of Jersey. The last thread was woven by the Germans who incorporated it into their fortifications during World War II, although the castle is currently undergoing a £3 million restoration programme.   ❑

LEFT: a display in Mont Orgueil Castle.

A stately fort

When plans for Elizabeth Castle were begun at the end of the 16th century the intention was to demolish **Gorey Castle ③**, or Mont Orgueil, as it is more commonly known (open Easter to Oct daily, 10am–6pm, last admission 5pm; admission charge). Walter Raleigh recommended to Queen Elizabeth I that it should stay since it was a "stately Fort of great capacytye" which he considered "were a pity to cast down". He wasn't the first to show concern over the fate of the castle at Mont Orgueil. Governors of Jersey continually sought money from England to maintain the castle. Some even had to dip into their own pockets.

The castle easily dominates the village of Gorey and the entire Royal Bay of Grouville. And many would say it has greater prowess than the two fortifications that were to follow: Elizabeth Castle and Fort Regent. They would say also that it is the most cherished of Jersey's monuments. With more than 100,000 visitors a year, it certainly gets its fair share of the tourist trade. If you visit during the daytime, make sure you return to Gorey after dark: Mont Orgueil, when floodlit, is even more picturesque, even more dramatic and even more memorable. Whoever decided the castle should be illuminated created a best selling picture postcard.

The castle has undergone many modifications over nearly eight centuries. During the latest restoration programme Jersey Heritage Trust opened up previously inaccessible areas of the castle but have come under attack by some historians for favouring commercially-viable speculative recreation above conservation and reparation of the existing fabric. New exhibitions have been created inside and out, and once you've negotiated the ancient passages and stairways to arrive at the highest point, the views all around are, not surprisingly, stunning.

Map on pages 134–5

Mont Orgueil Castle
is a lofty place
Within the Easterne
parts of Jersey Isle,
Seated upon a Rocke,
full large & high,
Close by the Sea-Shore,
next to Normandie;
Neere to a Sandy Bay,
where boats doe ride,
Within a Peere, safe both
from Wind and Tide
—WILLIAM PRYNNE
(1600–69)

BELOW: the castle towers over Gorey.

Gorey's bright lights

Sitting in the shadow of this great castle is the small, picturesque and un-assuming town of **Gorey**  the southernmost community in the parish of St Martin. Quaint and quiet, Gorey isn't much more than a line of tidy shops and pubs ringing the small harbour. But that isn't to belittle it. The village developed in the early 19th century when the flourishing oyster industry gave Gorey the sobriquet of "the pearl of the east". Oysters were so plentiful it is said that restaurants supplied them free of charge to customers. However, in 1820 English fishing fleets invaded the coast to share in the profits but by the middle of the century the oyster beds had been overdredged and the industry was all but over. Today the harbour protects a fleet of pleasure craft and, as the only official seaport in Jersey apart from St Helier, offers high-speed catamaran trips to the Normandy ports of Carteret and Port Bail.

Gorey Pier was built in 1820, though there must have been an earlier structure of some kind as there is a 17th-century reference to Gorey having "the most ancient harbour of all in the island". Today, Gorey is the only official port for Jersey after St Helier.

The Jersey Eastern Railway ensured Gorey was very much in the swing of things when tourism began to develop in the late 19th century. The present car park and bus-stand mark the site of the old railway station. The flowerbed running along Gorey's long promenade marks the site of the old railway track.

Geoffrey's Leap

On the seaward side, the parish of St Martin stretches all the way from Gorey up to Rozel Bay and includes what many consider to be Jersey's most beautiful

The novelist George Eliot and her companion George Henry Lewes stayed in Gorey for a few weeks in 1857 at Rosa Cottage (now Villa Rosa).

BELOW: Gorey has a quiet air.

coastline. On the coast road out of Gorey, just a few hundred metres beyond Mont Orgueil, is a site known as **Le Saut Geffroi** ❺ (Geoffrey's Leap). The name refers to the antics of a convicted criminal who survived his sentence of being thrown over the cliff. Not satisfied with one miraculous escape, he leapt over the cliff once more. This time he was killed. Some say this story is a romantic retelling of what really happened. The "truth" has Geoffrey showing less bravado. In the Middle Ages, it was the custom for condemned men to be pushed off the rock with their hands and feet bound. When Geoffrey was pushed, he managed somehow to free himself and swim ashore. Everyone regarded this as a miracle and he was pardoned. A short time later, when he was again convicted of a crime, he asked for the same punishment but was unable to repeat his escape and died.

This promontory, made famous by a medieval leaper, was also home to medieval lepers: records show that there was once a leperhouse in this locality.

Just beyond Geoffrey's Leap Café, a narrow lane on the other side of the road leads up to a site of even more ancient interest: the **Dolmen de Faldouet** (also known as La Pouquelaye de Faldouet). This passage grave, said to date from 2,500 BC, is 45 ft (15 metres) long, 17 ft (6 metres) high and has a capstone whose weight has been estimated at 24 tons. One of Jersey's more dramatic Neolithic dolmens, and one that retains an air of mysterious antiquity, it is well worth seeing.

When the Dolmen de Faldouet was discovered in 1839, pottery and polished axes (now on display at Jersey Museum) were found, together with the remains of adults and children.

La Hougue Bie's legend

Less than 2 miles (3 km) away from Dolmen de Faldouet along the B28 into the parish of St Saviour is Jersey's most famous ancient site, **La Hougue Bie** ❻ (open Easter to Oct, daily 10am–5pm; admission charge). This 33-ft (11-metre) long Neolithic passage-grave, now the reponsibility of the local historical body, the Société Jersiaise, is topped by a mound 40 ft (13 metres) high. The whole structure dates from about 3,000 BC. That's the easy part of the story. The origins of the mound and the larger of the two chapels above it are less certain. One legend, first found in a manuscript of 1734, provides an explanation for the name Hougue Bie at least.

The word "Hougue" refers quite simply to a burial mound. The word "Bie" might come from the family name of "Hambye". The legend says that Lord Hambye of Normandy crossed to Jersey to slay a dragon in the vicinity. Lord Hambye's servant, hoping that he would gain credit for this feat, murdered his master and buried him. When the servant arrived back in Normandy he induced Lady Hambye to believe that the dragon had killed her lord and that he had killed the dragon to avenge his master's death. He also duped her into believing that it was his master's dying wish she should marry him. The wedding followed, though the servant was eventually unmasked. As a memorial to her murdered husband, Lady Hambye had a mound built on high ground where he had been buried. It was named La Hougue Hambye.

A chronicle of 1585 is said to record this event, saying that the Lady of Hambye erected a mound in a

BELOW: the mound at La Hougue Bie.

conspicuous place to enable her to view her husband's burial place from the castle-keep at Hambye (in Normandy). She also built a small chapel. All that can be said in support is that on the opposite coast of Normandy, a few miles from Coutanche, on the heights above the village of Hambye, are the ruins of the castle which once belonged to the Seigneur of Hambye.

Magic, museums and a German bunker

It took around 30 years for the Reformation, begun in 1517 by Martin Luther, to begin making its mark on the Channel Islands.

The above account refers to the larger of the two chapels, **Notre Dame de la Clarté**. There is at least one other legend accounting for its construction. Archaeological and historical sources say that the simple design and primitive masonry do indeed show it to date from no later that the 12th or 13th centuries.

The origins of the smaller **Jerusalem Chapel** are more certain. It was built by Dean Richard Mabon around 1520, shortly after his return from the Holy Land. Until 1924 another structure stood on the mound as well. **La Tour d'Auvergne** was a mock medieval structure attached to the western end of the building by James d'Auvergne shortly before 1780.

The stones used to construct the two burial chambers came from Mount Mado, in St John's parish, which remained a quarry until the 20th century.

La Hougue Bie is more than just an ancient site. A museum of geology and archaeology displays some of the oldest rocks on the island and the bones and teeth of prehistoric animals discovered at La Cotte de St Brelade (*see page 107*). A legacy of more recent history is the German command bunker, housing a memorial to the slave workers who died in the Channel Islands during the occupation. The Germans also constructed a watchtower on top of the mound at the west end and dug 70 trenches within the grounds.

BELOW: ancient passage grave at La Hougue Bie.

North of Gorey

Given the number of military towers along the road approaching Gorey from the south, you might find the sight of one more as you leave Gorey to the north less than inspiring. But **Archirondel Tower ❼**, set in the little bay of Havre de Fer and built between 1793 and 1794, has the distinction of being the prototype for what is probably the best known tower in Jersey: La Rocco Tower in St Ouen.

At Verclut Point, **St Catherine's Breakwater ❽** is nothing less than a Victorian military folly. It forms the northern arm of what was to be one of two Channel Island naval bases (the other site is in Alderney). The southern arm was to reach out from Archirondel Tower. The perceived threat was once again the French, who around 1840 had strengthened Cherbourg and a number of other ports. A British Navy admiral warned that the site was ill-chosen because it would quickly silt up. Work started in 1847 nevertheless. The building programme succeeded in doing little more than absorbing £250,000 of taxpayers' money. The Archirondel arm was abandoned in 1849. When St Catherine's Breakwater was completed in 1855 to a length of half-a-mile, it did indeed emerge that the "harbour" was too shallow for British warships.

Archirondel Tower.

Rozel

One of the best views of **Rozel ❾** can be enjoyed from the slopes of Rue Fontenell, which leads in from the south. The village, small and unspoilt, nestles in a cove with a wooded hillside rising behind it. A single street of houses and seaside stalls fronts the promenade. You could walk from one end to the other in about as many minutes as it takes Rozel's curiously unperturbed resident flock of geese to saunter across the rocky beach at low tide. The harbour here was built in 1829 and shared some of the spoils of Gorey's 19th-century oyster trade. Overlooking the bay, Le Beau Couperon Hotel was originally a barracks, built in 1810 at the height of the Napoleonic threat. Being the closest point in Jersey to France, Rozel was considered a valuable defence site. However, no shot was ever fired here in battle.

BELOW:
waiting for the tide
at Rozel Harbour.

The lush **Rozel Valley** can be approached from behind the village. It owes some of its flora to a 19th-century naturalist, Samuel Curtis, who planted subtropical trees and shrubs, many of which can be seen today.

An important part of Rozel's history, though not open to the public, is the Manor south of Rozel, less than a mile from the Parish Church of St Martin. A seigneur from Normandy, home of the original "Rozel", owned land in Jersey and lent the locality this Norman name. The Lemprière family, one of Jersey's oldest, bought the Manor in 1360. Though the family was displaced from ownership at one time, it is today in the possession of descendants of that line. The Lord of Rozel (together with the Lord of Augrès Manor) holds the hereditary title of Royal Butler, which gives them positions of honour when there is a royal visit to the island.

The steep slopes leading out of Rozel make up part of **Le Câtel Rozel**, an Iron Age earthwork fortification. Coins from Gaul and Rome found in the vicinity suggest this must have been an important strategic site in the past.

Bouley Bay

Bouley Bay ⑩ contrasts strongly with Rozel Bay. Here there's no picturesque village, though the cliff slopes are higher and the landscape is altogether more grand. Not surprisingly, perhaps, the British Hill Climb Association adopted Bouley Bay as one of its championship venues. As long as you are a paid-up member of the BHCA equipped with either a motorcycle, saloon car, racing car, sports car, or even just a bicycle, you can join in the fray.

Exercising in the bay.

A more peaceful location is the **Jardin d'Olivet**, a flat common popular for walks and picnics. This was a battleground in 1547 when a French invasion force, having already seized Sark, confronted the Jersey Militia. Bouley Bay has seen no other struggles since then, though this might be due in part to 18th-century fortifications to the west and east: **Leicester Battery** and **L'Etacquerel**. Cliff paths either side of Bouley Bay provide delightful walks. In summer the hills are ablaze with heather and wild flowers, while shags, which nest in cliff crevices in the spring, can be seen flying close to the shore. The steeply shelving beach and deepest waters around the islands' shores make ideal conditions for scuba diving, and the Jersey Diving Centre offers lessons and facilities to divers of all standards.

Durrell Wildlife Conservation Trust

The highlight of Trinity Parish is undoubtedly **Durrell Wildlife Conservation Trust** ⑪ (open daily 9.30am–6pm, 10am–5pm in winter; admission charge; www.durrellwildlife.org). Make no mistake, though, about this family of animals; this is not the "jungle top-40" approach to zoo-keeping. There are no chimpanzee tea parties here, no dolphin antics, no polar bears to be gawped at, no elephants at which you can throw bread rolls.

BELOW: Bouley Bay.

It was never the intention of the Trust's founder, Gerald Durrell, who died in 1995, to set up a "simple, straightforward zoo" with the usual elephants and giraffes. "The idea behind my zoo was to aid in the preservation of animal life," he wrote, "to build up under controlled conditions breeding stocks... so that, should the worst happen and the species become extinct in the wild state, you have, at least, not lost it forever. Moreover, you have a breeding stock from which you can glean the surplus animals and reintroduce them into their original homes at some future date." Already, Jersey-reared pink pigeons and kestrels have been returned to their native Mauritius; thick-billed pepper-green parrots to Arizona; white-winged wood ducks to Thailand; brown rodents called *hutias* to Jamaica; and golden lion tamarins, one of the world's rarest primates, to Brazil.

Most should be sorry to leave, given the quality of care and scientifically formulated diets in Jersey's 23-acre (9.2-hectare) park-land complex. In the intensive recovery unit of the Trust's modern Vet Centre, you might find a Goeldi's monkey under observation after a bout of diarrhoea, or an ibis with a broken mandible recovering from surgery.

The enterprise had a shaky start. With three best-selling books (*The Bafut Beagles, My Family and Other Animals* and *The Drunken Forest*) under his belt and the prospect of more in the pipeline, Durrell put an unusual proposition to his publisher, Rupert Hart-Davis: why not borrow on these "as yet unconceived masterpieces"? Hart-Davis agreed to stand guarantor for £25,000 if Durrell took out a life-insurance policy for that amount ("just in case I got eaten by a lion before I could repay the loan").

In 1958 Durrell found Les Augrès Manor. It was "probably one of the most beautiful manor houses on the island," he recalled. "Here was a huge, walled

Map on pages 134–5

At one point Gerald Durrell considered Fort Regent in St Helier as a possible site for the zoo. But the economics were wrong: he estimated that it would cost £25 million to convert.

BELOW: Gerald Durrell's statue at the Trust.

THE COST OF CONSERVATION

Running Durrell Wildlife Conservation Trust and maintaining its involvement in far-flung conservation projects is an expensive business. It costs the Trust, which has a Jersey staff of more than 70, £1.8 million (US$2.7 million) just to tick over. Feeding around 2,000 animals of more than 100 species, meanwhile, costs over £90,000 ($130,000) a year. But in Gerald Durrell's own words, "You have to keep fighting, or what are we on earth for? I believe so much in what we are doing that I cannot let up". The island's farmers help by donating bull calves, apples and tomatoes; greengrocers supply the occasional lorry-load of bruised peaches; locals collect earwigs and snails; and the Trust has its own organic farm to help reduce the food bill.

Hundreds of trainees from 70 different countries have studied both at the Trust's summer school and at the International Training Centre for the Captive Breeding and Conservation of Endangered Species, opened in 1984 by the Trust's patron, the Princess Royal. It is through those students and the Trust that Gerald Durrell's work goes on, in every continent. Sometimes the sources of help are unpredictable: one Canadian grandmother was so impressed by the Trust and its charismatic founder that she moved to Jersey to assist as a full-time volunteer.

Some golden tamarins at the zoo became so prolific that they were put on the equivalent of the birth-control pill. "We'd prefer not to be giving them hormone implants," said one vet, "but there are a limited number of places in the world which can handle these endangered species."

BELOW: gorillas at Durrell Wildlife Conservation Trust.

garden dreaming in the thin sunlight; a great granite wall, thickly planted with waterfalls of rock plants; 15th-century arches, tidy lawns and flowerbeds brimming with colour. All the walls, buildings and outhouses were of beautiful Jersey granite which contains all the subtle colourings of a heap of autumn leaves."

Throughout the zoological park, Durrell tried, wherever possible, to cultivate the native habitat of the animals' wildlife – and with some success, thanks to the temperate Jersey climate. In the white-throated wallabies' paddock, for example, there are various species of eucalyptus from Australia. Elsewhere, there are dawn redwoods and other rare species. The gigantic red, rope-haired orang-utans, inveterate nest builders, have taken to their open-plan bedrooms. It's worth lingering at the park until closing time just to watch them prepare their beds, complete with canopies which they construct over their heads out of discarded newspapers and cardboard.

Other favourites are the Andean bears in the **First Impressions** section, featuring a moated enclosure for endangered species from South America. The only bears in South America, the Andean species until recently faced threat from farmers who blamed the bears for damaging their crops. Nowadays the chief hazard comes from Asian hunters who hunt the bears for their livers, which yield valuable bile for medicinal use. A glass-domed interpretation centre, partly sunken into the landscape, gives access to the enclosure and provides a "behind-the-scenes" insight into the role and techniques of breeding endangered species.

The latest addition to the Trust is the "Jewels of the Forest" walk-through aviary where you come face to face with a stunning array of brightly coloured oriental songbirds and the Cloud Forest, designed to convey the scents, sounds and sights of the rainforests. *(See also Trust feature, pages 166–7.)*

Eric Young Orchid Foundation

About a mile to the south of Jersey Zoo, near Victoria Village, is the **Eric Young Orchid Foundation** ⓬ (open Thur, Fri, Sat 10am–4pm; admission charge). Here you can see the fruits of a lifelong passion for orchids. Eric Young, the founder, came to Jersey after World War II and set up the basis of his collection in 1958. In the same year he bought the stock from a local orchid nursery that was about to close down. He transferred his newly acquired orchids to a run-down market garden near Howard Davis Park purchased around the same time. Less than a decade later this growing collection of orchids was described as "the finest private collection of orchids in Europe, possibly the world".

Eric Young's ambition was to have his extensive collection housed in a suitable location and opened to the public, but he died before the project was completed. It's a haven for would-be photographers armed with tripods, and its refusal to "go commercial" has endeared it to many visitors since it opened in 1986.

Map on pages 134–5

The Eric Young Orchid Foundation.

Steam trains, cliffs and caves

Trains may no longer be used for transport in the island, but this didn't stop enthusiast Don Pallot from running one on his own short stretch of track. Mr Pallot, who died in 1996, also assembled an intriguing collection of other steam-powered machinery, including traction engines used at the museum's autumn threshing fair. These can be seen at the **Pallot Heritage Steam Museum** ⓭ (open Apr to Oct Mon–Sat 10am–5pm) south-west of the village of Trinity.

Returning towards the coast, the highest point on Jersey is Les Platons, where, at 435 ft (133 metres) above sea level, there is a small cist grave. This ancient monument is set amid modern radio transmitter masts, which at least make **Les Platons** easy to find. Anyone with passions for rock-climbing, caves and prehistoric deer might wish to go out to the end of this particular headland. At the bottom of the steep cliffs (do not attempt the descent without ropes and a guide) is the cave at **Belle Hougue Point**. This site is of limited archaeological interest – the only remains ever found here were of a previously unknown type of ancient deer – but the 100-ft (30-metre) deep cave will reward the efforts of any dedicated speleologist.

BELOW: Don Pallot, founder of the Steam Museum.

Bonne Nuit Bay

The fetching name of **Bonne Nuit Bay** ⓮ comes from a chapel built by this stretch of Jersey's rugged northern coastline in 1150 – the Chapel of Santa Maria de Bona Nochte. The name, however, wasn't always passed down the centuries in its original form and the chapel is referred to once in ancient records as the Chapel de Mala Nochte. Goodnight or Badnight, Bonne Nuit Bay is scenic, secluded and peaceful. There is a tiny harbour, sand and shingle beach, sheltered below heather-clad hills. It's rocky too, and the inevitable stories of smuggling are easy to believe. The bay was fortified in the 18th and 19th centuries, although the only remaining structure is **La Crête Fort**, built in 1835 on the eastern headland of Bonne Nuit Bay. Today this is the holiday retreat of the Lieutenant-Governor of the island.

The rock in the middle of the bay, **Le Cheval Guillaume**, is named after Guillaume de Vauville, who gave the Chapel of Santa Maria to the Abbey of St Saveur de Vicomte in the 12th century. In centuries past, fishermen and other islanders rowed around the offshore rock on Midsummer's Day to protect them from evil spirits.

There is little else on the coast of the Parish of St John to entice you other than **Wolf's Caves ⓯** and Sorel Point. The caves are accessible only at low tide and you have to be fit to make the 400-ft (120-metre) descent and return ascent. A sign says that it takes five minutes to scramble down but 15 minutes to climb back up the 307 steps. Check at the bar at the top for tide times.

Route du Nord

The road leading north out of St John's Village, the **Route du Nord**, was built during the German Occupation to provide employment for those who wouldn't work for the Germans. In a public car park there is a memorial with the following inscription: "This road is dedicated to the men and women of Jersey who suffered in the World War 1939–1945."

Depending on which way you look at things, **Sorel Point** can be something of a sorry sight. True, the views out to sea from this windswept promontory can be magnificent – weather conditions permitting, you can see Alderney, France, Guernsey and Sark – but turn your back to the sea and look eastward to Ronez Point and you'll see some ugly cliff slopes quarried and scarred to provide raw material for a cement works nearby.

The natural archway cut into the cliffs south-west of Sorel Point is better known as the **Devil's Hole ⓰**. The present pathway, which starts discreetly in

the Priory car park, stops about 100 ft (30 metres) above the sea and allows for only a rather disappointing view of this yawning chasm in the cliffs. An older stairway, which has collapsed, once led much lower and clearly provided a better vantage point. The melodramatic name was acquired in the 19th century and probably derives from the menacing figurehead of a mid-19th century French shipwreck, which was found here and crafted into a wooden horned devil. Over the years various replicas of the devil have been placed on the path down, but each one has been stolen, The latest "devil" is marooned in a murky pond at the start of the cliffpath.

Map on pages 134–5

Wine and Cider

In St Mary's Parish you can enjoy the fruits of Jersey's first step into viticulture and winemaking at **La Mare Vineyards** ⑰ (open Apr to Oct Mon–Sat 10am–5pm; admission charge). The first commercial vineyard was planted here in 1972. Up to then there was no record of a vineyard on Jersey, though white grapes had been grown in abundance in the 19th century. Despite the negative perception of UK wines, La Mare manages to sell 30-40,000 bottles of wine a year from its 21 acres. Originally producing still whites only, it now makes sparkling white, sparkling Rosé and red wine. Jersey is on the same latitude as France's Champagne region and the same traditional method of secondary bottle fermentation is employed to make the successful sparkling Cuvée de la Mare.

Jersey Butterfly.

Wine is not the only liquid refreshment to flow forth from La Mare. This is also Jersey's largest cider producer, though here it is not breaking new ground: cider has been a tradition on the island since Tudor times. In addition, they distil an excellent if slightly pricey version of the Norman apple spirit calvados, Jersey Apple Brandy. La Mare also produces its own marmalades, jams, mustards, chocolates, fudge and traditional Jersey black butter. The entrance fee includes wine tasting, explanations of the wine-making process and an audio-visual show. Visitors can wander around the estate and visit the new cooperage to discover the art of barrel-making.

BELOW:
the Moulin Pub.

To the southeast of La Mare Vineyards at **Jersey Goldsmiths** ⑱ (open all year daily 10am–5pm) you can watch artisans at work, make your own jewellery, pan for gold – of couse – buy gold and gemstones. Permanent and temporary exhibitions include gold- and jewellery-related memorabilia belonging to international stores. If none of this appeals you can just relax in the gardens, by the lake with the swans and flamingoes.

Grève de Lecq

If Rozel is the most picturesque bay on Jersey's north coast, then **Grève de Lecq** ⑲ is the most popular – perhaps a little too popular. Grève de Lecq was attractive to ancient strategists, too. Overlooking the bay to the east, **Câtel de Lecq** is an Iron Age mound on which a hill fort is said to have stood.

Not quite so ancient, but certainly more attractive, is **Le Moulin de Lecq**, a restored mill (now a pub/restaurant) whose origins can be traced back to the 14th century. It was last used for grinding in 1929, though the

Clear signing at St Ouen.

BELOW:
St Ouen's Manor.

wheel still turns. Inside, the huge, creaking wood-varnished cog – bottles of spirits sitting precariously near it – forms an impressive backdrop to the bar.

Behind the bay the **Grève de Lecq Barracks ②** (Tues–Sat 11am–5pm, Sun 2–5pm; free) were built in 1810 as part of the web of military installations radiating from Fort Regent. Part of the British army garrison was housed here from 1810 to the 1920s. These neat granite buildings are kept in an excellent state of repair by the National Trust of Jersey and today include the North Coast Visitors Centre, devoted to the wildlife and history of the area. Another military remnant is the round tower dating from 1780, which today keeps company with a crowded car-park.

Grève de Lecq has all the trappings of a lively English tourist resort: there's a large seaside cafeteria and souvenir shop, another large carpark, and two further cafés on the quayside.

On to St Ouen

Le Moulin de Lecq marks another parish boundary, that between St Mary and St Ouen. The largest of Jersey's parishes, **St Ouen**, has a reputation for being windswept and at times remote. Thanks to the lack of vehicular access **La Grève au Lancon ②** (Sand-eel beach) remains unspoilt. Low tide reveals a wide expanse of fine sands, rock pools and a network of caves in the cliffs on the landward side; but at high tide the sea completely covers the beach.

The best known historic site in St Ouen, amid the barren heathland of Les Landes, is **Grosnez Castle ②**. This lonely medieval outpost above the sea certainly doesn't compare with Jersey's other great castles. Little is known about it either. References on 16th-century maps show that it was already in ruins

more than 400 years ago. An account of Bertrand du Guesclin's invasion of the late 14th century mentions two castles. One was certainly Mont Orgueil and it is possible the other was Grosnez. From this north-west tip of the island there are fine views, weather permitting, of all the other Channel Islands. From left to right these are Guernsey, Jethou, Herm, Sark, and in the very far distance, Alderney. France lies in the distance to the east.

Windswept clifftops and sunken forest

The coastline between Grosnez and L'Etacq provides splendid views. Along the way the five-storey observation tower is a prominent German landmark and a coastal artillery battery (open most Sundays April to Sept, 10am–3pm; admission charge) has been carefully restored with gun emplacements and bunkers. Further south, the 200-ft (60-metre) high menhir-like rock known as **The Pinnacle** was an ancient ceremonial site, occupied in turn by Neolithic, Bronze Age, Iron Age and Roman settlers.

An entire forest near L'Etacq was submerged when the sea level rose after the Ice Age. According to legend, more than a forest was lost: the drowned village of La Brecquette is believed to be located close by. Modern-day L'Etacq is a small community just a few hundred metres inland where the sea air mingles with the wafts from a fishmonger's shop, housed in an old German bunker nearby.

Sand and surf

When the weather is bad, the wide sweep of **St Ouen's Bay ㉓** is far from welcoming. Not that this put off Sir Admiral Blake in 1651: his fleet conveyed the Parliamentary forces that subsequently landed here and repulsed the disunited

Map on pages 134–5

TIP

For a gourmet meal, you can pre-order lobster already cooked from the fishmonger in the old German bunker at L'Etacq. Tel: Faulkner Fisheries, 01534-483 500

BELOW: windswept walk on St Ouen's sand dunes.

TIP

Boogie boards and surf boards can be rented at various places along St Ouen's Bay, and tuition is available.

Jersey royalist factions during the English Civil War. These days, the bay's invaders are usually surfers competing in local, national and international competitions. And they are seldom at a loss for a wave or two; normally the surf is fine even by Bondi Beach standards. There's a remarkable contrast between this huge wild beach and a small sheltered bay like that at Rozel, given that they are separated by only a few miles.

Wild, sparse and windswept though it might be, there's plenty to see and do here. Running along the bay's edge is the misleadingly named **Five Mile Road**. If you walk its length it may feel like 5 miles (8 km), though it's a little over 3 miles (5 km). Walk along the beach from the northern edge of the bay by the headland rock of **Grand Etaquerel** down to the slipway near **L'Oeillère** and you'll do a little better at 4 miles (6.5 km). After a walk like that, you'll appreciate just how large St Ouen's Bay is. Look at the map and you'll see it marks the western edge of no less than three of Jersey's parishes: St Ouen, St Peter and St Brelade.

Tourist attractions

At the northern end of the Five Mile Road, occupying a German bunker, lies the **Channel Islands Military Museum** ㉔ (open Easter to Oct daily 10am–5pm; admission charge). The little museum is packed with Occupation memorabilia, British as well as German. It's the only place in the islands where you will see one of the few remaining Enigma cipher machines. On the walls are copies of proclamations, Orders of the Commandant and Death Warning notices such as that of Louis Berrier, an unfortunate civilian shot in 1941 for releasing a pigeon with a message to England.

BELOW AND RIGHT: the Channel Islands Military Museum.

Across the main road, **Jersey Pearl** (open daily 10am–5.30pm) offers a wide

range of pearl jewellery, both cultured and crafted. There are guided tours five times a day, a "pick-a-pearl" tour where you choose an oyster guaranteed to contain its own cultured pearl and a small section on the history of pearls and their cultivation. However the main emphasis is on selling. Prices range from a few pounds to upwards of £30,000 for exclusive South Sea and Tahitian pearls – or you can commission a piece of jewellery to your own design from one of the artisans.

Map on pages 134–5

Les Mielles de Morville

In an area as empty and open as this, it's the flora and fauna that command most attention. Much of the land is now a protected environment. Towards the north, Les Mielles de Morville is a park and nature reserve. To the south, Les Blanches Banques, an extensive network of sand-dunes, has also been protected.

Les Mielles de Morville ㉕ were designated a "special place" in 1978 in recognition of the high wildlife and landscape value of St Ouen's Bay. More than 400 species of plant life have been identified in this small area. St Ouen's Pond, an important part of this nature reserve, is a well-established bird-ringing station. Since it was decided to conserve Les Mielles de Morville, the area has lost much of its unkempt appearance. It was formerly a landscape of disused sheds, broken fences, derelict dwellings and dumped rubbish.

Perhaps the Germans can take the blame for originally setting the dereliction in motion: their fortifications were preceded by the demolition of all the houses along this Sunset Strip. But the landscape helped the residents in one way: when fuel began to run low, peat was cut and dried here.

The full conservation story is told at **Kempt Tower Visitors' Centre** ㉖ (open May to Sept daily 2–5pm; free), another of the defences built during the Napoleonic Wars. A fine example of a Martello tower, this has a well-designed exhibition covering ecology, geology and history. The top of the tower gives the best view of St Ouen's Bay.

In autumn and winter tractors load up with seaweed from the beach here for use as a fertiliser on bordering farmland. Horses and carts were once used for the job, gaining access to the beaches via the slipways you can see all round the Jersey coastline.

BELOW: on the beach.

Les Blanches Banques

The dune plain of **Les Blanches Banques** ㉗, among the 10 largest in the British Isles and one of the most important systems in Europe, is thought to have existed for more than 3,000 years. Neolithic tombs and flint tools found on the dune plateau of **Les Quennevais** are said to be even older. There are likely to be more ancient artefacts buried beneath the sand-waves since there are a number of past references to the area being engulfed by sandstorms. It's a hazard you won't face today: the dunes have been made stable by vegetation, so much so that their southern edge is taken up by **La Moye Golf Course**.

If you enjoy tracking down traces of prehistory, finding **Dolmen du Mont Grantez** will present a worthwhile challenge. There's a distinct lack of signs pointing the way and maps seem to indicate little more than its being located somewhere or other in the meadows overlooking St Ouen's Bay.

If and when you do find it – it's about 600 ft (200 metres) from a roadside near St Anne's Church, cunningly concealed by a stone wall which is itself obscured by ferns – the setting and the view repay your

efforts. This is a passage-grave where skeletons dating back 5,000 years were found in 1912. Of the 10 Jersey dolmens, this is the second oldest site. Seven burials were found, together with limpets, animal bones, pebbles and pottery.

St Ouen's Manor and Chapel

This magnificent stately building (no access to the public) figures prominently in this parish's history. The de Carteret family have owned land here since before 1066, though the first mention of a manor is in 1135. The oldest part of the building is the south tower, built in 1380. The west and north wings followed in the 16th century and the south and east wings in the 17th. At one time, when the Manor passed into the hands of four female members of the de Carteret family, it looked as if the traditional line of possession would end; but in 1880 it was inherited by Edward Charles Malet de Carteret.

Inside the grounds, the **Chapel of St Anne**, built at either the same time or earlier than the oldest part of the Manor proper, has served as a barn in past centuries of neglect and during the Occupation as a storehouse and butchery. After François Scornet, a French patriot fleeing his homeland, was forced to land in Guernsey, he was sentenced to death, then executed at the Manor.

Wild shores and shipwrecks

St Brelade is Jersey's second largest parish. Its southwestern corner is marked by **Corbière Lighthouse** ❷❽ standing more than 100 ft (30 metres) above sea-level. It derives its name from *corbeau*, French for crow, a bird traditionally taken to be an ill omen. This wild and desolate corner of the island abounds with tales of shipwrecks. The first recorded disaster involved a Spanish vessel carry-

In St Brelade's Church, pebbles from the beach are embedded in the unrendered granite, and if you look up you can still see a limpet or two clinging to the roof.

BELOW: Corbière Lighthouse.

ing a cargo of wine in 1495. Many other boats have foundered here, including the Royal Mail Steam Packet in 1859, with loss of life. Marine traffic navigated these waters unaided by a lighthouse until 1874 when Corbière Lighthouse, the first in Britain to be built in concrete, was completed.

At full tide, the lighthouse is cut off from the land. You can walk down to it at half-tide, though you should keep an eye on the water-level. An inscription along the pathway reads "Take heed all ye that pass by," and recalls the fate of assistant lighthouse-keeper Peter Larbalestier who died trying to rescue a visitor cut off by the incoming tide. During the war the Germans built bunkers at Corbière and a massive observation tower to the east, now used by the local shipping radio. They used La Rocco Tower to the north for target practice, breaching its ramparts and damaging the main structure.

The Railway Walk

Until 1936, Jersey Railways ran a train service from St Helier to St Aubin and Corbière, between which there were four stations: Pont Marquet, Don Bridge, Blanches Banques and La Moye. Trains ran on a single line of standard gauge track and the service ran with remarkable efficiency. However, competition from buses and a fire at St Aubin's, destroying rolling stock, led to the demise of the service. The track was turned into a footpath and today makes a delightful 4-mile (6-km) walk across the western corner of the island, from Corbière to St Aubin.

Between Corbière and St Brelade's Bay lies the delightfully unspoilt bay of **Beauport** ㉙. This is a favourite among islanders and their yachts are often moored here on summer weekends. However, the climb down the hill and the absence of facilities on the beach deter most tourists, and it is seldom crowded during weekdays If you are going to spend any time here, take ample refreshments and a sun hat.

St Brelade's Bay

With its gently sloping, golden sands, sheltered setting and clear, blue waters, **St Brelade's Bay** ㉚ is justifiably the most popular beach on the island. Wooded slopes, covered principally by Monterey pines, were until recently an attractive feature of the bay, but a hurricane in 1987 devastated the century-old trees. Some areas have been replanted, but it will be many years before the new trees are mature enough to re-create the former effect. Pleasure-seekers are there in some force, but it hasn't been spoiled and is unlikely to be.

The **Winston Churchill Memorial Park**, with its tidy lawns and trim flowerbeds, typifies the care that goes into St Brelade's upkeep. While this mini-resort does have its fair share of guesthouses and hotels, it's generally a peaceful, quiet place. On the slopes above the bay lie some highly desirable tax-exile residences, set among manicured gardens.

At the western end of the bay the picturesque **Church of St Brelade** ㉛ sits on a rocky ledge, overlooking the little harbour. Built of pink granite boulders from the shore, the church dates back to the 12th

Map on pages 134–5

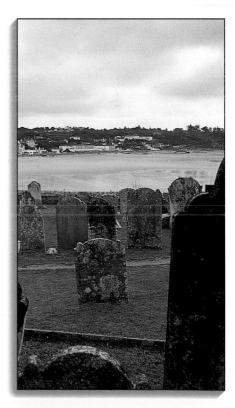

TIP

The start of the Railway Walk is signposted off the main road as it turns inland from St Aubin's harbour. Buses 12, 14 or 16 take you there.

BELOW: the burial ground at St Brelade's Chapel.

century and still retains its Norman chancel. Step inside and switch on the lights to reveal the enchanting interior with its warm, granite walls and intimate atmosphere. The church was named after Bren Gwaladr, a companion of St Sampson who came to Jersey in the 6th century.

Inland from the bay the **Jersey Lavender Farm** (open mid-May to mid-Sept, Tues–Sun 10am–5pm; free) is a family-run business which grows lavender for the purpose of producing oil for a fragrant range of lavender-based toiletries and perfumes. The spectacular swathes of lavender covers 9 acres (4 hectares) and provide a blaze of colour throughout the summer. Visitors can watch the distilling and bottling processes, see a short film explaining the work on the farm through the seasons, sample the fragrances and purchase oils and lotions. The edible range features lavender jelly, lavender fudge, lavender and honey mustard – as well as the lavender and strawberry gâteau served in the tearooms. A herb garden and a woodland walk add to the farm's attractions.

Jersey Lavender, St Brelade.

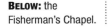

Medieval Frescoes and Perquage Path

The **Fisherman's Chapel** ㉜ is of much greater interest than the church. The exact date of its construction is uncertain, though recent excavations have suggested it is late 12th-century and that there was possibly a chapel on this site before then. The chapel escaped destruction during the Reformation, and was variously used as an armoury, a store room for the sexton, a carpenter's shop and a meeting room. It was not until 1880 that permission was given for it to revert to a church.

BELOW: the Fisherman's Chapel.

Restoration early in the 20th century brought to light the fragments of a series of beautiful medieval frescoes (1375–1425) decorating all four walls.

These were restored and today the scenes from the Old and New Testaments can be made out with the help of information plaques which reconstruct the missing outlines. Clearest of all is the scene of the Annunciation on the east wall.

The church and chapel are set in austere grounds with tall oaks, ancient cedars and neat rows of gravestones. Locals would certainly recognise some of the island's better-known family names. One of the tombs, a short distance along the road leading between the church and the cemetery, belongs to Jesse Boot, founder of Boots, the UK chain of chemists. His family has long been an important benefactor to Jersey.

The flight of granite steps linking the churchyard with the small harbour is the shortest Perquage (sanctuary path) on the island. Before the Reformation it was a convention that criminals could take temporary sanctuary in parish churches such as St Brelade's on the condition that they fled the island soon after. A perquage path was provided to ensure direct access to the sea.

Beaches and headlands

At low tide St Brelade's Bay forms a long continuous stretch of sand with **Ouaisné Bay** ㉝ and these together form the island's finest beach. Even on hot days in high season, the fine sands offer plenty of space. Behind Ouaisné beach, the gorse-covered **Ouaisné Common** is home to some rare species of fauna, including the Dartford Warbler, the Jersey green lizard and the agile frog; but sightings are rare. Portelet Common, an expanse of heathland above the beach, commanding splendid coastal views, can be reached by the cliff path that starts on the south side of the beach.

Further along the coast **Portelet Bay** ❹ is a pretty, sheltered beach with fine sands. Its little island, accessible at low tide, is properly called the Ile au Guerdain, but more popularly known as Janvrin's Tomb. It is the last resting place of Philippe Janvrin, a sea captain who in 1721 died of plague while on his ship anchored in Belcroute Bay. His body was not permitted to be brought ashore so his wife and a party of mourners attended his funeral service from a distance, watching from the beach.

Further south still, **Noirmont Point** ❺ is the site of a major German naval artillery installation. A four-storey emplacement, it was the command post for a number of gun positions on this headland. Although the bunker is only occasionally open to the public, it has been carefully restored by the Channel Islands Occupation Society. This windswept headland, once known as Niger Mons or Black Hill, after the dark clouds which gather here, was acquired by the States of Jersey to commemorate the islanders who died in World War II.

St Aubin, a pirates' haunt

The town of **St Aubin** ❻, on the opposite side of St Aubin's Bay from St Helier, is another of Jersey's "picture-postcard" communities. It takes its name from a 6th-century Bishop of Angers, patron saint of those seeking protection against pirates. It was an ironic choice. For the town, a thriving commercial centre long

Map on pages 134–5

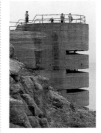

The German Observation Tower at Noirmont Point.

BELOW:
St Aubin's harbour.

before St Helier came to the fore, owed at least part of its wealth to piracy. The more polite term of "privateering" is preferred by historians who point out that confiscation of seaborne goods was legal.

St Aubin's first pier – the southern arm – was built in 1675 (the south pier you see today dates from 1754) in St Aubin's privateering heyday. Shortly after 1675, the diarist Dumaresq wrote: "The conveniency of the pier has occasioned a small town to be built, consisting of about fourscore houses." The Bulwarks, the houses beside the harbour, were built in 1790, while the pier was added in 1817.

St Aubin was never able to keep up with the growth of St Helier. At one time the only route to its "new" neighbour was across the beach of St Aubin's Bay at low tide. General Don's military road didn't reach all the way to St Aubin until 1844. It was the coming of the railway in 1870 that put the town on the map; the present Parish Hall, on the northern pier, was once the station.

The Shell House.

From its early days, St Aubin was more popular than St Helier. A guidebook published in 1911 paints an especially rosy picture: "For convenient and prompt access to beautiful scenery and lovely walks, St Aubin has the advantage over St Helier. The little town is in the very heart and centre of the best the Island has to offer… leading up from the town is a valley road beside the railway, with thickly wooded hills on either side, and cottages in picturesque untidiness smothered in a careless growth of roses, honeysuckle and greenery."

There is little to "see" as such in St Aubin other than take time to walk the back streets by the Royal Channel Islands Yacht Club and enjoy the relaxed atmosphere of the harbour setting. **St Aubin's Fort** ❸ is accessible only at certain times owing to the tide and is really worth visiting only for the view it provides of St Aubin itself. It's not open to the public. This building's long

BELOW: St Matthew's is known as the Glass Church.

BERGERAC'S LEGACY

The Old Court House, overlooking St Aubin's harbour, was frequently used as a setting in *Bergerac*, the BBC Television cops and robbers series popular in the 1980s.

So tranquil are such areas that it's hard to reconcile one's experience with the image of the island purveyed to the world in the series: just as a significant slice of Oxford's population seemed to be murdered in the course of another TV cop series, *Inspector Morse*, so skulduggery was rife in *Bergerac*'s Jersey.

The reformed alcoholic policeman Jim Bergerac caught the public's imagination, but islanders viewed the series differently. They tired of being asked, "Is it really like that in Jersey, and is it true that everyone is either a crook or a millionaire?", and they never ceased to marvel that, thanks to the miracle of the camera, when Jim drove his roadster into the tunnel under Fort Regent he often emerged not at the other end but half a dozen miles away in St Ouen.

There have, meanwhile, been plenty of attempts to jump on the Bergerac bandwagon. Bergerac coach tours which pointed out landmarks from the series were run by the major coach companies, and you don't need to look too hard to discover the Bergerac Hotel and the Bergerac Wine Cellar.

history of renovation and refortification since its original construction in 1542 hardly stands up to the glittering past of Elizabeth Castle less than 2 miles (3 km) across the water.

One place difficult to miss is the **Shell House** on the steep hill leading out of St Aubin to St Brelade's. The sloping garden outside this small bungalow has been decorated with a variety of seashells by its owner for over 30 years.

VALLEY EXCURSIONS

When Queen Victoria asked to see the most beautiful spot on the island, she was taken on a tour of **St Peter's Valley** ㊳. A convenient starting point for several of Jersey's most popular inland locations is **St Matthew's Church** ㊴ in the parish of St Lawrence, popularly known as "the Glass Church". The original was built in the mid-19th century so that people living in this neighbourhood didn't have to walk more than a mile (1.5 km) inland to the Parish Church of St Lawrence. In 1934, the church was renovated by Lady Trent in memory of her husband Jesse Boot, founder of the pharmacy chain. The main feature of this renovation was the art deco glasswork of René Lalique, a celebrated craftsman of the time. Windows, door panels, screens to either side of the altar, the font, a 12-ft (4-metre) cross and even the altar rail are all made from a frosted opaque glass. This was the only church Lalique decorated in its entirety with glass.

The church is adjacent to **Coronation Park**, also the result of Lady Trent's generosity. She gave it to the island in 1937 for use by the aged and the young.

At different times the stream running down through St Peter's Valley served eight mills. **Moulin de Quétivel** ㊵ (open mid-May to mid-Sept Tues–Thurs 10am–4pm; admission charge) is a fully restored example of how these would

BELOW: old milling technology at Moulin de Quétivel.

have looked. References to Quétivel Mill have been traced back as far as 1309, when it was a Crown Mill. The tenants of the king living in St Brelade had to supply the heavy timber, while the King provided iron, masonry, carpentry and the main sluice-gates. The mill's name derives from a now extinct family. Records dating back to 1307 refer to Rauf and William de Keytovel and other bakers having been fined without full adjudication.

Abandoned in the early 20th century, the mill was revived by the Germans during the Occupation, when they decided during the severe wartime food shortages to grind local-grown corn. The mill later fell into disrepair, but was brought back to working order by the National Trust in 1979. The top floor has an exhibition on the history of milling, the first and ground floors demonstrate how it works. There is also an explanatory video which shows you how cabbage loaves (still sold in some bakeries) are made in gorse ovens. The stoneground flour which is produced at the mill is sold in the ground floor shop. An attractive footpath, through woodland, runs form the mill to the mill-pond.

More than 60,000 tons of solid rock were excavated to create the complex – yet it was used as a hospital for only six weeks to care for Germans wounded on French beaches during D-Day.

Jersey War Tunnels

A right fork before Moulin de Quétivel leads you to an altogether different side of the island's history. If St Matthew's Church makes you feel closer to heaven, then the **Jersey War Tunnels** ❹ (open daily 10am–6pm, last admission 4.30pm; admission charge) will make you feel that much closer to hell. This extensive subterranean complex was built over a period of 3½ years with the aid of forced labour and slave workers, all of whom lived and many of whom died under inhumane conditions.

BELOW: the Jersey War Tunnels.

Intricately renovated and meticulously researched, the hospital has been turned into a huge and impressive museum. Even though coachloads of visitors disembark at Meadowbank to queue at the entrance to the tunnel, this site loses none of its dignity as a memorial. A plaque sums up the intention in three simple sentences: "Under these conditions men of many nations laboured to construct this hospital. Those who survived will never forget; those who did not will never be forgotten. This exhibition is a reminder of the five years of Occupation and is dedicated to all who suffered the hardship of that time."

The tunnel complex was originally intended as a bomb-proof artillery barracks to protect the entire garrison of around 12,000 men against assault from sea or air. Sixteen tunnels were planned for the use of ammunition storage, armoured vehicles, fuel and food. However, the complex was never completed, for in the weeks leading to D-Day, with an Allied invasion looming, orders were given for the complex to be turned into a casualty receiving station. Five wards were each designed to cope with 100 casualties. Unfinished tunnels were sealed off and the site was equipped with operating theatre, recovery room, hospital wards, doctors' and nurses' quarters, Officers' Mess, escape shaft, central heating, air conditioning and telephone exchange. The anticipated invasion never took place and the occupying forces surrendered peacefully on 9 May 1945. When the liberation came the tunnels exceeded about half a mile (1 km) in length. In addition there were nearly 1,600 ft (500 metres) of unfinished tunnels.

At first, no forced labour was used; the 319 Infantry Division set to work in 1941 excavating and drilling. When it became apparent that there weren't enough Germans to complete the job, the infamous Organisation Todt became responsible for the works and it wasn't long before Spanish Republicans (captured in France), North Africans, Alsace Jews, Poles and French were press-ganged into service. In late 1942 Russian prisoners-of-war were also put to work here. Walking around the "hospital" today, even in the company of a stream of tourists, is an eerie experience. A map detailing the planned extent of the tunnel complex shows that only about half of it was ever completed and is a reminder that the Germans intended the Channel Islands to be permanently fortified outposts of the Third Reich.

A copious cocktail of medical and military paraphernalia not only vividly illustrates what the hospital looked like but paints a broader canvas of the history of the Occupation. The Jersey War Tunnels is therefore the telling of two related stories. On the one hand there are the hospital wards, operating theatre, Kommandant's office, radio room and officer's mess. On the other hand several displays show what life was like under the Germans. The state-of-the-art, award-winning Captive Island exhibition has recently undergone major refurbishment and doubled in size. Located within the inner galleries of the tunnel complex, the exhibition is a poignant interpretation of Jersey under the Nazi yoke. Visitors are taken from "Threatend Island" through "Daily Life", "Resistance" and ultimately "Liberation". Through video and sound installations deportees, housewives and forced labourers relate their experiences. Above

Map on pages 134–5

Promoting the Jersey Experience.

BELOW: the Living Legend.

The island's rugged coastline has long been notorious. In 1873 The Times of London wrote: "Few places present greater attractions to tourists than the island of Jersey, and fewer still possess worse accommodation for landing and embarking passengers."

ground the War Trail takes visitors through woodland, past anti-aircraft gun positions, crawl trenches, barbed wire entanglements and personnel shelters; while the Garden of Reflection has been designed as a tranquil area for the public to contemplate the events of the Occupation and reflect on the effects of war in general. Over 50 plaques are engraved with a fact relating to either the Occupation itself or to conflict in general.

History and showbiz

The Jersey War Tunnels are in every sense an authentic relic from the island's past, but just over a mile a way on high ground on the eastern side of the valley is the **Living Legend** ❷ (open daily 9.30am–5pm; admission charge). This purpose-built and cunningly designed attraction is an interesting blend of history and tourist recreation.

At the heart of the Living Legend is the **Jersey Experience**, a spectacular and, it must be said, convincing audio-visual presentation which tells the island's story from the prehistoric era to the present day. Visitors start on the deck of a Victorian paddle steamer destined for St Helier, then descend down the dark winding tunnel of time encountering characters and creatures form local legends. Further down at "the Island in the Sea", secrets are revealed of smugglers, shipwrecks and maritime myths. The auditorium is a mock-up of the Manoir de la Brequette, a manor house lost beneath the sea centuries ago. This is where the story of the island begins.

If you pay a visit to the Living Legend, be prepared for some surprises. The same site, which is described as a village in the promotional literature, also offers shopping for crafts, gifts and leisurewear, a restaurant and children's play

BELOW: tableau at the Jersey Experience.
LEFT: the Living Legend.

area. It covers 9 acres (4 hectares) and incorporates go-karting and two adventure golf courses set among gardens, caves, waterfalls and lakes – a serious challenge to all ages.

St Peter's Church

St Peter's Village is at the centre of the parish of the same name, less than a mile (about 1 km) from Jersey's airport. St Peter's Church has the tallest spire on the island and hence a warning red light for planes. It is sometimes known as St Pierre dans le Désert, a reference to the sand-dunes of Les Mielles close by to the west.

The earliest recorded mention of this church dates from 1053, though much of the present structure was built in the 12th and 13th centuries. Its bell, cast in Normandy in 1649, is inscribed *Mon nom est Elizabeth la belle* – which may be simply a pun on "bell" or, alternatively, a compliment to Elizabeth, the wife of Sir George Carteret, who was closely connected with the parish.

On the road which leads to the airport is the very popular **Jersey Bowl**. As well as offering all the delights of ten-pin bowling, the complex has Laserquest, a kids' zone, a restaurant and bars and is next door to the well-appointed Jersey Rugby Football Club.

Waterworks Valley

An alternative, or additional, valley route from St Matthew's Church takes you directly north, up through **Waterworks Valley ❹**. More secluded than St Peter's Valley, Waterworks Valley at one time had as many watermills as St Peter's. But the growth of St Helier in the 19th century meant that the water supply had to be more extensively utilised. **Millbrook Reservoir** was built in 1898, **Dannemarche Reservoir** in 1909 and **Handois Reservoir** in 1932. A shady country lane takes you past the first two of these; the last is easily reached on foot. They're a reminder that, on islands, water can be precious.

Museum of Country Life

Close to Waterworks Valley in the parish of St Lawrence is **Hamptonne Country Life Museum ❹** (Easter to Oct daily 10am–5pm; admission charge). The cluster of faithfully restored farm buildings, the meadows and orchard portray Jersey life over the ages. The interiors of the two oldest houses have been recreated to illustrate living conditions of farming families in the 17th and 18th centuries. A third building is devoted to an informative exhibition showing the changes in farming in the past 100 years and the decline in the island's agriculture – from 2,600 farms in the 1880s to just 500 today.

Hamptonne also does its level best to keep traditional crafts and skills alive. One building holds a massive cider press, another a collection of horse-drawn vehicles, and another houses a bakery where bread, Jersey vraic buns and deep-fried Jersey pastries called "wonders" are produced. This is very much a living museum with a variety of farm animals and a traditionally garbed *goodwyf* on hand to chat to visitors or take them on guided tours. ❑

TIP

If you plan to be at Hamptonne Country Life Museum during lunchtime, hampers can be ordered for picnics in the apple orchard; ask at the café before you begin touring the site.

BELOW: a school party meets the Good Wife at Hamptonne, Jersey's Museum of Country Life.

DURRELL'S ARK

Like a hotelier, Gerald Durrell didn't expect guests at his zoo to stay indefinitely – his aim was to see them returned safely to their natural environments

Mention Jersey in some far-flung corner of the globe and it is a fair bet that someone there will have heard of the island's famous Wildlife Preservation Trust and its founder, Gerald Durrell, who until his death in 1995 devoted himself to the protection of endangered species and their habitats.

Although he travelled the world in search of rare creatures and seemed as much at home on the Russian Steppes as he was in the African rain-forest, evidence of the Durrell legacy to the world is concentrated in the landscaped grounds which surround the 16th-century manor of Les Augrès in Trinity. It was at the manor, in 1959, that Durrell, a conservationist long before conservation became fashionable, realised the dream of opening his own zoo, a venture which was ultimately to achieve a remarkable level of success in spite of its shoestring start in life *(see pages 146–8).*

SUCCESS BREEDS SUCCESS

The Durrell Wildlife Conservation Trust (as the zoo is now known) is not only enormously popular with visitors but has also won plaudits from experts on conservation. As Durrell's reputation as a naturalist, author and broadcaster, whose leonine features and huge enthusiasm became well known to TV audiences, grew steadily, the organisation he founded embarked on a captive breeding programme of unparalleled scale. It also launched research and educational facilities which are respected throughout the world. One Canadian grandmother was so impressed by the zoo and its charismatic founder that she moved to Jersey to help out as a full-time volunteer.

▷ **ROOM TO ROAM**
It's a principle that animals such as these gorillas are given space in which to roam, preparing them for an eventual return to their natural habitat.

△ **OWL ACQUAINTANCE**
Students from all over the world come here to learn about preserving species such as the smoky owl.

◁ **LIVE AS THE DODO**
The dodo, symbol of extinct species, is the logo of the Trust, which tries to prevent such extinction.

△ **NIGHT OF THE IGUANA**
Reptiles such as this iguana have their own quarters, where tropical habitats are simulated.

THE DREAM OF GERALD DURRELL

Smitten with "zoo-mania" from the age of two when he discovered a "zoo of sorts" in the central Indian village where he was born, he started assembling his first collection of "everything from minnows to woodlice" before he was seven. The collection became more sophisticated – "everything from eagle owls to scorpions" – when his family moved to Corfu during the 1930s. Back in London during the war years, he worked as a student keeper at the Zoological Society of London's country estate, Whip-snade Zoo in Bedford-shire. Then he struck out on his own, leading expeditions to collect animals on behalf of other zoos. In 1957, after financing and leading 10 major expeditions to various parts of the world, Durrell decided the time was ripe to start his own zoo, one devoted to endangered species.

◁ **BEAR ESSENTIALS**
The first spectacled bears were successfully bred in Jersey in the 1970s and other European zoos take part in the programme.

▽ **IN THE SWING**
The winsome rope-haired orang-utans like to build nests from any old cardboard boxes that come to hand.

△ **BIRDS OF A FEATHER**
Flamingoes add a splash of colour in the grounds of Les Augrès Manor.

▷ **GENTLE GIANT**
A sculpture pays tribute to Jambo, a silver-back gorilla who hit the headlines when he stood guard over a five-year-old boy who fell into the gorilla compound.

GUERNSEY

It used to be known for its vast expanse of greenhouses, but the island has had to seek other sources of income

While the newly rich go to Jersey, locals claim, the "old money" heads for Guernsey. The antagonism between the two islands is reflected in many small ways: in the different colour of telephone booths, the different helmets worn by the police, the different robes worn by the bailiffs, the different dialects. From the air, the island dazzles as the sun is reflected off thousands of greenhouses, in which the once dominant tomato is being augmented by such exotica as kiwi fruit. St Peter Port, a jumble of narrow streets with a busy harbour, has an almost Swiss air of neatness.

With an area of 24 sq. miles (62 sq. km) and a population of 60,000, Guernsey is the second biggest of the Channel Islands but is more densely populated than Jersey. It also has more cars per head of the population than anywhere else in the world – and parking, especially in summer, is a problem.

The island is roughly triangular in shape, and divides into two quite distinct parts: to the south and east is the cliff-fringed "high parish" region, where access to the beach is via deep wooded valleys or down steep rock-cut steps. The "low parish" region to the north and west of the island consists of flat land fringed by miles of sandy dunes. The capital, St Peter Port (population 17,000), is on the escarpment that marks the boundary between the highland and lowland zones.

Including the Parish of St Peter Port, Guernsey is divided into 10 parishes. It's an easier administrative arrangement than was the case in the past. At one time there were more than 70 fiefs in Guernsey – each presided over by a seigneur. To the west of St Peter Port, St Andrew is the only one of Guernsey's 10 parishes that has no coastline. Its western boundary is one of the oldest in the island. It marks a dividing line drawn in the 11th century by Duke Richard II of Normandy who created the boundary by separating Guernsey's feudal landholdings into two.

Apart from Guernsey cows, the island's best-known export used to be tomatoes. In recent years, however, cheaper Dutch imports have usurped "Guernsey toms" from English greengrocers' shops, forcing the island's horticulturalists to switch their greenhouses to cut-flower production. Now most of the freesias, roses and carnations sold in the UK come from Guernsey. Horticulture forms the theme of several visitor attractions, and the island's natural profligacy is celebrated each August in its biggest festival, the Battle of Flowers. ❑

PRECEDING PAGES: Gallic influence in St Peter Port; a Guernsey garden at Le Fariouf. **LEFT:** Saint's Bay.

Map on page 176

ST PETER PORT

Guernsey's capital has some splendidly preserved late-Georgian and Regency architecture, but the real attraction is its atmosphere, which could almost be Mediterranean

H owever hard you compare the merits of Jersey with those of its largest neighbour, there's one category in which Guernsey will always win: its capital. **St Peter Port**, hugging the slopes that rise back from the sea, has preserved a mixture of elegance and charm that St Helier could never pretend to match. In fact, you'd have to go much further afield than St Helier to find a town as endearingly quaint, tidy and well-preserved as St Peter Port. The neat lines of Regency and Victorian buildings, the numerous cobbled streets, the steep stairways and alleyways weaving their way up and down between houses, a forest of boat masts jostling for attention just a few metres from the buildings overlooking the harbour – all this gives St Peter Port a charisma that most would associate more with the Mediterranean than the Gulf of St Malo.

St Peter Port

The town has succeeded in fighting off many of the exterior signs of modernity. This doesn't mean it lags behind. Whichever historic buildings are occupied by the offshore banks and investment houses, a crucial part of the island's economy, they no doubt do business aided by the latest technology. Outside in many of the streets you get the refreshing feeling that time has stood still. In some areas around Hauteville and Clifton, and elsewhere, the street scene can look like a film set.

LEFT: St Peter Port harbour.
BELOW: traditional Guernsey costume.

There's more than tradition in St Peter Port. Much is made of the Frenchness of some parts of the Channel Islands, though all too often it's a quality that disappears behind crowds of unmistakably British holidaymakers. In St Peter Port, while the holidaymakers are very much evident, the Frenchness, the cosmopolitanism, is more discernible. And it's not just the street names that suggest you've left Britain.

Perhaps St Peter Port's greatest asset is that it makes you want to explore it. Walk along its streets and alleyways and you can't help feeling that something interesting will appear around the next corner. Visit the "tourist sites" such as Castle Cornet, the Museum, Hauteville House – all well worth seeing – and you'll still feel inclined to stroll around the town afterwards just for curiosity's sake. And, after you've done all that, look back at the town's wide skyline from a vantage point like Castle Cornet and you'll get the feeling there's still a bit you "missed".

A sense of history

Above all, it's St Peter Port's past that gives the town its enduring strength. For this is the oldest community in the Channel Islands – and it shows. The splendid Regency and Victorian dwellings hide much earlier chapters that go back at least to the 13th century.

Little is known about earlier periods, though the discovery of a Roman ship in the harbour in 1982

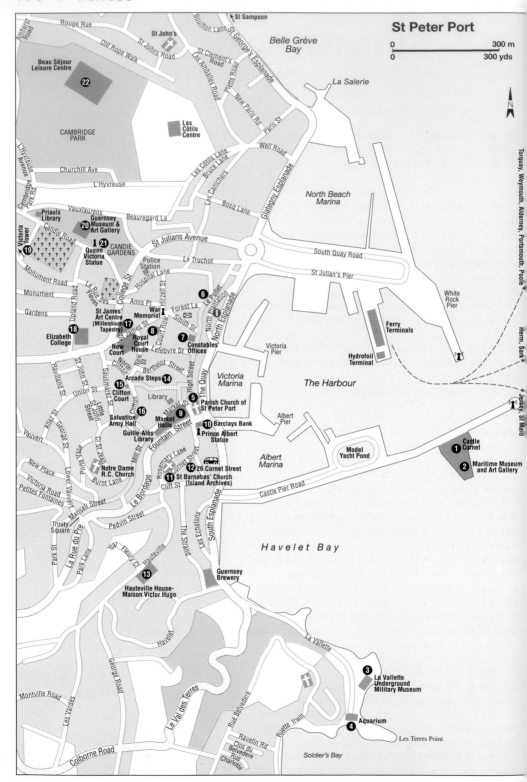

St Peter Port

0 —————————— 300 m
0 —————————— 300 yds

N

Torquay, Weymouth, Alderney, Portsmouth, Poole

Herm, Sark

Jersey, St Malo

St Sampson

Belle Grève Bay

Rouge Rue

St John's

Old Rope Walk

St Johns Road

Bouillon Lane

St George's Esplanade

St Clement's Road

Les Amballes Road

Piette Road

New Paris Rd

Paris St

La Salerie

Beau Séjour Leisure Centre

22

CAMBRIDGE PARK

Les Côtils Centre

Les Côtils Lane

Bruce Lane

Well Road

Churchill Ave

L'Hyvreuse

Les Canichers

Les Bosq Lane

North Beach Marina

Glategny Esplanade

South Quay Road

St Julian's Pier

Beauregard La

Vauxlaurens

Priaulx Library

Guernsey Museum & Art Gallery

20

Candie Road

21

Queen Victoria Statue

CANDIE GARDENS

Victoria Tower

19

St Julians Avenue

Le Truchot

Police Station

Hospital Lane

White Rock Pier

Monument Road

Le Rue des Frères

College St

Anns Pl

Hirzell St

Forest La

North Plantation

6

Le Pollet

North Esplanade

Monument Gardens

18

Elizabeth College

St James' Art Centre (Millennium Tapestry)

17

War Memorial

St James St

8

Court Row

Smith St

Royal Court House

Lefebvre St

7

Constables' Offices

Ferry Terminals

Victoria Pier

Hydrofoil Terminal

New Court

North Clifton

Berthelot Street

High Street

Victoria Marina

The Harbour

Havilland St

St John St

Union St

Little St John Street

Sausmarez St

15

Arcade Steps

14

Clifton Court

Library

Market Ln

5

Parish Church of St Peter Port

Albert Pier

Alland St

George St

Allez St

16

Salvation Army Hall

Guille-Alès Library

9

Market Halls

Fountain Street

10

Barclays Bank

Prince Albert Statue

Albert Marina

Model Yacht Pond

1

Castle Cornet

Vauvert

New Place

Victoria Road

Petites Fontaines

Lower Vauvert

Pont Vaise

Notre Dame R.C. Church

Burnt Lane

Le Bordage

Mill St

Clifton

Rosemary Lane

Cornet Street

12

26 Cornet Street

11

St Barnabas' Church (Island Archives)

Cliff St

Castle Pier Road

2

Maritime Museum and Art Gallery

Trinity Square

Park St

La Rue du Pré

Mansell Street

Pedvin Street

Val Fleury Ct

Hauteville

South Esplanade

Les Echelons

The Strand

Havelet Bay

Park Lane

13

Hauteville House–Maison Victor Hugo

Guernsey Brewery

Havelet

La Vallette

Montville Road

George Road

Les Yardes

Le Val des Terres

Rue Belvedere

3

La Vallette Underground Military Museum

Ravelin Rd

Clos du Belvedere

Rue Charlotte

Ruette Irwin

4

Aquarium

Les Terres Point

Colborne Road

Soldier's Bay

Map on facing page

showed that this part of Guernsey's coastline was a refuge for seamen even in ancient times. So before you set foot in St Peter Port today, it's useful to know something of what has gone before.

While it's known that the Town Church existed as early as 1048, one of the most important early developments was the construction of Castle Cornet, which started in 1206. A few decades later, in 1275, King Edward I ordered a new pier to be built (this was destroyed when the French attacked less than 20 years later) between the castle and the town. Guernsey, and St Peter Port, didn't wane in strategic importance: in the following century, King Edward III ordered that St Peter Port should be enclosed by a wall.

William Camden (1551–1623) wrote of "an haven within an hollow Bay bending inward like an halfe-moone, able to receive tall ships; upon which standeth Saint Peters, a little towne built with a long and narrow street."

Profiting from piracy

Some defence works were definitely built, the most notable of these being La Tour Beauregard – though, despite a second order from the King, it seems unlikely that St Peter Port's wall was ever erected. Local archaeologists, at least, have found no evidence of such a structure. There are clear markers, however, of the full extent of the medieval town; the small standing stones, or *barrières de la ville*, are alleged to have marked the sites of the gates in the "town wall". These stones don't date from medieval times. The one inserted in the wall near the Hansa Health Food shop, on the south side of Fountain Street, bears the date 1700.

Guernsey's early growth owed much to its position as a landmark to sailors. In an 11-month period in 1329, for example, it's recorded that 487 foreign ships called at St Peter Port. From the 12th to the 16th centuries, fishing was of prime importance, though the town remained compact. By the middle of the 16th century, St Peter Port consisted of little more than Cornet Street, Fountain Street, La Grande Rue (today's High Street), La Rue des Forges (today's Smith Street) and The Pollet.

It was the practice of privateering, which began in the late 18th century, that really saw St Peter Port grow in size and wealth. This was a form of legalised piracy by which privately owned vessels were licensed by the British government to seize and plunder enemy ships. The pickings were phenomenal: in 1778 alone local privateers brought in £343,500 in prizes.

By 1800, St Peter Port had grown from a small quayside settlement into a town of wealthy merchants. Many of the medieval buildings were beginning to disappear. St Peter Port's new-found wealth manifested itself in the form of fine Georgian and Regency buildings: **Elizabeth College** (1826); **Bonamy House** (1820); the **Church of St James the Less** (1818); **La Parte** (1801); **Lukis House** (1840); and the **Constables' Offices** (1787).

The growth wasn't just in grand public buildings like these. As in Jersey, the Napoleonic Wars brought an influx of new residents. There was such a demand for houses that new buildings spread up the slopes around the town and onto the plateau above.

The harbour was unable to keep pace with these new developments. By 1750 there were two small jetties enclosing an area roughly the size of today's Victoria Marina. But ships were frequently damaged in bad weather and there was no low-water landing place.

BELOW: indignity for Prince Albert.

When the steamship service between Guernsey and England started, the need for better facilities became even more pressing. In 1853, new jetties were begun and the harbour area grew from 4 acres (1.6 hectares) to more than 80 acres (32 hectares). By 1865, the two long breakwaters you see today were in place.

Castle Cornet

TIP

Castle Cornet stages organised activities for children during the summer, teaching them about life in an 18th-century garrison. There are also frequent Living History re-enactments at Castle Cornet, Fort Grey and Candie Museum.

BELOW: Cornet Castle as seen from the Havelet Hotel.

After the Town Church, this fortress sitting on an islet at the end of the southern pier, less than half-a-mile (1 km) from St Peter Port, is the oldest site in St Peter Port, embracing close to eight centuries of fortifications.

When King John lost Normandy to the French in 1204, Guernsey felt just as threatened as Jersey and **Castle Cornet ❶** was built. The fear was well-founded, though it was more than a century later that France succeeded in breaching the castle's defences. In 1338, shortly after the start of the Hundred Years' War, the French invaded the Channel Islands twice. On the second attempt they captured Castle Cornet and became masters of Guernsey, Alderney and Sark. Their occupation was shortlived: the castle was recaptured in 1345 after three days of fighting. The French recaptured it in 1356, but held it for only a few months.

Two periods of rebuilding saw Castle Cornet evolve into essentially its present form. The Tudors undertook extensive renovation between 1545 and 1558. During Henry VIII's reign, a prominent military engineer of the day, John Rogers, strengthened the castle's defences by building the Mewtis Bulwark on its southeast side. During Elizabeth's reign, under the Governorship of Sir Thomas Leighton, the castle took on an entirely new appearance; Paul Ivy, who drew up the plans for Jersey's Elizabeth Castle, was involved in the redesign. Ivy, the author of *The Practise of Fortification* (1589), was the first English military architect to incorporate ideas borrowed from Italy – thicker masonry to absorb cannon fire, as few vertical faces as possible (oblique and rounded faces were better at deflecting cannon balls) and bastions projecting at intervals along the curtain wall to provide gun platforms and protect the castle walls from direct attack.

During the English Civil War, Guernsey's Governor, Sir Peter Osborne, retreated to Castle Cornet in defiance of the rest of the island, which took parliament's side. The castle came under siege for nine years, during which time its garrison received supplies by sea from royalists in Jersey. The castle made a tempting target for the cannon in St Peter Port. Resistance eventually proved futile. When the castle surrendered in 1651, it was the last part of the British Isles to fall.

One of Guernsey's prominent landowners, the Seigneur of Sausmarez, Sir Amias Andros, played an important role by liaising between the King's forces which controlled Jersey and the loyalist garrison at Castle Cornet. After the restoration, Charles II made him Bailiff. He was one of only two prominent Guernseymen who were not obliged to seek pardon from the King for their conduct during the Civil War.

The buildings that remain are in excellent condition. It's only an accident of history that prevents it competing, visually at least, with Elizabeth Castle in Jersey. In the 17th century, Castle Cornet wore a lofty and majestic crown in the form of Donjon Tower.

When lightning struck it in 1672, it ignited gunpowder stored at its base. Donjon Tower, not to mention a number of important people and buildings, disappeared forever.

For most of its history, Castle Cornet was accessible only by boat – today's visitors can explore the castle (open Apr–Oct 10am–5pm, closed rest of year) by walking out along Castle Pier, which was built in 1866, as was the lighthouse at the end of the pier, from where optimistic anglers cast out their lines.

The castle is a delightful maze of buildings and courtyards, linked by steps and passageways, with little gardens tucked into sheltered corners. If you are around at noon, you can witness the daily **noon-day gun ceremony**, when an 18th-century cannon is loaded and fired. Several buildings within the grounds have been converted to museums. The first covers the history of the castle, and contains realistic tableaux depicting garrison life in the 18th century. Castle Cornet was then manned by invalid regiments, made up of soldiers disabled by wounds, but still capable of giving service, or those who were excused active service because of old age or length of service. The cramped conditions endured by ordinary soldiers are contrasted with the spacious accommodation enjoyed by the officers.

The oldest part of the castle survives only in fragmentary form – displays show the results of archaeological excavation to recover the form of the original medieval castle, while the present fortress is substantially Tudor in date. The success of this design was proved by the Civil War siege, when the castle proved all but impregnable, and again when, during World War II, the Germans occupied the castle and found it necessary to make very few modifications to fit it for modern warfare.

Three other museums within the castle grounds are housed in the 18th-century

Map on page 176

Gunner at Castle Cornet

BELOW: the noon-day gun.

barracks. The **Maritime Museum** ❷ looks at the relationship between St Peter Port and the sea, from Roman times, through to the era of the massive high-speed catamarans that cover the distance between Weymouth and Guernsey in less than 2¼ hours. The castle's most recent development is the **201 (Guernsey's Own) Squadron RAF Museum** celebrating the only RAF unit to retain such an affiliation. 201 Squadron's links with Guernsey date back to the 1930's, when their Southampton-based flying boats came on training flights and good-will visits. On the floor above this museum is the **Hatton Gallery**, full of portraits of governors and merchants, dramatic seascapes and some fine views of St Peter Port.

La Vallette Underground Military Museum

One of the local brewery's pubs.

Continuing along the Esplanade, you will pass the bus terminus and the **Guernsey Brewery**, on the right, with the town's main bathing beach to your left (sandy at low tide) before coming to the green end of St Peter Port, where gradens and trees cloak the steep hill above the undercliff footpath. After continuing along here for a short way, you reach **La Vallette Underground Military Museum** ❸ (open daily 10am–5pm, closed Tues and Wed Nov–March). The simple concrete-lined opening in the cliff leads into a complex of tunnels built by slave labourers during the Occupation. The tunnels served as a refuelling station for U-boats, and one of the huge oil storage tanks has survived.

The exhibition, like so many concerned with the war, consists of a mass of largely unexplained materials, with few labels, though the occasional letter, document or newspaper cutting offers clues to their significance.

BELOW: La Vallette Underground Military Museum.

It is remarkable that some objects have survived at all. The museum starts with a display of Red Cross food parcels delivered by the Swedish ship *Vega* towards

the end of the war when the population was starving. Next to these displays are posters detailing arrangements for the partial evacuation of the islands in 1940, when it was clear that the Germans intended to invade. Another exhibit reminds us that most of the islands' fortifications were constructed by forced labour – whips and rubber truncheons bring home the brutality of the wartime regime.

From the Underground Military Museum, the South Esplanade continues a short way to another tunnel. This one was built in 1861 as part of a scheme, never completed, to drive a road through to Fermain Bay. The Germans added some side tunnels, using Russian labourers who left their hammer and sickle symbol on the rocky roof. Today the tunnels house an **Aquarium ❹** (open Mon–Sat 10am–6pm Sun 10am–5.30pm), which displays examples of the various fish found in Guernsey's waters – from perfectly camouflaged baby soles and the tiny inhabitants of tidal pools to larger conger eels and dogfish. The most recent addition is a collection of reptiles in the vivarium. There are also prettily patterned tropical fish, with notes on their habitats and hints for their suitability for home aquariums.

The heart of town

The best-known thoroughfare in St Peter Port is the narrow pedestrian way of the **High Street**. It's also one of the oldest. Always busy during the day, the High Street is walled in by tall, elegant buildings to either side. Walk south down this ancient way and an even taller and more elegant building dominates the view ahead: the Town Church, more correctly known as the **Parish Church of St Peter Port ❺**. The first reference to this building was made by William the Conqueror in 1048. Subsequent extensions and renovations make it more modern than that. Some parts may date from the 12th century, though the earliest

Map on page 176

Aquarium inhabitant.

BELOW:
the architecture has a Continental air.

reliable record of construction is an inscription of 1466 relating to the south transept. The full history of this great granite building at the harbour's edge is uncertain, though two events are well-recorded. In 1721 the present steeple was built and in 1886 the church underwent a significant restoration.

However long you spend in St Peter Port, you won't tire of walking up and down the High Street and on into **Le Pollet ❻**, another narrow lane with the same old-world air about it. The High Street and The Pollet combined run for a little over half-a-mile. This route is marked by two *barrières de la ville*, one by the northeast corner of the Town Church in the High Street, another opposite Moore's Hotel. Important people made this thoroughfare their home. Moore's Hotel was a residence of the de Sausmarez family.

The Royal Court House.

An archway opens up off High Street, just before the junction with Smith Street, to Lefebvre Street and the **Constables' Offices ❼**, one of those grand buildings built at a time of new-found wealth in the 18th century. This Georgian mansion was once the property of the distinguished Le Marchant family. Near the top of Lefebvre Street, in Rue de Manoir, is the **Royal Court House ❽**, built in 1799. This replaced a more ancient building called La Plaiderie, which was situated near Moore's Hotel and was demolished in 1929. Guernsey's parliament, the Assembly of the States, holds its debates here. The public is invited to watch the proceedings from a public gallery whenever the States are in session.

Medieval St Peter Port was little more than a clutch of thatched buildings to the north and west of the Town Church, though little of the medieval town survives. The High Street was its constricted main artery. The Town Church marked the focus of much of the town's energies for this was where St Peter Port's markets set up shop. One pointer to the kind of produce that was sold takes the form of a street

BELOW:
music making.

name. Just a short distance from the Town Church is a small lane called **Rue des Vaches**. When there was no proper harbour cows brought for slaughter were driven out of boats at low tide, forced to swim ashore, and herded together in "Cow Street".

The markets

Today's **Market Halls** ❾, to the west of the Town Church, are all more than a century old. The Fish Market was completed in 1875, the Meat Market was designed in 1822 and the Vegetable Market was built in 1879. They are undergoing a major rebuild and are expected to fully reopen in 2006, although some traders are still to be found plying their fresh produce at the north end. **French Halles**, a market hall completed in 1782. John Wesley preached here in 1787 in the Assembly Rooms in what is now the Guille-Allès Library.

In medieval times, **Fountain Street** was remarkably narrow. With the buildings on either side projecting progressively at each storey, it is said that people could lean out of the windows and shake hands with their neighbours. The Fountain Street of today was laid out by architect John Wilson in 1833. This was originally a cobbled street. The Georgian elegance of **Barclays Bank** ❿ gives you a good idea of how this sloping road beside the Market Halls once looked before modern alterations were made to some shopfronts.

Beauregard Tower, built in 1357 on the orders of Edward III, is thought to have stood on the site of **St Barnabas' Church** ⓫, at the top of Cornet Street. The church (now the home of the Island Archives) was erected as a memorial to the Reverend Charles Guille, a former rector of St Peter Port. Before the Guernsey Art Gallery and Museum was built, it housed the Lukis and Island Museum. At **26, Cornet Street** ⓬ is a remarkable building that serves as the

Map on page 176

BELOW:
traditional Guernsey
sweaters for sale
at the market.

headquarters of the National Trust of Guernsey (open Easter–mid-Oct, 10am–4pm, Tues, Wed, Thur and Sat). The offices lie behind the well-restored 18th-century shop and parlour, where costumed shopkeepers sell toys and souvenirs from another era, though the prices are contemporary.

Victor Hugo's house

Maison Victor Hugo.

At the junction of Cornet Street, Tower Hill and Cliff Street, **Hauteville** does exactly as its name promises: it goes up to the top of the town – or at least to one of St Peter Port's "summits". One of the best vantage points is to be had from the top of Victor Hugo's house, itself one of Guernsey's star attractions (open for guided tours from 1 Apr–30 Sept, Mon–Sat 10–11.30am and 2–4.30pm). **Hauteville House**, also known as **Maison Victor Hugo ⓭**, is not so much a memorial to an exile and writer as a museum to an eccentric but nevertheless inspired interior decorator. Some knowledge of the man makes a tour of his house all the more meaningful.

Hugo was just one of over 200 political refugees who fled to the Channel Islands in 1852 following the coup of Louis Napoleon III in France in December 1851. He started his exile in Jersey and might never even have made it to Guernsey had not that same defiant spirit so boisterously expressed in his house led to his expulsion from Jersey. In 1855 the newspaper for the exile community, *L'Homme*, criticised Queen Victoria for having made a state visit to Paris. The people of Jersey, more than a little angered at this defamation of their sovereign, succeeded in getting the newspaper closed down and three of its senior staff expelled from the island. Victor Hugo led a petition signed by himself and 35 fellow refugees in protest. The petition ended: "And now expel us!" The lieutenant-governor of

BELOW: to enjoy the harbour view, Victor Hugo used to write while standing at this window.

Jersey obliged and all the signatories were quickly hustled off the island.

Hugo's single-mindedness is all around you when you take a tour of Hauteville House. He lived here from 1856 until 1870. During that time he created an interior that is nothing less than a triumph of the imagination. Here are just a few of his furniture innovations: ornate wooden chests and commodes dismantled and turned into wall panels; backs of chairs turned upside down and used as curtain pelmets; tapestries cut up and rearranged to line high and broad ceilings; and an enormous stately bed (intended for an expected visit by Garibaldi) made out of 25 other pieces of furniture.

The catalogue of eccentricities extends beyond the decor. Hugo's personal habits are just as revealing. He was, for example, fond of hanging a small flag outside his bedroom whenever he'd slept well so that his mistress, installed in a street nearby, could rejoice at his restful night. The guided tour finishes in Hugo's study where, aided by a panoramic view over St Peter Port, he wrote his prodigious output of novels, poems and essays while standing.

Despite its quirkiness, Hauteville House is stately and grand. You can view the building only on a conducted tour, though the eminently knowledgeable guides make this one of the best places you can visit anywhere in the Channel Islands.

Map on page 176

Old Town to New Town

When you walk back down Hauteville you have by no means tackled the most difficult of St Peter Port's slopes. There are plenty more to test you. One of the few "flat" streets in town is the square formed by the **Commercial Arcade**, behind the Town Church. This elegant and stylish 19th-century shopping mall, which attracts a steady stream of window-shopping tourists, would have been even more elegant and stylish had its developers not run out of cash: the original idea was to provide a glass roof to the arcades. The two Jerseymen who conceived the expensive scheme went bankrupt in 1833.

You can give your stamina a tough test by ascending **Arcade Steps ⓮** – all 111 of them. This stairway, which opens out on the western side of the arcade, climbs the steep cliff which was created when Commercial Arcade itself was excavated. As you go up, it's not too long before you are forced to stop for breath. That's just as well, for once you are above the level of the rooftops you can enjoy an uninterrupted view of St Peter Port's picturesque harbour.

At the top you are in **Clifton**, the border line of an important area of growth for the town in the 18th and 19th centuries. Before you turn left or right, take a look at the building nearly facing you. This is **Clifton Court ⓯** and dates from 1825. It started life as a Wesleyan chapel and later became Guernsey's first telephone exchange. Further along the road to your left is the **Salvation Army Hall ⓰**, dating from 1831.

There are two more heart-pounding flights of steps leading off Clifton: **Clifton Steps** and **Constitution Steps** (also known as Les Escaliers de Mont Gibel). At this point the strong may be tempted to go down one set and ascend the other. The weak will shun such bravado and head straight for the neat streets of Regency houses nearby that mark the New Town proper.

BELOW:
Hugo's statue in Candie Gardens.

Elizabeth College.

BELOW:
Candie Gardens.

Havilland Street, **St John Street**, **Saumarez Street** and **Union Street** boast some of the finest Regency buildings in St Peter Port. This small oasis of Georgian architecture makes for a landscape of white stucco, classical columns, cast-iron railings and wide sash windows. A minor landmark in Union Street has become something of a celebrity. A small plaque behind it states why: Victorian Pillar Box. The British Post Office installed its earliest roadside posting boxes in the Channel Islands in 1852–53, and this box is the oldest survivor still in daily use in the British Isles. It has been restored to what is believed to be the original livery of the past era.

The New Town wasn't the only part of St Peter Port to be identified with this new era of growth. In 1780, the Assembly Rooms, above the French Halles, were at first referred to as the "New Rooms" in order to distinguish them from the Old Assembly Rooms in The Pollet. Earlier, in 1764, the parish of St Peter Port purchased L'Hyvreuse as a military parade ground. Before it assumed the name of Cambridge Park (adjacent to Beau Séjour Leisure Centre) it was called the New Ground.

Three of the most visible points on St Peter Port's skyline are in the vicinity of the New Town. In **St James' Concert and Assembly Rooms** ⑰, the Bailiwick of Guernsey Tapestry, the Islands' Millennium project, occupies its own purpose-built gallery and recounts 1,000 years of local history through its ten embroidered panels (open Easter–Oct Mon–Sat 10am–4.30pm, Nov–Easter Thurs 10am–4pm). Also in College Street is the imposing building of **Elizabeth College** ⑱. Though founded in 1563 and named after Queen Elizabeth I, today's edifice dates from 1829. The college's first headmaster, Adrian Saravia, was one of the first translators responsible for the Authorised Version of the Bible. Less than a quarter-mile away is the heavily crenellated **Victoria Tower** ⑲. Built in 1848 on the

site of an old windmill, it marked Queen Victoria's first visit to the island in 1846.

Visitors looking for views and versions of Guernsey's past and its people should spend time in the **Priaulx Library**, in Candie House, and the **Guernsey Museum and Art Gallery** ⑳ (open 10am–4pm daily, and till 5pm May–Sept; closed 25 Dec–31 Jan). When this thoroughly modern museum was opened in 1978, it made a successful debut by winning the British Museum of the Year Award a year later. But its modernity hides some real historical pedigree. Many of the exhibits here were collected by F. C. Lukis, Guernsey's pioneering 19th-century archaeologist.

Once you have entered the museum through the barrel vault doorway, the open-plan design of the exhibition area gives Guernsey some exhaustive but easily digestible coverage. Geology, archaeology, horticulture, agriculture, industry and history are mixed and matched to good effect.

The Art Gallery

When history palls, the Art Gallery may beckon. Exhibits include Rodin's bust of Victor Hugo (1883), wearing a most expressive frown and wild beard, and Renoir's painting of *Fog on Guernsey* (also 1883). The great French Impressionist visited the island in 1883 and found inspiration for 18 paintings. The small collection of oils and watercolours you can view comprises work by a mixture of local and visiting artists. There are also numerous characterful sketches by Guernseyman Peter de Lièvre (1812–78), whose paintings of farmers and fisherfolk provide a valuable portrait of island life during Queen Victoria's reign.

Outside in the grounds you can't help noticing that the museum's tearoom bears an uncanny resemblance to a bandstand... which is precisely what it once was. In fact, the actual museum's design, a cluster of octagonal pavilions, takes its inspiration from the Victorian bandstand. The building diplomatically separates a **statue of Queen Victoria** ㉑ from a statue of her critic, Victor Hugo. From the time of his banishment, Hugo had little to say in praise of Jersey and saved his eulogies instead for the people of Guernsey. Words inscribed on the statue are from the dedication of his novel, *The Toilers of the Sea*:

> *Au rocher d'hospitalité et de liberté,*
> *à ce coin de vieille terre, Normande*
> *où vit le noble petit peuple de la mer*
> *à l'Ile de Guernsey, sévère et douce.*

Translated, this reads: "To the rock of hospitality and liberty, to his corner of ancient Norman soil, where live the noble little people of the sea, to the island of Guernsey, stern and gentle."

One of the town's most modern facilities, **Beau Séjour Leisure Centre** ㉒ and its grounds occupy about as much space as medieval St Peter Port once did. This forward-looking building stands in stark contrast to the centuries of history in the centre of town. Nevertheless, since it opened in 1976, it has proved popular to both visitors and residents. State-of-the-art fitness equipment, kids' activities and a range of sports are all on offer here; and save for the Merton Hotel in Jersey, Beau Séjour has the Channel Islands' only flumes – slides twisting high above the swimming pool down which youngsters tumble and splash. Guernsey's largest theatre and concert hall are also on the premises. ❏

Map on page 176

BELOW:
Queen Victoria.

AROUND GUERNSEY

Star attractions include sheltered bays and sandy beaches,
crafts exhibits ranging from woodcarving to jewellery making,
and yet more relics of the German Occupation

Map
on pages
190–1

St Peter
Port

Just 1½ miles (2 km) out of St Peter Port, the main road into **St Andrew**
passes the **Hangman's Inn ❶**; a site nearby was for many centuries a
place of execution. The best-known victim of the hangman's noose was a
certain Gaultier de la Salle. Two stories account for his fate on the gallows.
One tells how he illegally executed a fellow official (who had already received
a royal pardon) and was hanged for his crime. Another tells of an attempt by
Gaultier de la Salle to "frame" a neighbour for theft in order to gain the upper
hand in a dispute over rights to the use of a water well. He almost succeeded in
his deception but was exposed and hanged in place of the innocent man.

Near the Hangman's Inn is **Bailiff's Cross ❷**, a small commemorative stone
incised with a cross marking the spot where the condemned man is said to have
halted to take Holy Communion on his way to the gibbet.

The German Underground Hospital

Men were condemned to death elsewhere in St Andrew's. Many of the slave
workers who died building Guernsey's **German Underground Hospital ❸** are
said to have been buried in the concrete. It's a suitably unnerving thought to
ponder, for while Jersey's subterranean hospital has been extensively renovated,
the one here in St Andrew's, Guernsey, has been little
altered since the end of World War II. It saw a certain
amount of action in 1944 when it received soldiers
wounded during fighting in the D-day landings.

Nearly all the military medical equipment has since
been removed and as a result, the German Underground
Hospital is sombre and cavernous, echoing a network of
tunnels with only a handful of unintrusive displays to set
things in perspective. The dim lighting, the wet concrete floors and the very emptiness of the place all help
to make this a chilling experience indeed. You somehow feel closer to the past here, making it an entirely
different proposition to Jersey's counterpart; if you've
seen one underground hospital, don't assume you've
seen the other. These tunnels in St Andrew's took more
than three-and-a-half years to build but were operational
for only nine months. Today, renovated or not, this particular Nazi nest can still serve as an appropriately
solemn memorial to the slave workers who died here.

Blanchelande Girls College ❹ occupies the site of
a former boys' college, founded in 1904 by a French
religious order, the Brothers of Christian Schools. It's
not the college that the people come to see but the
famous Little Chapel (accessible all year) built in its
grounds. This miniature church is largely the work of a
monk, Déodat, who had the novel idea of decorating his
creation with thousands of pieces of broken china. The
result is one of the most outlandish mosaics you are

LEFT: the
shore at Fort Grey.
BELOW:
Little Chapel at
Blanchelande
Girls College

ever likely to see. Modelled on the grotto in the Church of Lourdes, the **Little Chapel** is barely 16 ft (5 metres) long and has difficulty accommodating even a dozen people. The chapel standing today is the last in a sequence of three. Déodat started work on a smaller first version in March 1914 but demolished it immediately after it was built. The second one stood until 1923; it was in that same year he started the present building. In 1939, when he returned to France due to ill health, the care of the chapel was entrusted to a fellow monk, Brother Cephas, who continued with the decoration until he retired in 1965.

Just beyond the chapel, some of the farm buildings on the estate are used by **Guernsey Clockmakers**, who make and sell a collection of clocks and barometers many of which easily match Déodat's creation for novelty value (open Mon–Fri 8.30am–5.30pm, Sat 10am–4pm).

The boundary of **St Martin's Parish** lies less than half-a-mile to the south of St Peter Port. The tricky and winding road of Val des Terres takes you to the **Aquarium ❺** (open Mon–Sat 10am–6pm, Sun 10am–5.30pm), still in the parish of St Peter Port (*see also page 181*). This started life in 1861 as a tunnel that was supposed to extend the road along La Vallette into Fermain Bay. The Aquarium has two sections: one for fish found in European waters, the other for tropical varieties. Despite the inclusion of oddities such as a fish found off Mexico whose name translates as "the fish that carries a needle and grunts like a pig", it's not especially inspiring.

Close by, La Vallette heralds the start of Guernsey's longest unbroken walk, almost 20 miles (32km) of undulating cliff paths which wend their way along the south coast as far as Pleinmont Point. The walk takes in such sights as the 100-metre high cliffs at Moulin Huet from which Renoir painted the rocky outcrops known as the Pea Stacks, and Le Gouffre, immortalised by Victor Hugo in *The Toilers of the Sea*. Walkers are never more than 1 mile (1½km) away from a bus route, and there are plenty of cafés and hotels en route at which to stop for a breather.

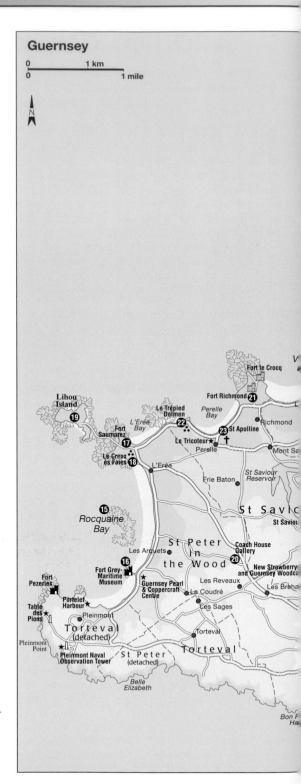

Guernsey

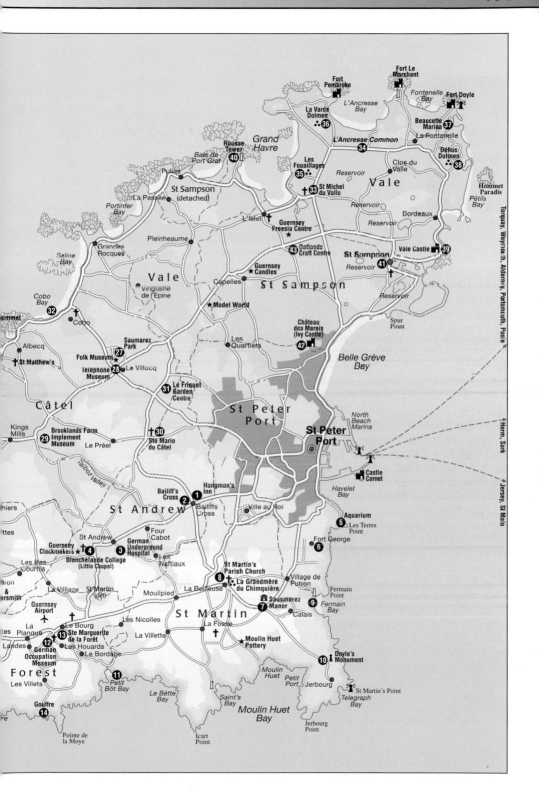

Fort Le Marchant

Fort Pembroke

Fontenelle Bay

Fort Doyle

L'Ancresse Bay

La Varde Dolmen ❹36

Beaucette Marina ❹37

La Fontenelle

L'Ancresse Common ❹34

Déhus Dolmen

Rousse Tower ❹40

Grand Havre

Les Fouaillages ❹35

Clos du Valle

Déhus Dolmen ❹38

Baie de Port Grat

Pulias

Reservoir

Vale

Hommet Paradis

Pétils Bay

St Sampson (detached)

La Passée

Portinfer Bay

St Michel du Valle ✝❹33

Reservoir

L'Islet

Guernsey Freesia Centre

Reservoir

Bordeaux

Grandes Rocques

Pleinheaume

Oatlands Craft Centre ❹43

St Sampson

Vale Castle ■❹39

Saline Bay

Vale

Vingtaine de l'Epine

Guernsey Candles ★

St Sampson ❹41 ✝

Cobo Bay ❹32

Cobo

★ Model World

Capelles

S t   S a m p s o n

Reservoir

Spur Point

ommet

Saumarez Park ❹27

Les Quartiers

Château des Marais (Ivy Castle) ❹42

Belle Grève Bay

Albecq

✝ St Matthew's

Folk Museum ★

Telephone Museum ❹28

Le Villocq

Le Friquet Garden /Centre ❹31

North Beach Marina

C â t e l

St Peter Port

Kings Mills

Brooklands Farm Implement Museum ❹29

✝❹30

Ste Marie du Câtel

Le Préel

St Peter Port

✝

Castle Cornet ■

Havelet Bay

Hangman's Inn ❶

Bailiff's Cross ❷

Bailiffs Cross

Ville au Roi

Aquarium ❺ Les Terres Point

S t   A n d r e w

Four Cabot

Fort George ❻

hiers

Guernsey Clockmakers ★ ❹4

St Andrew

German Underground Hospital ❸

Les Naftiaux

St Martin's Parish Church ✝❽ ✝✝ La Grandmère du Chimquière

Village de Putron

ttes

Les Bas Courtils

Blanchelande College (Little Chapel)

Fermain Point

aron &

La Villiaze

St Martin (ch)

La Belleuse

Mouilpied

Sausmarez Manor ❼

Fermain Bay ❾

ersmith

Guernsey Airport ✈

✝

Calais

La Plan que

Le Bourg

Ste Marguerite de la Forêt ❹13

Les Nicolles

La Fosse

S t   M a r t i n

La Villette

✝

Moulin Huet Pottery ★

tes

German Occupation Museum ❹12

Les Houards

Le Bordage

Doyle's Monument ❹10 ⛭

Landes

F o r e s t

Les Villets

Petit Bôt Bay ❹11

Le Bétte Bay

Moulin Huet

Petit Port Jerbourg

St Martin's Point ⛭

Telegraph Bay

Gouffre ❹14

Saint's Bay

Moulin Huet Bay

Jerbourg Point

Pointe de la Moye

Icart Point

Torquay, Weymouth, Alderney, Portsmouth, Poole

← Herm, Sark

Jersey, St Malo →

Statuary at Saumarez Manor.

BELOW:
Sausmarez Manor.

Sausmarez Manor

Once you've climbed the steep hill of Val des Terres you'll pass the site of **Fort George ❻**. Constructed between 1780 and 1812, it was used by the Germans in World War II and was bombed by Allied planes in 1944 in preparation for D-day.

Fort George is still in the parish of St Peter Port. Go to **Sausmarez Manor ❼** and you'll cross the parish boundary into St Martin's. The de Sausmarez family has for centuries been one of Guernsey's most distinguished dynasties. Over the years its sons have served as bailiffs, governors, naval officers and in the Foreign Office. There are recorded references, as long ago as 1254, to a forebear by the name of William de Saumareis, who was Seigneur of Samares in St Clement, Jersey. It is not known when he acquired his new fief in St Martin's parish in Guernsey, though it's likely its manor house occupied much the same site as today's.

Sausmarez Manor retains only a fragment of the ancient building in the form of an outhouse containing stonework that dates from the mid-13th century. Since then, the manor house has been added to many times. Its most distinguishing feature is the Queen Anne facade, which was erected between 1714 and 1718, and replaced an earlier Tudor building. The de Sausmarez family didn't always live here. In 1557, Seigneur George de Sausmarez died without an heir and the manor passed into the hands of John Andros. In all, six members of the Andros family became Seigneur, after which, in 1748, the manor returned to the original owners.

Sausmarez Manor is one of the best-preserved 18th-century buildings in the Channel Islands and the organised tours around the grounds and the house are

well worth taking. The refreshing lack of austerity is due to the fact that the manor is still lived-in. In fact, it's one of the most hospitable museums you're ever likely to come across (open daily 10am–5pm).

Though it is still eminently stately, with tapestries, paintings and a wealth of magnificent antique furniture and effects to fill you with envy. It was a refusal on the part of Sir Havilland de Sausmarez to keep up with the times that saved much of this heritage from the Nazis. In 1940, the Germans were intending to use Sausmarez Manor as a hospital but decided not to go ahead with their plans because the house did not yet have electric lighting.

Attractions in the grounds of Sausmarez Manor include a nine-hole pitch and putt golf course, and a dolls' house shop and collection.

St Martin's Parish Church ❽ is best known for the engaging and much-photographed menhir which stands outside it. The statue, most of which was carved around 2,500 BC, originally stood in the churchyard and was named La Grandmère du Chimquière (the Old Lady of the Cemetery). It later served as the left pillar of the churchyard gate. It is believed the crack through its torso was the result of an attack by a churchwarden who was angry over the worshipping of stone idols.

Saumarez Manor miniature railway.

Hugging the coast

Guernsey folk acknowledge 30 bays around the island, but there are others they keep to themselves. The finest are along the southeastern and southern coasts. They are a challenge to find and sometimes even more of a challenge to climb down to. But then that's half the fun.

Partly in the parish of St Peter Port and partly in the parish of St Martin is **Fermain Bay** ❾, one of the island's most popular summer haunts as well as the starting point of a long cliff walk that will take you right along the south coast to Pleinmont. During the summer months, a boat service links Fermain Bay to St Peter Port, and this is a romantic way to reach the beach, though most people approach the bay along the paths leading south from the main airport road from where there is a regular bus service into St Peter Port.

Like Fort George, **Doyle's Monument** ❿, a short walk beyond Fermain Bay, was a victim of World War II, though this time it was the Germans who were responsible for its removal. You pass the site of this erstwhile 100-ft (30-metre) tower on your way to **Telegraph Bay**. Today the memorial that has taken its place provides good views out to the Normandy coast.

Lieutenant-General Sir John Doyle (1750–1834) was to Guernsey what General Don was to Jersey. Doyle directed the building of Fort George and urged the States to reclaim Braye du Valle, the low-lying land in the north of the island which flooded at high tide and daily turned Clos du Valle into an island. The sale of the land that was thereby gained paid for the construction of Guernsey's military roads.

Doyle was also responsible for three Martello towers – Fort Grey, Fort Saumarez and Fort Hommet – which were built after a number of smaller towers

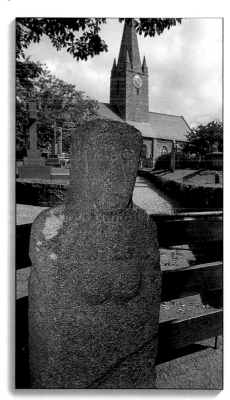

BELOW: Grandmère du Chimquière at St Martin's Parish Church.

Doyle's Monument.

BELOW: Napoleonic tower at Petit Bôt.

erected more than 20 years earlier had been criticised for being too small to provide effective firepower. Before Doyle arrived on the scene, the peninsula on which Doyle's Monument stood had already been fortified. You can still make out the three parallel lines of ramparts and trenches running to the cliff edge to either side of the site of the monument. These were originally thought to be Roman but are in fact part of an even older Iron Age fortification. The stone-walling west of the monument is the only remnant of Château de Jerbourg, a medieval castle much mentioned in ancient documents.

The next three coves along this stretch of coast, **Petit Port**, **Moulin Huet** and **Saint's Bay**, are all still within the parish of St Martin. A steep path near Doyle's Monument leads down to the first of these. Roads go down close to the other two and the cliff path also provides access.

Whether you are walking, cycling or driving around, the lanes weaving their way down near the coast are like a maze. As each lane leads into another, there's a signpost to **Moulin Huet Pottery**. If you can't find it at first, don't give up. It's a small, unassuming workshop turning out a tasteful selection of wares. You can watch the pottery being made at the back of the building and there's no pressure on you to buy (open daily 10am–5pm).

Petit Bôt ⓫ is one of the island's smallest beaches. A one-way road leads down from Forest Church and up again into St Martin. Petit Bôt attracts its fair share of visitors when the weather is good. With the Martello tower, and a tearoom occupying what was once an old mill, this tiny opening onto the sea is inclined to get crowded. Dotted around the island are old water lanes, and it is here, as in Moulin Huet, that the best-known ones are to be found. The water lanes follow *douits* (streams) down to a bay. Only a few remain and they give a feel of how the island used to be before the Occupation, when the Germans surfaced over most of the *douits*.

German Occupation Museum

The **German Occupation Museum** ⓬ (open Apr–Oct 10am–5pm, winter 10am–1pm) is not far from Route de Petit Bôt. Guernsey figured just as prominently as Jersey in Hitler's fortification of the Channel Islands (more than 66,000 mines were laid around Guernsey alone) and this museum has assembled an exhaustive collection of Nazi memorabilia. Its detailed collection of documents is a welcome change from the sight of guns, shells and all the paraphernalia of combat. The permits, orders and censored newspapers on display give you a good idea of what the day-to-day life of ordinary islanders was like. One exhibit, an excerpt from the States Memoranda to the German authorities, dramatically underlines the food and fuel shortage that gripped the island after the Allies had landed in Normandy.

The museum is also good on Guernsey's wartime domestic lifestyle. An "Occupation Kitchen" sets the scene in late 1944, curtains drawn for curfew at 9 o'clock and a crystal set brought out for the British Broadcasting Corporation news. In another room the reconstruction of an entire street depicts a number of sites – a bicycle store, a shop, a café and other buildings – in St Peter Port. The re-creation shows them as they looked during the Occupation.

Near to the Occupation Museum, the **Parish Church of Ste. Marguerite de la Forêt** ⓭ is thought to have been built on the site of a dolmen. The oldest part of the church, the southeast corner of the present building, rests on a series of boulders that seem to have formed part of a pagan burial chamber. The circular churchyard suggests that it does trace the shape of an ancient burial mound.

If you follow the road to the right of the Forest Church and turn left at a crossroads further on, you'll reach a mini-waterfall at the cliff edge called the **Gouffre** ⓮. The wife of Mr Guille, co-founder of the Guille-Allès Library, fell to her death here. There's an observation platform to protect you these days; you can walk beyond it to the end of La Moye Point right down to a small harbour at the end.

Western wrecks

Your first glimpse of **Rocquaine Bay** ⓯ as you cross Guernsey's southwestern corner is dramatic. At low tide it stretches more than 2 miles (3 km) to the tip of Lihou Island. Towards the southern end of the bay, sitting squat against a flat rocky shore, is **Fort Grey** ⓰, one of the island's three "true" Martello towers (open April–Sept daily 10am–5pm). Fort Grey's location, situated on a small islet and connected to the shore tower on the wide battlements, has earned it the nickname of "the Cup and Saucer".

Like all of the Martello towers in the islands, Fort Grey was built as a defence against French invasion. it was erected in 1804. There was, however a much

Map on pages 190–1

Much of Guernsey is best seen on foot.

BELOW: the German Occupation Museum.

On the lookout at the Maritime Museum.

BELOW: the Maritime Museum, known as "the cup and saucer".

earlier stronghold here. From the 17th century onwards there are references to a small castle known as Château de Rocquaine having stood on this site.

Maritime Museum

Today Fort Grey is Guernsey's **Maritime Museum**, and there could be no better site for it. The sea surrounding the island's western tip is a ship's graveyard which has seen countless vessels founder on the notoriously dangerous rocks of Les Hanois. Victor Hugo said of them: "These rocks – these midnight assassins – have filled the cemeteries of Torteval and Rocquaine." The earliest reference to them, however, concerns a wreck described more than six centuries ago in an Assize Roll dated 1309. When you stand behind the walls of Fort Grey today it's a sobering thought to ponder the loss of life that has taken place less than two miles away from you. There's a gun pointing out to Hanois Lighthouse that was salvaged from HMS *Boreas*, which sank in 1807. On that occasion alone 195 lives were lost. Local researchers have managed to locate and name over 100 shipwrecks in the vicinity between 1734 and 1974.

Guernsey was for a long time the cornerstone of two very important sea routes: the transatlantic run to the United States, and the southerly run from Britain and northern Europe down into the Mediterranean. Most disasters occurred in the 19th century when traffic on these trade routes had reached a peak and was as yet unaided by the Hanois Lighthouse, which wasn't completed until 1862.

Fort Grey's museum tells the shipwreck story in detail. The upper floor traces the history of navigation while the lower floor displays the finds of Guernsey's underwater archaeologists. It's a diverse display that features a whole range of

Map
on pages
190–1

finds from elegant silver candelabra that once graced the table of a naval captain serving in the reign of George III to a ship's bell, salvaged from the sea, which visitors are invited to ring as they climb the stairs.

The promontory of **L'Erée** forms the northern arm of Rocquaine Bay. From here, gravel paths run along the north of the island to St Peter Port; when combined with the coastal path of the south, these form the route for the 40-mile round-the-island charity walk that takes place each summer. **Fort Saumarez** ⑰ recalls Lord James Saumarez, one navigator who was unhindered by the hidden rocks in this bay. In 1794 he defeated five attacking French frigates with his ship, HMS *Crescent*. During World War II, the Germans crowned Fort Saumarez with a four-storey observation tower. Today this curious hybrid is on private land and is not open to the public.

While you are in this area you can visit **Le Creux ès Faies** ⑱ (Fairy Cave), Guernsey's third largest megalithic tomb, if you can find it. Locate L'Erée Hotel and you're about 1,000 ft (300 metres) away.

Pagan worshippers had also been busy on **Lihou Island** ⑲. When a handful of Benedictine monks arrived from the Abbey of Mont St Michel, probably in 1114, they found three dolmens and seven menhirs and used the stones as foundations for their chapel Notre Dame de la Roche. Catholicism ruled until the Reformation, when the chapel fell into ruins, some of which remain. Apart from a solitary farmhouse the island is windswept and barren, and although accessible via L'Erée twice a day at low tide, by Guernsey law only islanders were allowed to make that crossing until the States of Guernsey bought it from the owners for £435,000 in 1994. *(For detailed coverage of Lihou, see pages 275–77.)*

Within sight of Lihou Island and at the most southerly end of Rocquaine Bay, **Guernsey Pearl** and **Guernsey Coppercraft** is a tourist centre where, next to the in-house café and showroom, you can see the coppersmith busy in his workshop.

Take the road north again, to where the road divides at La Rue du Catioroc and La Route de la Perelle, and another kind of craftsman can be seen at work, one who works which a needle instead of hammer. For **Le Tricoteur** is a knitwear shop dedicated to Guernsey knitwear, including the traditional Guernsey, a hard-wearing sweater.

Further inland, south along L'Erée Road, and you will eventually arrive at the **Coach House Gallery** ⑳, where there's a tasteful selection of painting and ceramics from Guernsey and farther afield displayed for sale (open daily 11am–5pm). The Coach House is a sympathetically restored complex of old farm buildings. The gallery was started in 1975 at Braye du Valle, in the north of Guernsey, by a group of practising artists and enthusiasts. The Coach House Gallery has established a good reputation; past exhibitors here include Sir Hugh Casson.

St Saviour

The **Parish of St Saviour** is roughly rectangular in shape. It has the airport on its southeastern edge and a coastline that takes in all of **Perelle Bay**. "Perelle" is derived from the Celtic word for rock and at low

In centuries past, troops from nearby Fort Saumarez took to hiding in the "haunted" Creux ès Faies when too drunk to report for duty. To prevent them, an exasperated colonel had the ancient tomb filled with stones, to the chagrin of future archaeologists.

BELOW:
Perelle Bay.

tide the bay is a lunar landscape of rocks. This bay was always a good location for collecting ormers. Duncan's History of Guernsey quotes one observer who estimated that a crowd of 200 people on 9 March 1841 gathered an astonishing 20,000 in three hours.

When the tide is out and the rocks emerge Perelle Bay looks rather desolate and uninviting. **Fort Richmond** ㉑, a curious looking barrack house that gives the impression of having been dropped into a large hole so that its roof is not much higher than ground level, and **Fort Le Crocq** hardly compensate. Both of these fortifications were built in the 19th century and have long been neglected.

At the southern end of Perelle Bay, on Le Catioroc Point, is **Le Trépied Dolmen** ㉒. Less than 20 ft (6 metres) long, this dolmen, like many others in Guernsey, was excavated by F. C. Lukis in the 19th century, and is said to have been the scene for witches' sabbaths in the 16th and 17th centuries.

A much earlier and fortunately less neglected building lies a few hundred metres inland from the centre of Perelle Bay. **St Apolline's Chapel** ㉓ (open during daylight hours), which dates from the end of the 14th century, is the only medieval chapel surviving in Guernsey. Dedicated to a deaconess who was burnt alive by the Romans in the 3rd century, it's just 27 ft long and 13 ft wide (9 by 4 metres), and contains some restored frescoes. Before the Reformation this would have been just one of many similar chapels in Guernsey. Before it was acquired by the States in the 19th century, it was being used as a stable.

Among the island's Millennium projects was the path around St Saviour's Reservoir, or in less prosaic terms, the creation of a 2½ mile (4km) walk to the

Memorials in St Saviour's burial ground include one to 11 Irishwomen who were drowned in a shipwreck in Perelle Bay in 1819 on their way from Jersey to Falmouth.

BELOW:
St Saviour's Tunnel, as it once was.

Map on pages 190–1

water at Moulin du Beauvallet, where the old village mill used to be. Car parks are situated at either end of the dam wall.

There are references to the original **Parish Church of St Saviour** ㉔ as early as 1030. The building you see today conforms to the usual story of additions and renovations, though much of it dates from the 14th and 15th centuries and from rebuilding carried out in the 17th century after lightning struck the tower.

The New Strawberry Farm

Since its major overhaul, the **New Strawberry Farm** ㉕ (open daily 10am–5pm) has continued to grow only a small quantity of strawberries, destined for the cream teas served on-site, using gro-bags suspended in mid-air. The main thrust of the business now takes place at adjacent Aubrey's, a licensed 200-seat restaurant and café popular for children's parties, together with a small shopping mall and children's adventure activity areas. At weekends the restaurant is transformed into Aubrey's Showbar and features musical and comedy tribute acts. Outside is a pitch and putt.

Contiguous to the farm is the workshop of **Guernsey Woodcarvers** (open daily 10am–5pm), where craftsmen work on a variety of projects involving the restoration of antique furniture or the creation of new items, from lathe-turned bowls and lamps to cabinets, cupboards and music stands.

The **Bruce Russell Goldsmith, Silversmith and Jewellery Shop** (open Mon–Fri 9am–5pm, Sat–Sun 10am–5pm) feeds an entirely different appetite. When the Huguenots sought refuge in the Channel Islands in the 16th century they brought with them considerable expertise in silver and gold. Bruce Russell makes no particular attempt to link himself with that tradition, though his family has been engaged in this craft for two generations, making beautiful objects from gold and silver, including candlesticks, goblets, napkin rings and spoons, caskets and jewellery.

Fort Hommet and the Folk Museum

Guernsey's largest parish is **Castel**. Right at the centre of the island's northern coastline, it takes in Vazon Bay, Cobo Bay, Saline Bay and Port Soif.

The beach of **Vazon Bay** is a wide expanse of firm sand. Beneath it are the remains of a submerged forest, evidence of which is exposed periodically by storms. As well as being a good windsurfing bay, the wide flat beach is used in summer for motorbike racing. On the northern headland of Vazon Bay is the partly restored Martello tower of **Fort Hommet** ㉖. It still has German pillboxes and gun positions which can be seen clinging to its stonework.

A short way up the road is the best museum in the parish, the **Guernsey Folk Museum**, set up by the Guernsey National Trust in **Saumarez Park** ㉗ (open daylight hours) off Cobo Road (not to be confused with Sausmarez Manor in St Martin). The original part of the house was built in the early 18th century by William Le Marchant before it came, through

BELOW: Guernsey Woodcarvers.

The gardens at Saumarez Park, laid out in the 1880s, reflect the taste of St James Vincent de Saumarez, the fourth Lord Saumarez, who spent much of his life as a diplomat in the British Embassy in Paris. The less formal shrubberies are planted with the camellias and bamboos that he saw during diplomatic visits to Japan.

BELOW:
the Folk Museum
at Saumarez Park.

marriage, into the hands of the de Saumarez family. The main building, which belongs to the States of Guernsey, has been turned into a hostel for elderly people, though you may tour the downstairs rooms (open 10am–8pm daily). the grounds are open to all. The stables house the Folk Museum, a thorough exhibition of Guernsey's rural memorabilia (open 24 Mar–31 Oct daily 10am–5pm). Founded in 1968, it is based on a collection of agricultural implements collected by one of the Langlois family.

The museum recreates a number of period rooms such as a kitchen, a bedroom, a wash-house dairy, a cider barn and a cartroom. Many of the costumes and pieces of furniture are more than 100 years old and in excellent condition. With sepia-tone photographs of thick-whiskered farmers dressed in smocks and clutching hay forks helping to tell the story of Guernsey's rural life in the 19th century, the Folk Museum oozes rural nostalgia, and, while parents can enjoy a trip down memory lane inside the museum and tea rooms, outside in the grounds Saumarez Park houses the largest and safest outdoor playground in the island.

Telephones and other implements

If the Folk Museum is the best museum in the parish, then the **Telephone Museum** ㉘ (open June Mon–Sat 2pm–5pm, July–Aug Mon–Sat 10am–5pm; free), just a few hundred metres away, certainly deserved its reputation as the smallest up till recently. When it was inaugurated in 1976, it occupied a mere 650 sq ft (198 sq metres) of the ground floor of an unassuming suburban house and seemed bent on anonymity, situated as it was on a one-way system that meant many visitors would pass nearby without ever noticing it. Items returned to the

Map on pages 190–1

Guernsey Telecoms following the automation of the island's telephone system constituted its displays, and the museum was for confirmed phonophiles only.

Things changes in the mid-1990s when the museum underwent a complete refurbishment, simultaneously spreading out to occupy almost double the space it had once laid claim to – including the front garden, where a display of weather-defying exhibits took up residence. In 2001, the museum was once more extended. In its present incarnation it houses a collection of telephones, switchboards and telephone memorabilia tracing the history of telecommunications up to the fibre optics of today, with working models that will appeal to children.

Similarly, **Brooklands Farm Implement Museum** ㉙ (open Apr–Sept Tues–Sat 9.30am–4.30pm) at Kings Mill is primarily of interest to those with a love of the land. On this ancient site three water mills once stood, drawing their power from the Talbot Valley stream. The museum, set in a cluster of traditional farm buildings, explains the work of a typical mixed farm using displays of the tools and implements employed on the island before the war.

Brooklands Farm Implement Museum.

The correct name of Castel Church is **Ste. Marie du Câtel** ㉚. It's said the church was built on the site of a Viking fort, Le Château du Grand Sarazin, from which the parish takes its strategic name. The view today's church commands over the sea to Alderney, Herm and even the French coast suggests it would have been a strategically valuable site. There are references to Castel Church from 1155 in a document confirming that it was then under the patronage of Mont St Michel. The Neolithic menhir that stands outside the main door was excavated from under the chancel in 1878 during restoration work. Below this are the stone seats belonging to the officials of the medieval court of the Fief St Michel, with more recent archaeological finds on show inside the church.

Le Friquet ㉛ garden centre was once popular with tourists for its tropical butterflies, but it is still possible to enjoy the site, now comprised of a mini golf, a crazy croquet and a restaurant.

BELOW: Guernsey Folk Museum.

In praise of folly

Follow the Cobo Road coastwards and you'll reach **Cobo Bay** ㉜. If you recognise the distinctive pink-red hue of the rocks along the coast here and in Albecq Bay you should award yourself full marks for observation. This stone known as Cobo granite has long been a source of stone for buildings on the west side of the island; **St Matthew's Church**, at the southern end of the bay, is a striking example of its use.

One of the oldest dwellings discovered in the Channel Islands was excavated at **Ruette de la Tour**. The earliest of several houses, all built on the same foundation, was a longhouse dating from the 10th century. The **Ozanne Tower** is a recent acquisition by the National Trust and a feature of the Saumarez Nature Trail. This distinctive, square-shaped structure in grey granite dates from the mid-19th century, although it has been suggested that

the base stones of the tower might have been part of a prehistoric tomb. It was erected as a folly by the Ozanne family, whose coat of arms is clearly visible above the door to the tower, before passing into the hands of the de Saumarez family. It then served in turn as a museum to house the artefacts Lord de Saumarez picked up during his travels abroad and later, having been sold to the States of Guernsey, as a lookout tower during the German occupation. The tower does indeed afford enviable views of the west coast of the island and the National Trust plans to restore this worthy recipient of their care to its original use as a belvedere.

Hidden tombs

Guernsey's second largest parish is **Vale**, though you have to include both parts of it. Look at the map and you'll see that the northern part of Guernsey comprises two parts of Vale and two parts of St Sampson. There's little to see as such in the southern **Vingtaine de L'Epine**, but there's lots to keep you occupied in the northern **Clos du Valle**.

Until 1806, Clos du Valle wasn't even part of the mainland. La Braye du Valle was flooded daily at high water, making this northern extremity of Guernsey an island only reached by a bridge at St Sampson's. The reclamation of 300 acres (120 hectares) of land in La Braye du Valle was engineered by the building of an embankment at the head of Grand Havre in the north.

The clearest landmark you'll see as you approach La Braye du Valle around Grand Havre is Vale Church. More properly known as **St Michel du Valle** ㉝, the church was consecrated in 1117. Spare a thought for ancient worshippers ordinarily resident in Vingtaine de L'Epine who, before Doyle's interven-

BELOW: Cobo Bay.

tion in La Braye du Valle, were no doubt obliged frequently to negotiate the incoming or outgoing tide before they were able to enter God's house.

At Vale Church you are right on the edge of **L'Ancresse Common** ③, where golf reigns supreme. Your view across the common is barely interrupted by the gently undulating landscape – a mixture of common, rocky outcrops, pine trees, gorse, heather and numerous "Martello towers" dotted across the horizon. When you look at this, at times, rather bleak scene it's a little difficult to believe that you are just 6 or 7 miles (10 or 11 km) from the steep, craggy and beautiful cliff walks on the south coast of the island.

A Channel Islands travel guide published in 1911 made much out of L'Ancresse Common: "It is usual for visitors to pay one visit to L'Ancresse and to dispose of the district in an afternoon's ramble. So much the worse for the visitor. Many days can be well and profitably spent in exploring this out-of-the-way part of Guernsey."

Precisely how many days you spend up here on L'Ancresse Common will depend entirely on how successful you are in searching out some of the cunningly hidden ancient remains that lurk here. A few hundred metres north of Vale Church (ask any golfer for directions to the fifth hole) **Les Fouaillages** ③ were discovered in 1978. These small burial chambers set within a large triangle of stones in the ground have excited much archaeological interest. The layman is likely to be more impressed to discover that pottery found near this site is believed to date as far back as 4,500 BC.

A few hundred metres further to the north, **La Varde Dolmen** ③ is much easier to find. And so it should be, for it is the largest megalithic structure in Guernsey. This passage grave, running more than 40 ft (12 metres) into a high mound, is covered by six enormous capstones, one of which is over 16 ft (5 metres) long. The tomb was discovered in 1811 by soldiers while undertaking military exercises. The event was doubly significant because among those who came to have a look was F. C. Lukis, Guernsey's best-known archaeologist. It is said that the young Lukis went home with a skull under his arm – a prize that went to form the nucleus of the future Lukis Museum.

Rounding the tip

A perfect place enjoy a lofty view of Guernsey's north shore is from the roof of the restaurant overlooking **Beaucette Marina** ③. As you approach, all you'll see will be the tops of masts bobbing about. The marina was originally a quarry until somebody decided that it might make a good place to park an ocean-going yacht or two.

The restaurant here combines first-class seafood with surprisingly modest prices. After all, most of the clientele could no doubt afford much more. If you wonder where some of the tax exiles in the Channel Islands hang out, Beaucette Marina must surely be one of their haunts. On a good day the car park boasts more than its fair share of Porsches, Mercedes and other sleek cars, though the yachts in the marina put the motor cars to shame.

Fort Doyle, named after Guernsey's military road

Map on pages 190–1

Les Fouaillages burial chambers.

BELOW: waiting for the bus.

builder, is at the end of this promontory, but the modifications made by the Germans mean there's little to see.

Two other locations between Beaucette and St Sampson each recall famous Guernsey names. A few hundred metres offshore is an unassuming island called Hoummet Paradis, made famous by Victor Hugo as the home of a character in his book *The Toilers of the Sea*.

A short distance before you reach Vale Castle is another of the megalithic finds excavated by F. C. Lukis in the 19th century, **Le Déhus Dolmen** ㊳. This passage grave is the second largest on the island. More than 60 years before Lukis attended to this tomb's history, a resident of Guernsey bought the site for £4 10s (£4.50) to prevent it from being broken up and destroyed by quarrymen.

Another site of considerable antiquity is **Vale Castle** ㊴. It's unfortunate that so little of this fortress remains. The ramparts are solid enough, though the rest of the fortress doesn't live up to the promise it seems to hold you as you first approach. When Clos du Valle was effectively a separate island it would no doubt have been a strategic site; but now that the waters have been forced to recede, Vale Castle looks rather forlorn, like a stranded whale.

The earliest occupation of the hill on which the castle stands is said to date from the Iron Age, when, around 600 BC, a double-banked hill-fort is believed to have stood here. Excavations in 1980 revealed that the first medieval fortification was erected around the year 1400, when a number of buildings were constructed close to the existing walls. There are further references to the castle in the 16th and 17th centuries. During the French Wars in the late 18th century barracks were built; these were demolished in 1945 by the Germans and the miniature "street pattern" of cobblestones is all that remains.

Sir John Doyle, who served as the island's lieutenant-governor from 1803 to 1815, gave his name to Fort Doyle in Guernsey and Fort Doyle in Alderney and had a monument erected in his honour at Jerbourg.

BELOW:
Le Déhus Dolmen.

THE GREENHOUSE EFFECT

Greenhouses were originally built on Guernsey in 1805 to cultivate grapes, and by 1830 a gentleman just wasn't a gentleman if he didn't have a vinery in his garden. Originally, commercial greenhouses were set up to supply the demand for early season fruits – and tomatoes in particular.

The story of the tomato, in Guernsey at least, is one of decline. In 1957, more than 9 million 12-lb (5-kg) trays were exported, while in one recent year fewer than 500,000 red tomatoes in 6-kilo trays left the island. Although just under 2 million trays of cherry tomatoes (a "newer" breed in Guernsey) were exported, the biggest growth industry has seen growers switch from tomato to flower cultivation.

Over 1 million boxes of flowers are now being sent abroad, and postal flowers and pot plants represent a new avenue which Guernsey and Jersey growers are exploiting to the full. Today Guernsey exports 40 million roses to mainland Britain every year – apparently the high light levels enjoyed by the island encourage the growth of long straight stems, perfect for cut flowers of all kinds.

A shattering threat to Guernsey's greenhouses was posed in the 1970s by potential supersonic shock waves from early Air France Concorde flights en route to South America. Happily, they flew over the island subsonically.

Also in the Vale, behind the Peninsula Hotel at Les Dicqs is **Rousse Tower** ⑩ and battery, the first 18th-century sea defence which has been restored by the Heritage Committee and Tourism Board under their "Fortress Guernsey" programme. Several sites, including the German Naval Headquarters at St Jacques, the German Gun Casemate at Fort Hommet and the five-storey German Direction Finding Tower at Pleinmont have also been earmarked for restoration and as interpretation centres.

Map on pages 190–1

St Sampson

One of the clearest views to be had from Vale Castle is of the town of **St Sampson** ⑪, once the industrial centre of the island but now being spruced up. Although still a commercial working harbour, it has been transformed into a well equipped, £3.4 million marina whose surrounding shops and restaurants bustle in a way the parts of St Peter Port do not. Among the hidden treasures are the parish church, reckoned to be the oldest in the island. This site is where St Sampson, having studied in Wales, landed and brought Christianity to Guernsey in 550AD. Before the Braye du Val was filled in, the church stood on its shores. The Bridge Interpretation Centre, near to the Power Station, uses maps and audio-visual guides to show the reclamation of the Braye du Val and the building of St Sampson's harbour.

In all fairness to the town, St Sampson never set out to be good-looking; it was always working too hard. As the harbour from which Guernsey's granite was exported, it made a massive contribution to the island's wealth. In the mid-19th century the industry entered an unparalleled boom and St Sampson began to earn its reputation as the industrial north of Guernsey. It still plays that role to some extent. Today, most of the cargo coming into the island is off-loaded in

BELOW: cooling off.

St Sampson's harbour, and this port area will almost certainly be extended once the reclamation site at Longue Hougue has been filled in and developed.

The name of the town has charismatic origins at least. St Sampson crossed over to the Channel Islands from Brittany, where he was Bishop of Dol, in about AD 550 and is said to have landed on the shore of the natural harbour – which subsequently took his name. St Sampson, generally held to be the first to preach Christianity in Guernsey, is said to have built a chapel or oratory on the spot where the church stands today.

There's no reliable record of its construction, though it is referred to in a document of 1054. The church you see today originally stood practically on the seashore, in the same way as St Brelade's in Jersey. The most popular date claimed for the construction of this building is the year 1111.

The thoroughfare known as the Bridge, bordering the innermost part of the harbour, marks the spot where there was once a bridge connecting the mainland to Clos du Valle; reference to it is made in court records in 1204.

There are really only two or three places you are likely to want to visit in the Parish of St Sampson. Not much more than half-a-mile from the Beau Séjour Leisure Centre, and almost in the Parish of St Peter Port, **Château des Marais** ㊷ is arguably Guernsey's most curious site. Also known as Ivy Castle, this is a remarkably preserved small medieval structure. There's nothing especially curious about that, however, but to get there you have to make your way straight through a run-down and drab housing estate. The surrounding houses make for a very sorry sight – a street scene that those familiar with Britain's much talked about "inner cities" will recognise. The wealthy types patronising places like Beaucette Marina suddenly seem a million miles away.

BELOW:
the parish church.
RIGHT: brick kilns at
Oatlands Village.

The castle itself was built shortly after the loss of France by England in 1204 and is surrounded by a small moat. Late in the 18th century, during the Napoleonic Wars, the castle was refortified. The magazine and much of the existing stonework date from that period. Archaeologists believe that the mound on which Ivy Castle is built was part of a much earlier site, possibly dating from the Bronze Age. The castle itself, no longer ivy-clad, has been restored to illustrate a sequence of defences, from the earliest 13th-century moated bailey to the 18th-century powder magazine and the inevitable German concrete bunker.

The Oatlands Craft Centre

The **Oatlands Craft Centre** ❹ (open daily 9.30am–5pm), occupying what was once a brickworks, is a much more colourful alternative to St Sampson. Here you have the chance not only to acquire craftswork – glass and pottery mainly, silversmiths too – but also have a chance to watch it being made from close quarters. The potting seems tame in comparison to the glass-blowing, where you can step right inside the workshop and feel the full force of the glowing red furnace fires.

The glassblowers perform their delicate and practised task with a skill bordering on nonchalance. You can do little more than stand and stare at them work, wondering how they can take the brunt of the heat and suffer the deafening roar of the fans that feed the flames with oxygen. Sweated forced labour indeed, you might think – but you'd be wrong: the craftsmen you see here are their own bosses. The glassblowers and the potters set up Oatlands Craft Centre themselves and invited glass engravers, a silversmith and the proprietor of the patchwork shop to join them. Everybody involved expects to make a living through their wares.

Your children may persuade you to visit **Model World**, a model car and railway exhibition and shop on nearby Camp du Roi (open Tues, Thurs and Sat 2pm–5pm).

There's a further chance to indulge your taste for craftswork at **Guernsey Candles** (open daily 9am–5.30pm), located a few minutes up the road from Oatlands. While the candles here assume all kinds of extravagant, decorous and impressive configurations, there's little sense of this being a craft workshop in the same way that Oatlands is. But that doesn't matter: Guernsey Candles gets its fair share of the island's tourist traffic and the souvenir hunter could do worse than light a candle for Guernsey.

Alternatively you can choose to send a fragrant bunch of Guernsey flowers. Visit the **Guernsey Freesia Centre** (open daily 10am–5pm), and never again will you present a bunch of flowers in ignorance of the kind of expertise that went into growing them. Here you can see (and smell) freesias at different stages in their growth and watch a video detailing the history of the island's cut-flower industry. The statistics are impressive: for example, Guernsey now exports 40 million roses to mainland Britain each year. ❑

Map on pages 190–1

Guernsey Freesia Centre.

BELOW: waxing lyrical at Guernsey Candles.

THE PIN-UPS OF THE PASTURES

Jersey and Guernsey cows, long a vital part of the islands' economy, are known all over the world. Just what is it that makes them so special?

More than 100 years of carefully controlled breeding have made Channel Islands cattle among the most genetically superior livestock to be found anywhere, and the main shows (held in May and October in Jersey, July and November in Guernsey) celebrate this heritage. The breeding industry has played a vital role in ensuring the islands' continued prosperity. Animals were exported to the United Kingdom as early as 1700 and have since spread across all continents. One reason for their popularity is that they adapt easily to different climates, environments and conditions – whether the harsh winters of Canada and Scandinavia or the heat and diseases of the tropics.

Channel Islands cattle have demonstrated their efficiency at producing milk with a high butterfat concentration. They have been crossed with scores of different breeds; in India, for example, 25 million cows have been crossed with Jersey bulls.

IMPROVING THE GENETICS

No live cattle have been allowed into Jersey for close to two centuries and local farmers don't foresee this law being repealed. In Guernsey, the legislation was relaxed recently when some animals were crossed with bulls from abroad in order to improve genetics in the island's herds.

Today's farmer must be commercially-minded and understand the science of agriculture. No longer do they have to ship live animals all over the world. Instead, thanks to artificial insemination and embryo transplant techniques, Jersey and Guernsey cattle are sent overseas, 600 at a time, on board an aircraft in a vacuum flask of liquid nitrogen.

The islands' burgeoning populations and the expansion of the tourism and finance industries have fuelled local demand for dairy products and cattle are being raised more with milk, butter and cream liqueurs in mind.

▷ **ONE MAN'S MEAT**
Many people tend to rate Guernseys and Jerseys more "attractive" than some of the larger European breeds such as Holsteins and Friesians.

△ **ONE GOOD CHURN**
After the shows are over, it's the quality and quantity of the milk that counts. This Sark farmer prepares to export his milk via the daily ferry.

◁ **IT'S IN THE BREEDING**
Colour, appearance, size and shape are considered in assessing a cow for admission to the herd book. A complex points system has evolved.

KEEPING THE HERDS PURE

The Royal Jersey Agricultural and Horticultural Society was in 1833 and its Guernsey equivalent in 1842. Their introduction of official herd book registers signalled the true creation of the two breeds.

Only cattle conforming to an accepted general type qualified for the herd books, giving buyers the assurance that animals were free of disease and were of pure stock. Both islands went through a series of export booms.

Thousands of cattle went to the US and Canada. In 1919 a Jersey bull, "Sybil's Gamboge", one of the most prolific sires ever, was sold at public auction in the US, for $65,000 – a record still unequalled in real terms.

During the German Occupation (1940–45), as stocks of food ran low, hundreds of animals were requisitioned for food in Jersey. Fortunately, slaughter was controlled by the island's agricultural society officials and mainly inferior animals were taken, leaving a core of prime breeding stock at the end of the war. Today its reputation is enviable.

◁ **MUSEUM PIECE**
Dairy exhibits take pride of place at the Jersey Museum in St Helier, starring alongside Lillie Langtry memorabilia.

▷ **ROYAL APPRAISAL**
In a morale-boosting postwar visit, Princess Elizabeth and Prince Philip attend a cattle show at Saumarez Park in Guernsey in June 1949.

◁ **BEST HOOF FORWARD**
The Miss World show is amateur night compared with the intensity of a cattle show on the islands. The stakes are high.

▷ **SOUVENIR SURFEIT**
From cups to keyrings, from magnets to bookmarks, the cow's image is ubiquitous in souvenir shops.

SARK

*Its medieval ways are out of step in an age that values
democracy – and that's what attracts visitors*

Sark, the dropout's last retreat, is just 3 miles (nearly 5 km) long and 1½ miles (over 2 km) wide, and has the atmosphere of Victorian England. Cars are forbidden. The island, with a population of 560, is ruled in the manner of an independent feudal state by the Seigneur, who rides a bicycle and drives a tractor. The main settlement, "The Avenue", has the unreal air of a film set. Sark, which Victor Hugo regarded as *"la plus belle"* (the most beautiful) of the Channel Islands, has no income tax, property tax, import duty, export duty or death duty; but it does have 30 species of butterfly, 170 species of bird, plus wild orchids and sea anemones – and the world's smallest jail.

Consisting of a high flat-topped plateau, Sark is often described as two islands: Great and Little Sark are linked by a narrow natural causeway called La Coupée (the Knife), which has a 260-ft (80-metre) drop to either side. This causeway and the Seigneur's beautiful garden are the island's major tourist attractions.

The journey to Sark by ferry from St Peter Port takes 45 minutes and passes south of Herm before swinging northwards past the island of Brecqhou, bought in 1993 by the wealthy and reclusive Barclay Brothers, owners of the Ritz Hotel in London and various newspapers including *The Scotsman* and *The Daily Telegraph*. Their massive gothic castle, completed in 1998, is clearly visible as the ferry swings to the north of Sark and then comes in close beneath that island's towering cliffs, past rocks from which cormorants and shags launch themselves on fishing flights.

As you approach the harbour, you may also see fishermen laying crab and lobster pots, and numerous sea caves and evocatively shaped rocks, as well as the lighthouse on Sark's eastern flank. What you will not see is any sign of human habitation, for Sark's houses all lie at the centre of the island, in a sheltered hollow, hidden from sight as you approach by sea. To reach The Avenue, you must either climb the steep path from the harbour or hop on the "toast rack", an open-sided tractor-drawn cart given special dispensation on this car-free island. ❏

PRECEDING PAGES: the annual Jersey–Sark rowing race; La Coupée, the link with Little Sark. **LEFT:** Sark's standard public transport.

AROUND SARK

*In an island without cars, the easiest way to get around is by
horse-drawn carriage. On foot, you can explore unspoilt
beaches, smugglers' caves and abandoned silver mines*

Map
on page
218

To an extent Sark remains in its famous time-warp. At its best the island can still give you a feel of what it must have been like to have lived, not only in the Channel Islands, but in almost any rural community on France's Cotentin peninsula 100 years ago; to taste life as it was before the peace of the wooded countryside was shattered forever by the internal combustion engine and metalled roads. The Victorian poet Swinburne would probably continue to find Sark his "small, sweet world of wave-encompassed wonder".

All the same, a visitor should be warned that this last bastion of European feudalism can no longer claim to be almost entirely free of horseless carriages. It wasn't so long ago that the only powered vehicles permitted were the invalid car belonging to Dame Sybil Hathaway, whose rule during the German Occupation inspired a play in London's West End, and the tractor attached to an ambulance-van originally designed for a horse.

These days are long gone. There are now more than 60 registered tractors in Sark – about one for every nine of its 550 permanent inhabitants. John Michael Beaumont, the Dame's grandson and the present Seigneur, would like to see the number reduced, but it seems that the omnipotence of feudal rulers isn't what it used to be and the voice of the majority can't be silenced.

In fact, Sark was never feudal during the heyday of feudalism. During the 14th and 15th centuries it was raided by pirates so often that its only inhabitants were a few hermits living in the ruins of abandoned monasteries. It was reoccupied in the 16th century when Elizabeth I gave the Jerseyman Helier de Carteret the right to colonise it and thus prevent its seizure by the French.

After an initial reconnaissance convinced him that Sark was well worth cultivating, de Carteret arrived in force with 39 families and their retainers in 1565. He divided the island into 40 pieces (*ténéments*) and 39 of these were leased in perpetuity to his followers as feudal holdings. Most of the tenants built their homes as far inland as they could to shelter from the elements and hide from unwelcome visitors. To this day, the Sarkese seem to be able to live without a view of the sea.

The Seigneurie

Part of each tenant's feudal obligation to de Carteret was to mount a watch on a section of the coast as well as to provide at least one man armed with a musket for the island's defence. Elizabeth was so pleased by the way the Jerseyman had organised things that she gave him the gift of a cannon, which can still be seen, in the grounds of the present **Seigneurie ❶** (open Mon–Fri 10–5, and also Sat 10–5 in Jul and Aug).

You aren't allowed into the house itself but you can wander through its grounds and inspect the large

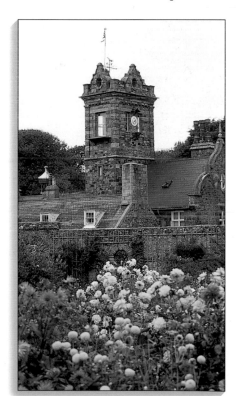

LEFT: the dovecote at the Seigneurie.
BELOW:
the Seigneurie.

*Dame Sybil
Hathaway's grave.*

walled garden where the gardeners strive to save, from the winter gales and frost, the exotic shrubbery introduced by the Dame and her grandson. (The islands have many charms, but don't let anybody try to fool you that they are almost subtropical, a silly image fostered in the days before most British holidaymakers knew what real heat was. It sadly misfired during World War II when some Britons rejected evacuees from the islands because they thought they'd be black.)

Some houses date from the 17th century, although the bulk of it was built about 1730. It wasn't conceived to any grand plan in the way of English stately homes but grew according to the quirks of succeeding seigneurs. Dame Sybil introduced a pets' graveyard with appropriate headstones on a wall where visitors can wonder at the longevity of her animals, "Mac – a gallant ratter, 1928–43", reads one.

Unfortunately, her grandfather's main contribution was even more startling. It is a square signalling tower for semaphoring messages to Guernsey because the original round one had become overgrown by trees which he was reluctant to cut down. The tower gives the house a Wodehousian "Blandings Castle"

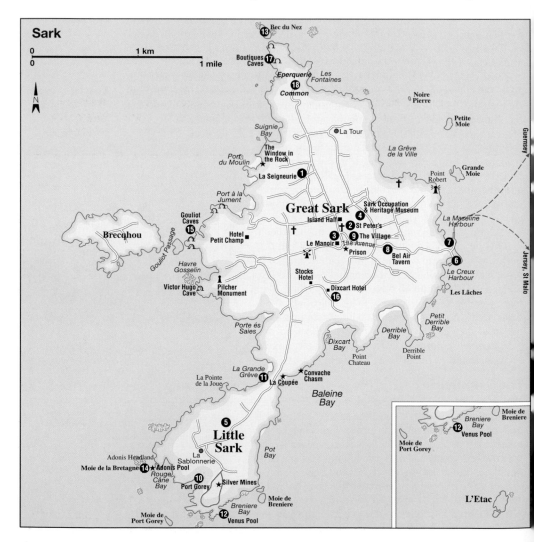

Map on facing page

theme, especially when the seigneurial standard (a St George with two gold Normandy leopards in one corner) is flying. Dame Sybil is reported to have hated this glowing example of the folly school of architecture, but could never afford to have it demolished. The seigneurial doves have made the tower their own. Only the Seigneur is allowed to keep a *colombier* (dovecote) in the same way that he or she is the only person permitted to keep an unspayed bitch.

St Peter's Church

Heading back from La Seignerie, you will pass to **St Peter's Church ❷**, built in 1820. The simple building has stained glass windows of various saints, including St Magloire, who came from Dol, in Brittany, in 565 to found a monastery on Sark. The monastery flourished, supporting 62 monks and serving as a school for the children of the Breton nobility, until marauding Viking pirates destroyed the buildings and killed the monks in the 9th century. Turning right out of the church, you will pass the inconspicuous **Island Hall**, which serves as a sports club for the island's children and as a centre for the island's social life.

Stained glass at St Peter's Church.

Alongside is the stone building that houses Sark's parliament, known as the Chief Pleas. Under the 1951 Reform (Sark) Law, the Seigneur's powers are much eroded. He can now merely delay for 21 days any proposal put by the Chief Pleas, the island's parliament, instead of vetoing it altogether. But he does still receive Le Trezième, a handy one-thirteenth part of any property deal done on the island. In 1980, shortly after he took office, Michael Beaumont was said to have received £34,000 from this ancient right. He himself pays a rent of £1.79 a year to the Queen; payment is not made directly to Buckingham Palace but to the Crown Receivers in Guernsey.

BELOW: the Seigneurie's defences

Sark's prison.

BELOW:
horse-drawn
carriages serve
as buses on this
island without cars.

The present seigneurie was originally one of the original 40 *ténéments*. Helier de Carteret himself lived at a place called **Le Manoir** ❸, on the opposite side of the road from the junior school and quite near the strange little building that looks like it might be a public lavatory, but which turns out to be the island's **prison**.

The Connetable and his assistant, the Vingtenier (so called because originally there was one for every 20 households), have greater powers than you would expect from part-time appointments: they can keep somebody in the jail for two nights, after which they have to be released or transferred to Guernsey. Its occupants are usually visiting day-trippers with bad hangovers who might be fined by the local magistrate, known as the *Seneschal*. Trippers, like tractors, are another grievous self-inflicted wound. In the high season, from July to September, they swarm ashore from Guernsey and Jersey on as many as 12 boats a day. During summer, at least 65,000 people, whose boat tickets include the landing tax demanded by the Chief Pleas, try to "do Sark" in about five hours. As a result, some of the better-known places become distinctly overpeopled. They take on a kind of Disneyland air and with it goes the sort of beerbottle-in-the-gorsebush littering often found in natural beauty spots in England.

One of the most visited spots on the island is the **Sark Occupation and Heritage Museum** ❹ (open Mon–Sat 11am–5pm). The displays include old farming implements, and photographs of island life, along with numerous relics of the Occupation. It is a short step from here to the popular Mermaid Tavern, which lies on the path that leads down to Point Robert and Sark's **lighthouse,** sat halfway down the cliff. On a clear day you can see to France from here.

Battle of the bicycles

Just how lucrative tourism has become may be judged by the saga of Sark's recent bicycle war. A great way to get around the island is by bicycle, for most of its 1,300 acres (520 hectares) is plateau fissured by narrow valleys running down to the sea. The smaller island, **Little Sark ❺**, is a bit bumpier and bicycles with gears are preferred.

For several years now it has been possible to hire machines by the day or week from two main establishments. In the summer of 1987 the former proprietor of one of these bicycle hire firms, a well-known local figure, was sent to prison in Guernsey for a month for employing children to damage or wreck the rival establishment's machines. This Fagin character laid down a scale of payments ranging from 50 pence for a puncture or cutting the brake cables to a fiver for the complete destruction of a bicycle by hurling it down the Corvanche Chasm from La Coupée, the precipitous isthmus improved by German prisoners-of-war that joins Great Sark and Little Sark. Names are withheld to protect the guilty; but it wasn't all that long ago that the perpetrator of these crimes sold his business which, under new management, now trades from Sark's main street, the Avenue.

Nowadays, if you want to avoid the trippers, it's probably best to visit during either side of the school summer holidays. Both spring and autumn are marvellous times in Sark, although the equinoctial gales that sometimes sweep the Channel can make mid-September a gamble. The tortured urban soul wishing to get the best out of the island and feel the tension drain away as he bicycles through the green tunnels or walks the cliffs, should stay at least a week.

Competition of a more beneficial sort is evident in the restaurants of the island's six hotels, and it would be invidious to pick any of them out for special attention.

Map on page 218

SARK OCCUPATION & HERITAGE MUSEUM

BELOW:
Mervyn Peake's novel *Mr Pye* was filmed for television on Sark and starred Derek Jacobi.

Pilcher Monument.

They all tend to have good *à la carte* dinner menus with plenty of locally caught fish prepared by imported young chefs anxious to make a name for themselves. Well-selected wine cellars are also a uniform feature, although prices can be disappointingly high, given the islands' carefully cultivated duty-free image.

How to get there

Sark lies 8 miles (13km) east of Guernsey and, since the only aircraft permitted to land on it are helicopters engaged in mercy missions and ferrying people to Brecqhou, the visitor must arrive by boat. There are three harbours, two on the east coast and one on the west, which is rarely used. Catamarans from Jersey via St Malo on the Brittany coast come to La Maseline Harbour while local boats and visiting yachts use **Le Creux Harbour** ❻ which was formed by blasting a tunnel through a rock wall into Baie de la Motte in 1588. It is thought to be one of the smallest harbours in the world. In the l930s a film company used it as the outdoor backcloth for Victor Hugo's *Toilers of the Sea* because they thought it was the next best thing to early 19th-century Guernsey. The company went bust and the film was never shown.

Creux is a well-sheltered place, a favourite of those yachtsmen experienced or foolish enough to sail the foggy Channel Islands' waters which wise sailors recognise as some of the most treacherous in the world. In Sark a law forbids the shooting of seagulls because of the guidance the birds' cries give mariners when the wind drops and their nesting rocks and headlands vanish into sudden sea mists. Until the mid-19th century, when it was finally conceded that another war with France was unlikely, the way into Sark's harbours was a closely guarded admiralty secret.

BELOW: Le Creux harbour, linked to the village by a tunnel and a steep walk up the hill.

Nowadays the main harbour for most shipping from Guernsey and Jersey is **La Maseline ❼**, just north of Creux in the neighbouring bay; it was begun in 1938 but, because of World War II, not completed until 1949. Overlooking it is the blue granite lighthouse at Pointe Robert. The harbour is Sark's main link with the outside world, the place where the supplies are received during the long winter months when gales bring grey seas lashing down onto its concrete quay (in summer, between boats, this is a favourite spot for line fishing, with sandeel bait).

On landing, the visitor is approached by carters whose flat-bedded wagons are pulled by tractors. The alternative to an uncomfortable, but mercifully short, cart-ride is a surprisingly steep walk to the top of the harbour hill road. Take the bus; but make certain first that your luggage is clearly identifed, for although the carters will deliver your baggage to the hotel it is not possible to travel with it all the way.

Fondly known as the "toast-rack" because of its twin benches, the main bus to **Bel Air Tavern ❽** at the top of the hill is a fairground-looking vehicle pulled by tractor. One of the bus companies, by the way, is owned by a man who first came to Sark with the British liberation forces to supervise, with prisoners-of-war labour, the clearance of 13,000 mines the Wehrmacht had planted. It is quite common on Sark to meet people who fell in love with the place on first sight, whether they be residents or holidaymakers who keep coming back year after year.

The real thing

At the top of harbour hill, just past the Bel Air pub, awaits a cab rank of horse drawn vehicles waiting to take you past the cluster of shops known as **The Avenue ❾** on a tour of the island. In most cases the drivers of these

Map on page 218

BELOW: the "toast rack", transporting visitors from harbour to hotel.

The schoolhouse.

Victorias and Wagonettes are horsestruck young ladies on a working holiday, but you may be lucky enough to be driven by a genuine Sarkee.

If you are and you have never heard a proper Channel Islands accent before – which is possible if you have simply passed through Guernsey or Jersey en route for the Sark boat – this may come as something of a shock. At one time all the inhabitants of the Iles Anglo-Normandes spoke a French patois which not only varied from island to island but from parish to parish.

The anglicisation of the islanders that started in earnest in the 1920s is now almost complete. Very few people under 50 speak patois and it will probably soon be as dead as Cornish. But it has left behind a distinct Channel Islands English, complete with French circumlocutions and local variations. Jerseymen, for instance, can sound remarkably similar to English-speaking South Africans. Both Guernseymen and Jerseymen can instantly spot a Sarkee by the way they roll their 'Rs'. And all those islanders whose speech still owes a lot to patois sauce their English with a generous lashing of aitches.

The route to your hotel may well take you down **The Avenue**, in which there are various shops, many of them selling such customary tourist tat as souvenir tee-shirts. A variation is the sale of "Sarkstone", an amethystine quartz made up into jewellery. Without VAT and other taxes, prices are quite reasonable – but don't imagine you are getting anything unique: the attractive purple stone is no longer mined on the island but comes from Zambia and China.

Mining has a rather unhappy history on Sark. Mute testimony can be found in the granite chimneys and craggy ruins growing out of the wild bracken and brambles down at **Port Gorey** ❿ on Little Sark, which is almost at the southern tip of the island.

BELOW:
The Avenue.

These are the abandoned silver mines and, without the tragedy that closed them, the present Seigneur would have never inherited his fief. Perhaps it would be best to read this tale where most of it happened.

Map on page 218

Mining for millions

To get to the mines you cross into Little Sark at La Coupée – the only dry-shod way there. There is a sign warning cyclists to dismount – though a head-on collision with another cyclist there would be a memorable experience. Before German prisoners-of-war labour put in hand-rails, school children used to have to crawl across the causeway in high winds. One day erosion will complete its job by cutting through the isthmus. **La Grande Grève Bay** ⓫ will become a strait, and the causeway itself will be transformed into a bridge. On your right a steep set of steps descends to the bay, which is good for bathing and surfing when the wind is in the right direction. The climb back up makes it only worth going down if you intend to stay a while.

Once across La Coupée, ride down to the **La Sablonnerie** and turn left up the lane just beyond it (the entrance to the hotel's tea gardens is on your right) and ride up to the point where there is a gate and a sign telling you that the track beyond it leads down to the **Venus Pool** ⓬. This pool, 10 ft (3 metres) deep and named by the Victorian artist William Toplis, who died on the island, is uncovered for two-and-a-half hours either side of a low tide. It has flat rocks around it suitable for sunbathing and in July or August, perhaps even September, a pleasant swim might be had without needing hot tea and blankets to ward off hypothermia. Perhaps it should be noted that throughout the islands small children and large ladies tend to stay longer in the water, apparently immune to its more bracing qualities.

La Coupée is 330 ft (100 metres) long and its path is 260 ft (80 metres) above sea level. It will eventually be eroded by the sea to leave Big Sark and Little Sark as separate islands in the same way that Jethou was cut off from Herm.

BELOW:
Grand Grève.

To get to the old mine-workings, do not go through the gate; descend instead through the gorse to the right of it towards the inlet called **Port Gorey**. The tracks go through bracken and brambles and, in September, bushes heavy with blackberries and sloes. A slope near the top is sometimes used as a rubbish tip and, if the smell doesn't give it away, the circling crows and gulls will. (Ordinary landbirds of the thrush and blackbird variety are, by the way, unusually tame on the island.) You can already see the first of the ruins. The chimneys are the most intact. They were the air vents.

Silver was discovered on Sark in the 1830s and Cornish miners were brought over to work it. One of the principal shareholders in the newly formed Guernsey and Sark Mining Company was the Seigneur, Pierre Le Pelley. Test bores promised an Arizona but the veins were narrow and, although the company kept a Sark silver tea set in their St Peter Port office to impress potential investors, the big vein of ore always seemed to be just around the corner. One of the eight galleries is now extended 200 ft (60 metres) under the seabed and sometimes the Cornishmen could hear an angry sea rolling bottom boulders along its roof. Maintenance expenses were heavy. There was a constant need to install bigger and better pumps to prevent flooding.

Then the first tragedy struck. Seigneur Le Pelley was drowned with two others off the **Bec du Nez ⓭**, the island's northern point, during a boat trip to Guernsey. His younger brother Ernest became Seigneur and, in order to raise more money for the mining venture, took a £4,000 mortgage on his fief from one John Allaire, a wealthy Jerseyman with an interesting past.

During the Napoleonic wars some 25 years before, Allaire had been a British privateer, licensed by the Crown to prey on French cargo vessels in the Chan-

In the 1560s Sark became a refuge for the notorious pirates, mainly English, who made a good living preying on the ships trading with Jersey and Guernsey.

BELOW:
the Bel Air Tavern.

nel. But it is believed that Allaire found it equally profitable to run up a *tricoleur* and capture an English ship since his patois-speaking Channel Islanders were just another bunch of Frenchmen to the average British sailor. They would take booty back to Jethou, the tiny island Allaire owned between Guernsey and Herm. Like most pirates, he had a reputation for not taking prisoners and there is a story of a curse being put on him and his descendants by a woman left to drown. This was the man to whom the Seigneur mortgaged his inheritance.

By 1845, 245 miners and Guernseymen had set up a tavern there, which soon acquired a reputation among the increasingly Methodist islanders as a den of iniquity. When the disaster came, some saw it as divine retribution. A gallery ceiling collapsed and gallons of freezing seawater came crashing in. There was a frantic scramble for the entrance shaft in the dark, for the lamps had gone out and the water was already chest-high and rising. Ten miners were drowned.

End of a dynasty

It was the end of the mining. It marked the beginning of the end of the Le Pelley dynasty of Seigneurs, too. Ernest died two years later, a broken man by all accounts. His son, Peter Carey Le Pelley, was unable to meet the mortgage repayments on the fief. By 1852 the old pirate Allaire was dead. It was left to his daughter, a widow called Marie Collings, to foreclose on it and become the next Seigneur.

So John Allaire, scourge of the Channel (when he died it needed a wheelbarrow to take his gold coin to a bank), is the present Seigneur's great-great-great-great grandfather. Thus even gentle Sark proves the theory that behind every great fortune lies a great crime. Or, in John Allaire's case, probably several great crimes were committed during the course of his life.

Map on page 218

BELOW: heading towards La Coupée.

There is a kind of natural jetty at Port Gorey, a finger of rough granite rocks going into the sea. If, on a fine day when the rocks are not too slippery, you go to the end of it you will discover the rusted hand-rail of a landing stage thought to be linked with the mining, although the Germans may have added to or repaired it during the Occupation. At least one Cornish miner remained on the island; his name was Remphrey and one of his descendants still lived there until recently.

Artists' haunts

From the silver mines it is best to go back to the La Sablonnerie for further exploration of this coast. Once at the hotel, turn left and follow the road its last 400 metres or so until you come to a farmyard where most of the outbuildings appear to have been turned into living quarters – at least in the summer. Go round the corner on foot (there is a notice telling you not to take your bicycle any further) and then you turn left through the fields until you reach the clifftop gorse. The Victorians who pioneered Sark as a holiday place were mostly artists and poets of varying talent, but to a man and a woman they all seem to have been classicists. So apart from the Venus Pool there is also the **Jupiter Bath** and the **Adonis Pool** which you are now approaching.

The pool faces a large rock called the **Moie de la Bretagne** ⓮ and, like Venus, is visible two hours from either side of a low tide. The tide rises very rapidly. It cannot be overemphasised that, however exhilarating scrambling around the Sark coastline can be, you must be constantly aware of the state of the tide and allow yourself some leeway for taking longer than you estimated.

A deep gulley has to be crossed to reach the pool where the clear waters are well over 7 ft (2 metres) deep. The pool contains a slowly beckoning garden of

The Adonis Pool, a natural indentation in the rocks, is visible for about four hours at low tide. It is 20 ft (6 metres) deep and fringed with seaweed.

BELOW:
going shopping.

FEUDS AND FEUDALISM

Having built their £60 million gothic-style castle on Brecqhou, the multimillionaire Barclay Brothers were dismayed to learn that, under Sark law (which extends to Brecqhou, 200 metres away), they were obliged to leave the estate to an eldest son. Demanding the right to bequeath the property to all four of their children, they threatened to take the battle to the European Court of Human Rights. In 1999 the island's government, the Chief Pleas, caved in and updated the constitution.

The case focused attention on Sark's medieval ways and British newspaper readers were bemused to learn that, under statutes unchanged for four centuries, a husband could legally beat his wife – as long as he used a stick no thicker than his little finger and did not draw blood. Since there was no right to divorce unless one first left the island for a year, there was little aggrieved wives could do except move out of the family home. The result: many couples split up and moved in with new partners – even though, in a tiny island of around 600 people, they were bound constantly to bump into their legal spouses.

Divorce was on the agenda again, despite the claim of one 79-year-old Chief Pleas member: "We don't want any more change. The administration of the island is perfect."

different coloured seaweeds. The rocks around it are a strange gold tint and have been gently sculpted into saltpans.

Tides have to be watched even more carefully if you want to explore Sark's caves. One is named after Victor Hugo, who climbed to it on a visit during his exile years in Guernsey, but it can be reached only by boat or by swimming and is dangerous without a guide. Just north of this, however, and also on the west coast, are the **Gouliot Caves** ⓯. These tunnel into the headland between Sark and the islet of **Brecqhou** (one of the original 39 *ténéments*). Nobody can visit Brecqhou without the owners' permission and, although it has become a millionaire's retreat, the Dame of Sark was glad to be rid of it when she sold it for £3,000 in the 1920s. It was then part of La Moinerie *ténément* and of little use to the Dame other than as an occasional venue for a picnic. It was owned in the 1980s by a millionaire who flew in by helicopter, and is currently owned by the secretive Barclay brothers, David and Frederick *(see page 275)*.

The Gouliot Caves are fantastically studded, almost like a glass mosaic with sea anemones of various colours from beetroot red to dark green. You can get to them by taking a track to the headland overlooking Brecqhou from the **Beau Regard** area in the **Hotel Petit Champ**, where the proprietor puts up a notice about the suitability of the tides. An obelisk near the sea is the **Pilcher Monument**, erected to commemorate Joseph Pilcher, drowned in a storm in 1868.

Just before the rocky headland overlooking Brecqhou, a footpath drops down through the bracken towards the right. Follow this. Your footsteps may fall on an incongruous concrete slab about 6 inches (15 cms) thick that has become part of the path; this is a German **mine marker**, III. There is another one back in the bracken about another 16 ft (5 metres) away. The mines themselves have long

Map on page 218

TIP

The Gouliot Caves can be visited during the low ebb of a spring tide, though the descent is difficult. Many interesting caves are dotted around Sark's cliffs. But the fast tides can easily cut off explorers and local advice should be sought.

BELOW: the "window" in the rock above Port Moulin.

gone; one German prisoner-of-war died in clearing them. Further down are some iron stakes where the Germans rigged their barbed-wire entanglements.

One British commando raid on Sark had far-reaching effects. The commandos took prisoner some Germans billeted at the **Dixcart Hotel** , which is in one of the island's loveliest valleys and is where the few remaining cider apple trees can be found. Some of the Germans tried to escape; one was later found with rope around his hands and knifed to death. It was because of this incident that Hitler issued his infamous order, not always followed by the Wehrmacht, that all commando prisoners must be treated as terrorists and summarily shot.

The northern tip

The **Boutiques Caves** ⑰, so called because they were once used by smugglers, need a torch to explore. Boots, or at least well-fitted training shoes with a good grip, are recommended for both caves, where the abundance of boulders over which to clamber give the ankles a lot of hard work and can be dangerous.

The Boutiques are near the **Bec du Nez**, the nothernmost tip of Sark. To reach them, you have to cross **Eperquerie Common** ⑱, which is thick with bluebells in the spring, There are two entrances to the Boutiques, well above La Grûne, but none easily negotiable into La Grûne channel which at high tide separates La Grûne from the rest of the island.

There's something really quite eerie about the Boutiques. You can imagine the sweating men, the kegs of brandy, the whispered oaths. For the first 650 ft (200 metres) or so, there are quite deep pools of water trapped in craters on the floor even at low tide. A reassuring factor is that there's nearly always a glimmer of light at the end of the tunnel. About halfway along, a side entrance leads to a small beach.

A tractor for every task.

BELOW:
the Dixcart Hotel.

Map
on page
218

On your way back across the common you might ponder that this quiet place saw, according to local legend, the *dénouement* of one of the strangest stories to come out of the German Occupation of the islands.

It seemed a straightforward case of murder followed by remorse and suicide; a German doctor was killed and, after his body was found, so was that of an officer's batman. The doctor, not unnaturally, was given a Christian burial. The batman, who was believed to have killed his fellow countryman before taking his own life, was buried in an unmarked grave on the common without the benefit of clergy. Then, a few months later, a badly wounded soldier in a field hospital on the Eastern Front confessed to being the killer. While serving in Sark, he had tried to persuade the doctor to declare him unfit for front-line duty. The doctor refused. He then murdered the batman to cover his first killing. Some Sarkees will say the soldier, having survived his wounds, was brought back to Sark and, before being executed, he was made to exhume the batman's body and give him a proper burial.

The locals like telling visitors stories. Some people insist that it is their favourite occupation – yet, like most Channel islanders, they are industrious. Many have two or three jobs, especially in summer when there are tourists' bags to be carted about and bars to be waited on. And, even if there are very few pure-blooded Sarkees left, there is an attitude to life that goes with living on a small island where winters aren't for the physically soft or easily bored.

There was a time when winter made a prisoner of those Sarkees who couldn't afford to decamp to Guernsey, as most seigneurs did, before the seas became too rough. Now a new tradition is catching on: the young men tend to disappear in the autumn but are back in December with money to spend. What is their welcome source of income? They go to England to cut Christmas trees. ❏

Before changes in UK company law, directors of a British company who held their board meetings on Sark could have their company deemed resident on the island and so subject to favourable tax laws. This device was known as the "Sark lark".

BELOW:
Sark's schoolhouse.

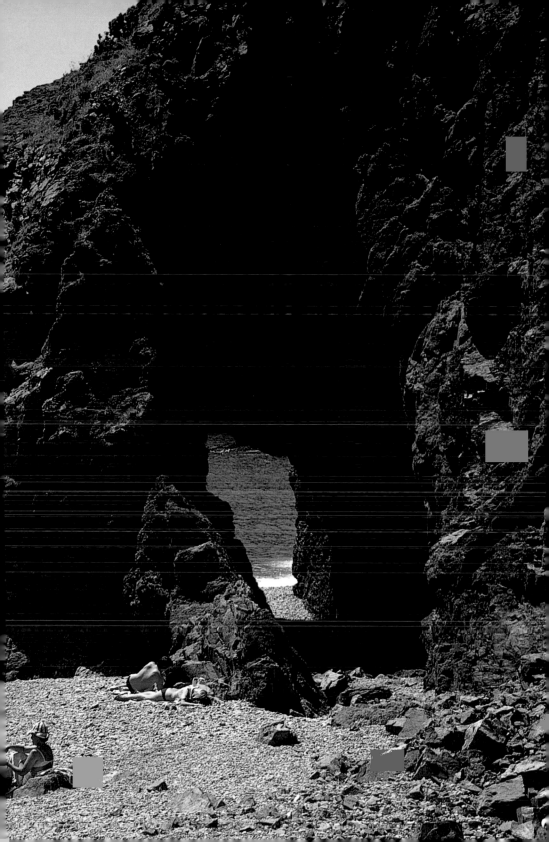

HERM

The island, leased to a single tenant, is run like a family business – a sort of bed-and-breakfast surrounded by sea

They used to bury people in Herm – not just one or two but thousands. Evidence of those burial can still be seen, although many of the graves have been swallowed by the sea and many more were desecrated in the 19th century. Why our early, pre-Christian predecessors should think that Herm, one of the quietest islands on earth, was an ideal place to bury their dead and to erect huge standing stones in their honour we may never be sure; but any visitor who believes that the old granite stones which adorn the island have arrived by chance should think again. Someone, long ago, moved them here. Herm was a neolithic graveyard and deserves the occasional archaeological dig

A tiny place, Herm lies just across the water from St Peter Port, a 20-minute ferry ride to the northeast. It is 1½ miles (2.5 km) long and ¾ mile (1 km) wide, and has a population of just over 100. You can walk round it in an afternoon, enjoying its wild flowers and archaeological remains. On summer Sundays, though, it can become one of the world's most crowded islands as 2,000 day-trippers arrive by ferry from Guernsey.

The island, which is leased from the States of Guernsey, has been run as a family business since 1949, first by Major Peter Wood and now by his heirs, with a dairy farm, a hotel and a number of farm buildings converted to form self-catering accommodation. It is a very pretty, meticulously run island where you can't pick the flowers, can't own a house, shouldn't play your ghetto-blaster or transistor radio on the beach and should wash your clothes only between midnight and noon. Who said that small islands spell freedom?

Herm's greatest attraction is the glorious Shell Beach, in the northeast of the island, composed largely of shells and shell fragments washed here by Gulf Stream tides. It's a paradise for beachcombers, who can spend their time identifying up to 200 varieties of shell. Bird lovers are also drawn to Herm because the island serves as a feeding ground for birds of passage during their summer and autumn migrations.

Then there are the smaller islands – Jethou, Brecqhou, Lihou, the Ecréhous, the Minquiers (*see pages 273–9*) – and, around them, reefs which, it's been said, can split a ship's hull like a hacksaw slicing through melon. ❏

PRECEDING PAGES: Dixcart Bay on Sark; Herm as seen from the sea.
LEFT: Shell Beach.

AROUND HERM

The island is a great place for people who like birdwatching, seashores, walking and food. It's so peaceful nowadays that its tiny jail is no longer needed

Map on page 240

Leased by the Wood family from the States of Guernsey, Herm is very different from the other Channel Islands. Major Peter Wood (1915–98), who came to the island with his Yorkshire-bred wife, Jenny, in 1949, was a New Zealander. He was also very conscious that his island home would stand or fall according to the whims of the tourist industry, and he devoted the rest of his life to carving Herm into the quiet little paradise it is today; that is, a civilised island 1½ miles long by half-a-mile wide with one large hotel (the **White House ❶**), two pubs, a row of cottages, two shops (including a post office) and two well-run beach cafés.

There are also the puffins, of course, and the chapel and the farm and the manor house. But everything (apart from the puffins) had to be built or rebuilt after World War II and now have to be maintained or modernised. Major Wood gave his life to the island and by doing so has created an island dynasty. His daughter, Pennie, and her husband, Adrian Heyworth, now run the island and recent initiatives have included the injection of £300,000 into the main hotel and, with the help of a Kew-trained gardener, the planting of thousands of trees to replace those lost by weather damage or sheer old age.

Herm has always lent itself to the moulding of personal visions, although one of the first people to leave a name behind, St Tugual, probably never wanted to settle in the Channel Islands in the first place. He (or she) provided the name of the small chapel on the hill above **Spring Meadow**, near to the farm and the manor, and this serves as a reminder of the days when Herm was a religious outpost, run by Catholic monks who founded a monastery, improved the land so that it could fatten livestock and produce grain, and stayed there under the control of French or English dioceses for hundreds of years. Later, during the 17th century, Calvinism drove them off the island.

LEFT: the walk home from the harbour. **BELOW:** St Tugual's chapel, a reminder that Herm was once a religious outpost.

St Tugual's chapel

By the mid-17th century the island was deserted, although the **chapel ❷** dedicated to the memory of St Tugual remained. It is a small, rounded, granite room with a high stained-glass window at the far end.

Window and chapel have been tastefully restored since the Wood family came to the island but no-one can restore forgotten knowledge of St Tugual, who remains an enigma. Indeed, it has been rumoured that Tugual was a Welsh woman who accompanied St Magloire to Guernsey and Herm in the 6th century, who died here and whose memory was perpetuated by the building of this holy shrine which has been well looked-after by the Wood family, despite woodworm in the school-style wooden seats, and which is used for morning service at 10.30am every Sunday.

For the rest of the time the chapel is left open, well-lit and flooded by lilting strains of recorded choral music. This changes to the real thing on Sunday mornings, although the organist might change from week to week. A notice in the White House Hotel proclaims: "If you would like to play the organ on Sunday, speak to the manager." Cliff Richard was one of many Christians who have taken part, leading the congregation in song and prayer.

Law and order

There is no rector on the island, which has a resident population of 97 (more than that in summer). Similarly there are no police, firefighters, nurses or doctors, although there are set procedures and selected people to deal with any emergency. These procedures involve mainly the island manager (Adrian Heyworth) and the resident accountant. Both are members of the fire-fighting team and honorary Herm constables, who between them carry the full weight of Guernsey law.

The last time the Wood family negotiated to extend its lease well into the 21st century, a report by the States of Guernsey revealed that "the finances improved dramatically from 1983 and are now achieving substantial profits". Increased prosperity means more modernisation, more holiday cottages (converted outhouses) and more electricity.

The main power source on the island is in the form of generators run with the aid of three diesel bus engines. This means that, at the height of the tourist season, the huge demand for electricity necessitates sacrifice. Hotel guests (and staff) are forbidden to use electric kettles and are allowed to turn on electric washing machines only in the morning. This power-saving routine has also

BELOW: it's hard to get lost on Herm.

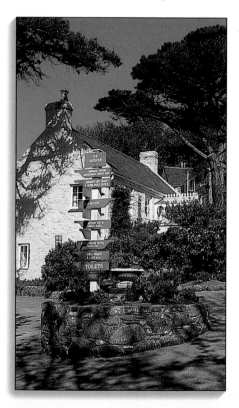

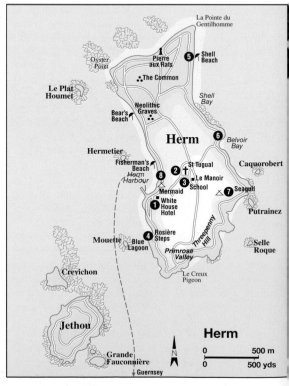

produced a quaint tradition: hotel guests are supplied with small gas burners in their rooms, complete with small kettle and teapot.

Map on facing page

The young ones

Despite having no doctor, fireman or uniformed policeman, Herm does have its own teacher and **school** ❸. Provided by Guernsey Education, a junior/infant school teacher commutes to Herm every day, teaches a class which changes in ages and numbers each year and then, in the evening, goes home.

By the time the children are at secondary school level their parents have a difficult choice to make: do they send them away to boarding school in Guernsey or does the whole family leave Herm, for the sake of a good education? Most parents usually leave and, for this reason, most Herm employees are in their twenties – in striking contrast to most of the White House Hotel's guests.

Before the summer season it is the retired or semi-retired traveller who makes his way to Herm, knowing that no television sets are allowed in the hotel (but they are in the self-catering cottages); knowing that an evening entertainment is likely to be bridge, Trivial Pursuit or a jigsaw puzzle; and knowing that, if ever a contemporary hotel was ideally suited for an Agatha Christie murder mystery set in the earlier part of the 20th century, this is it.

With stuffed, heavy armchairs in the White House, cottages with names like Bracken, Cherry, Puffin, Primrose and Forge (where the accountant lives) close by, and pubs called **The Mermaid Tavern** and **The Ship**, all that's required to complete the scene is a corpse, Miss Marple dithering her way to the solution ("nobody will leave this island until the murder is solved") and the police inspector – who, of course, would have to be sent over from Guernsey.

Archaeologists in 1840 found evidence that Neolithic people had lived on Herm in 3000 BC. Other excavated relics suggested that the Romans may have traded here.

BELOW: the White House Hotel, focus of island life.

Occasionally a policeman *is* required, but usually the island looks after itself extremely well. Any serious injury prompts the swift call-out of the ambulance boat *Flying Christine*, while the two special constables know that if any troublemakers arrive on Herm, they can call on volunteers to help them ship the offenders back to Guernsey, as convicts were once shipped to Australia. Alternatively, they can lock them up in one of the smallest jails in the world: a domed, beehive-shaped affair opposite the White House. This is a granite ornament these days, but that wasn't always the case.

Steps to London

Herm lends itself to autocratic rule. In the 19th century John Lindsay, his son-in-law Jonathan Duncan and then Ebenezer Fernie saw Herm not as a burial island or a tourist resort but as a working set of quarries. The harbour, opposite the hotel and the shops, was strengthened and enlarged; huge amounts of granite were exported to London (the steps that lead from Carlton House Terrace to the Mall were cut from Herm granite, as were the steps up to St Paul's Cathedral) and 400 labourers lived on the island with nothing else to do but work and drink.

The drinking led to fights, to gang warfare and to the prison becoming a popular place to spend the night. The search for granite and then copper, lead and silver led to many of the cromlechs and standing stones being destroyed. It was easier to take the granite from above the ground than to dig it out from below and bones were crunched underfoot or used as footballs.

Near **Rosière Steps ❹**, where ships bring passengers to the island at low tide, an experimental mine shaft was sunk into the cliff edge and a large monolith called Pierre aux Rats, at the northern end of the Common, disappeared

Pierre aux Rats obelisk, an aid to navigation.

BELOW: the Herm ferry on its way to the island.

completely. Its granite was shipped to London. As Guernsey fishermen used the stone as a navigational aid, they were none too happy, and the States of Guernsey ordered Herm Granite Company to erect a monument in its place. They did so and this odd, granite finger stands high above a grass and fern common to the north of the island. The scene is reminiscent of a badly neglected golf course.

The granite industry floundered. The granite men went bankrupt and it was left to Prussian Prince Blucher von Wahlstatt to bring his own vision to Herm at the end of the 19th century. Pine trees were planted, the manor hill was lined with dozens of eucalyptus trees and other exotic plants, and the manor at the top of the hill was extended, turreted and turned into a kind of corridored, Teutonic private asylum.

Wallabies and deer were brought to Herm and bred successfully. But neither they nor the Prince were present when the novelist Compton Mackenzie took over the lease in 1920, before moving to a tinier island nearby – Jethou (pronounced "Jetoo") – in 1923. He left an island populated mainly with rabbits, cattle, a few horses and many, many species of birds. This was as much as the island was when Major Wood took over the lease in 1949.

Bird island

When the RAF Ornithological Society conducted a seven-day bird survey in the early 1980s, they identified 92 different species, including Brent geese, guillemots, razorbills, shags and – on the "Humps", four small islands two nautical miles from Herm – puffins. There were around 90 or so pairs nesting there at the time but over the years the number has sadly declined, and a more recent sur-

The prolific novelist Compton Mackenzie, best remembered for "Whisky Galore" (1928), was tenant of Herm from 1920 to 1923. He once described the manor house as "the ugliest building in Europe".

BELOW:
fertile farmland.

vey showed that the puffin population treats the Humps more as a holiday home than as a permanent abode. From the beginning of March fewer than 20 puffins now arrive in the islands. Three months later, at the end of June (a month before the real tourist season starts), they head for quieter waters.

Thankfully, many of the remaining 91 species are not so shy and the island remains an ornithologist's delight. Herm bustles with visiting birdlife. It even contains a memorial to a well-loved bird, a parrot, owned by Sir Percival Perry who lived there before the World War II. The bird was strangled one night by a band of drunken fishermen and, to commemorate his passing, Sir Percival dedicated an outcrop of rock behind the hotel to honour his pet bird.

If it is bad form to kill the island's fauna (apart from rabbits, which overrun the place) it is terribly bad form to pick the flora. The policy of allowing it to grow, unchecked by anyone but those people who live there, has produced an island full of blooms during summer which may be hard to control (any garden the size of Herm would be), but which is immeasurably pretty. Royal Fern, peculiar to Herm, grows here, as do horned poppies and sea kale on the shores, and wild iris, primroses and foxgloves inland, along with more exotic plants, like New Zealand flax and Japanese cactus. These grow especially well towards the centre of the island and either side of the path which begins above the Harbour, leads uphill towards **Le Manoir** and then runs, spine-like, towards **Primrose Valley**.

During World War II the occupying Germans filmed tank and infantry landings on Herm and released the resulting film as "The Invasion of the Isle of Wight".

Shell Beach

Allied to the natural prettiness of the flowers is the natural beauty of the beaches, particularly **Shell Beach 5** and **Belvoir Bay 6**. Both have cafés which are maintained with scrupulous care by Herm Island Ltd., which Major Wood established

BELOW:
Shell Beach.

to ensure that Herm would be run as a family affair after his death. Indeed, the cafés are so well looked-after that, just after 4pm every day in summer, one of the island's few tractors arrives pulling a refuse skip on wheels. The day's collected rubbish is taken to the dump near Rosière where it is either burnt or unloaded into an old quarry. There is no litter problem on Herm. Residents say litter just isn't tolerated.

Both Shell Beach and Belvoir Bay (the smaller and more popular of the two) are neither entirely sand nor shell, but somewhere in between, and are ideal hunting grounds for the dedicated shell collector. They are clean and slope gently down to the sea. Occasionally they attract the attention of a passing sailing ship which moors in the calm waters a little way from the land. But beware, Herm has the highest level of sunburn in the Channel Islands. Sunbathers, apply a liberal coat of sun cream, especially to children.

Map on page 240

Popular campsites

No swimming at all should take place within 300 ft (100 metres) of Alderney Point because of strong currents, but camping and walking along the designated paths (*not* either side of them) are actively encouraged. There are two campsites, **Seagull** ❼ and **Mermaid** ❽, which are quite popular with Guernsey residents during the low season. They bring their own tents, put them up and live in them on weekends. This is a cheap way to enjoy two-day spring and autumn holidays for not much more than the price of a 20-minute boat fare.

The food at the White House Hotel, its three cafés (there is one larger one attached to the Mermaid Hotel), the pubs, restaurant and barbecue area is slightly limited, never poor and occasionally very good indeed. It is scrupulously served with the added attraction on the restaurant menu of oysters — a new, independent

BELOW: walking is one of Herm's great pleasures.

venture by a Guernseyman. This means that the local oyster beds provide visitors with Herm oysters at only £3 for six shellfish, which would fetch six times this amount in any major city.

Oysters are the island's main growth industry, apart from tourism, and the Wood family has cleverly linked the two together at the Mermaid Tavern, where visitors can choose their oysters to be cooked in any one of 12 different ways.

While the oysters will be straight-from-the-sea fresh, the only other home-grown foodstuff Herm produces is milk, for its herd of Guernsey cattle produces up to 450 litres of milk per day, with always between 20 and 40 cows in milk. The herd used to be one of the largest in the Channel Islands, but after one hot summer it became abundantly clear that the island could not produce enough grass to feed them all. The herd was reduced in size and will never again go above its current number, which is 70.

Only rarely does the milk boat fail to make its twice-a-day run to Guernsey, and while experience has shown the current tenants that there is a ceiling to the number of cattle which can live on the island, the Occupying forces during the war fully expected there to be double that number. Their intention was to use the land as a cattle-fattening store; all fattened cattle to be milked or eaten for the sake of the German army. In effect, it was a good idea which came to nothing. For most of the war only the Dickson and Le Barge families lived on Herm, tending a few livestock and at times oblivious to what was happening in Europe.

Letter of the law

Before tourism blossomed, one of the most lucrative ways of making money was from the sale of Herm stamps. The island established its own post office, designed

On the west coast, north of Fisherman's Beach, is a small cemetery with just two graves and a scarcely readable inscription. Local legend has it that a mother and child died of cholera in the early 19th century and were buried here by the crew of a passing ship.

BELOW: as well as tourists, the ferry brings milk churns back for refilling.

its own stamps and for nearly 20 years issued fresh covers which were franked, with a Herm island stamp, before being sent, via Guernsey, all over the world.

The British government allowed Herm this financial privilege until, in 1969, Guernsey intervened. The States told Major Wood that he could frank Guernsey stamps and sell stamp-size, sticky pieces of paper of a similar size to stamps (he was not allowed to call them "Herm stamps") and that, while one piece of paper could be placed on envelopes, the other could not. If ever a modern-day, Herm-issued stamp is franked at the sorting office (the hotel), Guernsey Post Office will want to know why.

Wood craft

Gravediggers, quarrymen, wallabies and now 1,800 holidaymakers a day at the height of the season – Herm has seen them all. But cars are a rarity. Three tractors, one Land-Rover and three buggy-type motor bikes with go-anywhere wheels are the only vehicles on the island.

When Major Wood took over the island he discovered that a ghost shared it with him. It was (is) supposedly the spirit of a 16th-century monk. In a similar fashion, though Major Wood died in September 1998, his spirit lives on because just about everything that the island is now can be traced to his vision. Tourism is the thing, at the moment, that brings in the money and the whole island is expected to realise it.

Herm is a wonderful tourist paradise – if you enjoy the high standards set for staff and guests. You get the feeling that, if you complained about the noise the seagulls were making outside your window, the next day they would still be there – but silent. ❏

TIP

Don't be tempted to accompany your walk round the island or beach picnic with music from a radio or ghetto blaster – both are banned on Herm.

BELOW: Herm is a popular weekend retreat for Guernsey people.

ALDERNEY

The island was turned into a labour camp during World War II, and this has given it a distinctly different character

Alderney, the least visited island, lies just 8 miles (13 km) from France and the cobbled streets of its only town, St Anne, have a very Gallic atmosphere. Some 3½ miles (5.5 km) long and 1½ miles (2.5 km) wide, it is a roughly rectangular island, with a cliff-fringed plateau to the south and a northern half that slopes gently to a series of sandy bays.

A cynic once described Alderney as a rock with 2,000 drunks clinging to it and claimed that its only export is empty bottles floating away on the tide; certainly, the pubs are convivial places when the gales are blowing. There is more than a grain of envy in the voices of Guernsey or Jersey people who purvey the drunken image of Alderney. Sour grapes make bad wine and it is their loss of a slow and peaceful way of life, Alderney's lack of bureaucracy and its relaxed attitude to visitors who drink too much that prompt the saying. More birds than bottles will be seen when bobbing on the sea in a boat, and the great demand to live on the island is the only reason Alderney's residents cling to the rock.

It is a retreat for islanders from Guernsey and Jersey, and many other places too; they leave families behind and flock to spend a few days fishing, playing golf, or enjoying a party. Spirits and glasses are raised and the tone of the place is lowered. Alderney people accept the fact with equanimity; indeed, they seem to become more welcoming every time the "I must get away from it all" ploy is used.

Alderney's character differs somewhat from the other islands, partly because it was deliberately depopulated during World War II and used as a forced labour camp. The island was massively fortified by the Germans – 12 forts ring its coast – and relics of the Occupation scar the island and evoke memories of suffering and death.

Although there are more immigrants than locally born people, a fact which is reflected in the make-up of the States of Alderney, the island's parliament, there is little animosity between either category of settler – although, come election time, more than one would-be candidate will stand on the "I am locally born and proud of it" ticket.

Meanwhile the island's parliament continues to fight a rearguard action against keeping the island in the black. With little to export and only tourism as a real source of income, no wonder they tried to steal a march on Guernsey by being first to allow publicans to open on Sundays, as well as every other day of the week.

The island is much visited by ornithologists – the adjacent Burhou Island has puffin colonies and a small bird sanctuary – and by beach lovers looking for privacy and an escape from the busy world. ❏

PRECEDING PAGES: Alderney's wild north coast; and its wide-open beaches.
LEFT: a ferry heads into Braye Harbour.

AROUND ALDERNEY

The capital, St Anne, is an attractive maze of cobbled streets and fortifications around the rest of the island are a reminder of both maritime and wartime threats

Maps:
Island 256
Town 259

Walking Alderney's wind-blasted cliffs in a squall, you may remember the island's reputation for conviviality and decide that sitting in a warm pub is the only thing worth doing. It's hard to avoid drink in Alderney. **Braye**'s welcoming pubs are the first – and often only – sight visiting boat people see after they leave the Yacht Club bar. The pubs are more like clubs than conventional watering holes – full of character and characters, they seem the natural place to be on an island which offers few places of entertainment.

Take the **Divers** Ⓐ, for instance – and many do. A huge old copper diving helmet hangs over the door, as if just raised from the shoulders of the person who preceded you. Warm chatter flows out of the bar as the next step is taken to enter the inner portal. Smiles on faces turned doorwards to greet the casual customer and a grey granite slab floor sprinkled with fine sand give a momentary shock. It's said the sand softens the fall when so much has crossed the bar that the swaying woodwork fails to support the drinkers; bar staff boast that the Divers is the only pub in Britain to have a new carpet daily.

Half hidden in the sand is a coin, cemented to a granite slab; unwary drinkers who try to retrieve it are pounced upon for a contribution to a charity aiding shipwrecked mariners.

Like Napoleon's army, Alderney marches on its stomach. There's a choice of menus ranging from the freshest of seafood to reasonably priced pub snacks or sunny garden barbecues. In May, the island's top chefs, restaurants, hotels and guest houses team up to produce the **Alderney Seafood Festival**, with the Channel Islands' **Tennerfest** taking up the culinary baton in October.

Sadly, one of the best-known *bon viveurs*, a wine buff whose commodious cellars of excellent wines was legendary, died before they relaxed the Sunday licensing laws. John Arlott, once His Master's Voice of BBC cricket commentaries, and a regular visitor to the island from 1951 onwards, retired to Alderney in 1981 saying it was a "desperately easy place" to live in, with a "pleasant absence of bores."

A game of cricket

It was Arlott who introduced another well-known cricketing character to the delights of Alderney and its only cricket ground, **Les Butes**, which is a spectacular pitch with sea views where you might expect a well-hit ball to reach the harbour half a mile below. For Arlott, once the chairman of the Alderney Cricket Club, invited Ian Botham, once of Somerset and England, to his house. Botham and his family liked what they saw and visited Arlott again, and even though the old master is now but a fond memory in Alder-

LEFT: the sign of a celebrated pub.
BELOW: beach picnic on the edge of Braye Bay.

*Patriotism extends
to the pubs.*

ney, a cricketing tradition was maintained when Botham bought a house on the island; although he sold it in 1996, he still visits regularly. He and his son, Liam, joined Alderney Cricket Club, and one particular stag night Botham senior hosted for a fellow England cricketer has become legendary.

The Bothams were able to settle in Alderney because there are no laws restricting purchase of property. If you can afford a house, you can buy. This has meant that the island has become popular with people in their sixties or seventies, who sell up in England and retire here with their best furniture and memorabilia. Enter some Alderney houses and you discover that the antiques are worth as much as the bricks and mortar that surrounds them.

Secrets of the sea

While Alderney Museum (*see below*) displays what at first sight appears to be a hotch-potch of island history in the old school house just west of Victoria Street, one of the most extraordinary finds ever recorded in British seas is gradually being pulled out of the water off the north coast of Alderney.

That the wreck of the 16th-century 60-ft (18-metre) vessel the *Makeshift* should have been discovered at all is a virtual miracle, for when local diver Bert Cosheril pulled up a heavily concreted musket with one of his crab pots in 1984, he left it sitting outside his house for a week until he took the trouble to cut a section through it, to find out what it might be.

It wasn't until more booty from the wreckage was brought to the surface and a team of professional divers went down that, with the help and advice of UK historians, it was decided that this was probably the wreck of the *Makeshift*, described by one eminent Oxford professor as being "of more historical

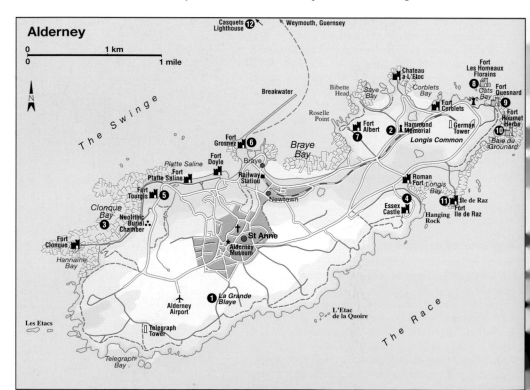

importance" than Henry VIII's warship the *Mary Rose*. In 1994 Mike Bowyer from Bangor University was appointed to oversee a long-term plan to recover as much as possible from the wreck, but wind conditions frequently blow up to 8 knots and divers only have 40-minute slots of still water in which they can work.

They are also hampered by the age-old question of "who will pay?" which presents a Catch 22-style problem. For if the States could afford to bring the wreck out of the water it could conceivably earn as much money, as a tourist attraction, as the *Mary Rose*. They don't have that kind of money. In the meantime it draws a few people to the museum, and to the shed near the harbour where cannon, matchlock muskets and helmets are stored, but its recovery created more financial problems than it solved. When one of the cannons was sent to York to be restored, for example, the Weymouth authorities tried to make the island pay VAT on it.

Like everyone in small communities, the islanders have to make their own entertainment. Alderney's 2,200 residents have clubs, choirs, theatrical groups and sports teams. Their footballers have not won the tripartite inter-island Muratti Vase for many years, but the squad is strong enough to take on teams of a semi-professional standard from Jersey and Guernsey and has even been known to score a goal occasionally against their much stronger neighbours.

The community spirit extends not only to the islanders' ambitions to raise money for their recently-found wreck (each cannon costs £9,000 to restore), it also can be seen in its voluntary lifeboat crew, recently reconstituted and already credited with several sea rescues.

Away from the sea and above the town, on the upper slopes, an ancient network of fields have been farmed in strip fashion through to modern times while

Maps:
Island 256
Town 259

TIP

Bikes can be hired from Puffin Cycles (tel: 01481 823725) on Braye Street. Another option is to hire a two-seater golf-style buggy capable of 10 miles (16 km) an hour; a full driving licence is required for this (tel: 01481 822606).

BELOW:
Braye harbour.

The railway uses old rolling stock from the London Underground.

land and sea are connected by a long steep road which runs from the high parts of the island to the pub-lined Braye Street.

St Anne a town built on the hillside connecting the farmers with the fishermen, is the capital. It is split by a cobbled road which drops from the High Street to the hipped-roofed Wesleyan Methodist Chapel – Victoria Street links the upper town with shops at Les Rocquettes and the cricket green on Les Butes. The hill continues steeply to the hotels and bars in Braye Street, and the harbour.

Old times

Much of Alderney is an agricultural wasteland; indeed, it is so poor that a strip farming technique, widespread in Europe during the Middle Ages, was employed to make best use of the 450 acres (180 hectares) of good land; there were no hedges or banks. It supported 700 people in the days of Queen Elizabeth I. Farm houses and buildings were clustered on poor soil around the top of St Anne, giving that part of town a rustic, rural look. The fields were separated into rectangular blocks called *riages*, each about 14½ acres (5.9 hectares), across the end of which ran *vaindifs* where the ox-team turned when pulling a plough. The *riages* were sub-divided into parallel strips, some running north and south, others east to west. Strips belonging to a family were scattered among the *riages* so that everyone had a share of good and poorer land. They have been split and amalgamated many times since then and now vary in size.

Modern life, of a sort, hit the ancient strip farming on the Blaye more than 50 years ago when the first Channel Island airport was opened. It has changed little since. A few prefabricated huts and a hangar surround the tiny airport in which departures are announced in a loud voice and arrivals are marked by the

BELOW:
getting to Alderney in an Aurigny Trislander is an experience in itself.

shouts of greeting as some island family is reunited. The island's lifeline routes are operated by one of the world's smallest and most successful airlines, **Aurigny Air Services**, which flies 17-seater Trislander aircraft from Guernsey and Jersey, Cherbourg and Southampton all year round, with **Rockhopper Aero** as the competition.

While the easiest way to travel to Alderney from the other islands is by plane (a 15-minute trip from either Guernsey or Alderney), during the summer season regular sea trips can be made from either island by catamaran. The island's heavy goods are carried from Guernsey in small freighters operated by the Alderney Shipping Company, or direct from Weymouth every two weeks, but the island is still waiting for a direct passenger service to be reintroduced between mainland Britain and Alderney harbour.

One benefit of the island's compactness is that you can easily walk into St Anne from the airport. The farming influence dominates as you enter **Marais Square B**. This was the centre of life for the farming folk – roads radiate from the square past old farmhouses, the architecture filled in with Georgian and Victorian dwellings. Alderney people maintain that, until the deportation during the German Occupation, they had their own breed of Channel Island cattle. They say that the Alderney cow was smaller than the Guernsey but it is doubtful if they ever existed as a separate breed. Undaunted, their story is told on the side of the Marais Hotel. "The legendary Alderney cow, now extinct, attracted buyers to the auctions held in this square from all over the world," says the sign next to a picture of a dairy maid and the island's Dodo. A sadly unused but beautiful granite trough occupies centre stage in the cobbled square.

Here, perhaps more than anywhere on the island, the vast number of cars can

Maps:
Island 256
Town 259

Telegraph Bay, on the southern tip of the island, is named after the Telegraph Tower that stands on top of the headland. It was used in the early 19th century to send semaphore signals to the other islands. When the tide is out, the bay is a good spot for swimming and sunbathing.

BELOW:
a thirst for history.

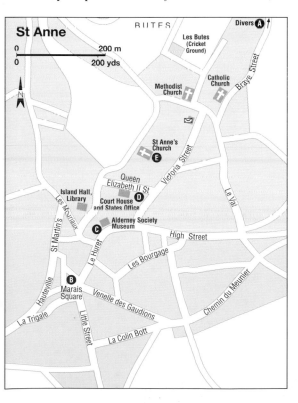

be best judged – almost every adult member of the population has one. It is impossible to get good pictures of the town anywhere between the Marais Square cow trough and the beautiful house-line of Braye Street as so many cars clutter the views.

Parts of the island have a strange feel. A regular visitor complained that the area around **La Grande Blaye ❶**, at the back of the airport, seemed always "to be quiet and spooky". It is where one of the island's four concentration camps was built during the last war, he was told chillingly. Many of Alderney's small community were evacuated to Britain before the German forces landed in 1940. Many of them joined up – some died fighting with the British – but the people who remained in Alderney were taken to Guernsey where they spent the Occupation. All livestock and possessions were left behind. One old farmer stayed and throughout the Occupation maintained his herd of cattle (it was taken from him after the Occupation) and so, too, did a recently-arrived Irish family. They were in a more enviable position than the old farmer, for Ireland was neutral during the war and they could not be accused of collaboration.

While residents were in exile atrocities of a fashion, now well-known, went on in secret. Russians, Poles and many French Jews from German concentration camps were imported to labour as slaves, under the notorious Organisation Todt. They worked on the brooding fortifications which were built as part of Hitler's Atlantic Wall – the massive concrete structures became tombs for many of the detainees who died of starvation, and stand as a lasting memorial. Other Todt workers were buried in unmarked graves around the island.

They are not forgotten. The **Hammond Memorial ❷** stands above **Longis Common**, once the site of hundreds of unmarked graves. It is said that the

BELOW:
the Hammond
Memorial.

island was silent of birdsong when the people returned after liberation. But while they were away gannets had colonised Les Etacs rock to circle Alderney evermore, like the souls of the Todt workers they are supposed to represent.

Maps:
Island 256
Town 259

History on show

The first steps of visiting natural historians should be to Le Huret, at the top of High Street, where the island's story is explained in the **Alderney Society Museum**  (open: daily 10am–noon and Easter–Nov, 2pm–4pm). The setting is old-fashioned with huge glass cabinets housing the last public remains of Alderney men from the time of neolithic settlers to the folk who returned after the Germans left. The collections are housed in the Old School which was opened as a museum in 1972. It was, almost inevitably, too small and a new extension was added in May 1984. On show are the crafts and trades of Alderney, its natural history, the misery of the Organisation Todt slave workers – illustrated with the blue and white striped shift worn by one wretched prisoner or more – a 4,000-year-old spear and the latest stamps.

Washed-up whales have appeared on Alderney's beaches and their pitiful pictures immortalise the poor beasts. The photographs include some of a sei whale, thought to have become confused by French warships' sonar. Kept alive by spraying water over its body, the anxious islanders waited for the tide to rise so the whale could return to sea. As the creature made grunts, pops and whistles, its school of relatives swam offshore until it was liberated and they all went out to sea together.

Alderney Museum.

Alderney's court sat outside the Old School in Le Huret until modern times; even today royal proclamations are read out there. It now sits a short distance

BELOW: St Anne – you can stroll to it from the airport.

away in the **Court House** which can be visited during office hours. The court room doubles as the meeting place for the States of Alderney, the island's 12-seat legislative assembly.

This curious body is neither town council nor parliament, as Alderney is governed by the States of Guernsey, who extend legislation to the island, when appropriate, and administer her health, postal and social services, police and education. This causes great resentment in Alderney whose population would prefer to be autonomous and control their own destiny.

After the war

The Occupation and deportation of Alderney families was the greatest instigator of change the island has ever seen. Residents returned in November 1945 to find many of their houses destroyed, the island in ruin, fields overgrown, the breakwater smashed by the sea in several places and breached across a 50-metre section. Their economy was non-existent and the island had no money.

The Labour Government, which swept into power in the UK under Clement Attlee in 1945, stepped in to help "our dear Channel Islands", as Churchill referred to them in his end-of-war speech. But a farming co-operative failed, the penalty for putting the airport on the fertile fields of the Blaye, and Alderney people were given the choice of becoming part of the county of Hampshire or of having their island administered by Guernsey. They chose the latter in an arrangement described by John Arlott as a "shotgun wedding".

This has given rise to the resentment felt by islanders for their southern administrators – nobody enjoys a shotgun wedding. Islanders grudgingly put up with the interference of a distant and, as it is seen, rather out-of-touch administration. Alderney has two seats in Guernsey's parliament and is able to influence those areas of budgeting and policy-making which affect the island. But because all Channel Island politicians are amateur and the island is far removed from Guernsey, the representatives visit the seat of their administration for the monthly meetings of the States, and only occasionally in between times.

BELOW:
St Anne's Church.

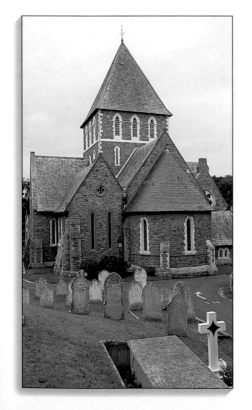

The **States of Alderney** meet in the Court House opposite the administrative offices in Queen Elizabeth II Street. They sometimes discuss street names – Queen Elizabeth II Street was New Street, renamed after a visit by the Queen in 1978 and now known as QEII. Victoria Street was changed from Rue de Grosnez for a similar reason in 1854, but Route de Braye, Grande Rue and La Petit Rue have become Braye Road, High Street and Little Street due to a general anglicising of the island.

St Anne's Church , the Cathedral of the Channel Islands, which has entrances from both Victoria and QEII Street, is one of the few architect designed places of worship in the Channel Islands. Luckily the later and better-known Gothic architecture of Sir George Scott – such as London's St Pancras Station Hotel and the Albert Memorial – cannot be guessed from the design of the church which is noble, with Norman influence. Completed in 1850 to accommodate the billeted garrison and large population of Irish labourers, it is dignified, light and spacious, with a pyramidal tower which acts as a landmark from the sea.

An unusual feature of the church is the Caen stone imported as a building material; most Channel Island churches make use of local stone only. St Anne's was built as a memorial to his parents by the last hereditary Governor of Alderney, the Rev John Le Mesurier. It became the centre of controversy during the Occupation. Some of the bells were shipped to France, where they were to be melted down to make munitions, and the church was used as a store and wine cellar, giving rise to accusations of sacrilege. Four of the six bells were recovered outside Cherbourg after the war and the other two were found in Alderney. All six were sent to the United Kingdom where they were recast to hang in the refurbished church.

Labourers for the building industry arrived in the late 1840s to produce materials for, and work on, the ring of forts built to protect the anchorage which was to mirror Portland Harbour on the other side of the Channel. Many Irish immigrants were fleeing the potato crop failure and the horrors of famine, and the number of workers trebled the local population. The Rue Neuve project to provide houses for the new residents was started – with it went a new Court House and prison cells to accommodate those with high spirits and a taste for the Alderney hooch.

Fort patrol

Fears of yomping French troops marching across Alderney so worried the early Victorians that every good beach is guarded by a fort. Built to create "the Gibraltar of the Channel", the 12 forts were a panic measure to counter and blockade the strongly fortified French naval base at Cherbourg. They were built rapidly

Map on page 256

German Fire Control Tower.

LEFT: Island Hall.
BELOW: one of the island's *jurats* (magistrates).

The Great Barrier

Alderney's breakwater along with the island's ring of 12 defensive fortifications, is a legacy of the hostility and suspicion that existed between England and France in the early 19th century, even though hostilities officially ceased after Napoleon was defeated. When the French began constructing a naval harbour at Cherbourg, alarm bells rang in the Admiralty, and the British government suddenly discovered the urgent necessity of building "harbours of refuge" at Braye, in Alderney, as well as on Guernsey and Jersey. The intention was to convert Braye harbour into a massive naval base, with two breakwaters at each side of the bay. Only the western wall was built, completed in 1847 and originally a mile long.

Planners designing the breakwater never consulted local fishermen who predicted that storms and winter gales would smash even the greatest structure built in that position. The prediction proved correct and the prob-lem gives island authorities their biggest worry to this day – continual maintenance is needed to keep the breakwater intact. Half the 4,680-ft (1,430-metre) length was abandoned many years ago and the resulting 600-metre reef remains a hazard to shipping entering the anchorage.

But it provides valuable shelter for hundreds of French and British yachts that visit the island each year. Their crews and skippers spend heavily on provisions and in the bars, often taking the opportunity to sleep ashore, filling the occasional gaps that occur in every hotel booking chart. Island fishermen take advantage of the shelter, and the sand of Braye beach is protected from erosion by the breakwater. It is the island's most valuable asset.

Within six months of its completion in 1864, two huge breaches were torn in the wall of the breakwater. The UK Treasury became increasingly worried: not only had the cost of building gone way over budget but the running expenditure was sky-high. A committee of inquiry was held in London eight years later to consider whether to destroy the structure, let the sea take it or continue maintaining the breakwater. A deputation from Alderney argued that the UK built it for its own advantage, destroying the former safe anchorage used by fishermen. It had to be maintained or the island would be ruined, they said. The committee agreed.

Responsibility for the maintenance of the breakwater remained with the UK until 1987, when the Guernsey States took it over as part of their contribution to HM Government's defence and international representation bill. The average maintenance costs ran to about £½ million a year. A report to the States in 1994 observed that the rubble mound was continuing to lose material and that there was the possibility of a breach. In 1997, the States published a document entitled "Long Term Strategy for Alderney Breakwater" which contained several proposals, including that of building a shorter breakwater inside the existing structure. The result was 300 letters and over 1,500 petitionary signatures of protest, since when the breakwater's future has remained uncertain. But as one Alderney fisherman commented 'Alderney is the Breakwater'. ❑

LEFT: the breakwater also aids fishermen.

between 1845 and 1861, but within a few months of completion the forts and breakwater were obsolete. Steam ships, better explosives and a rifled gun that brought Alderney within range of heavy artillery on the French coast, turned forts into follies.

The forts form a basis for an excellent walk. Designed by young engineer Captain William Jervois, the plans were clearly drawn by a person with a strong aesthetic sense. They fit smoothly into the landscape and incorporate not only the functions of Victorian military defence but also embellishments such as medieval machicolations and arrow slits.

Geographically, the first and possibly most striking is at **Clonque Bay** ❸ where a spectacular path, which runs from **Essex Castle** ❹ 3 miles (5 km) away along 300-ft (100-metre) cliffs, zigzags down to sea level. The path from Clonque passes **Fort Tourgis** ❺, a huge barrack block on the hillside, before joining the main road, which runs to the harbour.

Fort Platte Saline was a small battery built to protect the bay of that name from attack. It has been swamped by the sand and gravel works that exploit the tidal deposits on the beach.

The breakwater is protected by **Fort Grosnez** ❻, at its base, while **Fort Albert** ❼, the biggest, squats on the hillside overlooking the habour and Braye Bay. **Château à L'Etoc,** between Saye and Corblets Bay, where a tunnel helped *vraic tcherieux* (seaweed gatherers) to leave the beach with their ox-drawn carts, has been converted into flats – **Fort Corblets** on the next headland is also a private dwelling.

Three small abandoned defences protect the rocky east coast. **Fort Homeaux Florains** ❽ is on an islet off the lighthouse, **Fort Quesnard** ❾ makes the

Map on page 256

TIP

Half-day boat trips for birdwatchers are run by the MV Voyager (tel: 01481 823666) and the Lady Maris (tel: 01481 823532). These include close-up views of the puffin colonies on nearby Burhou Island.

BELOW:
Fort Clonque.

Local transport.

headland while **Fort Houmet Herbe** ❿ looks out over the Race towards Cap de la Hague. A fort on **Raz** island ⓫, connected to the mainland by a causeway, houses a collection of moth-eaten stuffed birds while **Essex Castle**, high on the cliffs above, guards Longis Bay.

Within earshot of Alderney's shores are the Garden Rocks, home to 2,000 pairs of gannets. Close by is the low-lying island of Burhou, where puffins nest. Elizabeth Beresford, the children's author, has written about Oscar Puffin and her cousins who nestle here, but these are children's tales. Adult tales of the rocks and the island include a story of a well-intentioned couple who lived in the lighthouse when the breakwater was being built. Not surprisingly, perhaps, they decided to send their teenage girl to mainland Alderney to broaden her education. She was not a worldly lass, having been born on the Casquets. Within days of her arrival to stay with friends, she paid a fisherman to take her back to the lighthouse – the pace of life was too fast, she said.

The story of the Hanging Rocks contrasts the overcrowded island of Guernsey with rural Alderney. The desperate islanders of Guernsey rowed to the UK, attached a rope to the Hanging Rocks and pulled Alderney into the sea, intending to take the lump of much needed land home. It stuck on the seabed and the rope parted when they were halfway, leaving the Guernsey people to return to their island empty-handed.

They certainly would not have chosen such a dangerous place to leave an island. The Channel Islands have a huge rise and fall in the tide – more than 35 ft (11 metres) on some of the big spring tides. These cause vast quantities of water to pour out of the English Channel where the maritime river is split by Alderney. One vast current, **the Race**, rushes between the island and Cap

de la Hague; another, **the Swinge**, passes through the narrow channel to Burhou. Beyond this flat island, the water surges and heaves to the distant **Casquets Lighthouse** as the tide rushes past.

Map on page 256

Laid-back approach

Alderney is described as the Cinderella of the Channel Islands – people coyly say it has no money and is extremely beautiful. What they mean is that it has two ugly sisters who are much richer – but who needs money when they have beauty and what could be called a laid-back approach to life's problems?

The island certainly has no easy access to funds (there are no cash points in the island although per head of population there are probably more in Jersey and Guernsey than anywhere else in the world), but it does have character.

It has also produced an ingenious population, including Major Palmer, nick-named Peabod who, in 1939, found himself stranded in Guernsey. At the time, the only way of travelling home was on the *SS Courier*, a 151-ton steamer that was licensed for only 12 passengers at a time. Palmer was told that she was fully booked for the next two weeks and that he would have to wait on the larger island while waiting for a lift to the small. A resourceful man, the major weighed himself at the Guernsey Post Office, bought the appropriate number of stamps for the weight recorded, and sent himself home, 1st-class parcel post.

Even though the proper GPO procedures had to be observed (once in Alderney he was taken to the sorting office for proper disposal and formal delivery) the island applauded his initiative as he arrived in the island 12 days earlier than his wife expected. For residents young or old share one common characteristic: they like a man who can beat the system. ❏

A château-like house, known locally as the Nunnery, stands on Longis Bay on the site where a Roman fort was discovered. Coins, pottery and bronzework from the site are on display in Alderney Museum.

BELOW: locals swear that Alderney's famous reputation for drinking has been exaggerated.

THE LITTLE ISLANDS

*Owning an island and keeping the rest of the world at bay
is a common fantasy. Rich men have made their
fantasy come true in the Channel Islands*

Map
on page
14

According to that great island-fancier, the late author Sir Compton Mackenzie, **Jethou** is the "most perfect small isle". He was tenant of the 45-acre (18-hectare) Crown property for seven years from 1923, wrote 14 books and innumerable articles there, and saw the music magazine, *The Gramophone*, for which he was responsible, thrive. He fled to Jethou after selling the lease of Herm – just 2,600 ft (800 metres) across the sea – to Ford motor mogul Lord Perry, when financial upkeep of the larger isle threatened to overwhelm him.

Lord Perry had also made an offer for Jethou, where he wanted to grow poisonous plants for the chemical industry. Sir Compton, who always maintained that the spirits of Jethou were a benign influence on his life, was later thankful that he resisted the plan. In 1958, when he heard that the island was again up for sale, he wrote: "Jethou is the most perfect small island off the coast of Britain. If I was younger, I'd buy it again."

Over the centuries many have coveted magical, hump-backed little Jethou, which includes the islets of **Crevichon** and **Grande Fauconnière** joined to it at low tide. It was the first Channel Island to fall into possession of the English Crown at the end of the 11th century, when the rest of the archipelago was still part of the Duchy of Normandy. The tenant (who has to be a British subject) pays no income tax – merely an annual rent of £100 (US$160). All mineral and wreck rights are the reserve of the Crown, and the tenant is forbidden to keep a brothel or a gaming house, and must allow Guernsey residents to collect seaweed and sand eels.

A private paradise

Under the present tenant and his predecessor, both wealthy men, Jethou has become a private paradise. Visitors can no longer readily explore the "haunted" Fairy Wood, smothered in bluebells each spring, nor wonder at the 275-year-old mulberry tree – said to be the oldest of its species in the British Isles. The 24th tenant was Anthony George Duckworth, a lawyer based in the Cayman Islands. He bought the lease in 1984 for a sum "in excess of £500,000" following the death of millionaire industrialist and philanthropist Sir Charles Hayward. The sale included a granite manor house, two staff bungalows, a boathouse, jetty and slipway.

Sir Charles acquired Jethou in 1971 for £90,000 at an auction held on the island that is now part of local history. Bidding started at £50,000 between a handful of interested purchasers, standing in October sunshine above Jethou's lonely foreshore. Bids rose at the rate of £1,000 a second until all but one contender had dropped out. The previous tenants were a Jersey family, Susan and Angus Faed, with their four children,

PRECEDING PAGES:
Lihou Island; the
Minquiers, off
Jersey.
LEFT: the Ecréhous
are run by Jersey.
BELOW: Jethou, as
seen from Herm.

Restald was a Norman ship master who was given Jethou as a reward by William the Conqueror's father, Duke Robert I of Normandy, also known as Le Diable.

who paid £25,000 in 1964 for the lease. The Faeds ran a café to help with the cost of running Jethou, and welcomed visitors in summer. The difficulty of education for their children was the main reason for the family's deciding to give up their Robinson Crusoe life.

In the more distant past, Jethou tenants had not always been so law-abiding. The Faeds' café was once the Admiral Restald Tavern, which had a hard-drinking reputation and was named after the island's first tenant of AD 1000 *(see margin note)*. The present tenants of Jethou are Peter Ogden and his wife Catherine, who seem intent on living entirely private lives. They have, however, indicated to the States of Guernsey that they would like to retain the island's lease until 2007.

Brecqhou

When millionaire industrialist Leonard Matchan bought the beautiful 100-acre (40-hectare) island of Brecqhou, just off Sark, for £44,000, he acquired a tax-free private kingdom at a knockdown price, a seat in Sark's parliament, and a transport problem. The previous tenant was J. Thomson Donaldson, who bought Brecqhou in 1949 with his brother, Alastair, for £15,000. The island, with its big house and farm buildings, had been neglected for nine years, the German occupiers of Sark having no interest in its fate. The Donaldsons, founders of the Donbros clothing firm, sunk large sums into restoring and improving the property. It was ill-health that drove J. Thomson Donaldson to put Brecqhou on the market for £120,000 – and to accept a much lower price for it in 1966.

Dame Sybil Hathaway, the late and famous Dame of Sark, created the little island into a *ténément* (one of 40 freehold properties in Sark that entitles the owner to a seat in Chief Pleas) when she sold it in 1929 for £3,000. Sark has no

BELOW:
avoiding the rocks.

income tax, and bans cars and planes. Mr Matchan, the busy boss of Cope All-man International, found that one of his early tasks as an island MP was to present the case for landing his helicopter on his own private domain.

Len Matchan, on reaching his seventies, also decided to sell – to the right buyer and at the right price – but he died in 1987 before the sale was completed. At that time his "big house" had seven bedrooms, five of them with bathrooms en suite, but that was clearly insufficient for the new owners, twins David and Frederick Barclay, owners of London's Ritz Hotel and *The Daily Telegraph* newspaper, who have created what has been described as a "gothic castle" on the island, which they bought for £2.3 million. The brothers, estimated to be worth a cool £1.2 billion, shrouded their plans in secrecy. True, they took out full-page advertisements in the *Guernsey Press* shortly after rumours began circulating about their plans, but that was just to deny that a massive nuclear shelter and/or a casino were part of the architect's brief. Even the small army of builders working on the new house were sworn to secrecy before they were hired, so clues about the development could be gathered only by the occupants of low-flying planes or the curious who peered across the narrow Gouliot Passage, which separates Brecqhou from Sark.

Lihou

The witches who, according to local legend, cavorted on their Sabbat around Le Catioroc headland on Guernsey's west coast would hurl defiance at the priory dedicated to the Virgin Mary on the tiny isle of Lihou. Only the ruins of the medieval Benedictine priory remain on the island, which is linked to the mainland at low tide by a causeway. But past and present tenants of the 40 acre

Map on page 14

BELOW: the "fortress" built on Brecqhou by the Barclay brothers.

(16-hectare) Crown property – the rent was set at £3.50 a year – along with many of the visitors who pick their way across the rocky causeway, maintain that Lihou has a peculiar serenity.

The priory itself was not always so tranquil. In 1304 a priory servant murdered a monk, and was subsequently slain by one of the Bailiff's men sent to arrest him. When a human skeleton was unearthed on Lihou in 1962, there was speculation that these might be the remains of the monk's murderer.

Lihou once had an iodine factory, using local raw materials, but it was forced to close when it couldn't compete with cheaper Chilean iodine.

Target practice

During the Occupation of the Channel Islands from 1940-45, the Germans used Lihou for target practice; after the war it was bought by two ex-RAF men. An American company that wanted to build a hotel there began negotiations to buy it, but abandoned the project because no source of water could be found.

Meanwhile, a wealthy landowner and farmer from Sussex had become spellbound by Lihou, seeing it as an oasis of peace in an increasingly frantic world. Colonel Patrick Wootton and his wife Ann eventually bought the lease in 1961, after tracing one of the owners who had emigrated to South Africa through an advertisement in the *Cape Times*. True to his earlier vision, Pat Wootton introduced in 1965 a summer series of youth camps that brought young people from many different countries to spend two weeks under canvas on the tiny isle. The Colonel believed that Lihou's remote, peaceful environment provided a spiritual breathing space for youngsters caught up with the whirling world and the need to make their way in it.

BELOW: Brecqhou, just the thing for the millionaire who has everything.

An effervescent, complex personality, Pat Wootton was one of two private individuals to sue the owners of the *Torrey Canyon* as a matter of principle

after oil from the stricken giant tanker badly polluted one of Lihou's bays. After a long fight, he was awarded £750 compensation. He was almost equally incensed when Guernsey decided to ban the smaller island's "stamps" (carriage labels) after the Channel Islands took over the running of their postal services from Britain's General Post Office in 1969. He had been issuing Lihou stamps since 1966 to help fund the youth project, and protested to the Guernsey authorities that Her Majesty's postmaster-general had given him *carte blanche* to run a postal service because the General Post Office was unable to do so. The Lihou postal service went down fighting with the issue of defiant last-day covers, supported by Len Matchan's helicopter flying in from Brecqhou.

The Colonel introduced a rare breed of seaweed-eating sheep from Orkney to Lihou – part of a survival operation mounted by the Rare Breeds Survival Trust. These engaging animals flourished only too well in their new home, and took to swimming across to Guernsey and back regularly to raid local residents' gardens. The flock was sold by the next owners of Lihou, the Honourable Robin and Patricia Borwick, who bought the islet in 1983 for £274,500 (US$412,000), after Pat Wootton moved to Prince Edward Island, Canada, where his wife had spent part of her childhood.

The Borwicks lived all year in the six-bedroom granite house built by their predecessors, sharing the island with their dog, a donkey, a horse, and 150 assorted ducks, peacocks, bantams and geese, which liked a daily dip in the sea.

In complete contrast to Brecqhou, Lihou became more open to the public than ever when, in 1995, it was bought by the States for £430,000 ($645,000) on behalf of the people of Guernsey. The States still have the option of leasing the island to a tenant, on the condition that the public would have access.

Map on page 14

BELOW:
you can walk to Lihou at low tide.

Les Minquiers and Les Ecréhous

The most recent major battle to repel French invaders in the Channel Islands took place as recently as 1953. Unlike previous conflicts up and down the centuries, this was a bloodless affair between Jersey (backed by the United Kingdom) and France, fought out in the cool ambience of the International Court of Justice at The Hague. The foothold in question was two groups of rocky islets, **Les Minquiers** (pronounced *Minkies*) and **Les Ecréhous** reefs. Les Ecréhous lie roughly halfway between Jersey and the Normandy coast of France, while Les Minquiers are situated to the south of Jersey on the way to St Malo.

The French government claimed that Les Minquiers were a dependency of their own Chausey group of islands, and that Les Ecréhous belonged to France by virtue of a gift in 1203. Legal arguments droned on for weeks, culminating in a 70-minute judgement favouring British sovereignty of the region under Jersey's jurisdiction.

Jersey continued to be responsible for maintaining customs posts on both reefs. The stone fisherman's cabin at Les Minquiers, bought by the Jersey authorities for £25 in 1909, is the most southerly customs station in the British Isles. Like a similar building on the Ecréhous, acquired for £52 in 1884, it bears the Jersey coat of arms.

The periodic visits of customs officers were unresented if not exactly welcomed by the man who, as "King of the Ecréhous", became the best-known Channel Islander internationally apart from the late Dame of Sark. Alphonse Le Gastelois was born in 1914, in St Martin, the Jersey parish to which Les Ecréhous belong, and he grew up to acquire a reputation as a loner and eccentric. He "emigrated" to Les Ecréhous in 1961 after coming under suspicion of being

In the 17th century Les Ecréhous became the meeting point for French and Jersey smuggling – a lucrative trade in which, it was said, everyone from Jersey's lieutenant-governor down was involved.

BELOW: rough seas around the islands have claimed countless vessels over the centuries.

Map on page 14

the perpetrator of terrifying sexual assaults on children – crimes for which Edward Paisnel, the notorious "Beast of Jersey", was convicted 10 years later.

A teddybear figure in woolly hat and wellies, Alphonse lived alone on the reef for 14 years. French yachtsmen and local fishermen would bring provisions for him when they visited Les Ecréhous, and owners of summer weekend cottages on the reef trusted him with their keys, asking him to keep an eye on their properties. At Christmas, a hamper from St Martin would arrive for the castaway aboard a Jersey government launch.

Absorbed in his rocky kingdom, he accumulated a mass of papers to prove that the reef did not belong to St Martin, but was held by him for the English Crown by right of long occupation. He finally gave up his claim in 1975 when he returned to Jersey to live in a boarding house in St Helier. Age and hard winters had caught up with Alphonse.

But he had a predecessor who outstayed him. Phillipe Pinel, a Jersey fisherman who lived on the reef from 1848 for 46 years, was the first "King of the Ecréhous". When Queen Victoria visited Jersey in 1857, he presented her – as one sovereign to another – with a basket he had made from dried seaweed.

Although the question of the ownership of the Minquiers and the Ecréhous has been settled in law, the decision of the court was not a popular one in France. From time to time a Tricoleur is found flying at the Minquiers, having been run up by visiting fishermen from Normandy or Brittany, and in 1994 the Ecréhous were "invaded" by a flotilla from the Norman port of Carteret. A thin blue line of Jersey policemen maintained order and kept the Jersey flag flying, but the dispute will almost certainly rumble on, given that it is less about real estate than fishing rights. ❏

BELOW: Les Ecréhous. **OVERLEAF:** a leafy lane in Guernsey.

INSIGHT GUIDES
TRAVEL TIPS

CONTENTS

Getting Acquainted

The Place

The Channel Islands, known to the French as Les Iles Anglo-Normandes, lie off the French coast in the Gulf of St Malo. The bailiwick of Jersey (capital, St Helier) is 45 sq. miles (117 sq. km) with a population of 85,150. The bailiwick of Guernsey (capital, St Peter Port) is 24 sq. miles (62 sq. km) with a population of 59,000 and has administrative responsibility for four smaller islands, Alderney, Sark, Herm and Jethou, which have a combined population of less than 3,000.

Time Zones

Like everyone else in the United Kingdom, Channel Islanders set their watches and clocks to Greenwich Mean Time (GMT), adding an extra hour in March for British Summer Time, and then reverting back to GMT in October.

When it is midday (GMT) in the islands, it is 7am in New York; midnight in Wellington; 1pm in Paris, Madrid and Rome; 8pm in Hong Kong, Manila, Beijing and Singapore; and 9pm in Tokyo.

Language

English is the language spoken and used by most people today, although the islands' tradition is very French. Each has its own dialect, forms of ancient Norman French called Jèrriais, Guernsiais, Aureogniais and Sercquiais. Basically they are conversational languages, and pronunciation and words differ greatly between the islands.

Until World War II these dialects were widely spoken and true French was used to conduct much written business. With the great influx of English-speaking people after the war, the dialects declined rapidly.

They are kept alive today by local societies, occasional letters in the newspapers, weekly talks on local radio and by two dictionaries produced by Dr Frank Le Maistre in Jersey and by Mrs de Garis in Guernsey. Signs at Jersey airport and harbour now welcome visitors: "Beinv'nue à Jèrri".

Street names in St Helier, Jersey, still carry their French names, often very different from the English ones they were later given – e.g. La Rue de Derrière (King Street), La Rue des Trois Pigeons (Hill Street) and La Rue Trousse Cotillon (Church Street, but in French "Pick up your Petticoat Street"). Most of the place names on Jersey retain their French names, and pronunciation still confuses many English-speaking visitors – e.g. Ouaisné is pronounced Waynay, and St Ouen St Wan.

Most surnames have French origins; Poingdestre, for instance, means "right-fisted". Many begin with 'Le' or 'L' meaning "the" (e.g. le Lièvre, the Hare; L'arbalestier, the Cross Bow; L'anglois, the Englishman – pronounced "Longwah" in Jersey and "Longlay" in Guernsey).

Others begin with 'De' 'De La' or 'D' meaning "from". These people were nobility who fled to the islands during the French Revolution (e.g. de la Mare, from the marsh; de la Haye, from La Haye in France, meaning hedge; de Gruchy, from Gruchy in France).

Older names have Frankish origins (e.g. Renouf, from Regenwulf; Mauger, from Maethelgaer).

Climate

The islands owe a great deal to their maritime situation. The surrounding waters, warmed by the North Atlantic Drift, reach 63°F or 64°F (17–18°C) in August. This helps reduce the risk of frost or snow, but it also keeps the summer temperatures a little lower than parts of England, with June to September maximums averaging 68°F (20°C).

The warm wet air can cause fog, – though the strong southwest winds soon cause it to disperse. Jersey and Guernsey usually vie for the highest sunshine totals in the British Isles. The islands average seven hours a day in the summer. Mean rainfall per year is about 100mm during each winter month and 50mm during each summer month. The islands, particularly Jersey, have one of the greatest tidal ranges anywhere in the world (40 ft/13 metres).

The Economy

Agriculture has traditionally been the main economic activity, with Jersey and Guernsey cattle famous all over the world. Tomatoes were a major export from Guernsey, although cut flowers are now growing in importance. In the past few decades, both bailiwicks have relied heavily on tourism and off-shore banking.

The Government

The islands are neither part of the United Kingdom nor of the European Union, though they have preferential relationships with both. The Queen appoints certain officials but the islands are left to run their own internal affairs independently, with Britain retaining a tacit responsibility for defence and external affairs.

The parliaments of Jersey, Guernsey and Alderney are individually known as the States. Sark retains a system dating to feudal times by which a Seigneur or Dame has wide responsibilities for the running of the island, with a legislature known as the Chief Pleas meeting three times a year.

Telephone Codes

The United Kingdom telephone code for Jersey is 01534. For Guernsey, Alderney, Sark and Herm, it is 01481. When dialling from outside the UK, preface these codes by 44 (for the UK) and omit the initial 0.

Planning the Trip

What To Bring

CLOTHING

Although you won't want to forget your sunhat, sunglasses and sun screen, the climate, being temperate, is unpredictable. Think about bringing some rainproofs and a couple of woollens just in case the weather changes.

Unwary tourists caught in a downpour can usually dive into the nearest shop and buy a plastic mac which, although unattractive looking, is cheap and gives good protection.

Leisure-wear is accepted almost anywhere, except in the better restaurants and hotels where men may feel more comfortable in more formal wear. In the towns, service might be refused to anyone clad solely in a swimsuit or not wearing a shirt. Smart, casual dress must be worn to gain admission to many night-clubs and discotheques. Those in jeans or training shoes are likely to be turned away.

One of the best ways of seeing the islands' beauty is on foot, so a stout pair of shoes is useful.

Topless sun-bathing, although not widespread, is accepted on the beaches, but baring all is not.

Electricity

Standard 240 volts AC sockets in most hotels take the standard UK three-square-pin 13-amp plugs. In older properties, in the smaller islands, round-pin plugs may still be in use. Good adapters should fit either type of socket.

Visas & Passports

British subjects and citizens of the Irish Republic do not require passports or entry visas. However a passport is required for day trips to France from the islands and as proof of identity for travellers using e-tickets at airports. EU members may travel on either passports or identity cards. Nationals of other Western European countries and North America need a valid passport but no entry visa. Citizens of other countries should contact the nearest British Embassy or Consulate about visa requirements.

Customs

As the Channel Islands are not part of the European Union, the maximum allowances for wine/spirits, cigarettes/perfumes brought from the islands into an EU country are:

Cigarettes 200 or cigarillos 100 or cigars 50 or tobacco 250 gms; still table wine 2 litres; spirits (+22% volume) 1 litre or fortified sparkling wine/some liqueurs 2 litres or additional still table wine allowance 2 litres; perfume 60 cc/ml; toilet water 250 cc/ml.

Persons under 17 years are not entitled to tobacco or alcohol allowances. The maximum personal allowance for other goods, including gifts, is £145. This may not be combined with other members of the travelling party. Items in excess are liable to VAT.

Animal Quarantine

Rabies is a very real danger to these small communities, especially because so many yachts sail to and fro between the islands and France. There is a total ban on the import of all animals from everywhere except the UK and Republic of Ireland.

Public Holidays

The Channel Islands enjoy the same public holidays as the UK with one extra – Liberation Day on 9 May to commemorate the end of the German Occupation in 1945. The

other holidays are: New Year's Day (1 January); Christmas Day (25 December); Boxing Day (26 December). Good Friday and Easter Monday fall in March or April. Two spring bank holidays in May and a summer bank holiday at the end of August also change annually. Alderney's summer bank holiday is at the beginning of August.

Getting There

BY AIR

In summer, direct flights operate to Jersey from around 25 regional airports in the UK. Fewer operate to Guernsey and Alderney. As UK holidaymakers look to more southerly destinations, the islands have begun a new campaign to appeal directly to their closer European neighbours.

The islands' policy of attracting out-of-season conference business means that flights can be fully booked at the most surprising times. Low-cost airlines have brought down prices but airport charges are high and there are few real bargains. The cheapest fares are normally secured by booking well in advance through the airline websites.

Direct Air Services

Airports from which it is possible to fly direct to Jersey are shown below with the airlines. A letter (G) indicates that the airline also flies to Guernsey.

Belfast City
flybe
Tel: 0871 700 0123
www.flybe.com (G)
Birmingham
flybe *(see above)* (G)
Bournemouth
Rockhopper
Tel: 01481 824567
www.rockhopper.aero (G)
Aurigny
Tel: 01481 822886
www.aurigny.com
Bristol
British Airways
Tel: 0870 850 9850
www.ba.com
Air Southwest
Tel: 0870 241 8202

www.airsouthwest.com
Aurigny *(details as before* (G)
Cardiff
Air Wales
Tel: 0870 777 3131
www.airwales.com
bmibaby
Tel: 0870 264 2229
www.bmibaby.com
Coventry
Thomsonfly
Tel: 0870 1900 737
www.thomsonfly.com
Durham Tees Valley
bmibaby *(see above)*
Norwich
flybe *(see above)*
Nottingham/East Midlands
bmibaby *(see above)*
Edinburgh
bmi
Tel: 00870 6070 555
www.flybmi.com
flybe *(see above)*
Exeter
flybe *(see above)* (G)
Glasgow
bmi *(see above)*
flybe *(see above)*
Inverness
flybe *(see above)*
Isle of Man
flybe *(see above)*
Leeds/Bradford
bmi *(see above)* (G)
Luton
flybe *(see above)*
London Gatwick
British Airways *(see above)*
flybe *(see above)* (G)
Guernsey Aurigny *(see above)*
London City
VLM
Tel: 0207 476 6677
www.flyvlm.com
London Stansted
Aurigny *(see above).* Jersey via
Guernsey.
Manchester
British Airways *(see above)*
bmibaby *(see above)*
flybe *(see above)* (G)
Aurigny *(see above)* (G only)
Manston, Kent
EUJet
Tel: 0870 414 1414
www.eujet.com
Newcastle
British Airways *(see above)*

flybe *(see above)* (G).
Plymouth
Air Southwest *(see above)*
Shoreham
EuroExec
Tel: 01273 446447
www.euroexec.com
Southampton
flybe *(see above)*
Swansea
Air Wales *(see above)*
Dublin
bmibaby *(see above)*
British Airways *(see above)*
flybe *(see above)* (G)
Aer Lingus
Tel: 00353 (0) 818 365000
www.aerlingus.com
Cork (summer)
British Airways *(see above)*
Manx Airlines
Tel: 01 260 1588
www.manx-airlines.com
Shannon (summer)
British Airways *(see above)*

BY SEA

Condor Ferries
(tel: 01305 761551 and 0845
3452000, www.condorferries.co.uk)
operates a high-speed catamaran
service from Weymouth and Poole to
Jersey via Guernsey. Cars can be
taken on any of the services. The
fastest service takes 2 hours to
Guernsey, 3 hours to Jersey. In high
season there are up to four crossings
a day, in winter the service is
reduced to one early morning
crossing from Weymouth.

　Condor also operates the
conventional Clipper ferry from
Portsmouth to Guernsey and Jersey.
The service takes 6 hours to
Guernsey, 10 hours to Jersey. For
the night crossings cabins should be
reserved well in advance.

　Fast catamaran services,
operated by Condor ferries *(see
above)* and **Emeraude Ferries**
(tel: 01534 766566) and **Manche
Îles Express** (tel: 01534 0000)
run between Jersey, Guernsey,
Herm and Sark. **Condor** and
Emeraude also operate fast
services to St Malo in France
(passport required).

TOURIST OFFICES ABROAD

The main VisitBritain offices can
deal with enquiries concerning the
Channel Islands. Alternatively
consult www.jersey.com. Some of
the VisitBritain offices in English-
speaking countries are:

Australia
Level 2, 15 Blue Street
North Sydney, NSW 2060
Tel: (61 2) 9021 4400
Fax: (61 2) 9021 4499
www.visitbritain.com/VB3-en-AU
Canada
5915 Airport Road, Suite 120
Mississauga, Toronto
Ontario L4V 1T1
Tel: Free toll 1 888 VISIT UK
(847 4885)
www.visitbritain.com/ca
Ireland
18-19 College Green Dublin 2
Tel: (353 1) 670 8000
Fax: (353 1) 670 8244
www.visitbritain.com/ie
New Zealand
17th Floor, 151 Queen Street
Auckland 1
Tel: (649) 303 1446
Fax: (649) 377 6965
South Africa
Lancaster Gate
Hyde Park Lane, Hyde Park 2196
Johannesburg
Postal address:
PO Box 41896
Craighall 2024, Johannesburg
Tel: (27 11) 325 0343
Fax: (27 11) 325 0344
www.visitbritain.com/za
United States
New York
7th Floor, 551 Fifth Avenue
New York NY 10176-0799
Tel: (1 212) 745 0200
Fax: (1 212) 745 3062
www.britainusa.com/ny
Los Angeles
10880 Wilshire Blvd
Suite 11766, Los Angeles,
California CA 90025-6538
Tel: (1 310) 481 0031
Fax: (1 310) 481 2960
www.britainusa.com/la

Practical Tips

Security & Crime

Neither Jersey nor the other islands have high crime rates. Most wrong-doers are apprehended by the police fairly quickly but not everybody can be trusted, so keep valuables out of sight and lock car doors.

Emergency Services

Useful Numbers: Dial 999 in an emergency for police, fire, ambulance or sea rescue. In Herm dial '0' for the operator.

JERSEY

Police HQ 01534 612612
Beach guards (summer only) 01534 482032
Bus information 01534 877772
Ambulance Emergency 999
Ambulance HQ 01534 622343
Fire Service 01534 737444
General Hospital 01534 622000
Samaritans 0845 7909090
Daily Diary 1882
Automobile Association 0800 887766
Flight Enquiries 01534 490999
Operator (telephone) 100
Directory Enquiries 192
International Directory 153
Weather 01534 745550

GUERNSEY

Samaritans 0845 790090
Weather Report 01481 12080
Alarm Call 1777
Directory Enquiries 118118
Island Coachways 01481 721210
Flight Enquiries 01481 237766

ALDERNEY

Island Medical Centre 822822
Flight Enquiries 822624
www.aurigny.com

SARK

Medical Officer 832045

Health

It is advisable to take up a medical insurance as private consultations and prescriptions are not covered by the reciprocal health agreements between the Channel Islands and many other countries. In Jersey, however, UK residents can get free treatment at special morning clinics held at the General Hospital (tel: 759000). This opens May–Sept Mon–Fri 9am–noon, Sat 10–11.30am, and Oct–Apr Mon, Wed & Fri only 9.30–11.30am. The General Hospital's emergency unit is open at all times for treatment, including emergency dental care.

Inpatient treatment is provided free-of-charge in Jersey, Guernsey and Alderney. The majority of visitors who seek treatment are those suffering from sunburn.

Banks

While there are around 100 banks in the Channel Islands, most are set up to take deposits or investments. Foreign exchange dealings, therefore, have to be carried out in one of the British High Street clearing banks such as Barclays, National Westminster, Lloyds TSB, HSBC or The Royal Bank of Scotland.

Hours of business for banks in Jersey and Guernsey vary from bank to bank and branch to branch, as the banks adjust the hours to suit the needs of their customers. Some banks in town open as early as 8.30am and close as late as 5.30–6pm. To be on the safe side one can assume that all branches will be open between 9.30 and 4.30pm.

In Alderney, banking hours are from 9.30am–3.30pm weekdays.

The banks having branches here are Lloyds, TSB, HSBC and National Westminster.

The two banks in Sark are National Westminster and HSBC. During the season NatWest opens 9.30am–1.15pm and 2.15–3pm Mon–Fri, and HSBC 9.30am–12.30pm and 1.30–3pm Mon–Fri. There are no automatic cash dispensers on either of these two islands.

Most hotels and shops will accept travellers' cheques or Eurocheques.

The most commonly accepted credit cards are Access (MasterCard) and Visa. American Express and Diners Club are not so ubiquitous. Most proprietors of the smaller hotels and guest houses will expect accommodation bills to be paid in cash or by cheque.

Currency

The pound is the official unit of currency and the bailiwicks of Jersey and Guernsey issue their own money. The notes are in £1, £5, £10, £20 and £50 denominations while coins are 1p, 2p, 5p, 10p, 20p, 50p and £1.

English, Scottish and Northern Irish money is also in circulation and both bailiwicks accept each other's currency. But make sure that you exchange all local coins and notes before leaving the islands; they aren't accepted as legal tender elsewhere.

Euros are readily accepted in a growing number of shops. Other currencies must be exchanged at a Bureau de Change office or bank.

Postal Services

Each bailiwick has its own postal system and issues its own stamps. Look out for red mail boxes in Jersey and blue ones in Guernsey. Only local stamps are valid for sending mail out of the islands. Guernsey postage is used in Herm and Sark, although mail will be franked locally. Alderney has its own postage but also uses Guernsey's.

Unlike the UK, mail is not divided into first and second class service – there is only one class. At the time of writing, the standard rate for a letter or card sent from Guernsey is 26p within the bailiwick and 32p to the UK. Letters weighing up to 20 grammes, or postcards, cost 34p to send to European countries and go by air automatically. Airmail rates to other parts of the world vary according to weight and size.

The main post offices are open from 9am–5pm during the week. On Saturday, in Jersey and Guernsey, the main offices are open from 9am–noon, in Alderney they open from 9am–12.30pm and in Sark they open from 9am–4.30pm. Many sub-post offices shut early one day a week.

Jersey and Guernsey stamps are sought after by philatelists and collectors throughout the world. There are five or six new issues every year, many coinciding with special anniversaries and events. These can be bought at philatelic bureaux in the main post office in St Helier and St Peter Port.

Telephone and Fax

Visitors should experience few problems making calls home or abroad, even from the smaller islands (whose services are handled by Guernsey Telecoms, Cable and Wireless and Wave Telecom). Area codes for the UK and main cities in most countries are found in the middle of the telephone directory. There are plenty of public call boxes in street kiosks, pubs, restaurants, hotel lobbies, shops and at the ports.

International calls can be dialled direct from any public phone. Most call boxes have card phones, which also accept credit cards. Pre-paid phone cards are available from post offices, newsagents and garages. Direct-dial codes for the UK are the same as those used within the UK.

In Jersey, faxes can be sent from the main post office in Broad Street, St Helier, or from the Jersey Evening Post, Charles Street, St Helier.

Internet access

In Guernsey, wireless internet access (WiFi) is available at the airport and a number of cafes in Town. There is free Internet at the Guille Alles Library after taking out a visitor membership; and 75p buys you 30 minutes at Allsorts, 32 Contree Mansell.

The Media

All English national newspapers and numerous foreign papers, together with a vast selection of magazines and periodicals, arrive daily on a special early-morning delivery plane, except during fog or bad weather.

High-powered transmitters relay clear pictures from the four British terrestrial TV channels into the majority of homes and hotels. More regional news can be obtained by watching Channel Television bulletins on ITV (Channel 3). Some sets can receive teletext information (such as Ceefax) and with special aerials French TV broadcasts can be picked up. Almost all hotels, guest houses, pubs and most homes now have satellite television.

For what's on, when, and where, consult the *Jersey Evening Post*, the *Guernsey Press* and the fortnightly *Alderney Journal*. In the summer, various holiday papers and publications are also produced.

Tourist Offices

The bailiwicks of Jersey and Guernsey compete with each other as holiday destinations so enquiries have to be directed to the appropriate tourist office and not to a central bureau covering the whole Channel Islands. Information on how to get to the islands and where to stay is normally sent free-of-charge (surface mail only) to any part of the world on request.

The tourism departments provide help in finding accommodation but do not make bookings or reservations. Public information and accommodation desks in Jersey and Guernsey are staffed during normal office hours out-of-season, during weekday evenings, all day Saturday and on Sunday mornings and evenings, in summer.

Enquiries in writing or by phone should be directed to:
Jersey Tourism, Liberation Square, St Helier JE1 1BB.
Jersey, Channel Islands.
Tel: 01534-500777. Fax: 500808.
e-mail: info@jersey.com
www.jersey.com
Guernsey Tourist Board
P.O. Box 23, St Peter Port G41 3AW, Guernsey, Channel Islands.
Tel: 01481-723552. Fax: 714951.
e-mail: tourism@guernsey.net
www.visitguernsey.com
Alderney Tourist Office
Victoria Street, St Anne, Alderney
Tel: 01481-8227811. Fax: 822436.
e-mail: tourism@alderney.net
Sark Tourist Office
Sark, Channel Islands.
Tel: 01481-832345. Fax: 832483.
www.sarktourism.com

Consulates

The Channel Islands are too small to warrant their own diplomatic representation overseas. The interests of foreign nationals living and working in the islands, as well as visitors, are handled by Consuls in each bailiwick.

Consular Offices in Jersey:
Belgium
Honorary Consul – Mr A. R. Binnington, PO Box 87, 22 Grenville Street.
Tel: 01534 609203 or 07797 715562.
Denmark
Honorary Consul – Mr G.R. Le Moine, St Helier Port Services.
Tel: 01534 870300.
France
Consul – Mr R Pallot, 71 Halkett Place, St Helier. Tel: 01534 726256.
Germany
Honorary Consul – Mr K. Sour, 1st Floor, Ingouville House Ingouville Lane, St Helier.
Tel: 01534 511513.
Ireland
Consul – Mrs. P. O'Neill, La Minou, La Rue de la Pigeonnerie, St Brelade.
Tel: 01534 745551.
Norway
Honorary Consul – Mr S.A. Adeler, Petit Bois, La Blinerie Lane, St Clement. Tel: 01534 30175.

Portugal
Consul – Mr C. Costa, Burlington House, St Saviours Road, St Helier. Tel: 01534 877188.
Sweden
Honorary Consul – Mr P. H Sturgess, 9 Esplanade, St Helier. Tel: 01534 780545.
Netherlands
Honorary Consul – Mr R. Jeune, PO Box 87, 22 Grenville Street, St Helier. Tel: 01534 609000.

Vice-Consuls in Jersey:
Finland
Honorary Vice-Consul – Mr T.J. Herbert, 22 Grenville Street, St Helier. Tel: 01534 609000.
Italy
Foreign Consular Agent – Mr Renzo Martin Fondafau House, La Route de la Côte, St Martin. Tel: 01534 853167 and 851250.

Vice-Consuls in Guernsey:
France
Vice-Consular Agency, 38 Hauteville, St Peter Port. Tel: 01481 729290.
German Federal Republic
Honorary Consul   Mr Drake, c/o Isle of Sark Shipping Co Ltd, White Rock, St Peter Port. Tel: 01481 733300.
Italy
Vice-Consular Agent – Mrs. J.A. Finetti, Montechiari, Petit Axce Lane, Vale. Tel: 01481 243759.
Netherlands Vice Consulate
Vice-Consul – Mr Geoff Norman, c/o. Norman Piette Ltd, P.O. Box 88, Bulwer Avenue, St Sampson's. Tel: 01481 241721; fax: 243265.
Switzerland
Albert F Good. Tel: 01481 710267; fax: 710275.

Getting Around

Inter-island Travel

Herm is only 2 miles (3 km) and Sark only 9 miles (14 km) from Guernsey, making them both easily accessible by ferry.

An air taxi company, Aurigny Air Services, has its operations base in Alderney. It's much faster to get one of their little yellow Trilander planes for a visit from Jersey or Guernsey to Alderney than to go by sea.

The French ports of Carteret, Granville and St Malo are just a short ferry ride from Jersey.

Services from Jersey

BY SEA

Passengers Only
To St Malo:
Condor Ferries (01534 872240). Crossing time 1 hr 15 mins. Emeraude Ferries (01534 766566; www.emeraude.co.uk). Crossing time 1 hr 15 mins.
To Carteret and Granville:
Manche–Îles Express (01534 880756; www.manche-iles-express.com) Crossing time 1 hr to Carteret, 1hr 10 mins to Granville.
To Guernsey:
Condor Ferries (01534 872240) There is no direct service from Jersey to Herm. For more information on passenger services from Jersey contact: Ace Travel (01534 488488).
To Sark:
Manche–Îles Express (01534 880756)

Car Passengers/Ferries
To Guernsey:
Condor Ferries (01534 607080). Crossing time 55 mins.

To St Malo:
Condor Ferries (01534 872240). Crossing time 1 hr 15 mins. Emeraude Ferries (01534 766566; Fax: 68741). Crossing time 1 hr 15 mins.

BY AIR

Travel from Jersey
To Paris and Cherbourg
Twin Jet (+33 0387 567 070; www.twinjet.net)
To Dinard, Caen, Guernsey and Alderney
Aurigny (01481 822886; www.aurigny.com)

Travel from Guernsey
To Alderney:
Aurigny Air Services (01481 822886; Fax: 729666; www.aurigny.com)
Condor Ferries (01481 729666)
Rockhopper Aero (01481 824567 www.rockhopper.aero)
To Dinard:
Aurigny Air Services (01481 822886 www.aurigny.com)
To Herm:
Herm Seaway Express (01481 721342)
Travel Trident (01481 721342)
To Jersey:
Condor Ferries (01481 726121)
To Sark:
Isle of Sark Shipping Company (01481 724059)
To St Malo:
Condor Ferries (01481 729666)

Travel to Alderney
By Air: There are daily flights from Southampton, as well as frequent services to Jersey and Guernsey, Dinard and Caen. For further information contact Aurigny Air Services (01481 822886) or Rockhopper Aero (01481 824567).
By Sea: For information on passenger services from the UK to Alderney and from Alderney to Jersey, tel: 01481 823737. To reach Alderney from the UK one should travel to Guernsey and then make a connection to Alderney.

Public Transport

BUS

While a car is the easiest way of getting around, buses are usually the only viable alternative for non-drivers. The Jersey Motor Transport and Island Coachways on Guernsey have invested heavily in a fleet of new buses and cheap fares – 50p a journey or Wave and Save smart cards. Anyone planning to use the buses regularly during their stay will find it cheaper to buy an Explorer ticket for 1, 3 or 7 days of unlimited travel. Off-season and Sunday services on both islands are reduced. Airport routes run frequently during the year.

Alderney has an almost hourly bus service which operates during July, August and September on a circular route taking in the town, harbour, camp site and many of the sandy beaches.

TAXIS

Waiting areas for rank cabs can be found at the ports and in the towns. Private taxis can be ordered by phone from one of the companies listed in the telephone directories, especially useful when planning an evening out. Extra charges apply for late night collection, waiting time, etc.

The taxi is the main transport link between the airport and St Anne in Alderney. Sark has no motorised vehicles – taxis there are literally horse-powered, as a horse-drawn van is one of the best means of touring the island.

Taxi Companies
Jersey: 1A Taxi service (07797 717122); A & R Airport Taxis (07797 716121); Arrow Cabs (01534 731111); A1 Rank Taxis (07797 716464); A.A.T (Adams Airport Taxis) (07797 720264); Bob's Airport Taxis (07797 716139); Citicabs (01534 499999); Clarendon Dragons (01534 871111 and 01534 888333); A to B Taxi

Services (01534 625033 and 07797 737347); Domino Cabs (01534 747047); Hail A Cab (01534 629600); Luxicabs (01534 887000); Première Cabs (07797 728749); Wheeler's (01534 858121); Yellow Cabs (01534 888888).

Guernsey: Delta Taxis are the biggest company and offer wheelchair-accessible cabs (01481 200000); Abba Taxi Service (07781 1047220); ABCAB (07781 13455); Best Friends Pet Taxi Service (01481257979); Bob Nicholson – early morning (07781 154713); Bruno's Taxi (07781 100228); Fonacab (01481 232919); The Hackney Cab (01481 121086); Island Taxis (01481 129090); Norman Le Messurier, with wheelchair-accessible cabs (07781 121086); Sunshine Taxis (01481 245675).

Taxi ranks: Airport (01481 235283); Bonded Stores, St Peter Port (01481 714106); Bridge, St Sampson's (01481 247131); Weighbridge St Peter Port (01481 714143); Vaudin's United Taxis (01481 725590).

Alderney: ABC Taxis (823760); Alderney Taxis, Le Banquage (822611); Island Taxis (823823); J.S. Taxis (01481 822269).

COACHES

An organised coach tour, with a guide, is one of the best ways to see the islands and to get a feel for what is worth seeing in depth. Tours can be for a full day, for a morning or afternoon only, or for an evening. Tickets can be booked either directly with the coach companies or with your hotel or guest house.

In Jersey contact either Tantivy Blue Coach Tours, 70–72 Colomberie, St Helier (01534 38877), or the Waverley Way, 20 Gloucester Street, St Helier (01534 58360).

In Guernsey, island tours are run by Island Coachways (01481 720210) www.island-coachways.demon.co.uk, at the bus terminus, South Esplanade.

TRAINS

Except for a couple of model railways and a short track run by a steam museum enthusiast in Jersey, the only passenger train in the islands is for tourists and runs from Braye to the northeast coast in Alderney. The diesel engine pulls former London Underground carriages on the route six times each weekend between Easter and the end of September.

In Jersey Le Petit Train runs guided tours along St Aubin's Bay, accompanied by a guide giving detailed commentary en route. A second Petit Train departs on a historical 35-minute circular tour of St Helier.

Private Transport

Car Hire
Self-drive rates are among the cheapest in Europe. One reason for this is that some car manufacturers have been using the islands as a back door into the British market; by registering the cars in the islands and hiring them out for a few months, dealers have been able to sell nearly new cars to mainland customers at quite a big discount because of the saving in car duty normally added to new cars in the UK.

A good "A" car can be hired on a daily basis from £30 per day (fully inclusive, with fuel). Most companies will offer 7 days' hire for the price of 6. Visitors must produce a valid driving licence with no endorsements for dangerous or drunken driving in the last five years and they must be aged 21 and over. Some restrictions may be imposed by the hire company's insurance agent in respect of the upper age limit.

Hire cars are instantly recognisable as a large letter "H" is affixed next to each number plate.

Signposting is often a problem as they are few and far between in many cases. Buying a map to help find your way around is always a good idea.

Cycling
Cycling has become more popular since the introduction of the Green Lane Scheme (*see Speed Limits*

section below). A little more puff is needed to circumnavigate Jersey than Guernsey by bicycle since distances are greater and the hills longer and steeper in Jersey. Cycles can be hired from a number of companies offering a wide range of cycles, some with baby seats.

Moped and motorcycle hire

Hiring of motorcycles, scooters and mopeds is generally restricted to people over 21. Some companies, however, may hire mopeds to anyone over 18. In all cases, the hirer must have held a full driving licence for at least 12 months.

VEHICLE HIRE

Jersey
Car Hire:
Aardvark A Z Zebra Hire Cars
9 The Esplanade, St Helier
Tel: 01534 736556;
www.zebrahire.com
Avis Rent-A-Car
Beaumont, St Peter
Tel: 01534 51900;
www.avisjersey.co.uk
Europcar
Jersey Airport
Tel: 0800 735 0735;
www.europcarjersey.com
Falles Car Hire
Beaumont, St Peter
Tel: 01534 495000;
www.jersey.co.uk/falles
Harringtons
Route des Genets, St Brelade
Tel: 01534 741363
Hertz Rent-A-Car
Jersey Airport
Tel: 0800 735 1014;
www.hertz-jersey.co.uk
Sovereign Hire Cars
27 The Esplanade, St Helier
Tel: 01534 608062;
www.carhire-jersey.com
Viceroy Hire Cars
59-61 Kensington Place, St Helier
Tel: 01534 738698; email:
info@norfolkhoteljersey.co.uk
Welcome Hire Cars
Three Oaks Garage, La Grande
Route de St Lawrence
Tel: 01534 863117; email:
cynthia@cigarages.co.uk

Moped and Motorcycle Hire
Sovereign Hire Cars
27 The Esplanade, St Helier
Tel: 01534 608062;
www.carhire-jersey.com

Bicycle Hire:
Aardvark A-Z Zebra Cycles
9 The Esplanade, St Helier
Tel: 01534 736556;
www.zebrahire.com
Harringtons
Route des Genets, St Brelade
Tel: 01534 741363
Jersey Cycletours
St Aubin
Tel: 01534 746780/482898

Guernsey
Car Hire:
Avis Rent-a-Car
P.O. Box 258
Les Caches, St Martin
Tel: 01481 235266
Baubigny Car Hire
Stanley Road, St Peter Port
Tel: 01481 729172
EuropCar Inter-Rent
Les Caches, St Martin
Tel: 01481 239696
Falles Hire Cars
Les Caches, St Martin
Tel: 01481 236902
Harlequin Hire Car
Les Caches, St Martin
Tel: 01481 239511
Hertz Rent-a-Car
Airport Forecourt, Forest
Tel: 01481 237638
Sarnia Car Hire
Stanley Road, St Peter Port
Tel: 01481 723933
Value Rent a Car
Braye Road, Vale
Tel: 01481 243547

Motor Cycle And Motor Scooter/Moped Hire:
Millard & Co. Ltd., Victoria Road, St Peter Port (01481 720777).

Bicycle Hire:
Cycleworld, Camp du Roi Crossroads, Vale, (01481 258285); Electra Ltd, North Plantation, St Peter Port (01481 726926); Le Courtil Bryart, Rue Sauvage, St Sampson's, *free delivery and collection*; (01481

58518); La Villette Garage, St Martin, (01481 37577); Millard & Co. Ltd., Victoria Road, St Peter Port (01481 720777); Rent-a-Bike, St Sampson's, Bridge (01481 49311).

Alderney
Car Hire:
AFS Hire
Braye, Alderney
Tel: 01481 823352
Braye Car Hire
Tel: 01481 823738
Central Car Hire
Tel: 01481 822971,
mobile: 04481 102971)
Mini-Moke Hire
Tel: 01481 822971.

Bicycle Hire:
J.B. Cycle Hire (822294); Pedal Power (01481 822286).

Sark
Bicycle Hire:
A–B Cycles (01481 832844); Avenue Cycle Hire (01481 832102, Fax: 832720).

Traffic Laws

Yellow lines painted across the roads at intersections mean "Stop and give way". It is sensible not to ignore them, particularly in Guernsey where many roads are of a similar size and the difference between a major and a minor road isn't always obvious. Yellow arrows before a junction in Guernsey and Alderney indicate that a junction is ahead and one should always be ready to stop.

The only stretch of road with more than one lane is Victoria Avenue in Jersey, the dual-carriageway coming from the west into St Helier.

The "filter in turn" is one of the most efficient systems in use and certainly helps keep traffic flowing at busy junctions. These occur at larger junctions where vehicles from each direction take it in turn to cross or join the traffic flow from other directions.

Long yellow lines painted the length of the kerb are areas where parking or stopping is prohibited day and night. A number of zones in St Helier, including the high streets, are pedestrianised and closed to traffic. In Guernsey, only permit holders can get access to the main street in St Peter Port.

Speed Limits

Jersey's speed limit is 40 mph but drops to 30 and 20 mph in certain signposted areas. A number of parishes have introduced "green lanes", smaller lanes on which priority has now been given to pedestrians, horses and bicycles. The speed limit on these is 15 mph.

In Guernsey it is not permitted to go faster than 35 mph on open roads, 25 mph in built-up areas and 5 mph in some places.

Alderney has a similar maximum speed of 35 mph, except in St Anne where 20 mph is the norm.

Parking

Parking in towns can be frustrating as visitors vie with local commuters to get spaces. It is free in Guernsey and controlled by a disc clock obtainable on the car ferries or from the police station, tourist information office and many garages and shops. Hire car firms should also provide them.

Time of arrival has to be set on the clock which must then be left on the dashboard for traffic wardens to see. Parking zones are indicated by blue signs and vary from 15 minutes to 10 hours.

Jersey operates a similar free disc clock system in some areas on the outskirts of St Helier and, depending on the area, parking is allowed for periods between 20 minutes and three hours.

Payment for other parking spots in St Helier (including in the multi-storey car parks, in some areas of St Brelade's and Gorey Pier), is by Paycard. The Paycard can be purchased in advance from Post Offices, garages and shops displaying the Paycard symbol but not in the carparks themselves. Instructions for use are printed on the cards.

Free disabled parking is allowed if you are an "Orange Badge" holder and some spots in the multi-storey car parks have been set aside for disabled drivers.

Fuel

Fuel is much cheaper than on the mainland. Unleaded fuel and Four-Star can be found everywhere; diesel oil is sold at most stations. Fuel cannot be purchased on Sunday in Guernsey.

Where to Stay

Many visitors return to the same hotel time and time again, mainly because they get value for money and a friendly welcome from staff who remember them from their previous holiday.

The choice of accommodation ranges across the spectrum – from the luxury international hotel with a string of awards displayed at its entrance to the humble British seaside guest house, quality self-catering apartments, holiday villages and campsites.

Controls are such that each of the bailiwicks has its own registration and grading system which applies to all premises taking paying guests. Some 500 establishments in both Jersey and Guernsey are graded and assessed annually by a team of Tourism Department inspectors.

The schemes are designed to ensure that basic standards are met and proper facilities provided; unfortunately, they aren't comparable with grading systems in other countries. Visitors can choose where they want to stay by consulting official lists of the registered accommodation in free annual tourism brochures.

The Grading System

The Jersey grading system separates the hotels from the guest houses. The hotel register, indicated by suns, has five grades and the guest house register, denoted by a diamond shaped mark, has three grades. The higher grade establishments usually have more facilities and generally higher standards of service.

In Guernsey the hotel register is denoted by crowns, with each hotel being awarded between one and five crowns. Guest houses have letter

Cycling Tours

No distance on the islands is too far to cycle and the network of quiet country lanes and coastal roads make for pleasant, if at times strenuous, cycling.

Since the introduction of the Green Lane Scheme, cycling on Jersey has become much more popular. Cycle routes have been established all over the island and clear signs enable you to explore the winding lanes without constantly referring to maps. If a rural lane suddenly ceases to be a Green Lane, the probability is you have cycled across a parish boundary; three pro-car parishes are still resisting the Green Lane scheme. For visitors who want to

plan their own cycling itineraries, Jersey Tourism publishes a useful map, marking the coastal circuit, inland links and connections to popular attractions. Jersey Tourism also publishes a cycling guide with five detailed routes, 15–18 miles (24–30km) in length. Refreshment stops are highlighted.

Jersey Tourism (tel: 01534 500700) offers guided cycle tours four times a week in season. The tours are free of charge, last two hours and cover the history and heritage as well as the natural beauty of the island.

The Guernsey Tourist Board (01481 723552) publishes a guide to waymarked cycle paths.

grades, from A to D. Over 20 percent of the accommodation available in Guernsey is in self-catering units, also graded A to D. Jersey's tourism industry relies more on conventional hotel accommodation and there is far less self-catering; but in recent years a number of high quality conversions of existing buildings have been carried out for this purpose.

There are not many accommodation choices in Alderney. Nevertheless, each establishment is inspected and approved ones are published. Details of the registered hotels, guest houses, holiday cottages and flats on Sark and Herm can be found in Guernsey's accommodation guide.

The hotel and guest house tariffs quoted below are approximate rates for a person sharing a room for one night on a bed and breakfast basis. In hotels with restaurants, half-board terms are normally available. The number of persons accommodated are shown.

Prices generally fluctuate according to the season and are usually subject to annual cost of living increases. Substantial savings are possible by booking accommodation and travel together as part of a tour package.

Because there is only a limited amount of space, reservations for a holiday between May and September need to be made well in advance, otherwise choice could be limited. During the season, only certain hotels accept midweek bookings.

Visitors who decide to take a break "on spec" during the season can usually find somewhere to stay, although it is likely to be in the higher or lower price brackets – check before travel is arranged.

The shoulder months, March, April, May or September and October, are, weather permitting, good times of year to travel to the Channel Islands – rates are lower and accommodation easier to find.

The islands prohibit the import of trailers or motorhomes and there are no caravan sites. Camping is allowed only on recognised sites where facilities are provided; no camping is permitted elsewhere.

Reservations for accommodation in Jersey can be made through JerseyLink (Tel: 01534 500888, Fax: 500808).

Jersey

Hotels

Apollo
St Helier
Tel: 01534 725441; Fax: 722120
www.huggler.com
Comprehensive facilities include indoor and outdoor pools. Situated around a quiet courtyard off one of St Helier's bustling streets. 85 rooms. £47–£57.

Atlantic
Le Mont da la Pulente
St Brelade
Tel: 01534 744101; Fax: 744102
www.theatlantichotel.com
Close to the airport, the hotel is set in extensive private grounds and has magnificent views over St Ouen's Bay. 50 rooms. £95–£112.

Beau Couperon
Rozel Bay, St Martin
Tel: 01534 865522; Fax: 865332
www.jerseyhotels.com
Part of a converted Napoleonic fortress overlooking Rozel Bay. Peaceful location and comfortable accommodation. £35–£58.

Beau Rivage
St Brelade's Bay
Tel: 01534 745983; Fax: 747127
www.jersey.co.uk/hotels/beau
Situated directly on the seafront in St Brelade's Bay with seafront conservatory, sun terrace and private sunbathing deck. 27 rooms. £18–£54.

Beausite
Grouville Bay, Grouville
Tel: 01534 857577; Fax: 857211
www.southernhotels.com
Close to the Royal Jersey Golf Course, and the sandy bay of Grouville. 76 rooms. £34–£52.

Bergerac Hotel & apartments
Portelet Bay, St Brelade
Tel: 01534 745991; Fax: 743010
www.southernhotels.com
Close to the picturesque Portelet Bay and Ouaisné Beach. All modern facilities. 50 rooms. £34–£52. Apartments £343–£1050 per week.

Château La Chaire
Rozel Bay, St Martin
Tel: 01534 863354; Fax: 865137
www.chateau-la-chaire.co.uk
This beautiful country house sits at the foot of Rozel Valley. 14 rooms. £66–£91.

Château Valeuse Hotel
St Brelade's Bay
Tel: 01534 746281; Fax: 747110
e-mail: chatval@itl.net
Set back from the seafront, Château Valeuse offers high quality service in a relaxed atmosphere. 34 rooms. £35–£54.

Cheval Roc
Les Nouvelles Charrières
St John
Tel: 01534 862865; Fax: 723684
Overlooking the beautiful, secluded beach and fishing harbour on the Island's dramatic north coast. 42 rooms. £25–£45.

Club Hotel & Spa
Green Street, St Helier
Tel: 01534 876500; Fax: 720371
www.theclubjersey.com
New, luxury "boutique" hotel in the centre of town, with stylish rooms and arguably the best restaurant on the island *(see under Bohemia Bar and Restaurant in Restaurant section)*, as well as the glass-domed "New York Café"-style restaurant and a luxury spa. 38 rooms, 8 suites. £88–£188.

Cristina
St Aubins Bay
Tel: 01534 758024; Fax: 758028
www.dolanhotels.com
A quiet location enjoying one of the finest views of St Aubin's Bay. 60 rooms. £38–£55.

Eulah Country House
Mont Cochon, St Helier
Tel: 01534 626626; Fax: 626600
www.eulah.co.uk
Former Edwardian vicarage in tranquil garden setting with lovely views over St Aubin's Bay. Luxurious guest rooms, each individually designed and all with Kingsize beds. Upstairs seaview lounge with a fully stocked "Honesty Bar". 15 minutes' walk to St Helier, 5 to the beach. No smokers or children under 14. 11 rooms. £80–£115

Golden Sands
St Brelade's
Tel: 01534 741241; Fax: 499366
www.dolanhotels.com
In the centre of St Brelade's Bay, virtually on the beach. Sea-view rooms all have balcony and splendid views of the bay. Good facilities for children. 62 rooms. £38–£55.

Greenhills
St Peter's Valley, St Peter
Tel: 01534 481042; Fax: 485322
www.greenhillshotel.com
Small and charming country house hotel set in its own gardens in the rural heart of St Peter. The house retains some of its original 17th-century architectural features. Family-run and friendly. 25 rooms. £49–£68.

Hotel de France
St Saviour's Road
Tel: 01534 614000; Fax: 614199
www.hoteldefrance.co.uk
Elegant and comfortable hotel. Well-equipped, with indoor pool, fitness centre and two restaurants. 272 rooms. £55–£73.

La Place
Route du Coin, La Haule, St Brelade
Tel: 01534 744261; Fax: 745164
www.hoteldellaplacejersey.com
One of Jersey's top-rated hotels. Exceptionally comfortable, traditional and built around the remains of a 17th-century farmhouse. High standard of cuisine and service. 40 rooms. £40–£94.

Laurels
Route du Fort, St Helier
Tel: 01534 736444; Fax: 759904
www.seabird.co.je
Close to town and the seafront. 37 rooms. £30–£50.

Lavender Villa Hotel
Rue a Don, Grouville Bay
Tel: 01534 854937; Fax: 856147
Small and friendly family-run hotel with access to the beach across the Royal Jersey golf course. Cottage-style public rooms and fresh bedrooms. Small heated swimming pool. 21 rooms. £25–£36.

L'Emeraude
Rue St Thomas, Longueville, St Saviour
Tel: 01534 874512; Fax: 759031
www.emeraudecountryhotel.com
Set amidst the peace and tranquillity of the Jersey countryside, yet only a short drive from town, l'Emeraude, once a stately home, is elegant and welcoming. 58 rooms. £30–£47.

L'Horizon
St Brelade's Bay
Tel: 01534 743101; Fax: 746269
www.handpicked.co.uk/lhorizon
Elegant and modern hotel with lovely views of St Brelade's Bay. Light, airy guest rooms, many equipped with plasma screen TVs, DVD and video players. Choice of three restaurants: Grill room, the Terrace for al fresco meals, or the more informal Brasserie. Excellent facilities include large heated indoor pool, saunas, spa and mini gym. 107 rooms. £65–£130.

Les Arches
Archirondel, St Martin
Tel: 01534 853839; Fax: 856660
e-mail: casino@itl.net
Overlooking a secluded bay with private access to the beach. Well equipped with pool, tennis and gym. 54 rooms. £27–£43.

Les Charrières Country Hotel
St Peter
Tel: 01534 481480; Fax: 485433
www.jersey.co.uk/hotels/lescharrieres
In pretty countryside at the top of St Peter's Valley. Popular for its carvery restaurant and indoor leisure complex with heated indoor pool, jacuzzi, steam room, sauna and gym. £28–£46.

Longueville Manor
Longueville Road, St Saviour
Tel: 01534 725501; Fax: 731613
www.longuevillemanor.com
The highest graded hotel on the island, this is an exquisitely decorated 13th-century manor set in 15 acres (6 hectares) at the foot of its private wooded valley. Award-winning gourmet cuisine is served in the oak-panelled dining room. 28 rooms. £105–£350.

Millbrook House
Rue de Trachy, Millbrook, St Helier
Tel: 01534 733036; Fax: 724317
www.millbrookhousehotel.com
Delightful country house hotel converted from a restored 18th-century residence, set in 10 acres (4 hectares) of park and garden. 24 rooms. £37–£42.

Moorings Hotel
Gorey Pier, St Martin
Tel: 01534 853633; Fax: 857618
www.themooringshotel.com
A small comfortable hotel offering the highest standards in service and cuisine. 16 rooms. £44–£58.

Mountview Hotel
St John's Road, St Helier
Tel: 01534 887666; Fax: 880746
www.channelshotel.com
Small hotel near the sea. Self-catering apartments also available. 35 rooms. £26–£40.

Old Court House Inn
St Aubin Harbour
Tel: 01534 746433; Fax: 745103
www.oldcourthousejersey.com
Fine harbour-view building dating to 1450. Meals served in the conservatory or the upstairs restaurant. Specialities are lobsters, prawns and crab. 9 rooms. £40–£85.

Old Court House
Gorey
Tel: 01534 854444; Fax: 853587
www.ochhotel.co.uk
Situated on the fringe of Gorey, the charming port on the island's tranquil east coast, the hotel is set in its own grounds away from the main road. 58 rooms. £45–£67.

Ommaroo
Havre des Pas, St Helier
Tel: 01534 723493; Fax: 759912
www.seabird.co.je
Traditional hotel within easy walking distance of the town centre and overlooking the seafront at Havre des Pas. 86 rooms. £32–£54.

Pomme D'Or
Liberation Square
St Helier
Tel: 01534 880110; Fax: 737781
www.pommedorhotel.com
Overlooking Liberation Square and the Yacht Marina, the Pomme D'Or has been refurbished to a high standard. 141 rooms. £54–£84.

Portelet
Portelet, St Brelade
Tel: 01534 741204; Fax: 746625
www.potelethotel.com
Situated overlooking two of the Island's most beautiful bays, the Portelet has a quiet setting, with

gardens, tennis and a heated outdoor pool. 86 rooms. £49–£63.

Revere
Kensington Place, St Helier
Tel: 01534 611111; Fax: 611116
www.revere.co.uk
A town hotel steeped in history, character and style. Centrally placed for town and St Aubin's Bay. 57 rooms. £38–£64.

Rex
St Saviour's Road, St Helier
Tel: 01534 731668; Fax: 766922
www.hotelrex.co.uk
A central location combined with the comfort and facilities which create a tranquil hideaway. 53 rooms. £24–£38.

Royal Yacht Hotel
Woighbridge, St Helier
Tel: 01534 720511; Fax: 767729
www.theroyalyachthotel.com
Thought to be the oldest established hotel in St Helier and with careful refurbishment it has retained its Victorian charm. 43 rooms. £45–£48.

St Brelade's Bay
St Brelade
Tel: 01534 746141; Fax: 747278
www.stbreladesbayhotel.com
Set in award-winning gardens and faces due south onto Jersey's most beautiful beach. Elegant rooms and high-quality cuisine. 74 rooms. £55–£94.

Samarès Coast Hotel
Samarès Coast Road, St Clement
Tel: 01481 873006; Fax: 768804
www.morvanhotels.com
Combining seaside position with a prize winning garden, the Samarès Coast Hotel offers an inviting restaurant and indoor and outdoor pools. 52 rooms. £36–£38.

Hotel Savoy
Rouge Bouillon, St Helier
Tel: 01534 619916; Fax: 506969
www.hotelsavoyjersey.com
Originally a Victorian mansion, now a modern hotel with pool. Stands in its own grounds, just a short stroll from central St Helier. 61 rooms. £30–£48.

Shakespeare
Samares Coast Road, St Clement
Tel: 01534 851915; Fax: 856269
www.shakespearehoteljersey.com
The most southerly hotel in the British Isles, overlooking St Clement's Bay. 32 rooms. £30–£47.

Silver Springs
La Route des Genêts
Tel: 01534 746401; Fax: 746823
www.silverspringshotel.co.uk
Beautiful grounds and gardens, combined with all the facilities you could want. 88 rooms. £44–£77.

Somerville
St Aubin
Tel: 01534 741226; Fax: 746621
www.dolanhotels.com
Nestling on a hillside overlooking St Aubin's yachting harbour and the expanses of bay beyond. A reputation of value for money. 59 rooms. £41–£61.

Uplands Hotel
St John's Road, St Helier
Tel: 01534 873006; Fax: 768804
www.dolanhotels.com
Family-run, based around old granite buildings and set in its own farmland a mile from the town centre. 43 rooms. £34–£46.

Washington
Claredon Road, St Helier
Tel: 01534 737981; Fax: 789899
www.washingtonhoteljersey.co.uk
Situated in a quiet residential area on the edge of town, the Washington is ideal for those on business or holiday wanting to be central but away from traffic and noise. 36 rooms. £30–£50.

Water's Edge
Bouley Bay, Trinity
Freephone: 0800 735 1003
Fax: 01534 863645
www.watersedgehotel.co.je
Panoramic position overlooking bay. 51 rooms. £40–£61.

Westhill
Mont l'Abbé, St Helier
Tel: 01534 723260; Fax: 766056
www.westhilljersey.co.uk
Large hotel set in 10 acres (4 hectares) of gardens on the town's rural outskirts. The St Helier seafront and St Aubin's Bay are a five-minute drive down the hill. 90 rooms. £33–£43.

Guest houses

La Bonne Vie Guest House
Roseville Street, St Helier
Tel: 01534 735955; Fax: 733357
www.labonnevie-guesthouse-jersey.com
A beautiful Victorian guest house with award-winning gardens; close to safe beach and swiming pool. 10 rooms. £18–£26.

Bon Viveur Guest House
The Bulwarks, St Aubin
Tel: 01534 741049; Fax: 747540
www.jerseyhols.com/bonviveur
In the old fishing village of St Aubin, close to shopping areas and a safe sandy beach. 19 rooms. £24–£36.

Des Pierres
Grève de Lecq, St Ouen
Tel: 01534 481858; Fax: 485273
www.jerseyhols.com/despierres
Delightfully situated in acres of woodland with magnificent cliff walks and only a few yards from the beach where bathing is possible at all times. 16 rooms. £27–£32.

Harbour View
St Aubin's Harbour, St Brelade
Tel: 01534 741585; Fax: 499460
www.harbourview.co.je
A charming, modernised olde-worlde inn, with garden bistro, in a superb position on the harbour in St Aubin. 13 rooms. £29–£49.

Haven Guest House
7 Kensington Place, St Helier
Tel: 01534 721619; Fax: 888842
www.havenguesthouse.com
Ideally situated for town, beach and parking. 10 rooms. £20–£30.

Panorama
La Rue du Crocquet, St Aubin
Tel: 01534 742429; Fax: 745940
www.panoramajersey.com
Appealing guest house with great views of St Aubin's Bay. Comfy beds and excellent breakfasts. Close to the picturesque harbour with plenty of restaurants within easy walking distance. No smokers or children. 14 rooms. £32–£55.

Peterborough House
Rue du Croquet, St Aubin
Tel: 01534 741568; Fax: 746787
www.jerseyisland.com/staubin/peterborough
Situated in a small cobbled street close to the harbour side with its restaurants, small shops and crafts. 14 rooms. £20–£31.

Prince of Wales
Grève de Lecq, St Ouen
Tel: 01534 482085; Fax: 485417
Close to a sandy beach, private sun
terrace overlooking the beach,
centre for scenic cliff walks. 14
rooms. £20–£33.

Sabots D'Or Guest House
High Street, St Aubin
Tel: 01534 743732
A select guest house in the
picturesque village of St Aubin.
Beach and watersports nearby. 12
rooms. £22–£30.

Seawold
Beaumont, St Peter
Tel: 01534 720807; Fax: 721631
e-mail: ciao@itl.net
Situated midway between St Helier
and St Aubin, just across the road
from the beach. 22 rooms.
£22–£32.

Undercliff Guest House
Bouley Bay, Trinity
Tel: 01534 863058; Fax: 862363
www.undercliffjersey.com
A peaceful guest house set in the
picturesque countryside of Bouley
Bay. 13 rooms. £28–£33.

Self-Catering

Prices are per property per week.

Bergerac Hotel & apartments
Portelet Bay, St Brelade
Tel: 01534 745991; Fax: 743010
www.southernhotels.com
Close to the beaches, the
apartments are centrally heated,
have private facilities and an indoor
complex with pool, sauna, and
many other facilities. 50 apartments. £343–£1050.

Boscobel Country Apartments
Rue des Vignes, St Peter
Tel: 01534 490100; Fax: 490200
www.boscobel.co.uk
Old Jersey farm with granite
buildings surrounded by 16 acres
(6½ hectares) of pastureland.
Purpose-built, well equipped
apartments with pine kitchens and
bedrooms, patio area and picnic
table. 2 minutes' drive from St
Aubin's bay. £295–£885.

Corbière Phare
Rue de la Corbière, St Brelade
Tel: 01534 744338; Fax: 7499298
e-mail: corbierephare@

jerseymail.co.uk
Spectacular views of the Atlantic
Ocean. 10 apartments.
£325–£600.

Highfield Country Hotel
Route d'Ebenezer, Trinity
Tel: 01534 862194; Fax: 865342
www.highfieldjersey.com
Situated in the heart of Jersey's
beautiful countryside. Facilities
include indoor and outdoor pools,
gym, sauna, games room and
restaurant. 16 apartments.
£546–£994.

La Rocco
La Pulente, St Brelade
Tel: 01534 743378; Fax: 746844
www.laroccoapartments.com
Across the road from a sandy beach.
All apartments have sea views and
are fitted to a high standard. 13
apartments. £345–£1625.

Samarès Coast Apartments
Samarès Coast Road, St Clement
Tel: 01534 873006; Fax: 768804
www.morvanhotels.com
Combining a seaside position with
prize-winning gardens, and a pool
area. 12 apartments. £489–£649.

Campsites

Prices are per tent per night.

Beuvalande
St Martin
Tel: 01621 784666; Fax: 785001
www.jerseyandguernsey.com
Good modern facilities, pool, games
room and family entertainment.
400 persons. £6–£8.

Bleu Soleil
Leoville, St Ouen
Tel: 01534 481007
www.bleusoleilcamping.com
Small, friendly site set in a quiet rural
area, with excellent facilities and
close to beaches. £6–£30.

Rose Farm
St Brelade
Tel: 01534 741231; Fax: 490178
www.jerseycamping.com
A secluded, long established family
campsite, a short distance from the
delightful harbour village of St Aubin.
500 persons. £10–£60.

Rozel Camping Park
St Martin
Tel: 01534 855200; Fax: 856127
e-mail: rozelcampingpark@

jerseymail.co.uk
Family-run and situated in quiet
countryside, close to the Jersey
Zoo. Bus service to St Helier. 200
persons. £6.80–£8.

Guernsey

Hotels

Auberge du Val
Sous L'Eglise, St Saviour's
Tel: 01481 263862; Fax: 264835
Set in 3 acres (1.2 hectares) of an
idyllic valley, this farmhouse has a
health suite and a bistro serving
fresh food, with herbs from the
garden. £30–£35.

Bella Luce
La Fosse, St Martin
Tel: 01481 238764; Fax: 239561
www.bellalucehotel.guernsey.net
Old-fashioned comfort and excellent
food. Situated near the south coast
bays. 31 rooms. £40–£59.

Bon Port Hotel
Moulin Huet, St Martin
Tel: 01481 239249; Fax: 239596
www.bonport.com
Set in the midst of Guernsey's
most beautiful scenery, offering
tranquillity, magnificent views and
unique walks. 18 rooms and
self–catering. £60–£199 per
room.

Cobo Bay Hotel
Cobo, Castel
Tel: 01481 257102; Fax: 254542
www.cobobayhotel
A warm welcome, comfortable
accommodation and an excellent
award winning restaurant overlooking the dramatic sunsets of Cobo
Bay. 36 rooms. £34–£89.

The Clubhouse @ La Collinette
St Jacques, St Peter Port
Tel: 01481 710331; Fax: 713516
www.lacollinette.com
Big sheltered garden and pool, hotel
rooms, cottages and apartments.
Set close to Candie Gardens, Beau
Sejour Leisure Centre and a short
walk to the centre of St Peter Port
£35–£150.

Duke of Richmond Hotel
Cambridge Park, St Peter Port
Tel: 01481 726221; Fax: 728945
www.dukeofrichmond.com
One of Guernsey's leading hotels,
within walking distance of the Beau

Séjour leisure centre and high street shops. 74 rooms. £45-£70.

Fleur du Jardin
Kings Mills, Castel
Tel: 01481 257996; Fax: 256834
www.fleurdujardin.guernsey.net
Restored 15th-century farmhouse in the heart of Kings Mills. Secluded gardens with heated pool. £37–£55.

Green Acres Hotel
Les Hûbits, St Martin's
Tel: 01481 235711; Fax: 235978
www.greenacreshotel.guernsey.net
A country hotel on the edge of town surrounded by green fields but situated in the beautiful parish of St Martin. 48 rooms. £22 £48.

Hotel de Havelet
Havelet, St Peter Port
Tel: 01481 722100; Fax: 714067
www.havelet.sarniahotels.com
This gracious Georgian house, situated in an elevated position overlooking St Peter Port harbour, has been converted into a luxurious small hotel with a reputation for fine food. 34 rooms. £53–£112.

Hotel Jerbourg
Jerbourg Point, St Martin's
Tel: 01481 238826; Fax: 238238
Set on the clifftops at Jerbourg Point with spectacular views of the other islands and France.

Hougue du Pommier
La Route de la Hougue du Pommier, Castel
Tel: 01481 256531; Fax: 256260
www.hotelhouguedupommier.com
This 18th-century farmhouse is set within a 10-acre (4-hectare) estate. Ten–minute walk to Cobo beach. £38 £91.

La Favorita Hotel
Fermain Bay, St Martin
Tel: 01481 235666; Fax: 235413
www.favorita.com
Family country hotel close to Fermain Bay, combining secluded charm with the comfort of a modern, professionally-run establishment. 36 rooms. £38–£50.

La Frégate Hotel
Les Côtils, St Peter Port
Tel: 01481 724624; Fax: 720443
www.lafregatehotel.com
Blends the charm of an 18th-century Manor House with the amenities of a modern hotel, set on a hillside overlooking the harbour. 13 rooms. £85–£180.

La Grande Mare Hotel
Vazon Bay, Castel
Tel: 01481 256576; Fax: 256532
www.lgm.guernsey.net
Set in private grounds incorporating a golf course, beside the beautiful, safe, sandy west coast bay of Vazon. Modern health and leisure suite. 25 rooms. £89–£129.

La Hougue Fouque Farm Hotel
Bas Courtils, St Saviour
Tel: 01481 264181; Fax: 266272
www.lhfhotel.com
Standing in 4 acres (1.6 hectares) of beautiful mature gardens in the heart of rural Guernsey and its countryside, this is a comfortable hotel with well-equipped bedrooms 16 rooms. £34–£89.

L'Atlantique Hotel
Perelle Bay, St Saviour
Tel: 01481 64056; Fax: 63800
A small privately owned hotel set in landscaped gardens in the rural parish of St Saviour, overlooking Perelle Bay. 23 rooms. £35–£50.

La Trelade Hotel
Forest Road, St Martin
Tel: 01481 235454; Fax: 237855
www.latreladehotel.co.uk
Situated in private grounds in the beautiful country parish of St Martin, La Trelade is only half a mile from Guernsey's south coast. 45 rooms. £45–£75.

Le Châlet Hotel
Fermain Lane, St Martin's
Tel: 01481 235715; Fax: 235718
www.chalet.sarniahotels.com
An Alpine style hotel is not only a few minutes' walk away from one of Guernsey's most attractive bays, but also close to some of the glorious south coast cliff walks. 40 rooms. £35–£102.

Le Friquet Country Hotel
Rue du Friquet, Castel
Tel: 01481 256509; Fax: 253573
www.lefriquethotel.com
Set in 6 acres of gardens, this is the ideal place for a relaxing holiday or short break. Recently refurbished. 19 rooms. £29–£56.

L'Eree Bay Hotel
St Peter's
Tel: 01481 26416; Fax: 266293
www.lereeguernsey.com
Across the road from and overlooking L'Eree Bay, so sunbathe and swim in the sea or the hotel's pool. 33 rooms. £19–£25.

Moores Hotel
Le Pollet, St Peter Port
Tel: 01481 724452; Fax: 714037
www.moores.sarniahotels.com
This old granite-built townhouse hotel is situated in the heart of St Peter Port and is an ideal base for either a holiday or business visit at any time of the year. 50 rooms. £38–£107.

Old Government House Hotel & Spa
St Peter Port
Tel: 01481 724921; Fax: 724249
www.theoghhotel.com
Situated in the heart of St Peter Port, offering breathtaking views over the town and the neighbouring Channel Islands. 72 rooms. £95–£145.

Peninsula Hotel
Les Dicqs, Vale
Tel: 01481 248400; Fax: 248706
www.peninsulahotelguernsey.com
A beach-front hotel overlooking Grand Havre Bay. Enjoy fine cuisine in the hotel's restaurant. 99 rooms. £55–£85.50.

St George's Hotel
21 St Georges Esplanade, St Peter Port
Tel: 01481 721027; Fax: 729259
Small hotel on the seafront a few minutes' walk from the marina and town centre. £28–£35.

St Pierre Park
Rohais, St Peter Port
Tel: 01481 728282; Fax: 712041
www.stpierreparkhotel.com
Set in its own parkland with a nine-hole golf course, tennis courts, three restaurants and indoor pool. 131 rooms £60–£165.

St Margaret's Lodge Hotel
Forest Road, St Martin
Tel: 01481 235757; Fax: 237594
Set in the heart of rural St Martin, yet only a short distance from the southern cliffs and beaches. 47 rooms. £25–£42.

Saints Bay Hotel
Icart, St Martin's
Tel: 01481 238888; Fax: 235558
www.saintsbayhotel.com
Situated at Icart's unspoiled headland, perched amongst the cliff-tops. 34 rooms. £23–£63.

Guest houses

Anneville Guest House
Les Vallettes, St Saviour's
Tel: 01481 236814
Small, friendly country guesthouse
£21.50.

Castaways Guest House
Bon Port, St Martin's
Tel: 01481 239010
On south coast with some of the best
views from the island, ideal for cliff
walkers. £20–£25.

Grisnoir Guest House
Les Gravees, St Peter Port
Tel: 01481 727267; Fax: 730661
www.grisnoir.co.uk
On the edge of Town; comes
recommended. £21–£33.

Longfrie Inn
Route de Longfrie, St Pierre du Bois
Tel: 01481 63107; Fax: 64041
An old Guernsey farmhouse set in
one of the prettiest parts of the
Island. Totally refurbished. Renowned
for good food. 5 rooms. £20–£32.

Maison Bel Air
Le Chêne, Forest
Tel: 01481 238503; Fax: 239403
www.maisonbelair.com
A family-run guesthouse close to
Petit Bôt Bay. On main bus route. 5
rooms, most ensuite, £22–29.50.

Self-catering

Prices are per property per week.

La Grande Mare
Vazon Bay, Castel
Tel: 01481 256576; Fax: 256532
www.lgm.guernsey.net
Sports facilities on site, beside the
sandy and safé west coast bay of
Vazon. 10 three/four person
cottages. Price on application.

La Madeleine Holiday Apartments
Saumarez Street, St Peter Port
Tel: 01481 726933; Fax: 727688
www.selfcateringgsy.co.uk
In the town centre but with gardens,
spectacular views over the Harbour
and Herm gardens. £260–£730.

Mille Fleurs
Rue de Bordage, St Pierre de Bois
Tel/Fax: 01481 2263911
www.millefleurs.co.uk
Peace and quiet of an old farmhouse
set in delightful valley gardens, as
featured on TV. Pool. 3 cottages for
2–5 persons. £325–£1050.

Campsites

Fauxquets Valley Farm Campsite
Castel
Tel: 01481 255460; Fax: 251797
www.fauxquets.co.uk
A peaceful site in the heart of rural
Guernsey. Fully equipped. Own tent
£5–£6 pp pn; tent hire from £224.

La Bailloterie Campsite
Vale
Tel: 01481 243636; Fax: 243225
www.campinginguernsey.com
Situated in the north of the island
and set in a quiet rural area.
Excellent facilities. Own tent £5–£6
pp pn; tent hire from £165 .

Le Vaugrat Campsite
Route de Vaugrat, St Sampson
Tel: 01481 257468; Fax: 251841
www.vaugratcampsite.com
Well-equipped site with plenty of
space for children to play. Fully
equipped tents to hire. Apply
directly for prices.

Alderney

Hotels

Belle Vue
Butes Road
Tel: 01481 822844; Fax: 823601
www.bellevue.alderney.com
One of the island's best known,
family-run hotels. 60 beds. £48–£60.

Georgian House
Victoria Street
Tel/Fax: 01481 822471
www.georgianhousealderney.com
Deservedly popular hotel offering
value for money rooms and a lovely
garden for summer dining. 6 beds.
£40–£55.

Harbour Lights
Newtown
Tel: 01481 822168; Fax: 824182
www.harbourlightshotel.co.uk
Friendly comfortable hotel a few
minutes' walk from Braye Bay and
Harbour and within easy reach of St
Anne. 17 beds. £25–£31.

The Town House
High Street
Tel: 01481 824897; fax: 824076
www.thetownhouse.moonfruit.com
Recently renovated in the centre of
St Anne's. £25–£35

Victoria
Victoria Street
Tel: 01481 822754; Fax: 824161
In the heart of the town and close to
Braye Beach. 17 beds. £30–£40.

Guesthouses

Bonjour
16 High Street
Tel: 01481 822152
Friendly guest house in the high
street. Families welcome and baby-
sitting can usually be arranged.
£24–£35.

Essex Lodge
Longis Bay
Tel: 01481 823557
Formerly the Longis Bay Guest
House, this is a French-style
farmhouse with spectacular views
over the bay, Raz Island and the
French coast. Peaceful and
friendly. Evening meals by
arrangement. No children under
12. £30–£40.

Farm Court
Les Mouriaux
Tel/Fax: 01481 822075
A collection of converted old farm
buildings arranged around a cobbled courtyard. Quiet location on
the edge of the town of St Anne. 17
beds. £35–£45 .

L'Haras
Newtown Road
Tel/Fax: 01481 823174
www.internet.alderney.gg/lharas/
Situated near the harbour and
Braye Bay. Within easy walking dis-
tance of St Anne and the shops. 10
beds. £24–£36.

St Anne's
Le Huret
Tel: 01481 823145
Ideally situated for both business
and pleasure in the heart of St
Anne, close to restaurants and
shops. 9 beds. £19–£22.

Simerock
Les Venelles
Tel: 01481 823645
Only minutes away from town, over-
looking farmland. 17 beds. £25–35.

Self-catering

Prices are per property per week.

Fort Clonque
Built in the 1840s, the fort sits on
its own rocky islet, cut off from
Alderney at high tide. It has been
converted into comfortable self-

catering holiday accommodation in four different buildings. Up to 11 people. Price on application to The Landmark Trust, Shottesbrooke, Maidenhead, Berks SL6 3SW (Tel: 01628 825925, Fax: 825417).

Pine Springs
La Vallée
Tel: 01481 822044; Fax: 822054
A private estate with four luxury Norwegian log villas in large garden surrounding swimming pool. 4 to 7 persons. Price on application.

Campsites
Saye Campsite
Tel: 01481 822556; Fax: 822436
The island's only campsite next to Saye Bay. Own tent £2–£4.50 pp pn and tents for hire.

Sark

Hotels
Aval du Creux
Harbour Hill
Tel: 01481 832036; Fax: 832368
www.avalducreux.com
Family-run hotel recommended by leading food guides. 31 beds. £49–£60.

Dixcart
Tel: 01481 832015; Fax: 832164
www.dixcartguernseyci.com
Sark's oldest hotel. Once a 16th-century farm longhouse, there is extensive acreage of medieval gardens, a cliff path through the densely wooded valley and a sheltered bay. 28 beds. From £30.

Hotel Petit Champ
Tel: 01481 832046; Fax: 832469
www.hotelpetitchamp.co.uk
Set in an unrivalled, secluded position on Sark's west coast, with breathtaking sea views. 32 beds. £40–£70.

La Moinerie Hotel
Tel: 01481 832089; Fax: 832459
Charming 18th-century house situated in a sheltered wooded valley close to cliff path walks with scenic views. 23 beds. £28–£37.

La Sablonnerie
Tel: 01481 832061; Fax: 832408
Unspoiled and scenic views, a haven of peace. Nestled in mature gardens. 39 beds. £36–£70.

Stocks Island Hotel
Tel: 01481 832001; Fax: 832130
www.stockshotel.com
A country house in the heart of Sark, in the wooded valley leading to Dixcart Bay. Poolside café serves homemade patisserie and Sark cream teas. Log fires for cooler days. 46 beds. £55–£85.

Guesthouses
Le Petit Beauregard
Tel: 01481 832940
www.petitbeauregard.com
Situated on the west coast with great sea views. 22 beds. £40–£45.

Beau Séjour
Tel: 01481 832034
Charming old-fashioned guest house. 7 beds. Bed and breakfast £26–£33.

Clos Princess
Tel: 01481 832324; Fax: 832563
www.cwgsy.net/business/clos.princess/
Modern family home in the centre of the island. £23–£26.

Hivernage
Tel: 01481 832000; Fax: 832472
Family-run guest house situated on the quiet west coast. 12 beds. £25–£29.

Le Petit Coin
Tel: 01481 832077; Fax: 832603
Small, family-run guest house in the north of Sark with comfortable rooms and excellent home cooking. 7 beds. £25–£30.

Les Quatre Vents
Tel: 01481 832247; Fax: 832332
Family-run with sea views. £30.

Notre Désir
Tel: 01481 832266
www.sercq.com/
Modern accommodation to the east of the island with easy access to the shops and cafés. 6 beds. £25.

Self-catering
Prices are per property per week.

Bel Air Inn
Tel: 01481 832052; Fax: 832663
Fully equipped chalets sleeping 4–6. Boules piste, beer garden and wide range of lagers, beers and wines. £210–£480.

La Vaurocque
Tel: 01481 832060; Fax: 832201

Fully equipped, children of all ages welcome. 7 units for 2 to 6 persons. £250–£750.

Le Vallon D'Or
Tel: 01481 832308; Fax: 832608
Situated at the head of an unspoilt valley. Fully equipped cottage-type accommodation. 2 units for 2–4 persons. £375.

L'Ecluse
Tel: 01481 832468; Fax: 832467
4 self-catering cottages. £325–£550.

The Dower Cottage
Tel: 01481 832112
One double and one twin bedroom, both with sea views, comprise this cottage. £380–£519.

Campsites
La Vallette Campsite
Tel: 01481 832066; Fax: 832636
Good facilities. 50 persons. Price on application.

Pomme de Chien Campsite
Tel/Fax: 01481 832316
Situated in fine surroundings with sea views. Close to beach and village. 40 persons. Price on application.

Herm

Hotels
White House
Tel: 01481 722377; Fax: 710066
Overlooking the island harbour and sandy beach, the hotel has an award-winning restaurant, swimming pool, tennis court, and croquet lawn. 85 beds. £55–£75 half-board.

Self-catering
Prices are per property per week.

Herm Island
Tel: 01481 722377; Fax: 700334
Charming country cottages, within a few minutes' walk of sandy beaches. Sea or rural views. 18 units. £165–£790.

Campsites
Herm Island Camping
Tel: 01481 722377; Fax: 700334
Panoramic views across the sea from terraced meadows. This peaceful and picturesque site conveniently offers hot showers and a washing area. Apply directly for prices.

Where to Eat

Eating Out

Places to eat in the Channel Islands cater for most palates and pockets. Variety is the thing: you can dine by candlelight, sip aperitifs on a seafront terrace, meet friends in a bustling bistro, go Greek, pick up a pizza, take away good old British fish 'n' chips or enjoy a simple pie and a pint in a country pub. The best menus feature high quality local produce, vegetables and seafood in particular.

Find the right restaurant specialising in marine cuisine and something close to a perfect meal is likely to be served. Bass, plaice, sole and shellfish are landed in the morning and are on the plate by lunchtime. A summertime feast might include mussels poached in white wine, a lobster or dressed crab salad with Jersey new potatoes, washed down with a chilled Muscadet, and a bowl of strawberries topped with a dollop of thick cream.

Because of so much healthy competition for the brisk, year-round trade from businessmen, locals and tourists, owners and chefs do not like to be outdone by the restaurant next door. The islands have a reputation for gastronomy that goes far beyond their shores. The number of excursionists from France who come over just to eat a good lunch is testimony enough to the quality and variety of food on offer.

Portion control is unheard of and long menus in many establishments should be scrutinised. Extra dishes of the day – *plats du jour* – are often chalked up on a blackboard in a corner somewhere and shouldn't be missed.

Chefs also tend to like writing their menus in French and a certain amount of inventiveness goes into describing a dish in that language. Sole Bonne Femme is understandable, Sole Deauville is not. Don't be afraid to ask what the ingredients are. Wine lists are normally comprehensive.

The traditional Sunday lunch is a great favourite with locals. Set menus in many hotels and restaurants are good value.

Time a trip to coincide with Jersey's annual Good Food Festival in May when many of the establishments put on special gastronomic menus and food fairs are held in St Helier.

The following restaurants and hotels have been chosen as good places to dine. Many restaurants offer extensive *à la carte* menus and feature set menus, normally four or five courses for dinner, three at lunchtime. Special Sunday lunch menus are cheap and popular with residents and visitors throughout the year.

House wines are usually available at around £8 a bottle, although delving deeper into a wine list will reveal better quality German, French, Italian, Portuguese or Spanish wines at extremely reasonable prices. Table bookings at all establishments during the tourist season are advisable.

Visitors could plan a gastronomic tour of the islands without running out of choice. The Jersey Restaurateurs Association alone has more than 250 members.

Jersey

St Helier

Albert J Ramsbottom's
90 Halkett Place
Tel: 01534 721395
The freshest fish, the best potatoes, huge portions and careful cooking ensure a visit here is always satisfying. Try the fresh, white fillets of cod in crispy, golden batter. **£**

Atlantique Seafood Bar
Beresford Fish Market
Tel: 01534 720052
Excellent spot for seafood specialities such as *moules frites* (mussels and chips), hot or cold *fruits de mer* (seafood), tapas and daily specials. Also champagne breakfasts and brunch. Picnics can be ordered by phone. No dinners. **£**

Bamboo Garden Restaurant
8 Burrard Street
Tel: 01534 767711
A delightful Chinese experience is guaranteed at this intimate town restaurant. The very attentive service complements the excellent quality of the traditional Chinese cuisine. The crispy aromatic duck is a must. **£–££**

Bella Napoli Restaurant
38 Kensington Place
Tel: 01534 720631
A deservedly popular trattoria where the atmosphere and welcome complement the wide choice of pizza and pasta. Very good value. **£**

Bistro Central
7–11 Don Street
Tel: 01534 876933
French-style bistro serving fish specialities. **££**

Bluefish
West Centre
Tel: 01534 767186
Informal, relaxed meals offering great gourmet pizzas as well as seafood and meat dishes. Bubbly staff add to the lively atmosphere. **£**

Bohemia Bar and Restaurant
Beaufort Hotel, Green Street
Tel: 01534 880588
Rated by Egon Ronay as one of the top 25 restaurants in the UK and awarded a Michelin star. Top quality ingredients are sourced from local and European suppliers: scallops and sea bass from Jersey, foie gras and poultry from France, beef from Scotland. Choice of bar snacks, set meals or à la carte. **£** (bar), **££** (set lunch) **£££** (dinner).

Café des Artistes
Voisin & Co, 32 King Street
Tel: 01534 639990
This in-store restaurant is a blessing for tired shoppers. There is a wide range of dishes from Jersey bean crock to crab and lobster salad. Lunch only. **£**

Chambertin
20 Beresford St
Tel: 01534 766678
Authentic French cuisine in attractive setting. **££**

City Bar
Halkett Place
Tel: 01534 510096
Contemporary bar and brasserie catering for all tastes and providing internet access at your table (free use if you have a meal here). **££**

Gio's Restaurant
58 Halkett Place
Tel: 01534 736733
Customers have expressed delight at their visit here, from their warm reception, through to the typically Italian décor and the outstanding food. Try the calves' liver in wine and sage. **££**

Harbour Room Carvery
Pomme D'Or Hotel, Liberation Sq
Tel: 01534 880110
The attractive split-level room affords extensive views of the harbour area. The freshly prepared joints of beef, lamb and pork are always succulent and tasty. **££**

Jersey Museum Brasserie
Weighbridge
Tel: 01534 510069
Home-made cakes, bread, good salads and light lunches. Popular, central meeting place. **£–££**

La Bastille
4 Wharf Street
Tel: 01534 874059
Lively ambience ensures the popularity of this central wine bar. Try the vegetable soup, bacon-wrapped scallops and fresh fish dishes. Lunch only. **£–££**

La Capannina Restaurant
67 Halkett Place
Tel: 01534 734602
This traditional Italian restaurant is a favourite amongst the business community at lunchtime and equally popular with the discriminating diner in the evening. There are always interesting Italian specials. **££–£££**

Lido's Wine Bar
4–6 Market Street
Tel: 01534 722358
You should book a table at this popular bustling town-centre wine bar. There is a marvellous range of home-made quiches, pies and sandwiches. Lunch only. **££**

The Mandarin Room
18 Gloucester Street
Tel: 01534 737038
A pleasant, traditional ethnic

restaurant offering a wide range of well cooked dishes principally in Cantonese style. The sizzlers are especially worth trying. **£**

Ming's Dynasty Restaurant
8 Cheapside
Tel: 01534 856886
A pleasant place to try your favourite Chinese dishes as well as experiment with Chinese wine and Chinese tea. **£–££**

Nelson's Eye Restaurant
Havre des Pas
Tel: 01534 875176
The emphasis is on fresh food. The room is decorated in a nautical style based on Nelson's HMS *Victory*, and has superb views of the bay. *Fruits de mer* are regularly featured on the menu. **££**

Price Guide

Prices are per person for a full evening meal, including wine and service, or a one- or two-course lunch where indicated:

££££	– over £100
£££	– £50–£100
££	– £25–£50
£	– under £25

Pizza Express
59–61 Halkett Place
Tel: 01534 33291
A pizzeria doubling as an art gallery is a unique experience. An excellent choice of pizzas including vegetarian fillings. Try the garlic pizza dough sticks. **£**

Rudee's Thai Diner
9 Caledonia Place
Tel: 01534 732548
The multi-course Thai meal, with daily changes, acts as a perfect introduction to Thai cuisine with an *à la carte* menu providing other options. **£**

Viceroy Indian Restaurant
76 Bath Street
Tel: 01534 876984
Excellent tandoori cooking and dishes made to authentic recipes. **£**

Out of Town

Atlantic Hotel
Le Mont de la Pulente, St Brelade.
Tel: 01534 744101

Stylish hotel restaurant with superb setting over St Ouen's Bay. Fine food and attentive staff. **£££**

Bistro Frère
Rozel Hill, St Martin
Tel: 01534 861000
This very popular Island restaurant serves French cuisine and has fine views of the coast. **££**

Bistro Soleil
Beaumont
Tel: 01534 720249
Beachside bistro with seaviews, renowned for lobster, crab and fresh fish. Set menus and à la carte. **££**

Borsalino Rocque
La Grande Route des Sablons, Grouville
Tel: 01534 852111
Best-known for its *fruits de mer*. Book in advance for a table in the delightful conservatory. **££**

The Brasserie
Hotel L'Horizon, St Brelade
Tel: 01534 743101
The Brasserie is situated within the hotel's leisure complex. The food is of a very high standard, featuring salads, sandwiches and a range of brasserie dishes. **£–££**

The Carvery
Les Charrières Hotel, St Peter
Tel: 01534 483968
This carvery and bar is popular with locals. For Sunday lunch booking is essential. The menu features a choice of freshly-cooked joints. **££**

Château la Chaire
Rozel Bay, St Martin's
Tel: 01534 863354
Quiet and peaceful, set in a wooded valley, it's important to look out for the signpost. Part of an hotel, it offers the best cuisine on the north coast. **££–£££**

The Crystal Room
Hotel L'Horizon
St Brelade
Tel: 01534 43101
Elegant modern dining room which offers standards found only in the best hotels. The menu is up-to-the-minute and the choice is extensive. **££–£££**

El Tico
Five Mile Road, St Ouen's Bay
Tel: 01534 482649
Beach café with good breakfasts,

sandwiches and home-made cakes and pies. Great views of St Ouen's surfers from the terrace. **£**

Frère de Mère
Le Mont de Rozel, Rozel Bay, St Martin
Tel: 01534 861000
Good-value seafood restaurant with superb sea views from the terrace. **££**

Goose on the Green
Beaumont, St Peter
Tel: 01534 888273
A pub restaurant that offers real ale and a wide range of daily specials, often featuring local fish, served in a bright room. **£**

Greenhill Country Hotel and Restaurant
Mont de l'Ecole, St Peter
Tel: 01534 481042
Elegant restaurant with imaginative cuisine. Menus are essentially British with a continental flavour. Emphasis is on local fresh produce and seafood. **££–£££**

Green Island Restaurant
Green Island, St Clement
Tel: 01534 857787
Facing Green Island, this rustic venue serves good-value seafood and fish, including char-grilled scallops, sand eels and sea bass. **££**

Harvest Barn Inn
Vallée des Vaux, St Helier
Tel: 01534 735897
A smart pub downstairs with a day-time carvery and a pub restaurant upstairs. Enjoy a warm welcome and a wide range of food. **£–££**

Jambo
La Route de la Baie, St Brelade's Bay
Tel: 01534 745801
Chinese bay-view restaurant featuring Peking and Szechuan dishes. **££**

Jersey Pottery Garden Restaurant
Gorey Village, Grouville
Tel: 01534 850850
This popular restaurant serves the very best lobsters, crabs, gambas, asparagus and strawberries. **££**

La Barca
Bulwarks, St Aubin
Tel: 01534 744275
Cheerful trattoria with views over St Aubin's Harbour. **£–££**

Longueville Manor
Longueville Road, St Saviour's
Tel: 01534 725501
Sophisticated yet welcoming. Long-established, award-winning restaurant serving gourmet food in oak-panelled dining room or the airy garden room. Seasonal produce from the kitchen garden. **£££**

Man's Garden
Sandybrook Lane, St Lawrence
Tel: 01534 888682 or 888683
Intimate Chinese restaurant in quiet valley setting. Choose from aromatic crispy duck, Mongolian lamb, lettuce wraps, ribs and vegetarian dishes. Take away and free deliveries are available. **£–££**

Price Guide

Prices are per person for a full evening meal, including wine and service, or a one– or two–course lunch where indicated:

££££	– over £100
£££	– £50–£100
££	– £25–£50
£	– under £25

The Moorings Hotel
Gorey Pier, St Martin
Tel: 01534 853633
The hotel/restaurant nestles beneath the towering walls of Mont Orgueil Castle overlooking Gorey Harbour. A popular place to eat. **££**

Old Court House Inn
St Aubin, St Brelade
Tel: 01534 746433
Although parking here can be difficult, it is worth making the effort to visit this small Inn. Amongst the specialities are lobster, spicy chicken, lemon sole, Jersey plaice and crab creole. **££–£££**

Old Portelet Inn
Portelet, St Brelade
Tel: 01534 741899
This old Inn, situated above Portelet Bay, is a popular place take the family. A good selection of pub food. **£**

Old Smugglers Inn
Ouaisné Bay, St Brelade
Tel: 01534 741510
A traditional inn serving keg beer and a separate restaurant serving

reasonably priced meals, including a children's menu. **£**

Pizza Express
St Brelade's Bay
Tel: 01534 499049
Good pizzas in a stylish glass building with fine views of the bay. **£**

Red Rose
Oaklands Lodge Hotel, Augrès, Trinity
Tel: 01534 861735
Specialising in traditional English and Continental food. A convenient stopping place when exploring the north of the Island. **££**

The Retreat
Hotel de la Place, Route du Coin, St Brelade
Tel: 01534 744261
International cuisine using good quality local produce. Elegant setting in one of Jersey's top hotels. **££–£££**

Samarès Manor Herb Garden Restaurant
Samarès Manor, La Grande Route de St Clement, St Clement
Tel: 01534 721983
Fresh herbs from the Manor garden feature strongly in the cooking in this delightful spot. Morning coffee, salad lunches and afternoon tea Easter to October only. **£**

The Secret Garden
Gorey Common, Grouville
Tel: 01534 852999
A very popular café and licensed restaurant opposite Gorey Common. Traditional English cooking plus local fresh seafood. Open in summer for late breakfast, afternoon tea and evening meals. The char-grilled Scottish salmon is delicious. **£–££**

Suma's
Gorey Hill, Gorey
Tel: 01534 853291
Fresh innovative cuisine in a stylish restaurant overlooking Gorey harbour and castle. English cusine with Mediterranean and oriental overtones. Good-value set lunch. **££–£££**

The Village Bistro
Gorey Village, Grouville
Tel: 01534 853429
The best of local produce and seafood, imaginatively cooked. Reservations a must. **££–£££**

Zanzibar
St Brelade's Bay
Tel: 01534 741081
International cuisine, plus fine
views over the bay. Seafood dishes
with Eastern flavours such as
steamed mussels in curry sauce.
££–£££

Guernsey

In and Around St Peter Port
Absolute End Restaurant
Longstore
Tel: 01481 723822
Highly renowned seafood restaurant
with views of the other islands. **£££**
Bar One and Bistro
I, Fountain Street
Tel: 01481 722017
Tapas, sandwiches and a la carte in
fashionable surroundings with
quick, friendly service. **££**
Café Renoir
St Pierre Park Hotel
Rohais.
Tel: 01481 728282
Informal, relaxed meals with healthy
options dishes and children's menu.
Open all day. **£££**
Court's Restaurant
Le Marchant Street
Tel: 01481 721782
Superb food in cosy wood-panelled
restaurant. Excellent wine list. **££**
Da Bruno
North Esplanade
Tel: 01481 721186
Friendly, relaxed Italian eatery with
views over the Harbour. **££**
Da Nello
46 Pollet Street
Tel: 01481 721552
Has a fine reputation for its locally
caught fish, charcoal grilled steaks
and friendly service. In a
modernised 15th-century inn. **£££**
Duke of Normandie
Lefebvre Street
Tel: 01481 721431
Pub catering for most tastes. Home-
cooked specials served daily and
barbecues in summer. **££**
La Frégate
Les Côtils
Tel: 01481 724624
Considered the finest by many,
excellent cuisine and service. The
restaurant enjoys panoramic views

of the harbour and neighbouring
islands. **££££**
La Perla
Norman House, South Esplanade
Tel: 01481 712127
Laid-back and good value with
pavement tables and plenty on the
plate. **£**
La Piazza
Trinity Square
Tel: 01481 725085
Specialises in fresh Italian dishes
and local fish. **££**
Le Nautique
Quay Steps
Tel: 01481 721714
International à la carte. The accent
is on local seafood. **£££**
Le Petit Bistro
56, The Pollet
Tel: 01481 735055
One of the newest eateries in Town
with a rural French menu. **££**
L'Escalier
6, Tower Hill
Tel: 01481 710088
Award-winning restaurant offering
the best of Guernsey and French
cooking. Vegetarians made
welcome but book well in advance.
£££
Les Rocquettes Hotel
Les Gravées
Tel: 01481 722146
A casual dining room setting that
offers fairly priced meals with
something for everyone. **££**
The Lemon Wedge
Prince of Wales, Manor Place
Tel: 01481 720166
Set inside what was architecturally
the best pub in the island, now
transformed into a modern
restaurant. Imaginative menu. **£££**
Number 44
44, The Pollet
Tel: 01481 723937
Indian food in exotic surrounding in
the heart of town. **£**
Old Government House Hotel
Ann's Place
Tel: 01481 724921
A traditional dining room serving
French cuisine in plush
surroundings. **££££**
Roberto's
1, Trinity Square
Tel: 01481 730149
Great atmosphere, excellent food

and attentive staff at this small
Italian restaurant. **££**
SaltWater
Albert Pier
Tel: 01481 720823
One of the best seafood restaurants
on the island. Dine with a view of the
harbour and castle. **£££**
Taj Mahal
North Esplanade
Tel: 01481 724008
Specialises in Indian, Thai and
Malaysian cuisine. Thoroughly
recommended. **££**
Sawatdi Thai Restaurant
North Plantation
Tel: 01481 725805
Friendly Thai restaurant open daily
for lunch and dinner. Thai dancing
on Tuesdays. **££**
Victor Hugo Restaurant
St Pierre Park Hotel, Rohais
Tel: 01481 728282
Offers seafood, fine wines and
discreet personal service. Try the
fresh lobster from the lobster tank
or a selection of local or exotic
fish from the trolley. **£££**

Out of Town
The Auberge
Jerbourg Road, St Martin's
Tel: 01481 238845
Cliff-top location at Jerbourg for this
winner of the Guernsey Restaurant
Competition 2004. Dishes with a
twist comprise the inventive menu.
££
Cobo Bay Hotel
Cobo, Castel
Tel: 01481 57102
Table d'hôte and *à la carte*
restaurant serving a wide variety of
dishes. **££**
CrabbyJacks
Vazon Bay, Castel
Tel: 01481 257489
With a wonderful setting on the
coast road, the liveliest restaurant
on the island is a hit with kids.
Sunday lunch a speciality.
££
Fleur du Jardin
King's Mills, Castel
Tel: 01481 57996
Very popular old farmhouse-style
eatery offering traditional food,
daily specials and freshly-caught
fish. **££**

The Hollows
Le Gouffre, Forest
Tel: 01481 64121
Quiet valley setting above the delightful Le Gouffre Bay. The café-restaurant's innovate menu includes many Greek-inspired dishes. Open for breakfast. **££**

Hotel Bella Luce
La Fosse, St Martin
Tel: 01481 38764
A well-established and popular restaurant offering an excellent *à la carte* selection. Daily seafood specialities. **££**

Hotel Bon Port
Moulin Huet, St Martin
Tel: 01481 39249
Day or night the Pierre Renoir Restaurant is stunning with panoramic sea views. Large range of dishes from all-day breakfasts to seafood sandwiches and more formal fare. **££**

Hougue du Pommier
La Route de la Hougue du Pommier, Castel
Tel: 01481 56531
Bar food and set dinners in a delightful old farmhouse near Cobo Bay. **££**

Houmet Tavern and Anchor Bar
Grand Havre Bay, Vale
Tel: 01481 242214
Great pub food with surf and turf a speciality, and an emphasis on using fresh ingredients. Enjoys a stunning view of the bay. **£**

La Barbarie Hotel
Saint's Bay, St Martin's
Tel: 01481 235217
Imaginative cuisine served in a friendly atmosphere in this gem of a hotel. Very popular with locals throughout the year. **££**

La Grande Mare
Vazon Bay, Castel
Tel: 01481 56576
Luxury hotel noted for its excellent food, wines and service. **£££**

Le Friquet Country Hotel
Rue du Friquet, Castel
Tel: 01481 56509
The Falcon Carvery is not only recommended for its succulent roast joints, but also for its seafood. **££**

Longfrie Inn
Route du Longfrie, St Peter
Tel: 01481 63107
Bar lunches and evening meals in this friendly pub and restaurant. Popular with families; has play area for children. **£**

Marina Restaurant
Baucette Marina, Vale
Tel: 01481 47066
As one would expect being situated above Guernsey's only private yacht marina, this French-style restaurant specialises in seafood. **£££**

The New Fisherman's Restaurant
Rocquaine Bay, St Peter's
Tel: 01481 263333
Watch the sun go down over Fort Grey and the Hanois Lighthouse at this rightly popular fish restaurant. **££**

Price Guide

Prices are per person for a full evening meal, including wine and service, or a one– or two–course lunch where indicated:

££££	– over £100
£££	– £50–£100
££	– £25–£50
£	– under £25

Restaurant L'Atlantique
Perelle Bay, St Saviour
Tel: 01481 264056
This award-winning sea-view restaurant is located at L'Atlantique Hotel. **£££**

Victoria's Bar
L'Atlantique Hotel, Perelle
Tel: 01481 264056
Bar meals and snacks, including home-made sausages, pies, stews, puddings and hot deserts. **£**

Alderney

Albert House
Victoria Street
Tel: 01481 822243
Home-cooked food and real ales in the heart of St Anne. **£**

First and Last
Braye Harbour
Tel: 01481 823162
Harbourside restaurant specialising in seafood, renowned for its *bouillabaisse*. **££**

Georgian House
Victoria Street
Tel: 01481 822471

Charcoal-grilled fresh fish and a range of interesting daily specials served in a delightful garden in summer. **££**

Mañana Victoria Street
Tel: 01481 824021
A café cum wine bar during the day, the Mañana favours bistro chic in the evening. **££**

Sark

AJ's Island Café
The Avenue
Tel: 01481 832580
Breakfast, lunch and teas at this café-deli bar with a coffee lounge and tea garden. Fresh local food and home-baked breads. **£**

Aval du Creux
Harbour Hill
Tel: 01481 8322036
Oyster bar and lobster restaurant at the top of Harbour Hill. Part of the Aval du Creux Hotel, with a pool open to non-residents. **££**

The Courtyard Bistro
Stocks Hotel
Tel: 01481 832001
Features a popular *à la carte* menu with daily specials, home-made patisserie and *al-fresco* snacks. **£**

Dixcart Restaurant
Dixcart Hotel
Tel: 01481 832015
Imaginative cuisine in a spacious candle-lit restaurant overlooking the gardens. Excellent value for money. **££**

Hotel Petit Champ Restaurant.
Tel: 01481 832046
Renowned for good cuisine and a comprehensive wine list. Lobster and crab dishes are a speciality. **££**

La Sablonnerie Hotel Restaurant
Little Sark
Tel: 01481 832061
The Sablonnerie has an enviable reputation, with a number of the ingredients coming from the hotel's own farm and gardens. Freshly caught fish and Sark lobster are both specialities. **££**

Maison Pommier Restaurant
Rue du Fort
Tel: 01481 832626.
A short but inspired menu promises some fine dining. Booking advised. **£££**

Herm

The Mermaid
Herm Harbour
Tel: 01481 722170
A popular spot for lunch, the
Mermaid has a large walled
garden and an extensive menu.
Specialties include lobster, crab,
fish and steaks. **£**

The Ship Inn
Herm Harbour
Tel: 01481 722159
Part of the White House. Serves
pub snacks and more substantial
fare. **££**

The White House
Herm Harbour
Tel: 01481 722159
Conservatory restaurant with
sunset views. Fish and seafood
are specialities, including oysters
from the local oyster farm. **££**

Recipes

For those who like to take home the
recipes of distinctive dishes, these
suggestions come courtesy of
Jersey's Federation of Women's In-
stitutes and Mrs Eva Le Page. The
metric equivalents of the measures
given can be worked out as follows:
1 oz = 28 g; 1 lb = 450 g; 1 pint =
0.6 litre.

Des Fliottes

A very filling Jersey speciality still
served in many island homes on
Good Friday, is known as *Fliottes*
(unlike the so-called "Wonders",
there is no anglicization for this
dish).
Ingredients: ½ lb. flour; 1 quart of
milk; ¼ lb. sugar; pinch of salt; 2
eggs; knob of butter
Method: Mix the flour, sugar, eggs
and salt, adding sufficient extra
milk to make a thick batter. Put
the quart of milk to boil in a
large saucepan, adding the knob
of butter. When the milk is
boiling, drop in batter by the table-
spoonful, allowing the *Fliottes*
to float separately. Simmer for
some minutes until cooked.
Serve hot with some of the milk or
sprinkle some sugar over it.

Des Mervelles (Jersey Wonders)

Ingredients: 1 lb. plain flour; ¼ lb.
butter; ¼ lb. sugar; 3 large eggs.
Method: Rub fat into flour, add
sugar, then eggs, allow to stand for
one hour. Cook in deep fat, the
same heat as for chips. Makes 25
to 30 wonders.

Guernsey Gache

Ingredients: 1½ lbs. plain flour;
pinch ground ginger; 10 ozs. butter
or margarine; ¼ oz nutmeg; 1½
teaspoons cooking salt; 12 ozs.
fruit and 2 ozs. peel; 1 oz. fresh
yeast and 1 teaspoon honey; ¼ pint
milk and ¼ pint warm water.
Method: Put flour, ginger and salt
into mixing bowl. Mix yeast and
honey in a cup until mixture is
creamy – add tepid water and
milk. Put into centre of flour,
sprinkle flour on top, leave until

it cracks. Cut butter into small
pieces, start to mix until it looks
like satin. Add fruit and nutmeg.
Re-knead, add more water if
needed. Cover, put to rise for one
hour until well risen. Knock back
again, put into well-buttered tin –
three 1-lb. loaf tins. Leave to rise
again for half an hour or until
well risen. Put into hot oven Reg. 6
or 425°F.

Guernsey Bean Jar (Serve four)

Ingredients: 1 pig trotter or piece of
beef shin; 1 large onion; parsley
and thyme; salt and pepper; 1 large
potato, cut into small pieces; 1 carrot, cut into small pieces; ½ lb.
butter beans or haricots (or halves
of each item).
Method: Soak beans overnight,
wash and drain. Put in large casse-
role, a layer of beans, onions,
parsley and thyme. Repeat until
filled. Put in meat, fill with water,
cover, put into oven at 300°C,
150°C or Reg. 2 for 7–8 hours. Add
salt when beans are nearly cooked.

Conger Soup

Ingredients: Head and tail of 1 conger; salt; 1 small shredded
cabbage; 2 shallots; 1 bunch of
mixed herbs; borage leaves;
marigold leaves; parsley and thyme;
plain flour; 2 pints of milk; petals of
marigold; 1 pint of green peas.
Method: Wash head and tail of conger well; put in a large saucepan,
cover with water, add salt, bring to
the boil and simmer for 1 hour.
Remove fish, strain liquid and
return to saucepan, add a small
shredded cabbage, the shallots
finely sliced, bunch of mixed herbs
chopped up, borage leaves,
marigold leaves, parsley and thyme
and boil until tender.

Thicken with 2 dessertspoons
of plain flour and cook for 5
minutes. Add 2 pints of milk and 1
oz. of butter and bring nearly to
boil (but do not boil). Petals of
marigold flowers are then thrown
into the soup which is now ready
to serve.

When green peas are available 1
pint of these added to soup
improves the flavour.

Du Nier Beurre (Black Butter)

This traditional apple preserve is still made in one or two Jersey parishes. Hundreds of pounds of peeled apples, gallons of cider, a huge pan and plenty of wood for an outhouse fire are needed to turn a real *Séthée D'Nier Beurre* or Black Butter Night into a special occasion with sing-a-longs and lots of merriment. In fact it takes a whole day for the apple, cider and spices to cook and reduce down to a thick, tasty jam, which is then put into jars and shared among the helpers and the surplus sold. The event happens in the apple season – late November – but not necessarily every year. It is sometimes difficult to get a sufficient quantity of fruit as commercial orchards are no longer a part of the agricultural scene. The preserve can be made in the comfort of a modern kitchen. The recipe is as follows:

Ingredients: 2 lbs. sour apples; 5 lbs. sweet apples; 8 pints cider; 10 lbs. white sugar; 4 lemons; 1 dessertspoon mixed spice; ½ stick liquorice.

Method: Boil cider until reduced to half. Add peeled, cored, sliced sweet apples, a basinful at a time. Add liquorice and lemons, minced. When all are well-cooked, add sour apples. Cook until thick, then add sugar and cook again, stirring frequently. When very thick and dark add spice; bottle and cover.

Historical Attractions

Jersey

Channel Islands Military Museum: Five Mile Road, St Ouen; Tel: 01534 723136. Display of British and German militaria in a restored German bunker. Open daily in season, 10am–5pm.

Elizabeth Castle: St Aubin's Bay; Tel: 01534 723971, www.jerseyheritagetrust.org. Jersey Militia Museum, tableaux depicting events during the 17th century. "Granite and Gunpowder" illustrates the defences of Jersey over the past 400 years and there is an audiovisual presentation of the "History of Elizabeth Castle". Pedestrians can walk across a causeway at low water or use the privately owned amphibian ferry service. (Fares do not include entry to the Castle). Visits take around two hours or more. Open daily Easter–late Oct 10am–6pm, last admission 5pm.

Jersey War Tunnels: Meadowbank, St Lawrence; Tel: 01534 860808, www.jerseywartunnels.com. Award-winning, extensive museum telling the story of the occupation in Jersey. The Captive Island exhibition is dedicated to the effect the occupation had on the islanders and the island. Open daily 10am–6pm.

Grève de Lecq Barracks: Grève de Lecq. Military barracks built at the time of Waterloo. Owned and restored by The National Trust for Jersey. Exhibition of militaria and Jersey horse-drawn vehicles. Houses the North Coast Visitor Centre. Open May–Sept Tues–Sat

11am–5pm, Sun 2–5pm.

Grosnez Castle: St Ouen. Ruins dating back to the 14th century.

Hamptonne Country Life Museum, near St Lawrence Church; www.jerseyheritagetrust.org. Three hundred years of the island's rural heritage, from buildings and exhibitions to farmyard animals and meadows. Open daily Easter–late Oct 10am–5pm.

Island Fortress Occupation Museum: 9 Esplanade, St Helier; Tel: 01534 863955. Occupation memorabilia. Open daily summer 9.30am–6.30pm, winter 10am–4pm.

Jersey Battle of Flowers Museum: La Robeline, Mont des Corvées, St Ouen; Tel: 01534 734 306. See award-winning floats made of flowers, straw and thistles. Open daily in season 10am–5pm.

Jersey Museum: The Weighbridge, St Helier; Tel: 01534 633300, www.jerseyheritagetrust.org. Four-storey refurbished museum made out of two Pier Road townhouses with restaurant, art gallery and audio-visual interpretation of the island's history. Open daily 10am–5pm, till 4pm in winter.

La Hougue Bie Museum: La Hougue Bie, Grouville; Tel: 01534 853823, www.jerseyheritagetrust.org. Agriculture, Archaeology, Geology and German Occupation Museums; massive Neolithic tomb; medieval chapels and railway exhibition. Open daily easter–late Oct 10am–5pm.

Maritime Museum: New North Quay, St Helier; Tel: 01534 811043. Exciting museum combining hands-on and historic exhibits. Open daily 10am–5pm, till 4pm in winter.

Mont Orgueil Castle, Gorey; Tel: 01534 853292, www.jersey heritagetrust.org. A dramatic fortress that towers over Gorey harbour, built in the 13th century as protection against the French. Floodlit at night. Open daily Easter–late Oct 10am–6pm, last admission 5pm.

Occupation Tapestry Museum: New North Quay, St Helier; Tel: 01534 811043 (same building as Maritime Museum). Tapestries depicting scenes from the Occupation. Open daily 10am–5pm, till 4pm in winter.

Guernsey

Brooklands Farm Implement Museum: Kings Mills, Castel. A private museum of agricultural equipment used in Guernsey over the past 100 years. Open Apr–Oct Tues–Sat 9.30am–1pm.

Castle Cornet: Castle Emplacement, St Peter Port. The castle was founded by King John in 1206; buildings date from the 13th to the 20th century and it was the scene of many battles. Royal Guernsey Militia Museum, Maritime Museum, Armoury, Picture galleries, 201 Squadron Museum and museum shop. Noonday gun fired daily. Open May–Sept 10am–5pm, Apr & Oct 10am–4pm. Closed Nov–March.

Château des Marais: Castle Lane, St Peter Port. Castle is surrounded by a moat and large outer bailey.

Folk Museum (National Trust of Guernsey): Saumarez Park, Castel; Tel: 01481 255384, www.national trust-gsy.org.gg. The National Trust of Guernsey's Folk Museum contains a rich collection of Victoriana, furniture, china and early household equipment set out in a series of rooms arranged around an attractive 18th-century farm courtyard. Upstairs is a display on Victorian childhood, and the outbuildings have a variety of tools and implements used in Guernsey 100 years ago. Open 10am–5pm (last tickets 5pm) daily. Closed mid-Mar.

German Coast Defence Gun Casement: Fort Hommet Headland. A fully-restored German bunker with an original 10.5 cm gun. Open Tues and Sat.

German Direction Finding Tower: Pleinmont headland. A re-equipped five-storey coastal artillery direction finding tower. Open Sun & Wed 2–5pm, Apr–Oct.

German Military Underground Hospital: La Vassalerie Road, St Andrew. Complex of concreted tunnels hewn out of solid rock by slave workers of many nationalities under the control of German Occupying Forces, 1940–1945. Occupation relics and newspapers on view. Open Mar & Nov Sun & Thur 2–3pm; Apr &

Oct daily 2–4pm; May, June & Sept daily 10am–noon & 2–4pm; Jul & Aug daily 10–noon & 2–4.30pm.

German Naval Signals HQ: St Jacques, St Peter Port. The powerful radio transmitters in this bunker provided the only communication with Berlin when the Channel Islands were isolated after September 1944. Open Mon, Thur and Sat 2–4.30pm.

Guernsey German Occupation Museum: Forest. Tells the story of the German Occupation of Guernsey, 1940–1945, with visual tableaux, a lifesize street, bunker rooms, cinema, tearooms and garden. Open daily 10am–5pm, till 1pm in winter.

Guernsey Museum and Art Gallery: Candie Gardens, St Peter Port; Tel: 01481 726518, www.museum guernsey.net. Opened in 1978, the island's first purpose-built museum made a big enough impact to win the national Museum of the Year Award in 1979. The exhibition depicts the story of the island and its people. Open 10am–5pm, till 4pm in winter (closed Christmas week).

Guernsey Telephone Museum: "Hermes", La Planque, Cobo Road, Castel. The State of Guernsey have run the local telephone service since it started in 1898. Run voluntarily by Guernsey Telecommunications staff, the Telephone Museum opened in 1976 at the former Castel Manual Exchange. Open June 2–5pm, July–Aug 10am–5pm.

La Valette Underground Military Museum: St Peter Port. Air-conditioned German tunnel complex plus militaria including Commander of the liberating troops, Brigadier Snow's uniform. Open daily 10am–5pm.

Loopholed Tower: Rousse Headland. 18th-century fully-restored tower and interpretation centre.

Maritime Museum: Castle Cornet, St Peter Port; Tel: 01481 721657. Built as part of the island's defences against Napoleon in 1804 on the site of an ancient castle. Restored in 1975 as a maritime museum featuring the shipwrecks on the treacherous Hanois Reef nearby. The fort is situated on a small islet connected to the shore by a stone causeway. Open May–Sept

10am–5pm, Apr & Oct 10am–4pm. Closed Nov–March.

Sausmarez Manor: St Martin's. The stronghold of the de Sausmarez family, one of Guernsey's oldest. Delightful gardens, sculpture trail, pitch-and-putt course, doll's house collection and silversmithing. Open daily 10am–5pm.

Victor Hugo's House: Hauteville, St Peter Port; Tel: 01481 721911. Home of the famous French political exile, Victor Hugo, Hauteville House is as unique as its former owner. Open daily, except Sundays and bank holidays, from 10–11.30am and 2–4.30pm. Closed 1 Oct–31 Mar.

Alderney

Alderney Museum: St Anne; Tel: 01481 823222, www.alderney society.org. Covers the history of the island from the neolithic age to the present day. Natural history section. Open Mon–Fri 10am–noon, 2–4pm; Sat–Sun 10am–noon.

Sark

Sark Occupation and Heritage Museum: Rue Lucas, Sark. Old farming implements and photographs of island life, plus relics of the Occupation. Open Mon–Sat 11am–5pm.

Art Galleries

Jersey

Sir Francis Cook Gallery (Jersey Heritage Trust): Route de Trinité, Augrès, Trinity; Tel: 01534 863333. Temporary exhibitions.
Jersey Arts Centre: Phillips Street, St Helier. Home of the Berni Gallery. Month-long exhibitions of local and national artists and photographers. Free admission.
Jersey Museum: The Weighbridge, St Helier. The first floor is devoted to works by Jersey artists. Admission charge.

Guernsey

Coach House Galleries: Les Islets, St Peter's; Tel: 01481 65339. Old farm buildings provide an attractive setting for an art gallery with etching studio. Open 11am–5pm all year. Free admission.
Guernsey Museum and Art Gallery: Candie Gardens, St Peter Port. Exhibits include Rodin's bust of Victor Hugo, Renoir's painting of *Fog on Guernsey*, and characterful sketches of islanders. The museum displays books on the Channel Islands, fine porcelain, antiques and furniture. Open daily 10am–4pm, and to 5pm May–Sept, closed 24 Dec–1 Feb.

Nightlife

In Jersey and Guernsey nightlife is mainly centred around pubs and discos, with occasional cabaret and dance shows. The Art Centre in St Helier has photographic and art exhibitions, touring theatre company productions and much more. St James Hall in Guernsey has an extensive programme of entertainment, mostly of a formal nature. *Beau Séjour Leisure Centre*, Guernsey, and *Fort Regent Sports and Entertainment Complex*, on Jersey, bring in international variety acts, comedians and bands, on a regular basis during the season. The theatre at Beau Séjour has touring acts and individual artistes.

Several hotels host their own shows, including Swansons, on the Esplanade in Jersey, and the Merton in St Saviour whose nightly entertainment includes dancing, cabaret and floor shows. Madison's, in the Hotel de France complex in St Saviour's Road, has the latest dance music. The only traditional theatre in the Channel Islands is the Opera House in Gloucester Street, Jersey.

Popular day and evening venues are Jersey Bowl in St Peter, Bowl Island in St Helier and the Guernsey Bowl in Vale Avenue, the only ten-pin bowling centres in the Islands.

Many of the clubs and societies in the islands add to the nightlife in pubs, particularly those associated with pure entertainment such as folk, jazz or country and western music.

The latest films are shown in the two cinemas in Jersey (the Odeon in Bath Street and Ciné de France next to the Hotel de France in St Saviour's Road), and one in Guernsey (at the Mallard Cinema complex) and Alderney's island hall.

For younger people, there are plenty of nightclubs and live bands play regularly. For the under-18s, who are not permitted to drink alcohol, some special discos serve soft drinks only.

Discotheques: Entrance fees for most clubs and discos are around £5 – sometimes cheaper if you arrive before 11pm. Some public houses double as nightclubs or places of entertainment, with live music at Chambers in Mulcaster Street, St Helier (nightly), the Cock and Bull and the Doghouse in St Peter Port, and Blind O'Reilly' in St Sampson's. Nightclubbing can continue until 2am.

JERSEY

Blarneys: 11 Cattle Street, St Helier. Live music and Irish nights.
La Cala: Esplanade, St Helier. Nightclub and restaurant.
Chambers: Mulcaster Street. Live music nightly.
Chicago Rock Café: Waterfront. "Live at the Rock" nights and DJs.
Les Folies d'Amour: The Esplanade. Bar and nightclub. Mainstream dance. Over 21s.
L'Auberge du Nord: La Route du Nord, St John. DJs and live bands.
Liquid: New nightclub at the waterfront. Resident DJ, current dance music, R&B, hip hop.
Madison's Nightclub: Hotel de France, St Helier. Club, disco and restaurant.
Pure: Weighbridge. Funky house and UK DJs.
The Q Club: James Street. Local talent as well as UK bands once a month. Dance, rock and indie nights.
Rock Galaxy: Castle Street, St Helier. Disco and theme restaurant.
Sands: Five Mile Road, St Ouen.
The Venue: Beresford Street, St Helier.
Vespas: 72 Esplanade, St Helier. Small and friendly nightclub.
Warehouse: Caledonia Place, St Helier. 1970s, '80s, '90s music.
Watersplash: Five Mile Road, St Ouen. Break beat and rock.

GUERNSEY

Baloo's Bar: 8, Fountain Street, St Peter Port

Barbados Beach Club: Lower Pollet, St Peter Port
Blind O Reilly's: English & Guernsey Arms, St Sampson's
Buzz Bar: St Julian's Avenue, St Peter Port.
Cock and Bull: Hauteville, St Peter Port
Club 54: 54 Le Pollet, St Peter Port
Les Follies d'Amour: North Plantation, St Peter Port
No 10: Anne's Place, St Peter Port
WKD Bar: Le Pollet, St Peter Port

ALDERNEY

Belle Vue Hotel: The Bute

Pubs

Quaint pubs with friendly landlords, offering a game of darts and a pint of the local brew, abound. Jersey is reputed to have a bar for every day of the year and it also possesses two breweries: Mary Ann (which brews award-winning beers like Mary Ann Special and keg beers like Winter Ale) and the Tipsy Toad Townhouse and Brewery, which claims to be the largest in-house brewery of real ales in the world. A smaller brewery owned by the same company operates from the Star, St Peter.

The only brewery in Guernsey is Randalls Ltd, which supplies Tesco supermarkets in the UK. Both islands have seen a change in "pubbing" in recent years with many inns now offering a selection of real ales thanks to a shift in people's likes and dislikes and a concerted effort by Camra (the Campaign for Real Ales) to influence landlords' policies. Many pubs have been modernised to attract a younger and more upmarket clientele. Most pub lunches range from a simple toasted sandwich to a full-scale feast of fish or meat.

Since 2003 Guernsey pubs have been able to remain open until 12.45am seven nights a week. However, the choice of closing time is up to the licensee and varies.

Pub hours for Herm and Sark are similar to Guernsey's but in Alderney publicans can, if they so wish, open all day, including Saturday.

Festivals

Jersey

Battle of Britain Week: The highlight is a spectacular air display. Mid-September
Battle of Flowers: A high spot for the holiday season, this internationally renowned floral carnival takes place on the second Thursday every August. Funfair and other events during the week culminate in a spectacular parade of large and small floats decorated with fresh and paper flowers, bands and firework displays. The Moonlight Parade, held on the day after the Battle of Flowers, features illuminated floats from the main parade. Tel: 01534 639000 for details and entry prices. August
Christmas Festival: A programme of festive events starting at the end of November and including carol concerts, late-night shopping and street entertainment.
Foire de Jersey: Traditional country fair offering entertainment for all the family. Cattle shows, country craft shows, ring-events, food tastings and traditional country games. Late May
Island Flavours: a Taste of Jersey in Springtime. A week of food demonstrations by local chefs, farm visits, themed 'foodie' walks, and wine- and food- tasting in the best hotels and restaurants. Special menus based on the island's Genuine Jersey Produce – Jersey Royals, wine, honey, fish, shellfish and other local delicacies (www.jersey.com/food). April
Jersey in Bloom: A chance to meet favourite gardening personalities at open-garden events, guided walks, talks and practical demonstrations at a time when the island is at its floral best. July

Jersey Film Festival: Blockbuster movies and classic favourites are projected onto a 37-ft (11-metre) screen in the grounds of Howard Davis Park. A different film every night for a week. Free admission. August
National Nines Golf Tournament: September
Portuguese Fair: Celebrate with Jersey's Portuguese community their wonderful food, wine and beer. August or September
Seafood and Cider Festival : A week of celebration with cookery demonstrations, tastings, displays and events featuring traditional Jersey menus and food from around the world. May
St Aubin Food Festival: Food stalls and themed menus in the restaurants, cafés and bars of St Aubin. July
Tennerfest: Dine in style for just £10 in over 40 restaurants on the island. Oct–mid-Nov

Guernsey

Agricultural and Horticultural Shows: The West Show, the North Show, the Battle of Flowers. Floats, lavishly decorated with real and paper flowers, provide a colourful climax to the weekend. August
Battle of Britain Week: A similar display to Jersey. September
Chess Festival: International Competition. October
Dance Festival: Attracts entrants from all over the world. Competitions and displays. June–July
Festival of Food and Wine: Cookery contests, lectures by well-known authors and TV chefs and special gourmet menus at many restaurants and hotels. April.
Floral Festival Week: A celebration of the island's flowers and garden produce, with displays and entertainment.
Guernsey Festival: A music festival, with classical, as well as jazz and other styles. September–October
International Folk Festival: An annual festival featuring a varied programme of lively musical events. October.

Liberation Day: Celebration of the island's release from the German Occupation. Local public holiday with street entertainment and fireworks. 9 May

Round Table Harbour Carnival: - Man-powered flight, tug of war, dinghy races and boat parade in Victoria Marina. July

St Peter Port Town Carnival: After an opening procession, there are street entertainers around the town, street fashion shows, fancy dress competitions, and food stalls; as well as fitness demonstrations and competitions. July

Via'r Marchi: A traditional Guernsey evening at Saumarez Park. Crafts are sold by costumed stallholders, and there are displays of traditional music and dance. July

Alderney

Alderney Week: Attractions include attempts at man-powered flight off Braye Quay, a daft raft race, flower-decorated floats, fancy dress competitions, knockout cricket and tug of war contests. The week is rounded off with a torchlight procession, bonfire and a spectacular fireworks display on the Butes. August

Aurigny Angling Festival: Attracts around 200 competitors from all over the country. October

Milk-a-Punch Sunday: A long observed tradition, milk-a-punch is made of milk and egg, given a little kick by a healthy tot of rum. It is offered free by every publican on the Island, who compete to see who can make the best drink. May

Sark

Cattle Show: The dairy farmers have a chance to display their cattle, to be judged by judges from Guernsey. July

Grand Autumn Show: Heralded by the careful selection of crops and garden vegetables, by baking and decorating of cakes and preparation of preserves. September

House and Pet Show: July/August

Midsummer Flower Show: Gives gardeners a chance to show off

their skills, as gardens are judged to find the best in the Island. There are also special exhibits and a flower arranging competition. June

St Peter's Church Fair: Stalls, sideshows and performing Guernsey dancers. First Saturday in August

Water Carnival: The main event takes two days. The first is land-based and features an open fancy dress competition, silly races and silly competitions. The next part is water-based, featuring a procession of decorated boats, swimming races, yak races, home-made raft races and the flight of man-powered aircraft. July or August, depending on the tides.

For Children

Jersey

With its sandy beaches, clean seas and rock pools, Jersey is ideal for children. Most of the museums and attractions on the island are geared to all ages. Learning is made fun at the hands-on **Maritime Museum** in St Hellier (see page 127) and the **Living Legend** (see page 164), bringing the island's history to life. A sure winner is **Durrell Wildlife Conservation Trust** (see page 146) where you come face to face with lowland gorillas and can explore 31 acres (12½ hectares) of parkland established for endangered species. Here, an excellent educational centre is specifically aimed at children. **Samarès Manor** (see page 137) has farm animals, craft demonstrations, and beautiful gardens to explore; while **Hamptonne** (see page 165) is a delightful country farm museum with restored buildings, farmyard animals and nature walks. **Amaizin Maze** at **La Hougue Farm**, on La Grande Route de St Pierre in St Peter (open summer only), is a specially designed maze made out of cereal maize. An adventure park with a water pistol range, pedal go-karts, tractor and trailer rides and activities that change yearly provide plenty of fun, and there are daily falcon and parrot shows. **Elizabeth Castle** (see page 123) is a favourite for the journey across to the islet in the amphibian ferry.

Young children will be quite content to spend the day messing around in rock pools, fishing for shrimps, crabs and devil fish. Every beach shop is well equipped with cheap nets and buckets. The best beaches for swimming are St Brelade's and St Aubin's where the sand shelves gently and the waters are normally calm. However, older children who are good swimmers will love body surfing on the waves at St Ouen's. Boogy boards are available for hire. At Treasures of the Earth (daily 9.30am–5pm), on La Route de l'Etacq, a journey through caverns, grottos and "The Magic Temple" reveals glowing crystals, gemstones, fossils and prehistoric creatures.

The island has several parks and gardens, many with play areas for children. **Coronation Park** at Millbrook is one of the most popular, with two playgrounds, a paddling pool and refreshments. **Sunset Flower Centre**, behind St Ouen's Bay, has a tropical bird garden with macaws and cockatoos, and a pond stocked with massive trout which feed on pellets sold on the premises.

Jersey's answer to a wet day is **Fort Regent** in St Helier (daily 10am–5pm; Tel: 01534 500200). The entrance charge at this huge leisure complex covers all the tourist attractions, live entertainment and play areas for young children. The extensive recreation and sports facilities (*see page 132*) are aimed at all ages, and include a skate park, funfair rides, Quasar (laser guns), softball, crazy golf, trampolining and a toddlers' gym. St Helier's main swimming pool is now **AquaSplash** in the waterfont complex (Tel: 01534 734524), where special play times for children are scheduled. A multiplex cinema and a number of fast food outlets are also here. For more information on family days out visit www.Jersey.com/family.

Guernsey

If you and your children are still young enough at heart to enjoy all the pleasures of the beach, then there is no better destination for a family holiday. Sea temperatures become comfortable for swimming in mid-July – coinciding nicely with school summer holidays.

At cooler times of the year, paddling is still an option, and beachcombing is fun year round – the huge tidal flows that take place in the Channel Islands (between 20 and 25ft/6–8 metres difference between high and low water mark) mean that huge expanses of sand and crab-filled rock pools are revealed when the water goes out. Shell Beach, on Herm, is a famous spot for shell hunting, but there are scores of other beaches to choose from.

For much of the year, Guernsey and the smaller islands enjoy a climate more akin to that of northern France than southern England – but rain can be a problem in spring as fronts come in off the Atlantic. This is the time to head for the **Beau Séjour Centre** (*page 187*), on the hilltop above St Peter Port, to enjoy the swimming pool, with its flume slides and floating islands, or to see a film in the adjacent cinema.

Other formal attractions in St Peter Port include the **Guernsey Museum** (*page 187*), which has friendly staff and a quiz that will keep older children quiet for an hour or so, **Fort Grey** (*page 195*), which also has a quiz focusing on the wrecks found hereabouts, and **Castle Cornet** (*page 178*), which puts on organised activities for children during the summer, teaching them about life in an 18th-century garrison.

Two attractions, with confusingly similar names, are perfect for children: **Saumarez Park** (*page 199*) has an adventure playground in the grounds, and the Folk Museum provides a fun introduction to the island's history – including the ancient practice of child labour! The tea rooms here are also very child friendly, with a disco area (for pre-teenage children) as well as freshly made and reasonably priced food. **Sausmarez Manor** (*page 192*), in a different part of the island, has pets, crazy golf, a miniature railway and a collection of doll's-house furnishings. Apart from these, you will find plenty of other attractions, from the **Little Chapel** (*page 189*) with its shell-encrusted walls, to the children's adventure activity areas at the Strawberry Farm (*page 199*). An exciting way to see the island is in a Rigid Inflatable Boat (RIB), suitable for all ages. Book your trip at Albert Pier (Tel: 01481 713031).

Going to Sark or Herm by boat is an adventure in itself, and the journey is short enough for children not to get bored. Once there, there are no cars to worry about, so children can roam in relative safety, and Sark can be enjoyed either by bike or by the more sedate horse and carriage.

Shopping

What to Buy

Pick up any brochure and the image created is that the islands are a paradise for bargain hunters. Duty is low and the absence of Value Added Tax (17½ percent on the mainland) in some shops makes luxury goods, perfume, tobacco, wines, spirits and jewellery relatively cheaper. But when it comes to buying cameras, clothing and electrical goods, the buyer should beware. Visitors sometimes find that the bulk purchasing power of the national chain stores enable them to buy goods cheaper in the UK than in the Channel Islands because discounts are greater than the sales tax savings. A freight surcharge is also added to many goods sold in the Channel Islands.

For traditional gifts or souvenirs, try some of the unusual items manufactured from giant cabbage stalks at L'Etacq Woodcrafts in Jersey; Guernsey or Jersey milk cans; and pottery, glassware, woodcarvings or soft toys produced by local craftsmen.

Many visitors also buy jewellery, especially in St Helier where the number of shops has proliferated. One chain of stores offers a cashback refund as an inducement to customers if they can find a similar item they have purchased cheaper in other stores in the island.

St Helier also has the splendid **Central Market** (1882), with forty flower stalls, traditional butchers, delicatessen and gourmet food and wine outlets. At the nearby **Beresford Fish Market** you can buy everything from seabass, conger eel and live lobsters to spider crabs, squid and shrimps.

Both islands have many craft centres, some selling traditional Channel Islands products such as Jersey and Guernsey knitwear.

The most famous of the centres is the Jersey Pottery at Gorey *(see page 139)* where you can watch artisans at close hand, purchase from the showrooms and lunch at one of the most appealing restaurants on the island.

Shopping Hours

Shopkeepers don't take long siestas, despite the continental influence. Most open their premises from 9am to 5.30pm, Mondays to Saturdays – although in Jersey and Guernsey, the markets and a few small establishments close on Thursday afternoon. There is limited Sunday trading on the islands.

Sport

Participant

Angling

With their varied coastlines and clear waters, the islands are ideal locations for sea anglers, especially from mid-summer to the end of autumn. More than 70 different species of fish have been caught, including sharks (not inshore!), conger, rays, turbot, bass and bream.

No permission is needed to fish from the coastline or harbours and fellow anglers and tackle dealers are always pleased to offer help on where to go. Boat trips with experienced skippers who know many of the marks are good value. Cost is about £25 per day per person and includes bait, tackle and refreshments.

The offshore reefs near Jersey like the Ecréhous, the Minquiers and Paternosters are rich grounds. Guernsey has become a mecca for deepwater wreck anglers.

Alderney is acknowledged to be one of the top places for shore fishing in the whole of the British Isles.

Freshwater fishing is limited but possible in reservoirs. Temporary permits are issued by the water authorities in Jersey and Guernsey. For boat fishing trips contact:
Jersey: MV *Anna II*, Tony Heart (888552); *Theseus*, Dave Nuth (858046).
Guernsey: B Blondel (39848); George and Gerry (724677, mobile 04481 101482); G. Le Tissier (52620, mobile 04481 100275).

Birdwatching

Wide ranges of habitat and a mild climate are reasons why birds use the islands during spring and autumn migrations. Look for Dartford warblers, short-toed treecreepers, firecrests, and Brent geese. For those who are not experienced enough to spot the difference, field guides containing location maps are available.

Botany

With their mild winters and warm summers, the islands boast nearly 2,000 species of flora, of which 400 or more are winter-flowering. Botanical societies on the bigger islands have published various leaflets and information packs which list contact names for guided rambles. Further details from Jersey Tourism (500700) and the Guernsey Information Centre (723552).

Flying

A company based at Guernsey Airport offers fulltime training courses for private pilots. For trial lessons, contact Guernsey Aero Club (265254). The Jersey Aero Club (743990) does not offer residential courses but gives flying lessons. Alderney Flying Club (822297) welcomes qualified pilots for social events. Qualified private pilots can fly into Jersey, Guernsey or Alderney.

Gardens

Gardens in the islands are rarely without colour. In spring, the fields and hedgerows are transformed by daffodils bursting into bloom. From then on tulips, camellias, magnolias, hydrangeas and many other plants can be seen in the parks and gardens. Once a week during summer, private gardens in Jersey and Guernsey are open to the public in aid of charity. Ask for Jersey and Guernsey Floral leaflets.

Golf

Demand for the game exceeds supply. Local residents wanting to join one of the top clubs in Jersey can expect to be on the waiting list for up to 15 years. However, visitors who are members of a recognised golf club and have a reasonable handicap are allowed to play at these clubs at certain times of day. Other clubs are open to players of any standard, but it's advisable to telephone in advance to check availability.

Alderney's only golf course (nine-hole) is normally quiet and un-crowded. Rates are very reasonable and clubs can be hired.

Further information:
Jersey
Fighteen holes:
La Moye Golf Club: St Brelade (747166). Men must have handicaps below 24 and ladies 30 and below.
Les Mielles Golf and Country Club: St Ouen's Bay, St Peter (482787).
Royal Jersey Golf Club: Grouville (854416). Proof of handicap needed.
Nine holes:
Jersey Recreation Grounds: Grève d'Azette, St Clement (721938). Also mini/crazy golf and putting.
Les Ormes, Mont à La Drune, St Brelade (499077).
Wheatlands, off Le Vieux Beaumont, St Peter (888844).

Guernsey
Fighteen holes:
Royal Guernsey Golf Club: L'Ancresse, Vale (246523). Visitors must produce a current handicap certificate from a recognised club.
La Grande Mare Hotel: Vazon Bay (253432). 18 holes but 14 greens.
Nine holes:
St Pierre Park Hotel: Rohais (727039).

Alderney
Nine holes:
Alderney Golf Club, Route des Carrières (822835).

Horse Riding
One way of reaching the heart of the countryside is on horseback. Treks and escorted hacks along a well-maintained circuit of bridle paths, through valleys and up small lanes, and along cliff tops or dunes, normally last two or three hours and can be arranged through several of the stables. Riding on the beach is also permitted in Jersey but not between September 11 to 30. For more information contact:
Jersey: Bon-Air Stables, St Law-rence (865196); Brabant Riding School, Trinity (861105); Rossmore Farm Riding School, Vallée des Vaux, St Helier (726210); Sorrel

Stables and Saddlery Centre, Mont Fallu, St Peter (742009).
Guernsey: Gillian Brock, La Corbière Riding and Livery Stables, Forest (264193); Caroline Jackson, Otter-bourne Riding Centre, Torteval (263085); Manor Rding Stables, Rue des Camps, St Martin (38275); Rose Dorey, Melrose Farm Stables, Castel (252151); Guernsey Equestrian and Saddlery Centre, Les Grandes Capelles, St Sampson (725257); Jenny Le Prevost, La Carrière Stables and Tack Shop (249998).

Scuba Diving
Qualified divers can explore the mys-teries of the deep in the clean, cold waters around the islands. Introduc-tory dives and certificate courses are also available for those who want to learn the sport. The currents are often strong so don't dive unac-companied. More fish will be seen with a mask and snorkel than with scuba gear – temperate species always seem to be scared off by the bubbles. For boat dives, equipment hire and courses, contact:
Jersey: The Watersports Centre, First Tower (732813); Bouley Bay Dive Centre (861817); Dive Buddies, St Aubin's Harbour (490180).
Guernsey: Dive Guernsey/Guernsey School of Diving (714525); Sarnia Skin Divers (722884).
Alderney: Brian Markell (822633).

Surfing/Windsurfing
Surfers from many places flock to St Ouen's Bay in Jersey to ride the big Atlantic swells. On several occasions the island has played host to major competitions.

Jersey surfers travel around the world in search of the perfect wave and are among the best at their sport in the British Isles. Surf can also be found on Guernsey's west coast and in Alderney. A number of beach concessions hire boards and wetsuits. Jersey also has surfing schools at the Watersplash (484005), Sands (483707) and the Atlantic Waves School (865492).

Islands are normally ideal loca-tions for windsurfing and this archipelago is no exception. Wind strength and direction varies from

day to day and it is quite feasible to move from bay to bay to find the best conditions. Beginners, intermediate and advanced wave sailors are catered for. Qualified in-struction is available at schools in the three largest islands. A basic certificate course lasts five hours. The following companies offer either surfing, or windsurfing, or both:
Jersey: Jersey Seasport Centre, St Aubin – including surf-jets and surf-skis (745040); Gorey Watersports, Grouville Bay (745040); St Brelade's Windsurfing and Sailing School (853250).
Guernsey: Fat Face, Oceana House, St Peter Port (729090).

Swimming
Apart from the three main swimming pools – at Aqua Splash in Jersey (734524), Les Quennevais in Jersey (490909) and Beau Séjour in Guern-sey (728591) – the Merton Aquadome in St Helier (67774), of-fers swimming plus flumes, for children, and the Havre des Pas outdoor pool, at Grève d'Azette, St Helier (23160), allows swimming plus canoeing in the safety of the large outdoor pool. There is safe free seawater swimming at the Bathing Pools, La Vallette, St Peter Port.

Yacht Charter
Some sailing experience is neces-sary to charter a boat, or alterna-tively, skippers who know the local waters are available. The freedom to sail between the islands or to France makes a holiday afloat a worthwhile proposition. All marinas offer pontoon moorings and support facilities. Boats can be hired by the hour, day or week.

Useful numbers include the Jersey Cruising School and Yacht Charters, the Marina, St Helier (888100 Fax: 888088); St Helier Yacht Club, South Pier (721307); the Royal Channel Island Yacht Club, the Bulwarks, St Aubin (741023); the Royal Channel Islands Yacht Club, Quay Steps, St Peter Port (725500, Fax: 712257) and the Guernsey Yacht Club, Castle Emplacement, St Peter Port (722838); Tiger Lily Tours, Sark, (833099).

Further Reading

General

The following list of books include some which are out of print but may be found in public libraries.

Balleine, G.R: *The Bailiwick of Jersey*. Hodder and Stoughton.

Balleine, G.R: *Biographical Dictionary of Jersey*. Staples Press.

Binney, M: *Victorian Jersey*. Save Britain's Heritage.

Bisson, S: *Jersey our Island*. Batchworth.

Bonnard, Brian: *Alderney at War 1939–1949*. Sutton.

Bunting, M: *The Model Occupation: The Channel Islands under German Rule 1940–45*. Pimlico.

Cochrane, J: *Life on Sark*. Seaflower Books.

Collins, D: *A Childish Memory of the Germans in Jersey*. Navigator Books.

Cruickshank, C: *The German Occupation of the Channel Islands*. Oxford University Press.

Dobson, R: *Birds of the Channel Islands*. Staples Press.

Garis, M: *Le Dictionnaire Anglais – Guernesiais*. Phillimore.

Geoff, D.: *Landscapes of Guernsey with Alderney, Sark and Herm*. Sunflower Books.

Hathaway, S: *Dame of Sark*. La Haule Books.

Hickman, T: *Neolithic tombs of Guernsey and their subsequent use*. Witmeha Press.

Hillsdon, S: *The Jersey Lily: The Life and Times of Lillie Langtry*. Seaflower Books.

Jee, N: *Guernsey Cow*. Elek.

Jee, N: *Landscape of the Channel Islands*. Phillimore.

Johnston, D.E: *The Channel Islands: An Archaeological Guide*. Phillimore.

Journeaux, D: *Raise the White Flag: A Study through one pair of eyes of the Occupation of Jersey by German Forces*. Ashford, Buchan and Enright.

Le Dain, J: *Jersey Alphabet*. Seaflower Books.

Le Feuvre, D: *Jersey: Not Quite British*. Seaflower Books.

Le Maistre, F: *Le Dictionnaire Jersiais – Français*. Don Balleine Trust.

Le Ruez, N: *Jersey Occupation Diary; Her Story of Occupation 1940–45*. Seaflower Books.

Lemprière, R: *Portrait of the Channel Islands*. Robert Hale.

Lemprière, R: *History of the Channel Islands*. Robert Hale.

Lemprière, R: *Customs, Ceremonies and Traditions of the Channel Islands*. Robert Hale.

Lemprière, R: *Buildings and Memorials of the Channel Islands*. Robert Hale.

Le Sueur, F: *A Natural History of Jersey*. Phillimore.

Le Sueur, F: *Flora of Jersey*. Société Jersiaise.

Lewis, J: *A Doctor's Occupation*. Corgi.

McCormack, J: *The Guernsey House*. Phillimore.

McLoughlin, R: *The Sea was their Fortune: A Maritime History of the Channel Islands*. Seaflower Books.

Mallet, R: *Jersey Under the Swastika*. The Hyperion Press.

Manning, J: *Glimpses of Jersey*. The Guernsey Press Co.

Marr, L. J: *A History of the Bailiwick of Guernsey*. Phillimore.

Marr, L. J: *Guernsey People*. Phillimore.

Marr, L. J: *More People in Guernsey's Story*. The Guernsey Society.

Maugham, R. C. F: *Jersey Under the Jackboot*. New English Library.

Mollet, R: *A Chronology of Jersey*. Société Jersiaise.

Ramsey, W.G: *The War in the Channel Islands Then and Now*. Battle of Britain Prints International.

Robinson, G. W. S: *Guernsey*. David and Charles.

Sinel, L. P: *The German Occupation of Jersey*. La Haule Books.

Stentiford, M: *The Birdwatcher's Jersey*.

Stevens, J: *Old Jersey Houses*: Vols. I & II. Phillimore. Vol. VI. Phillimore.

Stevens, J: *A Short History of Jersey*. Société Jersiaise.

Stevens, P: *Victor Hugo in Jersey*. Phillimore.

Stoney, B: *Sibyl, Dame of Sark*. Burbridge.

Syvret, M. and . Stevens J.: *Balleine's History of Jersey*, revised and enlarged edition. Phillimore.

Toms, Carel: *Guernsey's Forgotten Past*. Phillimore.

Other Insight Guides

Three distinctive series are designed to meet your varying travel needs.

Insight Guides

The 190-strong **Insight Guides** series includes the following titles covering UK destinations: *Great Britain, England, Wales, Scotland, London, Oxford, Edinburgh, Glasgow*. French destinations include: *France, Normandy, Brittany, Burgundy, Alsace, Loire Valley, Provence, Côte d'Azur, Paris*.

Insight Compact Guides

The 120-strong **Insight Compact Guides** series, which packs easily accessible information into a small format, together with carefully referenced pictures and maps, includes individual titles on *Jersey* and *Guernsey* as well as *Normandy* and *Brittany*. It also has especially comprehensive coverage of Great Britain, with titles including *London, Bath, Cambridge & East Anglia, Cornwall, Devon, South Downs, The Cotswolds, Shakespeare Country, Lake District, New Forest, Oxford, Peak District, Snowdonia, York, Yorkshire Dales, North York Moors, Northumbria, Scotland, Scottish Highlands, Edinburgh* and *Glasgow*.

Insight Pocket Guides

The **Insight Pocket Guides** series contains personal recommendations from a local host and comes with an invaluable fold-out map. Titles includes *Brittany, Paris* and *London*.

Insight City Guides

Insight City Guides come in an alluringly portable format and feature a pull-out restaurant guide.

ART & PHOTO CREDITS

Picture Spreads

INSIGHT GUIDE
Channel Islands

Editorial Director **Brian Bell**
Cartographic Editor **Zoë Goodwin**
Design Consultants
Carlotta Junger, Graham Mitchener
Picture Research
Hilary Genin, Britta Jaschinski

Index

Numbers in italics refer to photographs

Insight Guides Website
www.insightguides.com

*Don't travel the
planet alone.
Keep in step with
Insight Guides'
walking eye,
just a click away*

INSIGHT GUIDES

The classic series that puts you in the picture

Alaska
Amazon Wildlife
American Southwest
Amsterdam
Argentina
Arizona & Grand Canyon
Asia's Best Hotels & Resorts
Asia, East
Asia, Southeast
Australia
Austria
Bahamas
Bali & Lombok
Baltic States
Bangkok
Barbados
Barcelona
Beijing
Belgium
Belize
Berlin
Bermuda
Boston
Brazil
Brittany
Bruges, Ghent & Antwerp
Brussels
Buenos Aires
Burgundy
Burma (Myanmar)
Cairo
California
California, Southern
Canada
Cape Town
Caribbean
Caribbean Cruises
Channel Islands
Chicago
Chile
China
Colorado
Continental Europe
Corsica
Costa Rica
Crete
Croatia
Cuba
Cyprus
Czech & Slovak Republic
Delhi, Jaipur & Agra
Denmark

Dominican Rep. & Haiti
Dublin
East African Wildlife
Eastern Europe
Ecuador
Edinburgh
Egypt
England
Finland
Florence
Florida
France
France, Southwest
French Riviera
Gambia & Senegal
Germany
Glasgow
Gran Canaria
Great Britain
Great Gardens of Britain
  & Ireland
Great Railway Journeys
  of Europe
Great River Cruises:
  Europe & the Nile
Greece
Greek Islands
Guatemala, Belize
  & Yucatán
Hawaii
Hong Kong
Hungary
Iceland
India
India, South
Indonesia
Ireland
Israel
Istanbul
Italy
Italy, Northern
Italy, Southern
Jamaica
Japan
Jerusalem
Jordan
Kenya
Korea
Laos & Cambodia
Las Vegas
Lisbon
London

Los Angeles
Madeira
Madrid
Malaysia
Mallorca & Ibiza
Malta
Mauritius Réunion
  & Seychelles
Mediterranean Cruises
Melbourne
Mexico
Miami
Montreal
Morocco
Moscow
Namibia
Nepal
Netherlands
New England
New Mexico
New Orleans
New York City
New York State
New Zealand
Nile
Normandy
North American &
  Alaskan Cruises
Norway
Oman & The UAE
Oxford
Pacific Northwest
Pakistan
Paris
Peru
Philadelphia
Philippines
Poland
Portugal
Prague
Provence
Puerto Rico
Rajasthan
Rio de Janeiro
Rome

Russia
St Petersburg
San Francisco
Sardinia
Scandinavia
Scotland
Seattle
Shanghai
Sicily
Singapore
South Africa
South America
Spain
Spain, Northern
Spain, Southern
Sri Lanka
Sweden
Switzerland
Sydney
Syria & Lebanon
Taipei
Taiwan
Tanzania & Zanzibar
Tenerife
Texas
Thailand
Tokyo
Toronto
Trinidad & Tobago
Tunisia
Turkey
Tuscany
Umbria
USA: The New South
USA: On The Road
USA: Western States
US National Parks: West
Utah
Venezuela
Venice
Vienna
Vietnam
Wales
Walt Disney World/Orlando
Washington, DC

INSIGHT GUIDES

The world's largest collection of visual travel guides & maps